D0503020

The Blue Planet

The Blue Planet

a natural history of the oceans

Andrew Byatt, Alastair Fothergill and Martha Holmes

To the ocean, my family and friends and in memory of
Tim Bevan, who had just discovered the underwater world.
Andrew Byatt

To Melinda, Hamish and Will and my parents, who first
introduced me to the coast.
Alastair Fothergill

To my parents, Peter and Judy, who first took me swimming
in the sea.
Martha Holmes

This book was published to accompany the television series *The Blue Planet*,
which was produced by the BBC and first broadcast in 2001.

Series producer: Alastair Fothergill
Producers: Andrew Byatt, Alastair Fothergill and Martha Holmes

First Published in 2001 by BBC Worldwide Limited
Woodlands, 80 Wood Lane, London W12 0TT
Copyright: © Andrew Byatt, Alastair Fothergill and Martha Holmes 2001
The moral right of the authors has been asserted.

All rights reserved under International and Pan-American Copyright Conventions.
No part of this publication may be reproduced, stored in a retrieval system, or
transmitted in any form or by any means, electronic, mechanical, photocopying,
recording, or otherwise, without the prior written permission of the copyright owner.

ISBN 0-7894-8265-7

First US edition 2001

Published in the US by

DK Publishing, Inc.
95 Madison Avenue
New York, NY 10016

Commissioning editors: Shirley Patton and Sheila Ableman
Project editor: Rachel Copus
Academic consultant: Dr Penny Allen
Text editor: Trish Burgess
Editorial advisor for habitat spreads: Polly Boyd
Bibliography: Richard Beatty
Design concept: The Attik
Art direction: Sarah Ponder
Design: designsection, Frome, Somerset
Picture research: Frances Abraham
Maps: Olive Pearson
Illustrations: Annabel Milne
Habitat spread illustrations: Kevin Jones Associates
Graphic on page 347 (top): 422

Set in Albertina MT and Gill Sans
Printed and bound in the UK by Butler & Tanner Ltd, Frome and London
Colour separations by Radstock Reproductions Ltd, Midsomer Norton
Jacket printed by Lawrence Allen Ltd, Weston-super-Mare

Discover even more about our Blue Planet at www.bbc.co.uk/nature

All imperial equivalents are approximate and no equivalent for metric tonnes has
been given. One short ton (US) is equivalent to 0.907 metric tonnes.

Contents

Foreword by Sir David Attenborough   10

Earth and its oceans   12

1 THE WATER PLANET   14

With water generally so available to us at the turn of a tap, it is easy to forget how essential it is for life on Earth. Water, collected in the great ocean basins, regulates the planet's temperature and climate as well as providing numerous habitats for plant and animal life.

1.1   Water World

1.2   Forces of Nature

1.3   Living in the Sea

2 LIFE ON THE EDGE   58

Around the borders of the ocean, where the land meets the sea, lie some of the most challenging of the ocean habitats. From sandy beaches to rocky shores and river estuaries, waves and weather constantly erode coastal areas. While many creatures come here to breed, there are few permanent residents. Those that do live here must be hardy and adaptable enough to survive the daily ebb and flow of the tides, which transform their habitat on a daily basis.

2.1   The Dynamic Border

2.2   Surviving the Coast

2.3   The Need to Breed

Contents

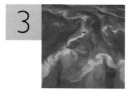

TROPICAL SEAS 100

The warm waters of the tropics are relatively poor in nutrients and oxygen, making substantial stretches of the shallows somewhat barren. However, in certain areas, where conditions are favourable, seagrass beds, mangroves and the most diverse marine communities of all – coral reefs – can be found. The efficient recycling of nutrients in these habitats allows them to flourish.

3.1 Coral Reefs
3.2 Mouths of the Reef
3.3 Sex on the Reef
3.4 Mangroves and Seagrass Beds

TEMPERATE SEAS 154

The green, algae-rich waters of the world's temperate zones are some of the most productive on the planet. These intensely seasonal areas see an annual cycle of boom and bust that depends upon the plankton: a bounty for which many animals will migrate thousands of miles to harvest. These waters are also home to most of the world's seaweed and the underwater cliffs are festooned with invertebrates that are as colourful as any coral reef.

4.1 The Richest Seas
4.2 Blooming Plankton
4.3 Ocean Forests
4.4 The Living Bed

FROZEN SEAS 212

The perimeters of the frozen seas of the Arctic and Antarctic attract surprising numbers of birds, seals and whales. But most of these migrate away as the annual sea ice forms in autumn; only a handful remain to cope with the rigours of a polar winter.

5.1 The Polar Regions
5.2 Antarctic Wildlife
5.3 Arctic Wildlife

6   THE OPEN OCEAN   **260**

Much of this seemingly limitless wilderness is a virtual desert, yet in the right conditions life explodes into intense productivity. This is a world in perpetual motion: plankton engage in an incessant daily migration from the dark depths to the surface and back, and many of the most powerful marine predators cruise these shelterless seas in search of prey. But simply finding food is not enough: somehow each species must ensure the survival of their offspring in this most unforgiving of habitats.

6.1   Ocean Wide, Ocean Blue
6.2   Ocean Drifters
6.3   Ocean Hunters
6.4   Ocean Birth

7   THE DEEP   **312**

Below 150 m (492 feet), where there is no longer enough light for photosynthesis, the deep ocean begins. By far the largest habitat for life on Earth, it is also the one about which we know least, since the enormous pressures and perpetual darkness make exploration extremely difficult. Until very recently thought to be barren, we now know that in these inhospitable waters lives a rich variety of extraordinary creatures that have adapted in a variety of ways for life in this challenging environment.

7.1   The Twilight Zone
7.2   The Dark Zone
7.3   The Deep-sea Floor
7.4   Life Without the Sun

Glossary   373
Acknowledgements   377
Picture credits   378
Index   380

Foreword

In an age when it is not uncommon for ten people to stand together on the summit of Everest, it might seem that every corner of our crowded planet has been explored. But that is far from the truth. The highest peaks on Earth are still unclimbed. We still have little idea of where the world's largest animal goes to breed and there are still thousands, maybe even millions, of animal species that remain undiscovered. All are hidden under the waves of the oceans.

Although the oceans constitute by far the largest habitat on Earth, we still know very little about them. It is their very inaccessibility that intrigued and challenged the makers of the BBC Natural History Unit's series *The Blue Planet*. The sea is not an easy place in which to film. If you sit for long enough beside a fruiting tree in the rain forest or a water hole in the tropical savannah, animals will eventually come to feed and drink. But where do you go in the vast expanse of the open ocean if you want to film blue whales on their migration, or tuna sweeping by at 71 kph (44 mph) in their search for prey? Sixty per cent of the oceans are more than a mile deep, but how do you get to the deep-sea floor? There are only five or six submersibles in the world that can dive as deep as that.

These were some of the challenges faced by the producers of the series who are also the authors of this book. Between them, they travelled to all the different ocean habitats and each writes individually about the ones they know best. The cameramen who worked with them have provided many of the illustrations, some of which, particularly in the chapter on the deep ocean, have never been seen before. Together, writers and cameramen have produced a uniquely comprehensive portrait of this astonishing and little-known world. I was lucky enough to see some of the film rushes as they came back and to share the excitement of both film-makers and research scientists as they witnessed new things and reached new understandings. I believe you can still feel the thrill of those revelations in the pages that follow.

David Attenborough

Sir David Attenborough
narrator, The Blue Planet

Sir David Attenborough surrounded by a colony of macaroni penguins in South Georgia.

Earth and its oceans

A quick glimpse at a world map will show just how important water is to our planet. In total, water covers just over 70 per cent of the Earth's surface, most of it being distributed between just five huge ocean basins. The largest of these is the Pacific and its associated seas, followed by the Atlantic, and the Indian Ocean, the Southern Ocean and the Arctic Ocean. Around and within these wide expanses of water lies a rich variety of habitats that support a huge diversity of life.

OCEAN HABITATS

On land it is relatively easy to pinpoint clear vegetation belts which show similar characteristics, but it is much more difficult to follow this principle with the oceans. Currents, wind patterns and changes in salinity all mean that many characteristics can be localised and variable. Nevertheless, it is possible to distinguish a number of general marine biological zones, as shown on the map, right, which are related to temperature. Warm water populations exist where the surface temperatures are about 18–20 °C (67–69 °F). Here there is a great diversity of species, but often the waters are relatively poor in nutrients, hence the total numbers of creatures may be quite low. On coral reefs, for example, the ecosystem is tightly organized and nutrient recycling is of the utmost efficiency in order to make the most of the small amount of nutrients available (▷ p. 115).

Cold water populations are found in the Arctic and Southern Oceans, where surface

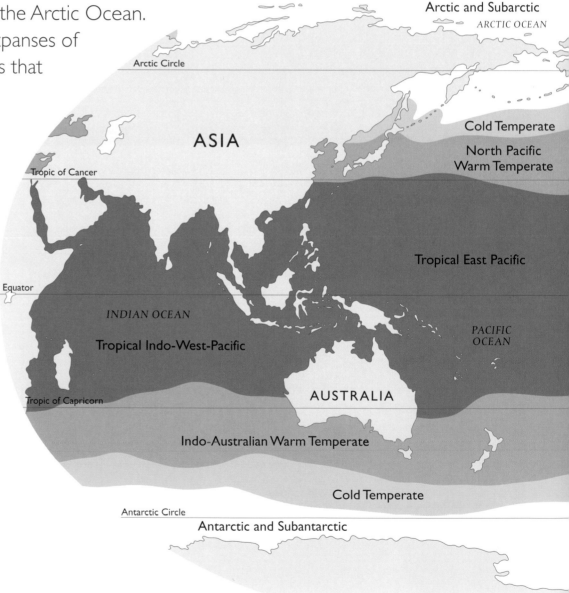

Arctic and Subarctic
ARCTIC OCEAN

Arctic Circle

ASIA

Cold Temperate

North Pacific
Warm Temperate

Tropic of Cancer

Tropical East Pacific

Equator

INDIAN OCEAN

PACIFIC
OCEAN

Tropical Indo-West-Pacific

AUSTRALIA

Tropic of Capricorn

Indo-Australian Warm Temperate

Cold Temperate

Antarctic Circle

Antarctic and Subantarctic

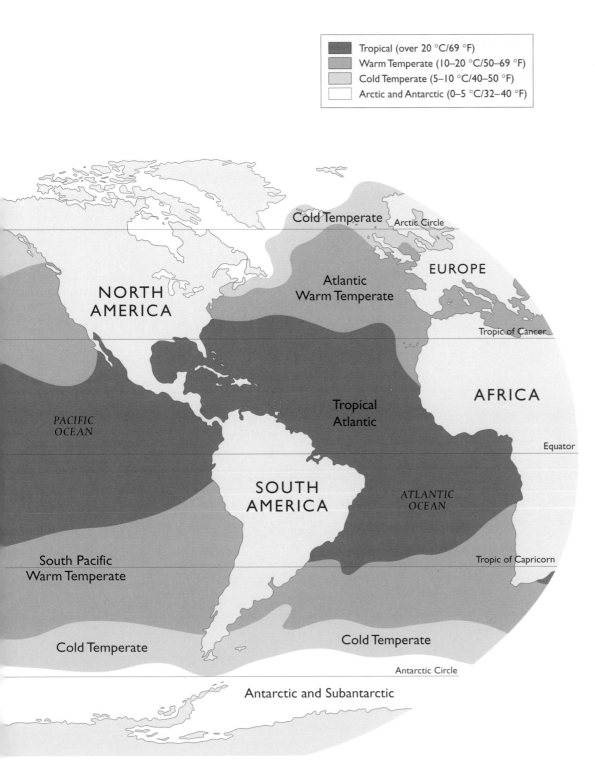

Tropical (over 20 °C/69 °F)
Warm Temperate (10–20 °C/50–69 °F)
Cold Temperate (5–10 °C/40–50 °F)
Arctic and Antarctic (0–5 °C/32–40 °F)

Cold Temperate   Arctic Circle

Atlantic
Warm Temperate

EUROPE

NORTH
AMERICA

Tropic of Cancer

AFRICA

PACIFIC
OCEAN

Tropical
Atlantic

SOUTH
AMERICA

Equator

ATLANTIC
OCEAN

South Pacific
Warm Temperate

Tropic of Capricorn

Cold Temperate

Cold Temperate

Antarctic Circle

Antarctic and Subantarctic

temperatures lie between 5 °C (40 °F) and just below 0 °C (32 °F). Here, there is a low species diversity – for example Antarctica has no land mammals, no freshwater fish and few plants – but there is still an extraordinary abundance of life. In spring, the ice melts and phytoplankton blooms with astonishing speed, attracting a host of other creatures that come to feed (▷ p. 225).

Between the tropical and the cold-water areas lie the temperate regions (▷ p. 154) where the surface temperatures are between 5 and 18 °C (40 and 67 °F) and the productivity of the oceans is markedly influenced by the seasons (▷ p. 160) because of the enormous variation in the amount of light energy. In midwinter the temperate regions can see as little as four hours of sunlight, while in the summer they can experience as many as 20 hours. When the light is most abundant, plants grow in profusion and temperature layers form in the ocean; both have a significant influence on marine life.

The ocean can also be divided into categories according to the distance from land and the depth beneath the surface. From the coasts, where the habitat is constantly changing due to the ebb and flow of the tide (▷ p. 72), to the enormity of the open ocean (▷ p. 260) and the mysterious darkness of the deep sea (▷ p. 312) each of these environments is blessed with a diverse range of life that is uniquely adapted for its particular habitat. The creatures of tidal areas have to cope with periodic exposure to air, those of the open ocean need speed and endurance, whilst in the deep, marine life has evolved to endure extraordinary pressures and long months of starvation.

THE WATER PLANET

1.1 WATER WORLD 16

Earth is a unique planet blessed with a vast quantity of liquid water. In prehistoric times, the ocean basins filled with water and became the cradle for the evolution of life.

SPECIAL FEATURE: Ocean exploration

1.2 FORCES OF NATURE 30

The combined effects of the sun, the moon and the rotation of the Earth govern the oceans and, in turn, our climate.

SPECIAL FEATURE: Waves

1.3 LIVING IN THE SEA 42

Numerous ocean habitats support varied and complex ecosystems; in them a great diversity of plant and animal life forms has evolved.

SPECIAL FEATURE: Blue whales

SPECIAL FEATURE: Prehistoric survivors

1.1 WATER WORLD

From space, Planet Earth is blue. It floats like a jewel in the inky black void. The reflection of the sun's light from the vast expanse of water covering its surface creates its gem-like blue colour. In the entire solar system, Earth is the only planet that has water in its liquid form in such quantities. That is what makes Earth unique. Water has been the cradle of life throughout most of the planet's 4600-million-year history. The earliest forms of life – a simple collection of organic compounds – evolved in water and stayed there. They were bathed in a nutrient soup that remained at a suitable temperature and never dried up. From these early beginnings, life on Earth evolved and diversified through the millennia. Fish, worms, amphibians, reptiles, birds, mammals and every plant, both above and below the water, started their evolutionary journey in the ocean. It is only because of water, and its combination of special properties, that life on Earth – as we know it – exists at all.

Previous page: The oceans are critical to life on Earth. They absorb carbon dioxide from the air keeping it cooler than it would otherwise be, they store heat and are the source of fresh water for all plants and animals on land.

THE BLUE PLANET

Planet Earth is special in our solar system because it is blessed with an abundance of life. One of the key factors in the evolution of life is the position of Earth in relation to the sun. Earth is 150 million km (93 million miles) away from the sun. Some planets within our galaxy, such as Mercury and Venus are closer, while others, such as Pluto, are further away. Because the sun radiates immense heat, conditions on a planet are determined by how close it is to the sun. Mercury, which is only 60 million km (37 million miles) from the sun, has daytime temperatures of 350 °C (662 °F) – hot enough to melt many metals – and any water that existed evaporated long ago. At the other extreme, Pluto, which is 5900 million km (3666 million miles) from the sun, is permanently frozen, with surface temperatures of about -230 °C (-382 °F). Fortunately, Earth lies between the extremes, and has a milder surface temperature. This, combined with the unique properties of the water molecule, results in a world where water can exist in a liquid state. As yet, no other planet in our solar system, or in the universe as a whole, has been found to have such a favourable set of conditions for life.

Ocean origins

As a result of a cosmic explosion known as the Big Bang, (an estimated 15 billion years ago),

1. Planet Earth as photographed from *Apollo 17*, showing Africa, Arabia and Antarctica. Despite our familiarity and fascination with the landmasses of the world, most of the surface of the Earth is covered by ocean.

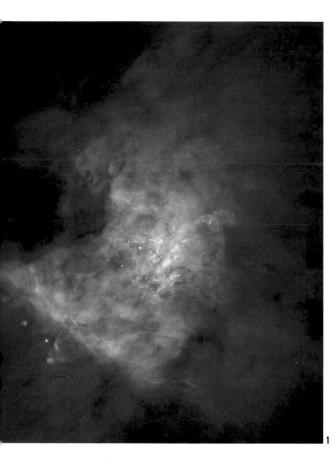

space, time and matter were created simultaneously; the universe was born. Over 10 billion years later, an interstellar cloud of swirling gas and dust condensed and began to heat up. Nuclear reactions began to occur in the intense heat, and pressure built up at its centre: what we now know as the sun began to shine. The young sun began to exert a gravitational pull on the rest of the cloud and grew, exerting a still stronger pull, until it contained all but a few bits of debris and some gases, which were both far away and travelling fast enough to remain isolated. These particles and gases eventually coalesced and the planets, including Earth itself, were formed. Our solar system is thought to have been created in this way about 4.6 billion years ago.

The great heat produced during the formation of the Earth probably meant that the entire planet was molten. The more dense materials sank to the centre, while lighter ones floated to the surface. As the planet gradually cooled, these lighter surface materials formed a thin crust. Volcanic activity continued unabated, with molten lava from beneath erupting up at the surface, releasing water vapour and other gases. Much of our water may have landed on Earth as ice-laden comets. About 4000 million years ago, the atmosphere was dominated by water vapour, but as Earth continued cooling, water vapour in the atmosphere began to condense and fall as rain. Streams developed into rivers, and gradually the low-lying areas filled with water. The oldest sedimentary (water-formed) rocks found to date suggest that these early seas formed about 3800 million years ago.

Today, just over 70 per cent of the Earth's surface is covered by water. If the Earth were flat and even, like a ball, the depth of the water layer lying on its surface would be 3.7 km (2.25 miles) deep. Luckily, Earth has a complicated topography, which includes extensive depressions – the ocean basins – which have filled with water. Most of the planet's water (nearly 98 per cent) is stored within these basins.

1. Orion Nebula – the creation of a galaxy. Ultraviolet radiation from the four huge, young stars near the centre ionizes the gases of the nebula, causing them to glow.

2. Water trapped in the Earth's crust emerges as steam during volcanic eruptions. Once swathed in water vapour, Earth has since cooled and the vapour has condensed to fill the ocean basins.

3. The salty oceans are the source of fresh water for most of the world. Water evaporates, is carried as clouds and falls as rain, snow or sleet elsewhere.

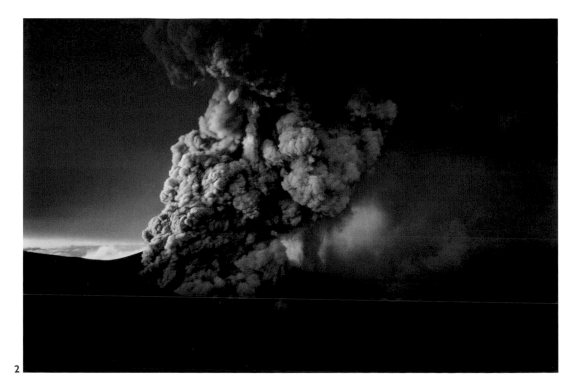

There is a constant and critical recycling of water around the planet. As the sun heats the surfaces of oceans, water vapour rising into the atmosphere forms clouds. These are driven around the globe by winds, and when the conditions are right, they condense and water falls as rain, snow or hail. This process of water changing from its liquid state in the oceans to gas in the atmosphere and back again to liquid is known as the hydrological cycle, and is essential to life on land. Without it much of the world would be barren.

The nature of water

The special properties of water, including the way it changes when heated and cooled, make it unique. Most substances expand when heated and contract when cooled, but water behaves differently. As it freezes, water increases in volume by about 9 per cent and becomes lighter, which is why ice floats. If this were not the case, we would not recognize the **3**

 ## THE ATTRACTION OF WATER

One molecule of water is made up of one atom of oxygen and two of hydrogen. However, the bonding between these three atoms is not symmetrical, and it is this feature of a water molecule that makes it so special.

The two hydrogen atoms lie at 105 degrees to each other rather than on opposite sides of the oxygen atom at 180 degrees. This arrangement results in the hydrogen end having a slight positive charge and the oxygen end a slight negative charge. Because opposite charges attract, water molecules come together: the negative oxygen end of one molecule is attracted to the positive hydrogen end of a neighbouring molecule. The weak bond that forms in between is called a hydrogen bond (see diagram, right).

When frozen, water molecules are held by the bonds in a hexagonal structure. As temperature increases and ice turns to water, the molecules move freely, forming and breaking hydrogen bonds. When the temperature rises further and the molecules vibrate faster, all the hydrogen bonds break, the molecules are set free and the liquid becomes water vapour.

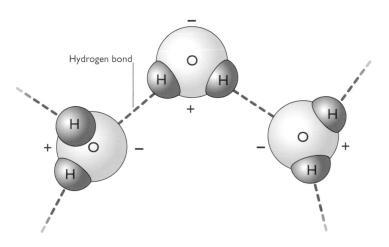

1

planet. Ice would sink to the bottom of high-latitude lakes, seas and oceans, and once shielded from the heat of the sun by the water above, more freezing would occur until these bodies of water would just be frozen blocks. There would be no ocean circulation on a grand scale, so warm water from the tropics would not reach the polar regions. The tropics would be intolerably hot, the poles permanently frozen and the temperature latitudes would freeze for much of the year.

Water can also dissolve more substances than any other solvent. It is especially good at dissolving salts. Sodium chloride, for example, is made up of one ion of sodium and one of chlorine, both with strong opposite charges. Without water, these ions form tight bonds, resulting in salt crystals. However, weakly charged water molecules are attracted to these strongly charged salt molecules and cluster around them, weakening the bonds between the ions. Gradually the ions separate and float off, surrounded by a cluster of water molecules. In other words, the salt dissolves.

Water has a great capacity to store heat. In order to heat up water just a little, a substantial quantity of heat is required and likewise, as water cools, a lot of heat is lost. The oceans store heat from the sun's radiation during the daytime, particularly in summer. On the other hand, they lose heat at night and during the winter. The process of heating up and cooling down is significantly slower for water than for land. As a result, oceans have an impact on neighbouring land, buffering the more extreme temperatures that would otherwise occur daily and seasonally. That is why coasts experience a milder climate than the inland areas of a large continental mass. Furthermore, ocean currents ensure that heat is transported around the planet. On a global scale, if Earth were not covered by such extensive oceans, we would experience blisteringly hot temperatures in the day and freezing cold temperatures at night.

The importance of water

Water's super-efficiency as a solvent makes it the basis for all forms of life. The chemical compounds and processes that make up what we call 'life' occur in water. It is not surprising then, that the bodies of most organisms are about 65 per cent water and most marine life contains about 80 per cent water and some, such as jellyfish, as much as 95 per cent.

Outside an organism's body, water's solvent properties are equally important. The salinity of water determines what animals can live there. Some can survive only in fresh water, where the salt content is very low; many can tolerate a higher salt content and live in the sea; yet others can eke out an existence in highly saline habitats such as salt marshes. Plants and animals that survive in places where salinity fluctuates dramatically, such as estuaries, have had to evolve more complicated ways of regulating their own internal body fluid concentration.

Water also contains dissolved gases, including oxygen. Oxygen in water comes from two sources: it is absorbed at the surface from air, or it comes from plants as a by-product of photosynthesis. This makes water an ideal place for animals to live, as they are bathed in a convenient solvent that provides them with oxygen. However, as water temperature rises, its oxygen content decreases, making the tropical oceans poorer in oxygen than the temperate oceans. Moreover, as water depth increases, the less surface-absorbed oxygen there is available; also, as there is no light, there is little or no oxygen from photosynthesis. At about 500 m (1640 feet) there is a layer of sea water that contains hardly any oxygen at all. Despite this, some animals, such as shrimps and fish, do manage to live here. To survive in such oxygen-poor water, they have had to adapt. First, they are relatively inactive, so they use less energy, and second, they have enlarged gills to extract as much oxygen from the water as possible.

▷ SIGNS OF LIFE

Fossil evidence of the first known organisms – resembling present-day blue-green algae or cyanobacteria – has been found in rock 3600 million years old. For about 1600 million years these single-celled life forms were possibly the only living things on the planet. However, there were significant changes during those years. Since Earth's creation, its atmosphere had probably consisted largely of water vapour, methane and ammonia. But the single-celled organisms now living in the oceans were photosynthesizing (creating simple sugars probably by using first chemical then later the sun's energy). A crucial by-product of photosynthesis is oxygen. Gradually the atmosphere changed as oxygen became available. Moreover, the ozone layer formed and screened the developing life from the effects of ultraviolet radiation. The stage was set for more complicated life forms. About 600 million years ago, the first, known multi-celled animals evolved.

1. Frozen water – ice – is less dense than liquid water and, therefore, it floats. If this were not the case, the polar oceans would be frozen solid.

2. All organisms contain water and rely on its solvent properties to live. Jellyfish are 95 per cent water.

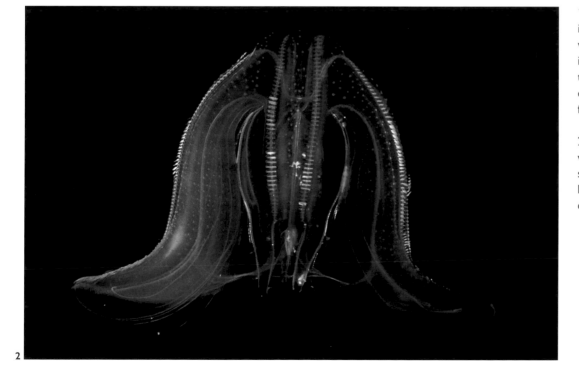

2

OCEAN EXPLORATION

The earliest evidence that man lived by the sea comes not from the remains of boats but from piles of discarded shells found in refuse tips dating from about 40,000 years ago. As the sea level rose after the last ice age, there is probably much more archaeological evidence hidden under water, but boats are unlikely to be found. Being made of wood, skin and fibres, they do not preserve well, but they undoubtedly played an important part in survival and exploration. As time went by, boats became increasingly sophisticated and people ventured further and further away from known territory, braving the open oceans in their quest for new land.

2. The *Challenger* expedition of 1872 was the first global venture dedicated to the study of oceanography.

1. The Arabs still build traditional dhows; ocean-worthy boats they have used to cross the Indian Ocean for thousands of years.

Early voyagers

One of the earliest sea voyages, at least 40,000 years ago, would have involved the migration of people from Southeast Asia to New Guinea and Australia. Although the sea level was then much lower and therefore the stretch of water they had to cross was probably only 40 km (25 miles) wide, they would have needed sturdier craft than those used on inland waterways.

Ocean-going vessels developed independently in many parts of the world. European trade was flourishing in the Mediterranean 5000 years ago. Ships also helped people to spread west through the Pacific, colonizing the islands some 4000 years ago. The Arabs, too had extensive trading networks with India, Arabia and Africa, demonstrating an early understanding of the monsoon wind patterns of the Indian Ocean and the use of stars as a navigational aid. With this knowledge they could cross wide stretches of open water without using landmarks as guides.

Mapping the world

Europeans had a hunger for both trade routes and knowledge in the middle of the last millennium. Money was made available to explorers who wanted to chart the oceans and open up trade. One of the first to make his name was Christopher Columbus, who, in 1492, was credited with having discovered the New World.

The Portuguese explorer Ferdinand Magellan set off in 1519 to circumnavigate the world, but was killed in the Philippines. The journey was completed under the leadership of Juan del Cano, and the vastness of the Pacific

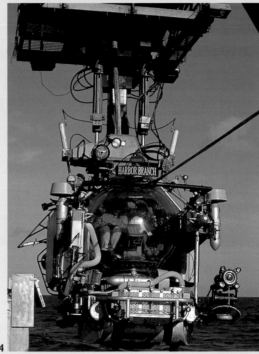

3. This Mappa Mundi is a map of the known world in 1459, as drawn by an Italian monk. Exploration and discovery flourished in the following 100 years with navigators such as Columbus and Magellan.

4. The *Johnson Sealink II* is one of the modern submersibles designed and equipped to investigate the deep ocean.

Ocean was officially discovered. Although these early explorers could measure latitude accurately, they struggled with longitude because a clock that could keep reliable time at sea had not been invented. It was not until 1760, when a clock-maker called John Harrison perfected his chronometer, that the problem was solved. Soon after, James Cook set sail with the best navigational equipment the world had known. During his three voyages, between 1768 and 1780, Cook mapped the Pacific Ocean, charted the east coast of Australia and surmised that there was a continent of ice to the south.

A science is born

Exploration of the oceans sank into insignificance behind the great and exciting new continental discoveries; strategic and commercial interests dominated. However, when the problem of longitude was solved, and accurate positioning of both marine and coastal features could be given, information about the seas and oceans became valuable to both traders and naval commanders. Understanding of the oceans progressed in fits and starts, but a major turning point was the *Challenger* expedition in 1872. Under the guidance of two British biologists, this ship circumnavigated the globe and many important discoveries were made. They dredged up animals from 8000 m (26,000 feet), thus demonstrating that the abyssal depths were not lifeless. The foundations for the modern science of oceanography had been laid.

Equipment used today is highly sophisticated. It includes submersibles, which can be manned or remotely operated, and even satellites which can study the oceans from high above. Despite great advances, our understanding of the oceans is still superficial. We know more about the surface of Mars than we do about most of the sea floor.

◆ TOPIC LINKS

1.1 Water World
p.24 Mid-ocean Ridges

1.2 Forces of Nature
p.31 Winds

5.2 Antarctic Wildlife
p.238 Finite Bounty

7.4 Life without the Sun
p.364 Exploring the Abyss
p.367 Variety of Life
p.370 Cold Seeps

A GIANT JIGSAW

For many centuries people thought that the Earth was established, stable and unchanging. But this view could not have been further from the truth. It was as early as 1596 that the Dutch map maker Abraham Ortelius pondered the fact that the coasts of Africa and Europe might fit snugly against the Americas on the other side of the Atlantic, and proposed that they might have been joined at one time. Supporting evidence mounted over the centuries. Coal deposits and other geological features were found to be similar in Africa and the Americas, and fossils of the extinct reptile *Mesosaurus* have been found both along the west coast of southern Africa and the east coast of South America. In 1912, a German scientist called Alfred Wegener collated all this evidence and proposed the idea of continental drift. He suggested that there used to be one supercontinent, which he named Pangaea, and that in geological time this continent had broken apart, its various pieces separating out to their modern-day positions. At first, his ideas were received with scepti-cism because there was no known mecha-nism by which continental drift could occur. It wasn't until the late 1960s that a solution was found and his ideas were truly accepted.

Mid-ocean ridges

After World War II, the use of sonar revolution-ized surveys of the sea floor. Accurate mapping of the ocean basins was now possible. Far from being merely the flat plains previously imag-ined, gigantic mountain ranges, isolated seamounts and deep trenches were discovered. It was the mapping of a great mid-ocean moun-tain range that, incredibly, extends through all the ocean basins that was the key to under-standing continental drift. This continuous mid-ocean ridge is by far the largest geological feature on Earth, but we only ever see glimpses of it where the tips of its submarine mountains break the surface, creating islands such as the Azores and Iceland in the Atlantic.

As geologists began to investigate part of the range that extends up the Atlantic (the Mid-Atlantic Ridge), they found evidence that the ocean floor was spreading apart, thus support-ing Wegener's idea of continental drift. Rocks near the centre of the ridge were younger than those further away. Moreover, the further away from the ridge the geologists looked, the more overlying sediment there was, suggesting the rocks beneath had been there longer. The final piece of evidence came when the magnetism of the rocks was examined. Every so often, in geological time, the Earth's polarity reverses so that the magnetic north switches to the south. Magnetic particles in molten rocks align them-selves to the new direction. Geologists found a series of parallel bands or stripes in the rocks of the mid-Atlantic ridge, each one signifying a change in Earth's polarity. These bands run along the length of the ridge. They also discov-ered that the bands on either side of the ridge are mirror images of each other. Here, then, was the evidence that continents were moving apart; Wegener's theory was accepted.

Plate tectonics

It is now recognized that the surface of the Earth is divided into 13 major plates and a number of smaller ones, all floating on the

1. A simplified map of known lithospheric plates indicating their direction of movement. The details of some areas are still not fully understood.

2. The Andes were formed by the oceanic Nazca Plate moving beneath the South American plate. The lighter materials from the Nazca Plate rise to the surface as they melt, erupting as volcanoes in the Andes.

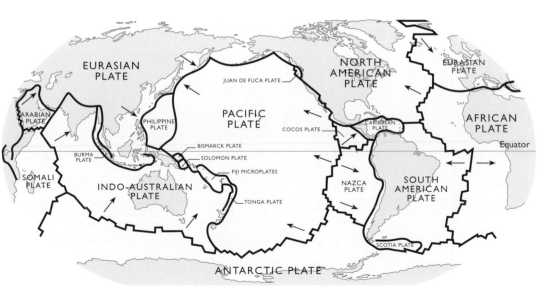

THE DIVISION OF THE EARTH INTO LITHOSPHERIC PLATES

EURASIAN PLATE
NORTH AMERICAN PLATE
EURASIAN PLATE
JUAN DE FUCA PLATE
PACIFIC PLATE
AFRICAN PLATE
ARABIAN PLATE
PHILIPPINE PLATE
COCOS PLATE
CARIBBEAN PLATE
Equator
BISMARCK PLATE
BURMA PLATE
SOLOMON PLATE
FIJI MICROPLATES
SOMALI PLATE
INDO-AUSTRALIAN PLATE
NAZCA PLATE
SOUTH AMERICAN PLATE
TONGA PLATE
SCOTIA PLATE
ANTARCTIC PLATE

Plate boundary
Plate movement

1

partly molten layer of the mantle beneath. Some of these plates carry continents, but others are purely oceanic. Those that do carry continents are responsible for continental drift. Continents move at the same rate as the plates are moving apart or together – 2 cm (0.75 in) per year in the Atlantic and 18 cm (7 in) per year in the eastern Pacific. It is thought that currents within the fluid rock of the mantle below cause the plates to move. Where a current rises up, molten rock breaks through the crust at a mid-oceanic ridge; where it moves down through the mantle, a plate does one of two things, depending on its nature.

Plates which are 50–100 km (30–60 miles) thick, consist of the surface crust of the Earth and a part of the upper mantle, both of which are rock. The crust part varies in nature. Continental crust, or land, is thicker (30–40 km/18½–25 miles deep) but less dense than oceanic crust (only 6 km/3¾ miles deep). This difference in density accounts for the oceans themselves. Despite being thinner, the denser oceanic crust floats lower in the liquid rock of the mantle than the lighter continental crust. Water flows by gravity to the lower areas, thus creating the oceans.

With the ocean floors spreading along the mid-ocean ridges, Earth would be expanding unless somewhere material were being forced back into the mantle. When an oceanic plate collides with a continental plate, the heavier, oceanic plate moves beneath. At this point – or subduction zone, as it is called – deep oceanic trenches are created and a line of volcanic activity is found along the continental edge. This is best illustrated in the East Pacific. The expanding East-Pacific Rise (a mid-ocean ridge) is pushing the Nazca plate towards South America. This oceanic plate is being forced under the lighter South America plate, causing many earthquakes. The continental crust of South America is buckling under the pressure, creating the Andes mountains, and as the less

2

1. View from space, looking west along the Himalayan mountains. As the Indian sub-continent (on the left) pushes northward into Tibet (on the right) the land in between has buckled, creating the highest mountain range in the world.

2. The last super-continent to exist was Pangaea. Some 200 million years ago it began to break up by a process known as continental drift. The continents are still moving today.

3. The sediment fan at the mouth of a big river extends many kilometres through the ocean. Here, only a little of the Mississippi river fan can be seen through the turbid waters.

dense materials contained within the Nazca plate melt, they rise and burst out as volcanoes.

But when two continental plates collide, both are light and neither sinks back into the mantle. As the landmasses are pushed together, tremendous pressure builds, rocks distort under the force and great mountain ranges are squeezed up. It is the collision of the Asian landmass and the northward-moving Indian sub-continent, for example, that has created the Himalayas.

The break-up of Pangaea

The continents have been floating around for many hundreds of millions of years, colliding to form supercontinents, which then break up again. The last supercontinent that existed was the one named Pangaea by Wegener. Pangaea was surrounded by a single super-ocean he called Panthalassa, the predecessor of the Pacific Ocean. There was also a shallow, tropical ocean he called the Tethys Sea.

About 220 million years ago, Pangaea began to break up. North America began to separate from the fused continents of South America and Africa, creating a gap which was the start of the northern Atlantic Ocean. The line of separation marked the beginning of the mid-Atlantic ridge. As the split widened, two giant continents were formed: Laurasia to the north, which combined North America and Eurasia, and Gondwanaland to the south, which consisted of South America, Africa, India, Australia and the Antarctic continent.

Then, some 170 million years ago, Gondwanaland began to break up. South America and Africa moved to the northeast, while India, on its own, started to move north. Some 35 million years later, South America and Africa broke apart, creating the southern Atlantic Ocean. The mid-ocean ridges of the north and south Atlantic joined up to form one long, continuous ridge. As the Atlantic continued to spread, the remains of Panthalassa, now the Pacific, began to shrink. It is still shrinking to this day.

The Tethys Sea was gradually closed by the northward movement of Africa and what we know as southern Europe. India finally reached Asia, and the Himalayan mountains were born. The mid-Indian Ocean ridge extended down to separate Australia and Antarctica, as it does today, causing Australia to move north.

THE BREAK-UP OF PANGAEA

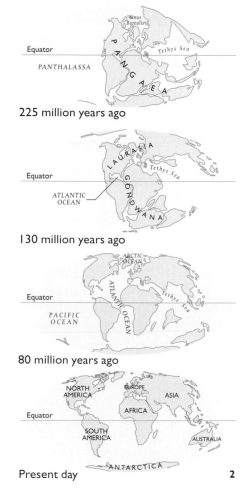

225 million years ago

130 million years ago

80 million years ago

Present day

SEASCAPES

On a global scale, plate tectonics shape the topography of the Earth's crust. This is true for both continental crust (land) and oceanic crust (the ocean floor). It also means that all around the world very similar features can be found under water. In broad terms, there are only two zones: the edges of the continents and the ocean floor.

Continental edges

Sea level is much higher today than it was 15,000 to 20,000 years ago, so the margins of all continental crusts have been flooded.

This has created extensive, new, shallow underwater habitats which are ideal for colonization by plants and animals. Although these regions, known as continental shelves, make up only 8 per cent of the world's oceans, they are where the majority of marine life is concentrated.

Continental shelves are nearly flat and typically about 150 m (500 feet) deep, though their range is 120–400 m (400–1300 feet). This uniformity of depth is explained by the fact that they are simply the outer edges of flat continents which have become flooded. However, they do vary greatly in width. Some continental shelves are very short because an oceanic plate is butting up against the edge of

the continental crust and compressing it. The Pacific edge of South America, for example, has a very short underwater continental shelf of only 1 km (0.6 mile). Most of the continental edge has been squashed to form the Andes range. Indeed, much of the Pacific rim is characterized by short continental shelves with active volcanic and earthquake zones. By contrast, the Atlantic continental shelves are much wider and non-volcanic; they are simply the flooded edges of the continental crust. The Atlantic Ocean is expanding, and the four plates that are separating carry the continents of Africa, South America, North America and Eurasia. Therefore, as the edges of the Atlantic are not marked by zones where

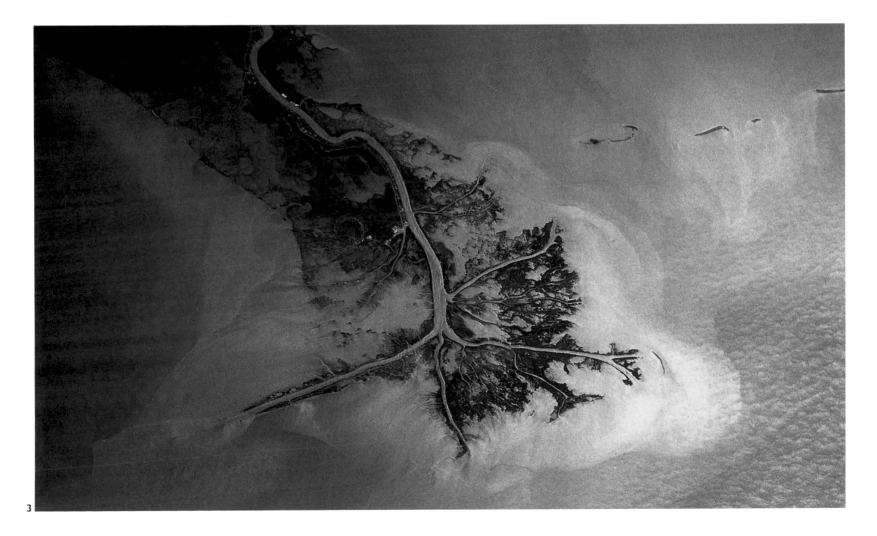

3

an oceanic plate is being pushed beneath a continental plate, there are no volcanoes or earthquakes around its perimeter.

The true edge of all continents now lies under water and is called the continental slope. The slope extends steeply from 150 m (500 feet) or so down to about 3000 m (9850 feet). Deep canyons riddle the slope, many of which are carved by the sediment from a river. Sediments flow down the slope and into the canyons, forming great fans at the bottom. These are so extensive that they merge to form an immense band of sediment (called the continental rise), which runs along the base of the slope. The Ganges fan is the most impressive, having a colossal cone extending some 2500 km (1550 miles) beyond the edge of the continental slope and reaching a depth of 5000 m (16,400 feet).

The ocean floor

At the bottom of the continental slope and beneath the sediment of the continental rise is the rock of the ocean floor. This is where the continental crust ends and the oceanic crust begins. Further out to sea, beyond the sediment of the continental rise, much of the sea floor is smothered in a blanket of ooze-like sediment. This does not originate on land, but comes from dead plants and animals that rain down from above. These extensive, usually flat areas are called abyssal plains.

However, abyssal plains are not utterly featureless. They are peppered with submarine volcanoes called seamounts, which, if they rise to surface waters, form important oases for marine life in an otherwise relatively barren ocean. When seamounts are high enough to break the surface, they form volcanic islands, such as the Galápagos Islands and the Hawaiian chain. Another feature of the abyssal plains are guyots – seamounts with strangely flat tops. Opinion varies as to how guyots became truncated, but as they are drowned volcanic islands, the most plausible argument is that their tops were eroded away when they were islands.

1

▷ LIGHT IN THE SEA

One of the reasons that the oceans are so full of life is that sea water is largely transparent. Plants need light to grow, and if light did not penetrate beyond the surface, there would be only a thin scum of life in the oceans. However, not all light penetrates very far; the amount and type of light that gets through depends on the quality of the water. Turbid water at a river mouth lets in less light than the clear water of the open ocean, for example.

Of the sunlight striking the ocean surface, between 3 and 30 per cent is reflected off immediately, depending on the angle of the sun to the water. Light that penetrates the surface does not do so equally. Sea water absorbs red wavelengths quickly, so objects that appear red at the surface look grey or black at depth. Underwater photographers, such as the one shown left, use flashlights for this reason. If they did not, their pictures would turn out mostly blue, for it is blue light that penetrates the furthest.

Trenches are also a feature of the deep ocean. Formed at the point where an oceanic plate collides with a continental plate and descends into the mantle, their sides plummet to phenomenal depths. Most oceanic trenches are found around the Pacific rim because the oceanic plates that make up the Pacific are being forced beneath continental plates along their perimeters. The bottom of the deepest trench of all, the Marianas Trench in the western Pacific, lies 11 km (7 miles) beneath the surface of the sea. Mount Everest would fit inside this trench and its peak would still be 2000 m (6500 feet) beneath the surface.

The abyssal plains have an almost unde-tectable rise towards the mid-ocean ridges. Closer to the ridge there is less sediment as the rocks are younger, and at the ridge itself the nature of the seabed changes altogether.

When two oceanic plates separate, there is a gap or valley in the middle. This is called the central rift valley, and within it is a whole new world. Sea water seeps down through the cracks and crevices of the broken crust, heats up to extreme temperatures (as much as 350 ° C/662 °F) in the hot rocks beneath and is forced out again in deep-sea hot springs or hydrothermal vents. Dissolved in the emerging water are minerals, paticularly sulphides. As this mineral-laden hot water makes contact with the surrounding, cooler sea water, it rapidly cools and the minerals solidify. Chimneys of solidified minerals build up, with black 'smoke' or sulphide particles pouring out of the top. These hydrothermal vents are one of the very few habitats on Earth where life does not rely on the energy of the sun.

1. The Galápagos Islands are submarine volcanoes that are so large they have emerged above sea level to form dry land.

★ Sea level has changed throughout time. Since the last ice age, sea level has risen about 120 m (400 feet) – a direct result of the extensive ice caps melting.

We swim, sail and surf in the sea. We build sand-castles on the beach and stand on cliff-tops to let the wind blow through our hair. We ski on snow, fish from rivers and drink pure water from springs without a thought. We enjoy the warmth of summer and cold of winter. In short, we take salt water, fresh water and the changing seasons for granted. But they are all products of the rotation of the Earth and its orbit around one particular star, the sun. Despite being 150 million km (93 million miles) away, the sun is the heat engine of the planet. Its power is awesome. Even after travelling so far through space, the sun's rays release 130 trillion horsepower per second on Earth. It creates all the winds, from light zephyrs to rampaging hurricanes, and drives ocean currents; it controls our climate and, in partnership with the moon, it influences tides. Almost all life in the sea and on land is directly or indirectly affected by it.

SUN POWER

Of the sun's energy that reaches the Earth, about 30 per cent is reflected back immediately, the remainder being absorbed by the atmosphere and Earth's surface. This energy fuels the planet and, most importantly, the oceans.

Winds

In the days when sail was the only means of moving across the ocean, mariners were well aware that to cross from Europe to the Americas it was necessary to sail south to catch the northeasterly winds, which would blow them west across the Atlantic. These winds were so reliable and so often used for trade, they became known as the trade winds. To return, mariners had to sail north up the Gulf Stream and catch winds known as the westerlies, which blew them back to Europe.

Winds are driven by heat from the sun, most of this energy being absorbed in the Tropics. Here, the sun's rays strike the atmosphere at right angles, which has two effects, both of which ensure more heat is absorbed by Earth. First, fewer rays are deflected off the

1. Heat from the sun drives our weather patterns. It causes evaporation and clouds to develop; it creates wind as air heats up and these winds then drive both the clouds and ocean currents.

1

1. The main wind fields of the world are consistent. They are created by hot air rising and cooler air rushing in to replace it.

2. Sandwiched between the equatorial trade winds is an area where air rises slowly and the winds fail. Called the doldrums, this belt of calm water was dreaded by sailors in the days of sail.

3. Where there is wind there are waves: the stronger the wind and the longer the fetch, the bigger the wave.

WIND PATTERNS OF THE WORLD

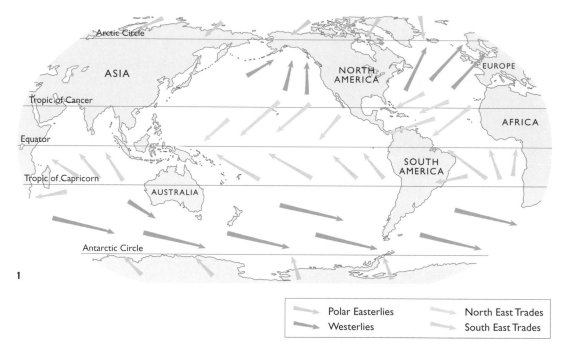

→ Polar Easterlies	→ North East Trades
→ Westerlies	→ South East Trades

 ## HURRICANES

In tropical oceans, where water temperature can rise to over 27 °C (81 °F), water evaporates and heat is transferred to the atmosphere. As the air warms, it becomes less dense and rises in a spiral, drawing yet more air upwards. (The picture, right, shows the formation of Hurricane Bonnie in September, 1992.) This rising air has a heavy load of moisture which, as it reaches higher altitudes, cools and condenses, releasing heat. The energy from this heat increases the speed of the air, creating spiralling winds. In the centre of the spiral is a calm region of low pressure. This contrasts dramatically with the high-pressure, fast-moving, cloud-filled air of the surrounding spiral. While the developing hurricane is over the ocean, it is fed with energy from the warm, moist, rising air, and its speed and ferocity increases.

Hurricane Gilbert, which swept through the Gulf of Mexico in 1988, was vast, measuring 1500 km (930 miles) across. Although the hurricane travelled at only 20 kph (12.5 mph), wind speeds near the centre of the storm were over 320 kph (200 mph). The extreme low pressure in the eye of a hurricane can cause houses to explode as it passes over them because the air at higher pressure within the house expands very suddenly. Once over land, the hurricane begins to lose power. It is no longer fed by the warm ocean and the increased friction over land disrupts the spiral.

atmosphere, so more pass through. Second, the distance the rays have to travel through the atmosphere before they hit the surface of the Earth is shorter. As air at the Equator heats up, it becomes less dense and rises. To fill the gap being produced beneath, air rushes in from adjacent areas, creating winds. These are the trade winds.

Instead of the trade winds simply blowing south in the northern hemisphere and north in the southern hemisphere, both these sets of winds blow slightly west as well. This affect, caused by the rotation of the Earth, was what made them so useful to early sailors. Known as the Coriolis effect (after the French scientist who first described it), it applies to all moving particles on the Earth's surface. Those in the northern hemisphere move slightly to the right and those in the southern hemisphere to the left. Imagine standing at the North Pole and throwing a ball to someone at the Equator. At the Pole, even though the Earth is spinning (in an anti-clockwise direction), you are turning only slowly, but the person at the Equator is moving at about 1500 kph (930 mph). By the time the ball you have thrown reaches the Equator, the person will have moved left of his starting place. So it appears that rather than travelling straight towards the other person, the ball has curved to the right. On a day-to-day basis in our own lives, the Coriolis

effect is too small to be noticeable, but it has dramatic consequences on the winds and currents, which move great distances over the Earth's surface.

Surface currents

Ocean surface currents are driven by persistent winds. The movement of the air literally pushes the water along. However, because of the Coriolis effect, currents do not move in the same direction as the winds that drive them, but at 45 degrees to the wind. In the northern hemisphere it is 45 degrees to the right, and in the southern, 45 degrees to the left. The equatorial currents driven by the trade winds do not move towards the Equator, but flow parallel to it.

The Coriolis effect is negligible on water particles at the surface, because they are moved by wind friction and therefore in the same direction as the wind. But once out of the wind, under the surface, the Coriolis force takes effect. Indeed, the deeper you go, the more effect it has and the further the water is deflected from the path of the prevailing wind. This is because the drag between each layer of moving water causes a deflection. The strength of the water motion also decreases with depth, so the end result is a narrowing spiral of water movement, turning away from the direction of wind. At about 90 m

(300 feet) – the depth at which winds no longer have an impact – the water can end up flowing in exactly the opposite direction to the wind. However, the overall result is that a body of water moves at right angles to the wind pushing it.

When prevailing winds blow parallel to a coast (particularly a west coast), the top layers of water move offshore at right angles to the wind and cold, deep water rises to replace it, creating an upwelling. This cold water is full of nutrients, which nourish marine life. The upwelling on the Peruvian coast of South America is very large and supports a massive fishery. By contrast, California has an upwelling that is unpredictable and short-lived. Less significant, certainly in terms of fisheries, are equatorial upwellings. These occur more commonly in the Pacific. As the equatorial currents on either side of the Equator move west, the water beneath moves north (or right) in the northern hemisphere and south (or left) in the southern hemisphere and deep, cold water rises in the middle to replace it.

A combination of global winds and the Coriolis effect produces huge gyres or circular movements of surface water in the ocean basins. The Atlantic, Pacific and Indian Oceans each have two – one in the north, which rotates in a clockwise direction, and one in the south, which rotates in an anti-clockwise direction.

WAVES

Waves are perhaps the most familiar feature of the ocean. We sail on them, play in them, surf them and scare ourselves when they get too big. But as well as providing entertainment and thrills, waves can be very destructive. They store a lot of energy, which is released as they break. The bigger the wave, the more energy released, and sometimes we are not ready for the impact: boats sink, piers are destroyed, houses get washed away and even human life is lost. Waves, like many aspects of the ocean, are not always as predictable as we would like them to be.

2

1

1. In April, 1946 a tsunami hit Hilo, Hawaii. The devastation and loss of life provided enough incentive for a tsunami early-warning system to be established.

2. Occasionally a massive, rogue wave may swamp and even sink a ship at sea.

Making waves

Waves are created by wind. As a breeze blows over water, surface tension, which holds the water smooth, breaks and ripples are created. The wind pushes the back of each tiny crest, and eddies form at the front, reinforcing the shape of the developing wave. Within the wave itself, water is moving in circles, riding up and forward as the crest passes over and down and backwards through the trough. So energy from the wind is not being used to move a body of water through the ocean, rather it is being stored and transported through the ocean itself. As the wind continues to blow, more energy is transferred, stored and moved.

The height of waves is determined by the fetch, or distance, over which the wind is blowing. Being the largest ocean on the planet, the Pacific has the longest fetch and therefore,

usually the highest waves. In a big storm waves can reach 15 m (50 feet) high, although the highest wave ever recorded was 34 m (112 feet).

Breaking waves

As waves approach the shore, they make contact with the seabed and the resulting friction slows the waves down. They get closer and closer, stacking up against each other. As this happens the height and steepness of the waves increase. As water at the top of the waves keeps going at the same speed, and water at the bottom slows down even more, the crests spill over themselves and the waves break. The energy carried in them is released on to the shore.

Different types of shoreline produce different types of wave. A very gentle gradient will create waves that spill over a long distance. By contrast, a steeply shelving shoreline creates

3

waves that break very suddenly and violently as they hit the shallows.

Tsunamis

Sometimes called tidal waves, these giant waves have nothing whatsoever to do with tides. and are now more commonly called tsunamis (from Japanese: tsu = harbour, nami = wave). They originate in submarine earthquakes, volcanic eruptions, or sometimes giant mudslides. When a shift occurs along a fault line on the sea floor, or a volcano erupts, the shock wave produced radiates outward, travelling at speeds of up to 700 kph (435 mph). At the surface of the open ocean the wave created is small – 1 m

(3.25 feet) high at most – and often goes unnoticed by ships. But as it reaches the continental slope, the wave slows down and in places the energy of the wave is channelled by the seabed. With enormous power behind it and great speed propelling it, the wave builds in height very quickly, and the results can be devastating.

Tsunamis are most common in the Pacific Ocean because of all the volcanic activity around its rim. The explosion of Krakatoa in Indonesia in 1883 sent tsunamis halfway around the world, killing 36,000 people. In 1998, an earthquake produced a tsunami 10 m (33 feet) high, which destroyed villages along the coast of Papua New Guinea, killing over 3000 inhabitants.

3. When the sea floor rises to a shoreline, a wave coming in from the ocean slows down, builds in height and then breaks.

 TOPIC LINKS

1.2 Forces of Nature
p.31 Winds

2.1 The Dynamic Border
p.61 The Shape of the Coast

2.2 Surviving the Coast
p.73 Smashed by the Waves

4.3 Ocean Forests
p.189 Wild Water

1. Spiral eddies form along the shear zones of strong currents, such as the Gulf Stream.

2. Black-browed albatrosses rely on the stable winds and waves of the Southern Ocean to fly great distances in search of food without expending much energy.

3. The main surface currents of the oceans. In the five ocean basins the currents merge to form gyres.

Gyres

Gyres are characterized by having strong currents along their western boundary which carry the water towards the poles, and a gentler, less definable current, running east. The spiralling movement of water in ocean gyres creates a centre where the sea level is higher than the rest of the gyre. In the Northern Atlantic Gyre, for example, is the Sargasso Sea, where sea level is about a metre or so higher than the surrounding ocean. The centre mound of water in a gyre is not right in the middle, however: owing to the rotation of the Earth, the centre is nearer its western boundary. This squashes the western current against the land and means that the water flows faster through the narrow gap. In the north, the speed of most ocean currents is about 10 km (6 miles) per day, but western boundary currents, such as the Gulf Stream in the North Atlantic and the Kuroshio Current in the North Pacific, may reach speeds of 90–160 km (60–100 miles) per day. These currents are strong and consistent, but as they head north and are gradually deflected east, they lose the land barrier, the pressure eases off, the water moves more slowly and the currents begin to meander. These meandering bodies of water can become isolated from the main flow of the current and form little satellite gyres, called 'rings'. These remain adrift within the main ocean gyre.

Ocean currents in the southern hemisphere tend to be slower than those in the north. The centre of the gyre is less pronounced, so the effect on the western boundary is reduced. Moreover, gyres in the south are bordered by a continuous cold current, which sweeps around the Southern Ocean, uninterrupted by any landmass. This current is called the Antarctic Circumpolar Current and is responsible for keeping Antarctica isolated from the warming effects of global currents.

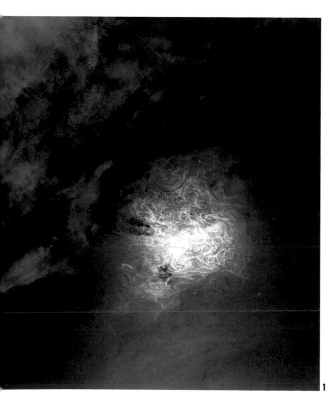

CLIMATE CONTROL

OCEAN CURRENTS

The difference in temperature between Antarctica in the grip of winter and the hottest desert in summer may seem considerable to us, but far from being a place of extremes, Earth is benign compared to what it would be without the oceans. These massive bodies of water act as storage heaters, slowly soaking up heat from the sun, and gradually releasing it in other places around the globe. They play a key role in regulating climate.

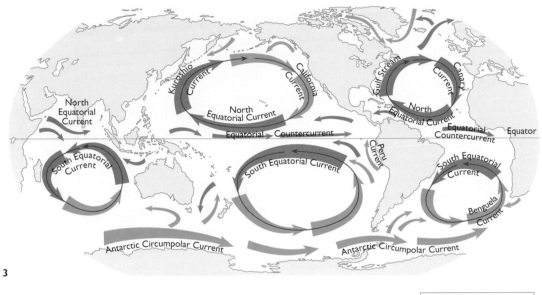

3

Warm current
Cold current
Gyre

Deep ocean circulation

In 1751 a British captain by the name of Harry Ellis heaved up a bucket of water from the depths while off the coast of West Africa. Noting how cold it was in comparison to the balmy temperature of the surface waters, he subsequently used it to chill his wine. No scientist could be sure where this cold water

GREENHOUSE GASES

The nature of Earth's surfaces – the oceans, landmasses and ice-caps – are important in regulating the amount of heat from the sun that is reflected and absorbed. Only 4 per cent of the incoming radiation is dispelled straight back out. The rest is used, bounced between the Earth and its atmosphere until it is also eventually lost. However, some atmospheric gases impede this process. The so-called greenhouse gases (carbon dioxide in particular) are transparent to incoming, longer wavelengths of light, but are more opaque to the outgoing shorter wavelengths of light (infrared) or heat. It is estimated that without this greenhouse effect, Earth would be 33° C (59 °F) colder. The amount of carbon dioxide in our atmosphere has increased by 25 per cent in the last century, and Earth's overall temperature is believed to be changing as a result. As more heat is trapped by the atmosphere, global temperatures will rise and the currently frozen ice-caps will begin to melt. An increase in sea level, which will flood many low-lying areas, is only one of the predicted outcomes. Global climate will change and with it some valuable habitats such as sea ice will shrink.

1. The oceans act as giant storage heaters, absorbing heat from the sun and redistributing it both in time and geographically. The mild, damp winters experienced in Ireland are a result of the warm Gulf Stream sweeping up its coast.

2. Along the coast of Peru, huge colonies of boobies rely on a supply of anchovy to feed their growing chicks. These fish depend, in turn, on a rich upwelling that fails during El Niño years – a disaster for the boobies.

1

came from, but they guessed that it had to have originated in the freezing waters of the poles.

In polar regions the sun barely heats up the water at all so it remains cold and dense. Polar water is also saltier than other waters, because when it freezes, its salt content stays in the unfrozen water, making it more concentrated. The combination of extreme cold and extra salt makes this water so dense that it sinks to the bottom of the ocean. As it descends, it displaces the cold, dense, salty water already there and pushes it along the ocean floor towards the Equator. Over many years, cold water from both poles spreads through the oceans, pushed along by new water descending. It gradually mixes with the warmer waters above and, over centuries, eventually reaches the surface.

In addition to these movements, water is also circulated around the globe by what is called the Great Ocean Conveyer Belt. The two main places where cold water from the polar regions is known to feed this conveyer belt are in the Atlantic near Greenland and in the south

around Antarctica. Water from the Gulf Stream cools as it reaches Greenland, sinks to the deep ocean, passes down the length of the Atlantic and combines with cold water from the Antarctic. The water then moves east. Channelled by deep sea trenches and mid-ocean ridges, some water peels off and runs up the western side of continents – the cold-water Humboldt Current alongside South America and the Benguela Current running up southern Africa being examples of this. The bulk of this conveyer belt of water moves eastwards, branching up into the Indian Ocean, and the rest continuing around until it reaches the Pacific, where it travels north around New Zealand. This cold, oxygen-rich and nutrient-laden water emerges as upwellings just south of India and in the northern Pacific respectively, creating areas of great productivity. Once at the surface the water heats up and travels west again, the two loops of the current meeting in the southern Indian Ocean, before it moves back into the Atlantic and up to Greenland. This

multi-ocean circulation transfers heat around the globe and helps regulate the planet's climate.

Giant thermostat

The oceans absorb and lose heat slowly, the surface changing no more than 1 °C (2 °F) a day in any one place, and only 10 °C (18 °F) in a year. (By comparison, land can change as much as 80 °C/144 °F in a day.) The process is slow because water conducts heat away from or to the surface. As the water surface heats up, heat is transferred to deeper water and stored there. The reverse happens on cooling: heat is lost to the atmosphere slowly because it has to travel up from the depths. There is a further delay in redistributing the heat because ocean currents take time to move around the globe.

Despite the time lag, the heat storage capacity of water combined with both the vertical and horizontal movement of currents around the globe provide efficient means of transferring a lot of heat from one part of the

2

world to another. This has a big impact on the surrounding landmasses. For example, as warm equatorial water moves to the cold north, via the Gulf Stream and North Atlantic Drift it begins to lose heat to the atmosphere. The air is gradually warmed and blown across western Europe by the prevailing westerly winds. So in winter, when the sun's rays are too weak to give much warmth, the North Atlantic Ocean acts as a radiator, producing relatively mild winters and a so-called maritime climate, rather than the freezing winters and scorching hot summers of the rest of the continent.

El Niño-Southern Oscillation (ENSO)

The role of winds, currents and oceans in regulating the world's climate is fundamental, but often we are blithely unaware of it. Only when the pattern is altered do we take notice, and the El Niño-Southern Oscillation, which affects the whole world has made us do just that.

In the waters off the coast of Peru is an upwelling that supports huge numbers of anchovy exploited by humans, as well as large seabird colonies. Towards the end of the year, the winds die down, the upwelling decreases for a while and the water warms up. This annual event is called El Niño. In some years, however, the effect is very pronounced. Without winds driving water offshore, the warm, nutrient-poor equatorial waters flow back east, smothering any remaining cold water. The surface water becomes a few degrees warmer and the anchovy that thrive in cold water disappear. The fishery collapses, thousands of birds fail to breed and many die. Water level rises too, causing flooding in low-lying coastal areas, while torrential rains batter parts of South America and others suffer drought.

It was some time before El Niño became linked to what is called the Southern Oscillation – a giant seesaw-like system of high and low pressure between the Pacific and Indian oceans. When there is exceptionally

high pressure in the Pacific, it is matched by exceptionally low pressure in the Indian Ocean and vice versa. During normal conditions, predictable Indian monsoons bring rain for the crops. But when there are major changes in pressure, the rains fail and famine results. On the other side of the Pacific, El Niño events occur at the same time, so rather than there being a number of localized vagaries, there is one big global atmospheric and oceanic event.

In 1982–83 the strongest ENSO in living memory occurred. South America's anchovy fishery collapsed and the continent endured drought and floods. Hawaii and Tahiti were battered by cyclones while Australia, India and southern Africa suffered droughts, and in some areas famine ensued.

However, not all the effects are disastrous. Warm-water fish, such as skipjack tuna, yellowfin tuna and Spanish mackerel, were caught off Peru, which helped fishermen through the disaster.

MOON POWER

Sea level has been rising and falling each day for billions of years. This phenomenon has a huge impact on marine life, particularly on the plants and animals living on the coast, which are alternately submerged and exposed with each tide. Life just offshore is also affected, as tides are important in water circulation: even far away from land, marine life uses tides to synchronize behaviour, most commonly reproduction.

Daily tides

Tides are created by the gravitational pull of the moon and the sun, and by the rotation of the Earth and moon. Everything in the universe exerts some gravitational pull on everything else, but in order for there to be an effect, these objects must be relatively close to each other. The gravitational pull of the moon on Earth, which is on average only 376,000 km (234,000 miles) away, is stronger than that of

the sun which is 150 million km (93 million miles) away. Centrifugal force, caused by the Earth's rotation, pushes outwards and balances the pull of gravity, so the distance between Earth and the moon stays the same.

Centrifugal force and the moon's gravitational pull vary at different points around the world. On the side of the Earth that is nearest the moon, the moon's gravity literally pulls the water in the oceans towards it. On the opposite side of the planet, the centrifugal force exerts a stronger influence than the moon, and that too pulls water with it. So water is pulled in opposite directions. These opposing forces create bulges, or high tides, in the oceans on opposite sides of the Earth at the same time. Between the two bulges are areas of water where the impact of the forces is even. Because water has been pulled away to the bulges, these areas experience low tides.

As the Earth is spinning on its own axis in a 24-hour cycle, every point on it passes through the 'bulges' twice a day. On land the

SUN, MOON AND TIDES

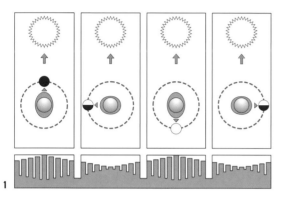

1. Diagram to show how the gravitational pulls of the sun and moon create spring and neap tides. When the sun and moon pull together, or directly oppose each other, the tides are more extreme (spring tides), when they pull in different directions (i.e. at right angles to each other) tidal range is reduced (neap tides).

effect is not noticeable, but we can clearly see the effect on oceans in the tidal highs and lows. However, tides have other forces working on them. Friction between water and the Earth's crust slows the movement of water down, thus high tides are a little offset from a line drawn between the Earth and the moon – they occur a little behind it. Also, the moon's orbit around Earth is not in time with the Earth's own 24-hour spin. In fact, the moon gains by 50 minutes each day, which means that a spot on the Earth is 50 minutes into its next day before it is in direct line with the moon again. Tides, therefore, also slip by 50 minutes each day.

Spring and neap tides

Despite the sun being so much larger than the moon, it is 400 times further away, which means that its gravitational pull on Earth is only about two-fifths as strong as the moon's. Nevertheless it does exert an influence on the oceans, and produce bulges in the same way as the moon.

When the sun is directly in line with the moon (and the Earth) its gravity either pulls with the moon or against it, depending on where the moon is. For example, if the moon is between the sun and Earth (new moon), the gravitational pulls of both the moon and the sun act together to produce particularly high and low tides. Equally, if the moon is full and on the opposite side of the Earth to the sun, both will be pulling water and working with the centrifugal force, so tides will also be higher. These twice-monthly tides are called spring tides, which relates to their height rather than the time of year when they occur.

It is when the moon is at right angles to the sun, either waxing or waning, that the tides are less extreme, the tidal range is low and we have neap tides. This happens because the moon's and the sun's gravitational pulls are partly cancelling each other out.

Real tides

Tidal patterns are not easily described, partly because huge landmasses get in the way and partly because of the topography of the ocean floor. Most coasts do experience two high tides and two low tides each day, but they can vary in strength, and some places have only one tide per day rather than two.

When the moon is directly over the Equator, this is the area most strongly affected by its gravity; it has less impact towards the poles. Likewise, when the moon's orbit takes it away from the Equator, the further north (and south) it orbits, the greater the pull in those places. Combine this with the Coriolis effect, mid-ocean ridges and other underwater features that disrupt the flow of water, and the result is a range of different tidal patterns across the globe.

Throughout most of the Pacific Ocean, for example, one of the two high tides each day is higher than the other. By contrast, most of the Atlantic Ocean has relatively even tides occurring twice a day. Other places, such as the Gulf of Mexico, much of Antarctica and a few isolated areas in the western Pacific experience only one tide per day.

In most of the ocean basins, tides affect the height of the water by 1–3 m (3.25–10 feet). But in areas where water flow is restricted, such as a partly enclosed bay, tidal range can be more. In the Bay of Fundy, Nova Scotia, for example, the tidal range is 15 m (49 feet) on spring tides, and a strong tidal current is present much of the time as a lot of water has to move in and out of the bay. This current mixes nutrients in the water, and as a result, the sea is very rich. Summer plankton blooms feed krill, which in turn feed humpback whales, which return each year to take advantage of this bounty.

3

2. The gravitational pull of the moon on Earth is twice that of the sun, because although the moon is much smaller, it is 400 times closer to Earth.

3. In some estuaries, as an exceptionally high spring tide rises, water will rush in like a wave, causing extensive damage along the banks. This is called a tidal bore.

Tsunamis (often called tidal waves) can travel across very deep oceans faster than a jumbo jet. In 1960 an earthquake in Chile sent a shock wave across the Pacific which reached Japan just 21 hours later.

LIVING IN THE SEA

The number and variety of animals and plants that can be found in the oceans is overwhelming. From the tiniest bacteria (only thousandths of a millimetre across) to the largest animal on the planet (the 33-m/108-foot blue whale), marine life comes in all shapes and sizes. Moreover, it all survives, feeds and reproduces in equally diverse ways. One of the reasons the oceans sustain so many life forms – many more than can be found on land – is that they offer three dimensions for occupation: a fish easily achieves neutral buoyancy in water, whereas birds expend a great deal of energy simply staying aloft. Thus, the available living space for marine life forms is an estimated 250 times greater than for those on land. Nevertheless, although the oceans offer a vast area to live in, most marine life is concentrated near the surface, in the upper 200 m (656 feet) where sunlight penetrates. Even within this shallow zone, life is not evenly distributed – most of it lives near land, on or above the continental shelf.

WHERE TO LIVE

Conditions vary greatly in different parts of the ocean, so there are numerous places to live and ways to make a living. Clearly, there are great differences between living in an icy world, in open water, on a coral reef or in the abyssal depths. In some places, life appears effortless for plants and animals; food is abundant, mates are numerous and so long as predators are avoided the living is easy. In other places it seems more of a struggle.

On the edge

Coastal regions are among the hardest places to survive. Land animals that rely on the sea for a living spend part of their time in water for which they are not necessarily well designed. Few plants and animals do well both on land and under water; there always has to be some compromise. Birds that feed by swimming under water, such as guillemots, are not good fliers. Penguins have given up aerial flight altogether for more efficient 'flight' under water. Similarly, marine animals that have to breed on land often move very inefficiently when out of the water. Seals and sea lions manage an ungainly shuffle at best.

The intertidal zone is probably one of the toughest places to live. Plants and animals on a rocky shore suffer great physical stress when the tide goes out. They are left literally high and dry. Some such as crabs and snails, run from the problem, seeking shelter in tide pools or in damp cracks and overhangs. Seaweeds remain stuck where they are, and some survive only if they originally settle in a place that keeps them moist during low tide. Molluscs such as mussels and limpets shut themselves

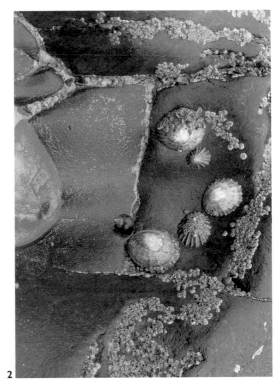

2

1

1. Coral reefs are the most diverse habitats of the marine world. In warm, shallow, sunlit waters, where conditions are stable all year round, competition for living space is intense.

2. Living in the inter-tidal zone is hard. Limpets and barnacles seal themselves into their shells to avoid drying up while the tide is out.

Phytoplankton are responsible for nearly half of the photosynthesis in the world, producing half the oxygen in the atmosphere.

in to reduce water loss. Others are adapted to tolerate it; the seaweed *Fucus* can cope with losing a remarkable 90 per cent of its water content with each low tide.

It is not only drying out that organisms have to deal with. They get battered by waves and during low tide they may be exposed to extremes of temperature, they may experience a drop in salinity if it rains and, of course, many of them rely on water for food, so when the tide is out they cannot feed. Life in the intertidal zone of a rocky shore is far from easy.

Polar regions present another set of extremes. For part of the year the polar seas are in total darkness, and during the summer they enjoy 24 hours of sunlight. Temperatures hover above freezing in the summer but can plunge to below -50 °C (-58 °F) in winter. Many

warm-blooded animals escape the dark and bitter cold of winter by migrating away as the sea freezes over. However, some hardy types, such as Weddell seals in the Antarctic and walruses in the Arctic, stay behind, enduring the severest of conditions. In order to breathe they have to use holes in the ice that are kept open by currents or, in the case of Weddell seals, use their teeth to keep a hole open.

Bathed in water

The richest, most diverse habitats occur in shallow, rocky places in both temperate and tropical seas. Enough sunlight reaches the seabed to allow plants to grow, and stable ecosystems can be built on such foundations. Coral reefs are the most diverse of all.

Although the water surrounding them is low in nutrients, recycling on a reef is so efficient that the community is largely self-sufficient. Temperate habitats are also exuberant, but are restricted by their seasonality.

Marine life is concentrated in coastal water for good reason: all the advantages of a solid, three-dimensional living space are on offer. By contrast the vast open ocean has one severe disadvantage for animals: there is no place to attach to, nothing to burrow into or hide behind. Nevertheless, compared to the intertidal zone or the freezing poles, it is an easier place to live – often warm, well lit and with no shortage of water. The only thing creatures have to do is stay afloat and avoid being eaten.

Staying afloat can be achieved in two main ways: by increasing water resistance to slow the inevitable sinking process, and by increasing buoyancy. Microscopic plants and animals (which form plankton) have large surface areas for their size, which increases drag as they sink; extra appendages and a flat shape add resistance. Greater buoyancy can be achieved by storing fat, which is less dense than water and therefore floats. Many small plankton, such as tiny crustaceans and fish larvae, have little fat droplets. Even larger, open-ocean swimmers, such as tuna and sharks, use fat to increase their buoyancy. Marine mammals do too, and the stored blubber also helps to maintain their body temperature. Most fishes use air for buoyancy, having evolved swim bladders (pockets of air) to regulate their depth in the water. Avoiding predators is far more demanding. In the open ocean, where there is plenty of light, most animals have very well-developed eyes, both for finding food and spotting predators. Transparency is a great advantage used by many jellyfish and smaller creatures.

Go below the sunlit surface waters to a depth of 200 m (656 feet) and life becomes harder. The pressure exerted by water is considerable, but most critically there is not enough light to support plant life. Without plants, animals depend on the rain of food from above, and that is hardly abundant. Only about 5 per cent of food produced in the sea above is not used there and sinks to support animals living at depth. Because food is so limited, there are comparatively few animals living in the twilight zone (200–1000 m/656–3281 feet), and fewer living in the inky blackness beneath.

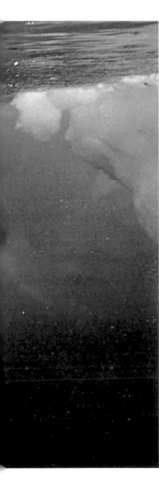

1. Guillemots are seasonal visitors to the icy seas of the Arctic. Only when the ice recedes in late spring do these migratory birds fly north to feed and rear their chicks.

2. Marine mammals, such as these South American sea lions, have a layer of blubber under their skin. This both keeps them warm in the water and helps with buoyancy.

BLUE WHALES

Twice the size of the biggest dinosaurs, blue whales are the largest animals that have ever lived on Earth. In every dimension their size is incomparable. Adult females are the largest, able to weigh as much as 200 tonnes and measure 33 m (108 feet) in length. Their tongue alone weighs the same as an elephant. When they exhale, the thunderous blow reaches 9 m (30 feet) high and, on a quiet day, can be heard miles away. Because they are so big, so rich in blubber and so audible, blue whales were once hunted to near extinction.

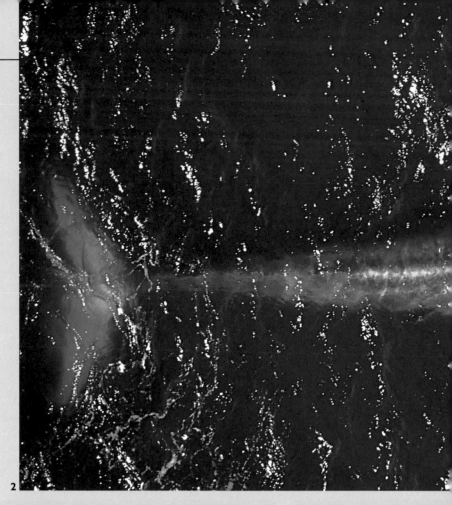

2

Hunting whales

For many years blue whales were not sought by whaling ships. Swimming at a remarkable 20 knots, they were simply too fast to be caught by sailing boats. On the odd occasions they were caught, they were too powerful to overcome and, in any case, when a blue whale is harpooned and dies, it sinks, which made them hard to handle. It was not until 1864, when a Norwegian whaling captain commissioned a purpose-built steam-powered boat, that blue whales were targeted. Soon the North Atlantic and Pacific stocks began to be depleted.

When shore-based whaling stations sprang up in 1904, the Antarctic population suffered. But it was the advent of factory ships which processed the dead whales from a fleet of many smaller ships, that heralded disaster for blue whales. The whalers had the speed to chase them, the harpoons to kill them and the freedom to stay at sea for long periods because they no longer had to return to shore after each catch. The southern summer of 1930–1 marked the peak of the slaughter: 28,325 blue whales were killed by only 41 ships.

It is thought that a total of 350,000 blue whales have been killed worldwide, 90 per cent of those in Antarctic waters. At last, in 1965, the International Whaling Commission decreed that blue whales should be protected. But by then, for most populations, it was already too late. An estimated 650 were left in the Southern Ocean, and there has been no visible recovery. It appears that the Alaskan population was wiped out altogether. Only in Californian waters, since 1980, has there been

1

a marked comeback, and now approximately 2000 blue whales feed there.

Big eaters

Blue whales have big appetites. In order to maintain such a huge body they probably need about 1.5 million calories each day. But as they feed for only half the year (the other half is spent in warm tropical water where they breed and where there is little or no food), they actually need 3 million or more calories per day.

Blue whales eat mostly krill, a small shrimp-like crustacean. They feed by engulfing huge mouthfuls of krill and water. In order to consume enough with each gulp, they have throat pleats stretching from their lower jaw along their body, which distend enormously when a mouthful is taken. In order to sieve the krill from the water, the enormous tongue forces water through the 270–400 tightly spaced, 1-m (3.25-foot) -long baleen plates that hang from the upper jaw.

Loners

Blue whales are usually seen alone. Occasionally, two or more adults can be seen feeding together, but most sightings of two blue whales are mother and calf. Very little is known about their breeding behaviour, and what we do know comes from records kept during the whaling days. Females mature at five years old. After mating, the gestation is 11–12 months and a calf of 7 m (23 feet) and 3 tonnes is born. After only seven months of feeding on rich milk, the calf is weaned and starts to feed on krill. At this stage it is 16 m (52.5 feet) long and weighs 23 tonnes. That means that a calf grows 4 cm (1.5 in) and gains 90 kg (198 lb) per day while nursing. To achieve this it drinks up to 100 litres (22 gallons) of milk each day. This extraordinary transfer of energy takes a toll on the mother, who loses about one-third (50 tonnes) of her body weight. When the pair return to higher latitudes for the summer, the mother can resume feeding and regain her fat stores.

1. The blow holes of a blue whale are exceptionally large – the size of a small child.

2. Seen from the air, a blue whale is torpedo shaped – the perfect design for swimming at speed and for long distances through the open ocean.

3. A blue whale forces air and water out of its mouth after having taken a giant, krill-filled gulp. Its throat pleats gradually concertina in again until they lie flat under the lower jaw.

◆ TOPIC LINKS

4.2 Blooming Plankton
p.180 Planktivorous Giants

5.2 Antarctic Wildlife
p.229 Krill – Staple Diet
p.235 Large Visitors

6.4 Ocean Birth
p.308 Baleen Whales

PYRAMIDS OF LIFE

On land, the plant world is dominated by trees, bushes and grasses, but in the oceans it is dominated by microscopic cells. Whatever size and shape they come in, the key thing that plants the world over have in common is the ability to photosynthesize. This chemical reaction uses energy from the sun to combine carbon dioxide and water to produce simple sugars, the building blocks of carbohydrates. Oxygen happens to be a by-product of the reaction. Apart from a few extraordinary habitats, such as the hydrothermal and cold vents in the deep ocean, photosynthesis makes the biological world go round.

Most of the ocean's photosynthesis occurs in plankton, a community of microscopic single-celled plants (phytoplankton) and animals (zooplankton), that drifts around in surface waters. Only the plants photosynthesize. However, plankton can refer to anything that lives by drifting in the sea, so large jellyfish and floating seaweed can also be included.

Marine pyramids

Viewed simply, a food chain or web is just a series of links between living things that depend on each other for food. The plants, or primary producers, are the first in line. Next come the first group of consumers, the herbivores, followed by various other consumers each feeding on the group before. However, not all energy is passed on to the next level. Some of the energy created by phytoplankton is lost in simply living, and not all phytoplankton are eaten before they die. Similarly, herbivores and carnivores use energy to live and to reproduce, and some of what they eat passes through them without being digested.

This loss of energy between each level is substantial and, on average, only 10 per cent is passed on. As a result there are fewer animals at each level. On land, this typically creates a pyramid of life: there are more plants than herbivores, more herbivores than carnivores and so on. In the ocean, however, the pyramid is normally inverted. The number of primary producers is lower than the herbivores, which in turn is lower than the carnivores. But if you look at actual *production* within any one level, a pyramid does exist. Phytoplankton reproduce within a matter of hours or days (but the standing stock is low as they are eaten very quickly), zooplankton take weeks, and fishes can take a year. So in terms of how much is actually produced at any one level, the pyramid still stands.

Because each level has less energy, there is a limit on the number of levels that can exist. At the top of the food chain, energy runs out, so animals such as sharks and killer whales, are fewer in number and reproduce less often, and are therefore less commonly seen than those lower down, such as smaller fishes.

The best strategy for animals at the top of the pyramid is to bypass as many levels of consumer as possible and feed nearer the bottom of the food chain; that way they harness more energy for themselves. Not surprisingly, it is the largest animals in the oceans that have achieved this. Whale sharks, the largest fish of all, feed on plankton, as do blue whales, the largest mammal.

Phytoplankton – the first link in the chain

Bathed in water, which contains dissolved carbon dioxide, and, because of their size, needing only a minimal amount of sunlight to fuel their photosynthesis, phytoplankton are pretty well cared for in most places. The only other nutrients they need in any quantity are nitrogen, phosphorus and silica, all of which are found in sea water. Being so minute, some as small as 0.0002 mm, their individual requirements are not large.

Phytoplankton are essential to life in the oceans: a staggering 90 per cent of primary production (the creation of organic

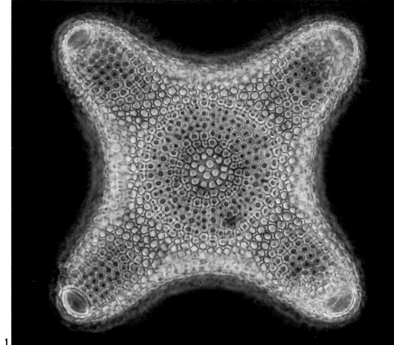

1

1. Diatoms are microscopic marine plants that are particularly abundant in temperate waters. Along with other phytoplankton, they form the first stage in the food chain.

2. Whale sharks are the largest fish in the sea. They bypass other trophic levels and feed directly on plankton, simply by opening their cavernous mouths and swimming through the soup of microscopic life.

2

The recycling of carbon between the ocean, the atmosphere and land is an essential ongoing process for life on Earth. Most carbon in its inorganic form, carbon dioxide, is found in the atmosphere and dissolved in sea water; thus the oceans are an immense carbon dioxide store. When plants photosynthesize, they convert inorganic carbon into organic carbon compounds or simple sugars. In the oceans it is the microscopic plants called phytoplankton, that are responsible for nearly all the conversion of carbon dioxide into useful sugars.

Most of the organic carbon moves up the food chain as one animal eats another. In order to live, organisms use the sugars for energy and by doing so convert the carbon back into carbon dioxide. This is released into the water or the air, where it can be reabsorbed by plants. But some organic carbon takes another path. Phytoplankton might die before being eaten, some carbon is excreted as faeces by animals and, in the end, the animals themselves die. All this dead organic carbon rains down on to the sea floor, where much of it is converted back to carbon dioxide by decaying bacteria. When not used by bacteria or eaten by scavengers, dead organic carbon builds up, layer upon layer, and over geological time is converted into deposits of fossil fuels, oil, gas and coal.

compounds from carbon dioxide) in the oceans occurs in these microscopic plants. In shallow coastal waters, a community can develop based on larger marine plants – seaweeds and algae – which grow on the sea floor. Indeed, in nutrient-rich water that receives a lot of sun (even if only seasonally), plants, such as the giant kelp forests of California, rival the productivity of phytoplankton. But coastal waters make up a tiny percentage of the oceans, and these small productive zones cannot begin to support the abundance of life found in the oceans.

Since phytoplankton needs light, it exists only in the upper 200 m (656 feet) of water. Here it flourishes and soon uses up all the available nutrients unless they are replaced. Clearly, it is not limited by water, and nor is it limited by carbon dioxide, as more is continually being absorbed from the atmosphere. It is nitrogen and phosphorus (and in some places silica and iron) that are the limiting nutrients. In areas of upwelling, where

nutrients are constantly replenished, phytoplankton do well. Similarly, seasonal storms, which affect temperate latitudes, mix the water thoroughly, ensuring that when spring returns, there are enough nutrients in the water for phytoplankton to bloom. The polar regions also have a plankton bloom, but it comes later in the year when the annual sea ice has all but melted.

Tropical water might be expected to have the highest primary productivity as the water is warm and there is year-round sunlight. But tropical waters are characterized by having a low nutrient content, and this limits phytoplankton numbers. Indeed, productivity in tropical water is only a quarter of what it is in temperate seas.

Zooplankton – the first consumers

Where there is a source of food, there is nearly always an animal to eat it. Zooplankton are animals of the plankton world and many of them graze on phytoplankton. In contrast to

⭐ Whales and dolphins produce greasy tears that protect their eyes from the stinging effects of salty sea water.

1. The baleen of a gray whale. It would hang from each upper jaw and be used to sieve crustaceans from sediment and water.

2. (opposite) On reaching maturity, at about 30 years old, turtles, such as this green turtle, may swim for thousands of miles to return to their breeding beaches.

land herbivores, few plankton are strict vegetarians; most zooplankton will indulge in a little animal flesh occasionally.

The most abundant tiny herbivores are copepods, making up about 70 per cent of the zooplankton. They are minute crustaceans that use their legs like paddles to draw water towards their mouth so that they can extract phytoplankton. Far from being unselective in their diet, they actively seek out phytoplankton using both sight and 'smell'. Copepods are also carnivorous, catching other zooplankton (and sometimes each other) with claw-like appendages.

On land, plants grow large and store food. Some of it is eaten, but most plant matter eventually dies and is decomposed by bacteria and fungi. In the ocean things are very different; most phytoplankton get eaten. Being single-celled, their growth potential is small, so they turn excess energy into reproducing by simple division, which they do frequently. That is why, in higher latitudes when spring arrives and there is enough light for photosynthesis, the phytoplankton population increases, sometimes explodes, before the zooplankton population has had time to graze it down.

Most zooplankton do not last long either. They live only a few weeks which gives them time to collect enough energy to breed before

dying (if they are not eaten first). In the tropical oceans, zooplankton can breed all year, but at higher latitudes, where the feeding season is short, the breeding season is correspondingly curtailed. Those animals in the zooplankton that are not permanent residents but merely larval stages of other animals do not reproduce at all. These zooplankton spend only a short part of their lives in the plankton community, but this period is important in dispersal, ensuring the colonization of new places.

Swarming the oceans are carnivores, which feed exclusively on zooplankton. Some are zooplankton themselves, being merely a little bigger or a little more aggressive than those they eat. Other feeders include fishes, jellyfish and even some of the biggest animals on the planet, the baleen whales.

Nekton – the swimmers

Members of the plankton are at the whim of ocean currents, but larger animals, some of which depend on the plankton community for food, are free to swim where they please. Fishes, marine mammals and squid are the most numerous of the group known as nekton, which also includes turtles, sea snakes and penguins.

Animals that feed exclusively on plankton range from small fishes, such as sardines, anchovies and herring, to manta rays and whale sharks. Their style of acquiring food varies as much as their size. Fish usually pick off individual zooplankton drifting by, while whale sharks simply open their mouths as they swim along and let the plankton enter. Whale sharks have fine, comb-like structures on their gills to sieve out larger planktonic animals as the water passes through.

The ability of these animals to swim means that they can move between the best feeding grounds as the productivity of each place changes with the seasons. Tuna, for example, make long journeys right across the Pacific and Atlantic, following the areas of highest productivity. Whales migrate from the tropics, where they breed, to the polar regions to take advantage of the huge plankton boom that occurs each polar summer. Many sea birds time their breeding to coincide with phytoplankton blooms, for shortly after zooplankton numbers increase, small fishes arrive to feed, and birds rely on an abundance of small fish to satisfy their growing chicks. In most ocean habitats, simple food chains like this do not exist; instead, there is a complex web of dependence, creating a more stable ecosystem.

EATING AT SEA

Water provides a three-dimensional habitat in which to live and feed. That fact alone vastly increases the methods by which animals can obtain their food. Many of them simply strain it from the water passing by, probably the easiest method, while others scrape it off rocks, eat it out of the sand or hunt it down.

Filtering food

Given that so much of the food in the ocean is plankton, many animals have evolved ways of filtering it out of the water. Whales do it by using baleen, whale sharks and fishes use their gills, while copepods use hairs. But many filter feeders live on the sea floor and cannot swim around to find food. These include barnacles and some tube worms, which use modified legs to snatch particles floating by in the water and pass them to their mouth. Even the anemone crab collects suspended particles using efficient, net-like appendages which it throws into the oncoming current.

Plankton are trapped by numerous coral reef invertebrates. Sea fans grow in flat, lattice-like structures at right angles to the prevailing current. When the individual animals or polyps of the sea fan, extend their tentacles, very little escapes the trap. Basketstars unfold their highly branched arms and spread their extensive net, trapping larger plankton and unwary small fish. Numerous little hooks then impale their prey before it is fed down to the mouth.

Other animals are more active and actually create a flow of water by tiny beating hairs. These armies of hairs draw water through the body of the animal so that particles can be extracted. Both sea squirts and sponges use this method, but some are also designed to maximize water movement by using the chimney technique. In the same way that air blowing over the top of a chimney draws air up through it, so water passing over sea squirts and tall sponges draws water through their bodies. In sea squirts a strand of mucus inside the body traps the passing particles, and the mucus is then bundled up and digested. In sponges, the water is moved along in small tunnels by whip-like hairs, where cells along the tunnel walls trap and ingest particles of floating food.

1

Eating off the floor

What little plankton is missed by the innumerable traps, joins the rain of faecal matter and dead material that falls from above. The ocean floor is littered with organic matter, which is soon eaten by the bacteria that thrive there. As on land, bacteria play an important part in breaking down organic matter for recycling.

Bacteria, in turn, provide a valuable food source for animals living within the sediment. These microscopic animals move between grains of sand hunting down bacteria. The combination of fine sediment, detritus and living animals creates a grainy soup, which is ingested wholesale by a wide range of larger animals. Little fish called sleeper gobies live and feed on sandy sea beds. They spend much of the day simply scooping up mouthfuls of sand, from which they extract food. Sea cucumbers – sausage-shaped animals which come in many varieties – are a familiar sight to divers. Some of them are filter-feeders, spreading branches into the water to trap passing food. Others are detritus-feeders, inching their way across the sea bed using an array of busy feeding tentacles to pick up food from the sediment.

In the same way that filter-feeders keep the water clearer of suspended matter than it might otherwise be, detritus eaters keep the sea floor in good shape. Sediment is turned over, passed through their guts and the organic matter extracted, leaving a cleaner sea bed in their wake.

Sponges are the vacuum cleaners of sea water. They filter water so fast that a small sponge, the size of a fist, will process about 5000 litres (1100 gallons) of water a day.

2

1. Porcelain crabs have specially modified mouth parts, which are thrown out like fans into the oncoming current. Fine hairs trap plankton floating by, and the food is brought down to the mouth and 'brushed' in.

2. Sea cucumbers collect debris off the sea floor on their sticky, branching tentacles. One by one the arms are cleaned of their catch by the central mouth.

Grazing

In shallow water, where sunlight penetrates, nutrients abound and there is a solid sea floor to provide anchorage, algae grow profusely. Algae can be single-celled and appear like slime, or they can grow in short clumps or in mats. They can even grow to 30 m (98 feet) or so, like the giant kelp of California. Algae are one of the most important components of all shallow-water communities but are often overlooked. Where they grow luxuriantly, numerous animals have evolved to exploit them. Some, such as snails, limpets, sea hares and abalone, literally scrape off the surface film of algae. These molluscs have teeth arranged along a muscular tongue, which works rather like a file. As they crawl over rock, they scrape the algae off into their mouths, but by doing so they wear down their teeth, which have to be continually replaced.

Sea urchins also graze algae, and are important in many habitats because they clean the sea bed, making room for colonizing animals to grow. However, they can become a problem. With such a steady supply of food, if their numbers go unchecked by predators, they proliferate and can eat their way through huge stands of seaweeds or kelp. In areas of California where sea urchin numbers have increased due to a low sea otter population, forests of giant kelp have been temporarily reduced to rocky 'deserts'.

Fishes are also important grazers, particularly on coral reefs where, among others, parrotfishes and surgeonfishes graze away at the flourishing algae and keep them in check. It is only because of these grazing fish that coral can grow at all: algae grow so fast on shallow reefs that coral larvae settling out of the plankton and trying to make a start on the reef would soon be overgrown.

1. Scorpionfish come in all shapes and colours, but are always cleverly camouflaged against the substrate on which they are lying. These predators lie still and wait for an unsuspecting fish to swim close by.

▶ BREATHING UNDER WATER

Gills are the underwater equivalent of lungs, absorbing oxygen and getting rid of carbon dioxide. Gills are also important in regulating the salt content of a fish's body. They lose a lot of water to the sea by osmosis, and as sea-water is the only source of water available, fishes are obliged to drink it. They then have to get rid of the salt taken in, so they excrete it via their gills. As sharks swim, water passes through their mouths and over their gills. When at rest, sharks actively pump water over their gills by opening and closing their mouths. They also have small holes called spiracles just behind their eyes through which water enters, before it passes over the gills. In rays and skates, which spend most of their time on the seabed, spiracles are the only way water can get in as their mouths are usually buried in sediment. (The spiracle of a blue-spotted stingray is illustrated, right.)

Other fish also pump water over their gills, but in a more efficient way. They have flaps covering their gills which effectively seals them. As they open their mouths and close these flaps, a vacuum is created which fills with water. Subsequently they close their mouth and water is forced over the gills and through the flaps.

Predation

The world of predators and prey is an arms race, each player developing weapons and tactics accordingly. In the marine world there are essentially two types of predators – those that feed on sedentary animals and those that feed on freely moving animals. Most invertebrates fall into the former category, while most vertebrates are in the latter.

Feeding on creatures that cannot move is more like grazing than hunting. Nevertheless, the animals that do this are true predators. The crown-of-thorns starfish, for example, everts its stomach over coral and digests it in situ.

Since they cannot move to avoid predation, most sedentary animals have some form of protection. Bivalves, such as mussels and oysters, have hard shells which they can close, but predators have found a way around this. Some snails have drill-like mouthparts which bore a hole in the oyster's shell. Digestive enzymes are secreted into the hole, and the resulting soup is sucked out. By contrast, starfish open bivalves with brute force and evert their stomachs to digest the contents.

Most free-swimming hunters of the ocean track down their prey using sight, but once within range, they use a wide variety of tactics to catch their food. Camouflage, stealth and ambush often play a part, but in open water, where there is nothing to hide behind, speed is most often used. Tunas and billfishes are all remarkably fast swimmers, attacking their prey at lightning speed.

Ambush predators are usually found on or near the sea floor. They sit and wait for their prey to come ever closer and, once the striking distance has been reached, they pounce on their unwary victims. Some ambush predators, such as stonefish, can be so well camouflaged they are almost impossible to see.

1

PREHISTORIC SURVIVORS

Few animals provoke as much fear as sharks. While their speed and fearsome teeth certainly equip them to be efficient predators, their reputation as ruthless, irrational killing machines far exceeds reality. Never has a group of animals been so misunderstood and maligned. True, some sharks do occasionally attack people, but attacks are infrequent and by no means always fatal. More people are kicked to death by donkeys each year than are killed by sharks. We should respect them certainly, but for their extraordinary evolutionary success and their design, rather than because we fear them.

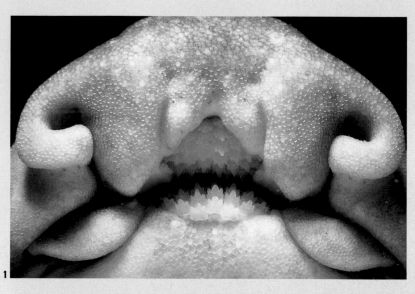

1. The bizarre-looking mouth of a horn shark is effective in handling and crushing small crustaceans.

2. The great white shark can exert a biting pressure of 3 tonnes per sq cm.

3. The megamouth shark was only discovered in 1976. Little is known of its behaviour as it lives at depth.

4. Hammerhead sharks have flattened heads which increases the sensory area used for detecting prey.

Sharks and their relatives

There are about 1100 species of sharks, rays and skates in the world. They differ from other fishes in that their skeletons are made of cartilage rather than bone, and also they have been around for a very long time. Over 100 million years ago, creatures similar to the sharks we know today were hunting in the ocean. The design was obviously good because, although they have diversified considerably, unlike many of their prehistoric contemporaries, their line did not die out.

Sharks live throughout the oceans at almost all depths. Some, such as the megamouth, which lives in the deep ocean, are rarely seen. Very occasionally they are brought to the surface in nets, usually dead. Another little-known shark is the smallest, the spiny pygmy shark, which is only 25 cm (10 in) long and also lives at depth. The slow-moving Greenland

shark inhabits Arctic waters and is seldom encountered. By far the majority of sharks are concentrated in tropical coastal waters where the water is warm and prey is plentiful.

Jaws

Not all sharks have big teeth. Some, such as whale sharks and basking sharks feed on plankton and do not need substantial teeth. Ironically, these are the largest of the group: whale sharks grow to 12 m (39 feet) (although individuals of 18 m/59 feet have been seen), and basking sharks reach an amazing 10 m (33 feet).

Smaller species, such as horn sharks, which live in temperate waters, have rows of tiny teeth. Similar in size to very coarse sand, they grow so close together that they form a rough, hard plate, perfect for crushing small crustaceans. Stingrays have a similar set of minute teeth.

Nevertheless, the large predatory species, such as bull sharks, tiger sharks and great white sharks, are famous for their teeth, which are triangular, serrated and very sharp. When a tooth gets damaged or lost during feeding, there is always another one just behind ready to replace it. Rows of teeth are continually forming at the back and slowly moving forward to the leading edge of the mouth. Tiger sharks are thought to get through an astonishing 24,000 teeth in ten years.

Hunting

Sharks have a number of ways of hunting down their prey. They can hear well, detecting sounds many kilometres away. They have an extraordinarily good sense of smell, particularly for blood. At distances of 100 m (328 feet) or so they can feel vibrations in the water. Homing in on any of these cues, they begin to use sight. Their vision is very good, and most of them can see better in dim light than their prey. Great white sharks hunt well in poor visibility by swimming low in the water and watching for the silhouette of an elephant seal or fur seal swimming near the surface.

Close to, sharks pick up very weak electrical charges that radiate from all animals. Even a tiny fish hiding in the sand, moving its gills slightly to breathe produces an electrical signal. A small hammerhead shark scanning the sea floor for any electrical cue can home in on such a signal.

3

◆ TOPIC LINKS

1.3 Living in the Sea
p.54 Breathing Under Water

3.2 Mouths of the Reef
p.127 Nocturnal Hunters

3.3 Sex on the Reef
p.132 Shark Babies

4.2 Blooming Plankton
p.177 'Blooming Jaws'

4.4 The Living Bed
p.205 Demersal Hunters
p.210 Shocking Fish

6.2 Ocean Drifters
p.287 The Biggest Mouths

6.3 Ocean Hunters
p.289 Sensory Warfare
p.295 Open-ocean Sharks

6.4 Ocean Birth
p.305 Abandoning the Babies

7.3 The Deep-Sea Floor
p.358 Deep-sea Sharks

4

2

LIFE ON THE EDGE

2.1 THE DYNAMIC BORDER 60

The coast is a dynamic border between land and sea, shaped by the wind and the waves and dominated by the cycles of the tide.

HABITAT ILLUSTRATED SPREAD: Life on the edge

2.2 SURVIVING THE COAST 72

The different coastlines – be they rocky, sandy or muddy – present the animals and plants that live there with different challenges.

SPECIAL FEATURE: Scavengers along the coast

2.3 THE NEED TO BREED 86

Most of the animals found along the coast are only visitors, returning each year to breed.

SPECIAL FEATURE: Out of their element

THE DYNAMIC BORDER

The coast is the dynamic border between land and sea. Of all the ocean habitats, it is the coast that is always on the move, being constantly shaped by waves and weather. The meeting of land and sea has produced a wide variety of environments, from sandy beaches to rocky shores, from river estuaries to mangrove forests, from sand dunes to salt marshes. For the animals and plants that try to survive here, life is arduous: salt spray fills the air and waves buffet the coast. The constant ebb and flow of the tides transforms the habitat on a daily basis. But contending with the elements has made the inhabitants hardy and opportunistic. Scavengers come to pick through the flotsam of life thrown up by the waves, and plants have evolved ways of coping with salt spray. During the breeding season, quiet coastlines are thronged with countless birds, turtles and mammals. The constant activity along the coastline means that its only predictable feature is its unpredictability.

Previous page: Nesting gannets crowd on to Bass Rock in the Forth of Firth, Scotland. Like 95 per cent of the world's sea birds, gannets always breed in colonies.

THE SHAPE OF THE COAST

Coastal scenery is as varied as it is spectacular. Anyone who has driven south from San Francisco along the coastal highway will testify to the breathtaking views from the massive cliffs of the Californian coastline. In the Galápagos islands off the coast of Ecuador the young volcanic shore is constantly battered by massive Pacific rollers crashing into the blow-holes they have eroded, sending great plumes of surf hundreds of metres into the air. In the Bahamas the azure blue sea laps quietly against gently sloping white sand beaches. On the east coast of England the wide skies and flat expanses of mud and salt marshes welcome thousands of geese and wading birds every autumn. Despite this apparent variety, there are basically just two different types of coastline – rocky and sandy.

High-energy coastlines

If you want to see massive waves crashing against the land, the most spectacular places are usually rocky coasts. These are areas of high wave energy, where sediment quickly washes away and erosion dominates. Eroding shorelines often have high cliffs and dramatic rocky features, such as arches, blow-holes and sea stacks. The Old Man of Hoy in the Orkneys, a tall pinnacle of rock sticking straight out of the ocean, or the stepped basalt of the Giant's Causeway on the Irish coast are both good examples.

1. Rocky coastlines are shaped into spectacular cliffs and dramatic rocky features by the eroding power of waves.

1. Sandy beaches constantly change shape under the influence of wind and water.

2. The falling tide in the Wash estuary, England exposes mudflats that provide rich feeding grounds for wading birds, ducks and geese.

Overleaf: A female common eider leads her ducklings out across the mudflats.

Rocky shores tend to be steep coasts that have usually been recently uplifted, or are still rising as a result of geological events. These uplifted coasts, of which the west coast of North America is a good example, have not had much time to be eroded or accumulate sediments. During the last ice age, huge sheets of ice covered much of the north of that continent. These scraped the sediments from the continental shelf, leaving bare rock beneath. When the ice melted, the coast slowly rose, leaving the rocky exposed coastline for which California is noted.

Geology and topography are important factors in determining the landscape's ability to resist the erosive force of waves as they hurl the sand, pebbles and gravel against the cliff face. Most erosion takes place along weaknesses in the rock, such as faults and joints, and eventually the cliff face will collapse into the sea. If the sea currents are not too strong, an offshore terrace of eroded material may form. Usually made up of pebbles, cobbles or even boulders, these beaches are very transitory, changing their form and shape with the seasons. Any fine material or sediment is washed away, moved to more sheltered coastlines where sandy beaches can form.

Low-energy coastlines

Being protected from the full force of the ocean, low-energy coastlines have less dramatic wave action, so the material eroded from rocky shores can be deposited there. These depositional, or sandy coasts, which make up 75 per cent of the world's ice-free coastline, are dynamic environments, changing shape under the influence of wind and water. Where wave action is minimal, the result tends to be muddy shores; greater wave action produces a sandy beach. In high latitudes sandy beaches are made up of minerals, mostly quartz. The white sand beach of the Tropics has a biological origin, coming from the eroded skeletons of corals and other marine animals. In fact much of that beautiful white sand has emerged from the guts of creatures which specialize in eating coral.

Just as with rocky shores, the shape of sandy beaches depends entirely on the forces of wind and water. In the few places where more sediment is being deposited than eroded, the beaches march steadily out to sea. Hastings in the south of England is a good example. In 1066, when the Normans invaded, the town was right on the coast: now it lies several kilometres inland. Normally the cycles of

erosion and deposition roughly balance each other through the year. A big winter storm may wash away a lot of sand, but it will gradually return as conditions get back to normal. In this way the shape of sandy beaches is constantly changing, with sand moving up and down the beach and being transported along the coastline.

Sand brought ashore by the waves will eventually get pushed right up the beach until it comes under the influence of the wind. Then it may be blown into ripples, which gradually build into dunes. Vegetation, such as marram grass, often helps to trap the wind-blown sand and stabilize it. These dunes can grow to huge proportions. The highest in the world, on Moreton Island in Australia, have reached 250 m (820 feet), while the Alexandria dune field in Algoa Bay, South Africa, covers over 120 sq km (46 sq miles) and is still advancing.

Estuaries

The other key coastal habitats where sediment is being deposited faster than it is being eroded are estuaries – the places where rivers meet the sea. These vast, flat expanses of salt marsh and mud-flats are among the most productive coastal habitats. Their rich waters provide nurseries for millions of young fish and shellfish, and migrating birds use them as refuelling stations on their long journeys. Human beings have also taken advantage of the sheltered conditions they provide and built ports in them.

Many estuaries were formed at the end of the last ice age when rising sea levels drowned river valleys. The Thames estuary in England and Chesapeake Bay near Washington DC, were both shaped in this way. Others, such as the Waddenzee in the Netherlands, are formed by a bar of sediment that gradually built up across the mouth of the river, eventually forming a barrier. The spectacular fjords of Norway, New Zealand and Chile are a third type of estuary. Retreating glaciers cut deep valleys which were partly submerged when sea levels rose. At their mouths a sill or step of rock remains, partially isolating the fjord from the sea. Finally, as in the case of San Francisco Bay, volcanoes or movements of the Earth's crust can cause the depression of an area of coastline, which floods to become an estuary. As all estuaries have relatively narrow mouths, they are usually sheltered from the force of waves. They are, none the less, strongly influenced by the tides. The meeting of seawater and fresh water creates a special coastal habitat where the key challenge is dealing with changing salinity.

★ Lugworms are probably the most common large invertebrates on sandy shores in Europe; up to 70 creatures can be found per square metre (just over a square yard).

2

⭐ Low-pressure weather systems suck up water beneath them producing bigger tides, while with high pressure systems the reverse is true.

IN THE GRIP OF THE TIDES

More than any other factor, it is the cycle of tides that dominates life along the coast. This is well illustrated in places such as the Bay of Fundy in Canada or The Wash on the east coast of England. At low tide, it is possible to walk huge distances across their expanses of mudflat with only wading birds and the occasional seal for company. Suddenly, though, the tide will turn and the ocean that seemed so far away comes rushing in. Like a galloping horse, the tide reclaims the land, and within just a few hours, the habitat is completely transformed.

The rise and fall of the tide varies a great deal around the world. In the Mediterranean, for example, the difference between high and low tide is as little as a metre, while in the Bay of Fundy, which has the world's largest tides, the vertical drop can be as much as 15 m (50 feet). The Severn Estuary in the west of England comes a close second, with a 13-m (40-foot) fall. The tide's ability to totally transform the physical appearance of a habitat presents real challenges for the animals and plants that try to live there.

Highs and lows

Animals and plants living between the high- and low-tide marks find their environment completely changed by the daily ebb and flow. Spending part of the time under water and part of it exposed to the air makes great physical demands. For a start, there is the constant risk of drying out when exposed to the desiccating effects of sun and wind. Then there is the variation in temperature to contend with. While the ocean's temperature, in any one place, tends to remain relatively constant, air temperatures can vary enormously with the seasons, rising and falling

▷ THE BAY OF FUNDY

The highest tides on Earth occur in the Minas basin, the eastern extremity of the Bay of Fundy in Nova Scotia, Canada. Twice a day 100 billion tonnes of sea water – the combined daily flow of all the rivers on Earth – pour in and out of the bay with dramatic effect. At low tide the fishing boats in the small harbour at Wolfville rest high and dry on the mud, but just six hours later they have 14 m (45 foot) of sea beneath their keels.

At high tide, the Hopewell rocks look just like any other small rocky islands covered with a handful of pine trees. But at low tide these same trees are left almost suspended in mid-air, supported by tall pillars of rock that tower over the, now exposed, mud way below (illustrated, left).

The currents entering the funnel-shaped bay from the Atlantic exceed 8 knots, and as the water squeezes its way through the 5-km-(3-mile-) wide channel, it is pushed to incredible heights. Today a tiny part of this energy is trapped in the only commercial tidal power plant in the western hemisphere. The peak output of this generator is 20 megawatts, about 1 per cent of Nova Scotia's electrical needs.

by several tens of degrees. The salinity of a habitat can also change drastically with the tidal cycle. In estuaries, for example, the rising tide pushes a wedge of denser salty water into the fresh water twice or even four times a day. No other ocean habitat undergoes such drastic physical changes on such a regular basis, and any creatures hoping to survive there must be able to deal with such a dynamic environment.

Feeding opportunities along the coast also vary enormously with the tides. As the tide retreats, for example, the barnacles, mussels and sea anemones that encrust the rocks along the coasts of Europe and North America are exposed and no longer able to filter their food out of the water. They also run the risk of drying out in the air. On sandy shores many animals face similar problems. The sediment is full of filter-feeding animals, such as cockles and razorshells, which live in burrows to avoid drying out at low tide. They can collect their food only when the tide is in.

The tidal cycle on sandy shores and estuaries is rather like the opening and closing of a larder door. The low tide allows terrestrial animals to exploit food sources hidden in the sediment: massive flocks of wading birds fly in to feed on worms and snails. But the larder door closes for them when the tide returns. Now it's the turn of marine animals to eat their fill.

Worms living in burrows can start filter-feeding again and bivalve molluscs can extend their siphons out into the water column to catch passing food particles. But they have to be careful, because those same siphons make a tasty meal for flat fish that swim back into the estuaries with the returning tide. These fish are, in their turn, the favourite food of ospreys. The advance and retreat of the tides is the dinner gong in the lives of most of the animals living along shallow coastlines.

1

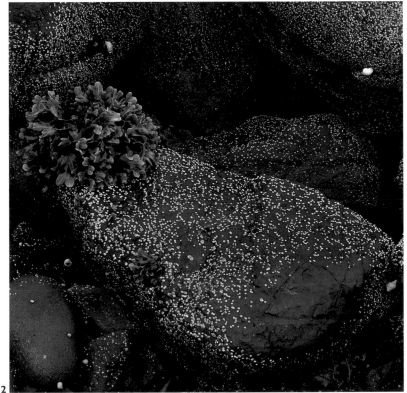

2

1. For grizzly bears living alongside Alaska's remote estuaries, low tide provides an opportunity to dig up clams that live in the mudflats.

2. Low tide on a rocky shore in Scotland's Loch Broom exposes seaweed and barnacles to the risk of being dried out.

LIFE ON THE EDGE

One of the pleasures of going to the seaside is swimming in the sea and riding the surf. For the creatures that live in this environment, however, life is not so much fun. The coast is the only part of the marine world to face regular exposure to air and consequently is one of the most demanding habitats. Each day, waves and weather gradually erode the cliffs and the ebb and flow of the tide regularly transform the habitat. From rocky coasts, to sandy shores and muddy estuaries, all of the creatures that live in these habitats must be hardy and opportunistic, timing their feeding and breeding to fit in with the coming and going of the tide.

Time and tide

If you visit the same beach at different stages of the tidal cycle, you'll notice a range of marine life appearing at different times. When the tide is out, creatures such as sea birds and racoons come to the beach to search for mussels, worms and clams, which hide in burrows beneath the sand or mud. When the tide returns, the animals that have been taking refuge from the sun come into their own; mussels open their shells, seaweed becomes moist again and moves in the water and sea anemones unfurl and wait for prey to approach.

Influenced by the moon and sun, however, tides vary in height from day to day and creatures, particularly those that are static, have had to adapt. If you look on the side of a rocky cliff you'll notice that marine life forms distinct stripes or zones (see main illustration, right) all the way up the cliffside. By spacing out in this way, each individual species finds a position where their needs are met. Filter feeders, for example, cluster where they will be covered by the tide for at least part of the day.

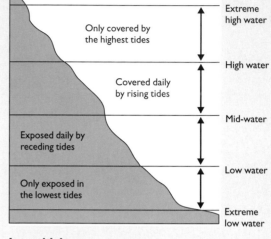

Extreme high water

Only covered by the highest tides

High water

Covered daily by rising tides

Mid-water

Exposed daily by receding tides

Low water

Only exposed in the lowest tides

Extreme low water

Intertidal zone

The intertidal zone is the area between the high and low-water mark. Marine life is distributed between these two extremes in a series of distinct bands – a phenomenon known as zonation.

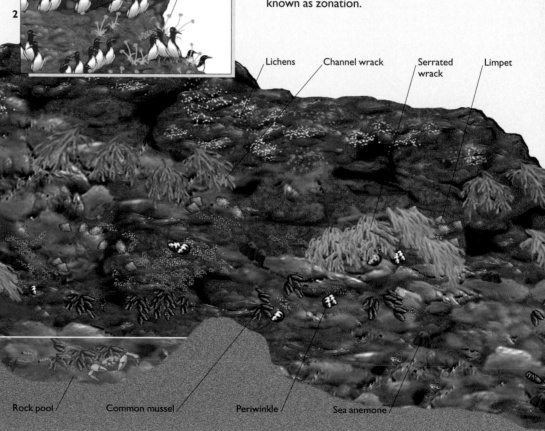

Guillemot

Single egg

Pink thrift

2

Lichens   Channel wrack   Serrated wrack   Limpet

Rock pool   Common mussel   Periwinkle   Sea anemone

1

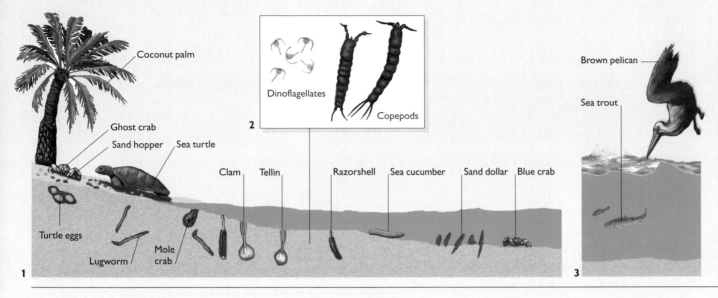

Coconut palm

Dinoflagellates

Copepods

Ghost crab

Sand hopper   Sea turtle

Clam   Tellin   Razorshell   Sea cucumber   Sand dollar   Blue crab

Turtle eggs

Lugworm

Mole crab

2

1

Sandy coast

1. Sandy shores are unstable and constantly shifting. As a result, many creatures burrow for protection. This also prevents them from drying out at low tide.
2. Millions of micro-organisms live hidden between the sand grains on the beach.
3. The surf zone attracts a great variety of fish and diving birds.

Brown pelican

Sea trout

3

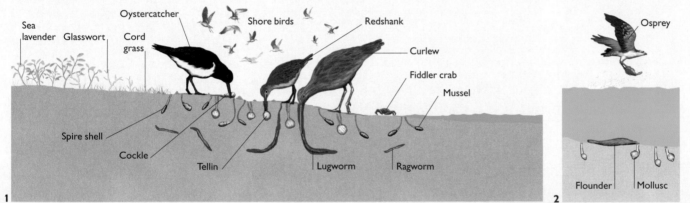

Sea lavender   Glasswort

Oystercatcher

Cord grass

Shore birds

Redshank

Curlew

Fiddler crab

Mussel

Spire shell

Cockle

Tellin

Lugworm

Ragworm

1

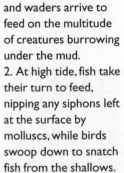

Osprey

Flounder   Mollusc

2

Estuary

1. At low tide, massive flocks of shore birds and waders arrive to feed on the multitude of creatures burrowing under the mud.
2. At high tide, fish take their turn to feed, nipping any siphons left at the surface by molluscs, while birds swoop down to snatch fish from the shallows.

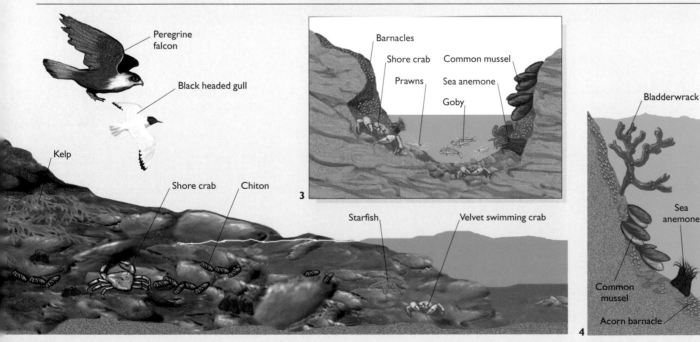

Peregrine falcon

Black headed gull

Kelp

Shore crab   Chiton

Barnacles

Shore crab

Prawns

Common mussel

Sea anemone

Goby

3

Starfish

Velvet swimming crab

Bladderwrack

Sea anemone

Common mussel

Acorn barnacle

4

Rocky coast

1. At low tide, many creatures are exposed and at risk of drying out. Some, e.g. mussels, have hinged shells that close to seal in moisture. Many sea anemones withdraw their tentacles, turning into jelly-like blobs.
2. In summer, rocky cliffs are filled with nesting sea birds such as guillemots.
3. Rock pools provide a haven for many animals that suffer from exposure at low tide.
4. At high tide, mussels and anemones open up.

1. Low tide in Loch Sunart, Scotland and groups of mussels keep their shells firmly closed to ensure that they do not dry out.

2. When the tide returns, mussels can open their shells and start filtering their food from the water, while plumose anemones extend their tentacles to trap passing prey.

Zones on the beach

The tidal cycle is more complex than its daily retreats and advances suggest. At different times of the month and at certain times of year the strength of tides can vary enormously, ($\triangleright$ p. 40) and this is the key factor in determining the distribution of life along coasts. Racoons hoping to search for mussels have to be careful to avoid the highest spring tides. Those mussels, in turn, tend to live in the middle of the shore, because they are filter-feeders and need to spend at least part of their day under water. When exposed at low tide, their shells form such a perfect seal that they are able to survive without drying out. Few mussels are found at the bottom of the shore because there they are eaten by marine predators, such as dog whelks and starfish. These in their turn are restricted to the water's edge because they cannot survive long out of the water, and need to live below the lowest spring tides.

On coasts worldwide it is the fascinating interaction between the physical forces of the tide and the biological factors of competition and predation that has produced different communities of animal and plants at different levels on the shore. This vertical zonation is particularly obvious on steep, rocky coasts where the different animal communities leave clearly visible bands of different colours on the rocks.

Time to breed

Many of the plants and animals that live between the high- and low-tide marks use the sea to fertilize and distribute their eggs, and they are careful to reproduce only when the tidal conditions are at their best. A high spring tide may well be the time to spawn for static coastal creatures, such as corals and some seaweeds, who want to wash their larvae well out to sea. Others who return to the land to breed are also careful to synchronize with the tides. The Californian grunion, for example, is a small, silvery fish that arrives in thousands during the spring and summer, literally riding in on the surf. By timing their spawning to coincide with the highest tides, the grunions ensure that their eggs are laid on the uppermost parts of the beach, where they are less likely to be eaten by intertidal animals. In addition, because the tides are just starting to recede, the grunion can be sure that their eggs will not be washed away. In a final act of synchronization, the eggs hatch out of the sand just in time for the next high spring tide, which reaches far enough up the beach to wash them out to sea.

Olive Ridley turtles also seem to co-ordinate their egg-laying with the tidal cycle. On just a few nights each year, tens of thousands of females emerge together on just a few beaches worldwide in a breeding spectacle called an arribada. These arribadas always start when the moon is in its first or last quarter. This is the time of neap tides, when the sea tends to be calmer and more of the beach remains exposed, making egg-laying easier.

3. Dawn on Costa Rica's Pacific coastline, and the last of the female Olive Ridley turtles are returning to the sea, after laying their eggs in the sandy beach.

SURVIVING THE COAST

The coast is one of the most demanding ocean habitats. Though many come here to visit, there are very few permanent residents. To live here animals and plants have to be able to withstand the constant battering of waves and weather and cope with the continual cycle of change imposed by the tides. All the residents of the coast originally came from either the land or the sea. For them, living in this borderland has meant compromise, forcing them to adapt to life out of their normal element. Temperature and salinity fluctuate constantly and opportunities to feed come and go. The animals and plants that cannot move easily are carefully arranged into different zones from the top to the bottom of the shore, depending on how well they can cope with the continual change imposed by the tidal cycle. And as each type of coastline – rocky, sandy or muddy – presents a different set of survival challenges, the adaptations are many.

THE ROCKY SHORE

The Muckle Flugha Lighthouse on Shetland is the most northerly point in the British Isles. In the winter, its lonely beam illuminates a wild and rugged coast of steep cliffs and bare sea stacks that stand like massive gravestones in the sea. It is difficult to imagine a less welcoming place, and in winter it seems almost completely devoid of life. Yet come the summer, thick clumps of pink thrift burst into flower and these same cliffs fill with hundreds and thousands of sea birds. Gannets turn the sea stacks white, guillemots and razorbills crowd every suitable rocky ledge, puffins pop cheekily in and out of rabbit burrows, and peregrine falcons return to prey on the other sea birds. For a few short months, it is all noise and action, but as autumn approaches, the activity abates almost as quickly as it started.

Cliffs like those in the Shetlands make a sudden transition between land and sea. Their steep sides make them inaccessible to most animals, but it is the salt spray more than anything else that makes life difficult. Breaking waves and strong winds continually douse the cliffs with salt and few permanent residents can put up with such conditions. Most of those that do cling precariously to cliff-side life, rely on the return of the summer visitors for some crucial part of their existence. Where soil accumulates in cracks and crevices, small salt-tolerant plants, such as sea campion and thrift, may cling to the cliff all year round. The occasional dropping from a summer nesting sea bird is vital in enriching this soil with nutrients. A few small snails or insects will survive among the cracks, and some ingenious ticks that feed off the blood of sea birds will spend a whole winter without a meal, waiting on the cliffs till their hosts return to breed in the summer.

Smashed by the waves

At the top of rocky beaches, where spray from breaking waves is thrown above the high tide levels, is a habitat called the splash zone. Life forms here must be particularly tough to survive, and a good place to observe the challenge is Cape Douglas on the western edge of the Galápagos. Uninterrupted by any land, great swells develop out in the Pacific Ocean and come crashing on to the Galápagos shores.

1. The marine iguanas of the Galápagos are the world's only marine lizards, feeding off the algae that grow on the rocks.

1

The islands' marine iguanas feed off algae that grow on the rocks just below the tideline and they have no option but to brave the pounding waves. As cold-blooded reptiles, they have to wait for the heat of the morning sun to warm them up and give them energy to venture down to the splash zone. Special claws on their feet allow them to cling to the rocks even when it seems as if a massive wave must completely wash them away. Most of the females cannot withstand life in the ocean because it is too cold, but the larger male iguanas can survive under water for 10 minutes or so. Knowing that there are richer algae pickings on the submerged rocks, the males launch themselves out through the massive surf to the slightly deeper water below the splash zone: they know it's worth the risk.

The iguanas share the splash zone with the beautiful Sally light foot crab, another species unique to the Galápagos. These brightly coloured crabs can scamper ahead of the breaking surf at surprising speed, and their highly flattened bodies seem to protect them in the waves. But the real master of the splash zone has to be the aptly named surf bird. This migratory wader specializes in feeding on tiny invertebrates along the tideline. One moment it is calmly feeding on the rocks and then, just as an enormous wave is about to break, it flies straight up into the air like a tiny jack-in-the-box, avoiding the impact.

But many splash zone residents are not able to run or fly away from the breaking waves. Instead they do everything possible to stay firmly attached. Barnacles have developed a glue so strong that many commercial companies have failed to synthesize it. Mussels hold on with a 'beard' of strong protein fibres produced by a special gland in their feet. More mobile molluscs, such as limpets and chitons, have developed a powerful muscular foot, which they use like a suction cup to fix them to the rocks. There are even fish, such as gobies and clingfish, which use a similar technique, having modified their pelvic fins to act as suction cups. The few seaweeds that cling on in the splash zone have a network of strong roots called a holdfast with which they clamp themselves to the rocks. Staying put is an essential survival technique on the rocky coast, particularly below the tideline.

Exposed by the tide

Venture a little further down the steep sides of a rocky coast and you are soon below the tideline, the highest point reached by the tide. Here, it is not just waves that are a problem, animals and plants have to deal with regular exposure and submersion for many hours, sometimes even days.

With the exception of a few bivalve molluscs that can bore into rock, most animals and plants have nowhere to hide, and those living near the top of the beach are subject to the greatest physical stress. The first big problem is temperature change. While temperatures remain relatively constant and mild in the water, they can vary enormously on land, ranging from intense heat during the day to freezing conditions at night. Fish living in

▶ HIGH-RISE HOMES

The massive cliffs of the North Atlantic are home to literally millions of birds, each species having its particular preference for which level to live on. Near the bottom of the cliffs are the broad ledges and flat-topped stacks favoured by shags and cormorants. These birds have short, ineffective wings and prefer not to venture too high. On the main flat cliff-face are guillemots, razorbills and kittiwakes, who nest together, seeming to find safety in numbers. The top of the cliffs, where the gradients flatten out and there are often areas of soil and grass, is the favoured nesting site for puffins and petrels which dig burrows into the soft ground. While auklets, such as those illustrated, right, nest in crevices amongst the boulders. The thugs of the cliff-face are gannets, who will nest at any level so long as there is sufficient space. In fact, they will happily prod smaller guillemots out of the way or throw their eggs over the cliff. The only birds they will not mess with are fulmars, who defend themselves by spitting out an oily substance that damages the gannet's feathers, reducing their water resistance.

1. Starfish and seaweeds that typically live in the middle of a tidal range, can survive short periods of exposure as the tide retreats.

tide-pools have had to become much more tolerant of changing temperatures than their relatives below the tides. So long as the pool does not actually freeze up, the temperature will not drop below −1 °C (30 °F). The problem is overheating. One species of periwinkle is known to have survived temperatures of up to 49 °C (120 °F). In the Tropics some snails living on the rocky coast have developed special ridges along their shells that act like cooling ribs on a car radiator. Colour also helps to prevent overheating: the dog whelk, for example, has evolved a white form as well as a brown one because white better reflects heat from the sun. The white dog whelk also predominates on sheltered Atlantic coasts where the risks of overheating are greater.

The danger of drying out

Creatures exposed on the rocky shore at low tide run the risk of drying out in the sun and wind. To avoid this, many tidal animals have developed a protective shell. Barnacles and mussels have shells and can seal in moisture by simply closing them. Others, such as limpets, have a single shell. To get a watertight seal, they clamp themselves on to the rock and even dig a little depression to make the seal more effective.

Animals that cannot clam up, such as crabs, choose to run and hide. Moist cracks under rocks will suffice, but the perfect havens are rock-pools. These oases are vital at low tide for a wide range of animals as they wait patiently for the sea to return. If running and hiding are not options, some animals and plants simply allow themselves to dry out. Chitons, which are small molluscs with eight overlapping plates on their backs, can survive losing 75 per cent of the water in their body tissues, and certain seaweeds can lose as much as 90 per cent of their water, becoming completely dry and crunchy. When the tide returns, they quickly recover.

THE SANDY SHORE

Walk along a sandy beach and the apparent absence of life is striking – nothing but the occasional wading bird chasing the surf and a handful of shells washed up on the beach. First impressions, however, are misleading. Although sandy shores lack the variety of animals and plants found on rocky coasts, those that do survive there often occur in very large numbers. The challenge is finding them.

Many of the animals are too small to be visible to the naked eye. Hidden between the sand grains, are literally millions and millions of microscopic organisms. Practically every group is represented, including diatoms, protozoa, algae, nematodes (roundworms), copepods and gastropods. Although tiny, these animals are very mobile, constantly migrating up and down through the sand with the tides or changing temperature and light.

Of the slightly larger animals at the top of the shore, crustaceans seem to have adapted particularly well. If you have ever had a picnic on a sandy beach you may remember that sand is not the only thing that can get into the sandwiches. Sand hoppers – amphipods just a few millimetres long – can reach plague proportions and specialize in feeding on the rotting vegetation that often washes ashore. On tropical beaches, exactly the same job is done by ghost crabs, which emerge every evening from their burrows in the sand to scavenge. They get their name from their white colour and their rather spooky habit of appearing from nowhere whenever a potential food source appears. They will eat practically anything, and will even drag unfortunate turtle hatchlings down into their burrows. Some types of crab occur in really spectacular numbers. Australian soldier crabs, for example, march across stretches of sand in organized groups hundreds strong, while the activity of swarms of sand bubbler crabs can cover the entire surface of a beach with thousands of tiny balls of sand. They specialize in sieving for microscopic life forms that live between the sand grains. Having passed the sand through their mouths, they leave the waste product as distinctive 'calling cards' – perfectly round balls of sandy waste.

Within the surf

Along the water's edge, where the waves break, is the surf zone – a much more active

1. The surf line on a sandy beach is a good place to search for washed-up shells and other flotsam and jetsam.

2. Ghost crabs live in burrows on tropical beaches and emerge every evening to scavenge.

1   2

1. Sanderling are small wading birds that specialize in feeding right alongside the breaking surf on sandy beaches.

2. The two entrances of a u-shaped burrow made in the sand by a polychaete worm. Water is drawn down through one hole, while waste sand is expelled through the other.

area. Among the wading birds that forage here is the small sanderling which chases along the very edge of the surf like a tiny clockwork toy. Each year sanderling migrate to and from their nesting grounds in the high Arctic right down to the very tips of South Africa and South America where they spend the winter.

As many fish establish their nurseries among these shallows, the surf zone also attracts a variety of diving birds. Little terns, for example, hover for minutes over the breaking waves before diving in to grab a fish with their dagger-like bills. Much larger pelicans ride the breeze created by the waves before suddenly diving into the sea with their massive beaks wide open. Because food is so abundant at the water's edge, a number of animals have taken to surfing up and down the beach with the tide. Whelks, beach clams and plough snails all use their expandable mollusc foot as a kind of surfboard. Real masters of the art are the surfing snails of South Africa. If a dead fish or other tasty meal washes up, these snails emerge from their burrows having scented the odour of the rotting food on the current. They then ride the waves up the beach before the fish is washed beyond their reach by the rising tide. The wealth of flotsam and jetsam deposited on these low-energy coasts ($\triangleright$ p. 62) makes them a surefire attraction to all sorts of scavengers.

Within the sand

Unlike rocky coasts, sandy shores are very unstable and constantly shifting in response to waves, tides and currents. Below the tide-line, there are no solid places for attachment. With the exception of seagrasses ($\triangleright$ p. 148), no plants have solved this problem, and animals that live here usually burrow into the sediment for protection. The variety of life depends very much on the type of sediment, and that in turn depends on the power of the waves. In calm, sheltered areas, where fine sediments can settle, the shoreline tends to be muddy; where the waves are strong, the beach will be sand.

Burrowing in the sand has the advantage that you are less likely to dry out than in the open. But grain size is very important. Coarse sand tends to drain water faster than mud which is one of the reasons sandy beaches have relatively little animal life. Grain size also affects the amount of oxygen that filters through. The smaller particles found in muddy sediment pass water and thus its dissolved oxygen less well. That is why many animals living in the sediment have developed ways to bring the oxygen to them. Cockles that hide just below the surface extend a siphon up above the mud. Water is inhaled on one side and expelled out the other. Another bivalve mollusc, the thin tellin, has a long inhalant siphon, which resembles an elephant's trunk. When the

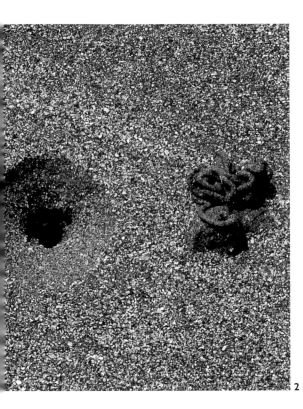

tide is up, the tellin extends this trunk over the surface of the mud, using it to suck up particles of food. While the annelid worms like ragworms dig u-shaped burrows in the sand, maintaining a constant circulation of oxygenated water with the array of bristles on their bodies.

Finding food in the sand

The main source of food for all the animals living in sand is dead material washed in with the tide. There are various different ways of collecting it. Some like the sea cucumbers and the worms simply act like hoovers, sucking up the sediment. As it passes through their guts they digest any valuable particles or small organisms in the sand. The worm castes you find on sandy beaches at low tide are the final product of this process as the worms expel the processed sand from their burrows.

Others are more selective, taking only certain particles. Sand dollars browse the surface of the sand, picking up tasty particles with their tube feet, while the bivalve molluscs extend their siphons out of their burrows to make their selection. Others still choose not to wait until the potential food has settled. These suspension feeders use a variety of techniques to pick out particles from the water column. An olive shell from Central America makes a mucus net it suspends just above the bottom, while the mole crab has a large pair of bushy antennae that it can hold up in the water to catch food. Cleverly, the mole crab also uses these antennae to catch a ride on the surf when it wants to move up or down the beach.

 ## WHALE AND DOLPHIN STRANDINGS

Every year a number of whales and dolphins seem to lose their way and get washed up on beaches worldwide. Sometimes mass strandings occur, when tens, even hundreds, of animals wash up together. The most common victims of stranding are toothed whales, such as sperm, killer and pilot whales (see right), and bottle-nosed dolphins. Exactly what causes whales and dolphins to end up on the beach remains a mystery. Individual strandings may occur simply because an animal is injured or old. Mass strandings seem to arise from errors in navigation made by the whole group. This might explain why toothed whales, which tend to travel together in tightly knit social groups, are the usual victims.

But what causes the navigational error? Storms, reduced visibility and even noise pollution may all be factors that interfere with the whales' sonar. It has also been suggested that whales may follow magnetic contours and occasionally blunder into dangerously shallow waters. It is even possible that parasitic ear infections could damage the whales' sonar. Whatever the cause, it is a distressing sight to find groups of ocean-going animals trapped in this way. Often, people try to help by attempting to re-float the whales, but sadly the physiological stress is so great that most die within hours.

SCAVENGERS ALONG THE COAST

You can never be certain what will wash up on the tide: it might be clumps of seaweed, the bodies of jellyfish or even, now and again, a stranded whale. As all beachcombers know, the strand line can be a very profitable place to search, and a range of different animals has learnt to exploit this unpredictable bounty.

2. A dead humpback whale washed up on the coast of Alaska is an unexpected bonus for a range of different scavengers including these bald eagles.

Treasures of the surf

Along the water's edge on almost every beach in the world there is always an enormous quantity and variety of washed-up material, most of it biological in origin. Common finds are whelks' yellow egg cases and fragile black mermaid's purses. Sometimes an old piece of marine timber containing hole-boring ship-worms may wash up. But the real prizes, which regularly appear on beaches in the

Tropics are sea beans. These incredibly hard and beautifully smooth black seeds are dropped into rivers by tropical lianas and travel out to sea. There they can survive for months, even years, before they wash up and germinate on a distant beach.

Strand line undertakers

Many different animals have learned about the rich pickings to be had from the water's edge,

and regularly trawl the strand line. Scavenging sandhoppers will eat almost anything, but are particularly fond of seaweed. Many land-dwelling beetles and flies also help to clean up the debris. Larger scavengers also join the feast. North American racoons, for example, have learnt that the tideline can provide unusual snacks, while South African baboons will venture right down to the waves in their search for the egg cases of sharks and dogfish.

Whale of a prize

The ultimate find for nature's beachcombers has to be a stranded whale or dolphin. So many tonnes of meat dumped on the beach at once are a real bonanza. Exactly why whales end up stranded above the tideline remains something of a mystery. Injury, parasitic infection, disease, social factors and errors in navigation are all among the possible explanations.

Each year a number of humpback whales wash up on Alaska's remote beaches and their bulk provides a feast lasting several months for local scavengers. Bald eagles and ravens fly in to pick at the carcass, while black bears are strong enough to bite through the tough skin. Even packs of wolves may emerge from the forest to dine on rotting whale.

3

Breeding bonanza

Scavengers come into their own when sea creatures visit the land to breed. In Costa Rica the mass nesting of thousands of Olive Ridley turtles supports hundreds of black vultures which patrol the beach each morning. As the rising tide washes turtle eggs out of the sand, the vultures snap them up. Sea bird colonies also provide good opportunities for the scavenger. The burrows of many sea birds contain blood-sucking ticks that feed only when their hosts return to nest. In Antarctica the only permanent land-based bird is the sheathbill, which lives by scavenging round the colonies of breeding penguins and seals. Although it

prefers to steal penguin eggs or food, the sheathbill is famous for eating everything and is quite happy surviving on penguin droppings. Antarctica's most impressive scavenger though has to be the giant petrel. These vultures of the south often emerge from the carcass of a dead seal with their heads bright red with blood.

Sea mammal colonies worldwide have their own particular scavengers. The sea lion colonies on Peru's Pacific coast attract Andean condors that land and take dead pups. And fur seals breeding along Namibia's Skeleton Coast suffer the attention of hyaenas, jackals and even the occasional lion.

1. A whale carcass attracts a shy, black bear out of the woods behind the beach. It will be several months before all the rotting meat is consumed.

3. Giant petrels are the vultures of Antarctica. This one has just pulled its head from the carcass of an elephant-seal pup.

◆ TOPIC LINKS

1.3 Living in the Sea
p.43 On the Edge

2.1 The Dynamic Border
p.66 In the Grip of the Tides

2.2 Surviving the Coast
p.79 Whale and Dolphin Strandings

WHERE RIVERS MEET THE SEA

With their vast expanses of salt marsh and mudflat, estuaries can seem dull and lifeless. But there is a certain magic in the maze of tidal creeks, the wide horizons of a wet mudflat reflecting the pattern of clouds and the constant threat of the chasing tide. Life is everywhere. Pick up a handful of mud and it is full of weird worms and shapely snails. Little fiddler crabs chase along the surface and massive flocks of wading birds darken the sky. Of all the coastal habitats, estuaries are among the most productive – vital feeding and breeding grounds for many fish, birds and other animals.

Although estuaries are formed in various ways (▷ p.62), they all consist of a more or less enclosed area where a river enters the sea. Large amounts of sediment are carried into estuaries by their rivers and, sheltered from the forces of currents or waves, this fine sediment settles as mud. As the sediment is rich in organic material, estuaries are tremendously productive places, home to large numbers of organisms. However, life there is not easy and the key problem is changing salinity. At the top of an estuary, where fresh water from the river washes in, there is far less salt than at the mouth, where the daily rhythm of the tides introduces much more salt. Life in an estuary depends on adapting to these fluctuations in salinity.

Most of today's estuary animals originally came from the sea, so they have difficulty coping with fresh water. With their high internal salt concentration, there is a constant threat that, due to osmosis, their bodies will flood with the surrounding water. Different animals have come up with different answers to this problem. Soft-bodied molluscs and polychaete worms, for example, actually change the constitution of their own body fluids to match the salinity of the water around them. Many fish and crabs, on the other hand, regulate the amount of water or salts in their bodies using gills, kidneys and other special adaptations. Salmon and sea trout, which migrate from oceans to rivers in the breeding season, are masters of this technique, regulating their body fluids with their kidneys.

Unlike the animals that came from the sea, estuary plants tend to have invaded from the land, so the problem for them is too much salt. Cord grass, commonly found on temperate salt marshes in the northern hemisphere, can excrete excess salt with special glands on its leaves. Samphire, on the other hand, has fleshy stalks, which are designed to accumulate large quantities of water and dilute any salts they take up.

1. The Tees estuary in the north-east of England. Like many estuaries worldwide, it provides a sheltered haven for both man and wildlife.

2. An otter hunts at sunset in Loch Fleet, Scotland. Otters are frequent visitors to estuaries, searching for the fish that come up on the tide.

3. Glasswort is a typical salt-marsh plant, which is better known as samphire. It is thought by many to be a culinary delicacy.

Life at the top

Just like rocky and sandy coasts, estuaries are made up of a series of different communities of animals and plants that change as one walks nearer and nearer the sea. And being flat means that they are enormously influenced by even a small rise or fall in the tide.

In temperate regions, estuaries are bordered by large grassy areas of salt marsh, which are usually dry being covered by water only at the highest spring tides. They are particularly extensive in places where the coastline is gently sloping, such as the Atlantic and Gulf coasts of North America and the east coast of England. Exploring these marshes, leaping across the little mud creeks and searching all the hidden places, can be a great deal of fun. Skylarks fill the air with song on a summer's day and, if you are lucky, you might spot the tracks of an otter that has spent the day hunting for flatfish. In the winter, skeins of grey geese arrive from their breeding grounds in the Arctic.

At the top of the salt marsh the tide is a rare visitor, so this less changeable habitat is often invaded by land animals, such as rats, snakes, insects and birds. Among the many plants that like this environment are samphire or glasswort, sea meadow grass, sea aster and thrift. Any attempt by these plants to move further down the beach is thwarted in a constant battle with the tide. Being submerged by sea water makes it hard to survive and only cord grass achieves this, living right down to the edge of the mudflats. This plant has an extensive system of stems that form a horizontal network under the mud to hold it secure. Even when the tide comes in, the tops of the leaves remain exposed to the air. Eventually, though, it gets too deep even for cord grass, and the vegetation gives way to the stark expanse that lies at the heart of every estuary.

2

3

Mudflats

Below the tideline, where it is very difficult for plants to get a foothold, are vast bare expanses of mud. Just as on the sandy shore, the key problem here for all life forms is the enormous variation in physical conditions caused by the tides. To escape these extremes, and to avoid the dangers of life on the surface, most animals burrow downwards, but this poses problems of its own. Compared with sandy sediment, mud is rich in organic material but, because it is dense, it is also very short of oxygen. Get your boot stuck on a mudflat and it is difficult to forget the smell of rotten eggs released when your foot finally escapes the mire. That smell is hydrogen sulphide, typical of oxygen-poor sediments.

Dead matter is the main source of food. Dig up the mud and you will discover a range of worms, molluscs and crabs hiding in their burrows. The sheer numbers of animals living on mudflats is enormous. Lugworms are probably the most numerous large invertebrates inhabiting the sandy shores of northwest Europe, with densities of up to 70 individuals per square metre (just over a square yard). These numbers pale into insignificance, however, next to the tiny snail *Hydrobia*, which can reach population peaks of over 100,000 per square metre (just over a square yard).

This wealth of food attracts numerous predators. Carnivorous worms, snails and crabs hunt within the mud itself, while others burrow down in search of clams, before drilling into their shells to eat the flesh within. On the returning tide, flatfish, such as flounders, slip in and nip off any siphons left at the surface by unwary molluscs. When the tide retreats, even bigger predators venture on to the mudflats. Alaskan brown bears like nothing better than to dig clams out of the mud with their enormous paws.

The most important predators on the mudflats are probably birds. Ospreys dive down to snatch flatfish from the shallows, while herons and egrets benefit from the enormous numbers of fish that use estuaries as nurseries. Ducks and geese are also regulars, but the real spectacle has to be the millions of wading birds that rely on estuaries for food. Massive flocks, containing hundreds and thousands of birds, come and go from the mudflats following the cycle of the tides. Each wader species comes equipped with a different shape of bill, perfectly designed for feeding on their particular choice of food (▷ p. 68).

1. Ospreys regularly visit estuaries and will dive for the fish that arrive with each returning tide.

2. A group of willets wait patiently for the tide to turn on a beach in Florida. As soon as the mud is exposed again they fly out to probe for worms and molluscs.

THE NEED TO BREED

Above the tideline, there are relatively few permanent residents. Most of the animals we find along the coast are only visitors, returning each year to breed. The constraints of their evolutionary biology force them back to the element from which their ancestors came. The ancestors of today's sea turtles, for example, were originally land-based reptiles, and as they still lay eggs with shells, they have no option but to deposit them on dry land.

In just the same way, millions of sea birds have to find a firm surface to bring up the next generation. Similarly, many sea mammals must also leave the water to have their pups. By contrast, land crabs, which have adapted so well to a terrestrial existence, cannot breed without returning their eggs and larvae to the sea. All these animals attract predators and this pressure, and often the lack of suitable breeding sites, encourages the coast's visitors to gather in enormous breeding aggregations – some of the greatest spectacles in nature.

REPTILES RETURN

The tiny island of Ascension, which lies in the middle of the Atlantic Ocean, is just 11 km (7 miles) wide. While most of it is an inhospitable volcanic wasteland, it has a few sandy beaches that provide the only nesting sites for thousands of green turtles. These creatures, who spend most of their lives in a solitary pursuit of food along the coast of Brazil, make an annual 2400 km (1500 mile) migration out into the Atlantic Ocean. Exactly how they navigate their way to the tiny pinprick of rock that is Ascension still remains something of a mystery. However, year after year the females return to exactly the same rookery at which they themselves were hatched.

1. A female green turtle struggles up the beach to lay her eggs in the sand on Heron Island, Australia.

A safe place for the eggs

Sea turtles produce the soft, leathery eggs typical of most reptiles. As they evolved on land, they are not able to withstand the rigours of salt water, so they must be laid on land where the warmth of the sand incubates them. The traditional nesting beaches are known as rookeries, but why particular beaches are favoured is far from clear. It may be that current nesting choices reflect historic patterns that have existed for hundreds or thousands of years. Many suitable beaches may now be untouched simply because the local turtle population has been over-exploited or disturbed by man. Certainly tagging experiments and DNA analysis have shown that females not only return to the same beach every year, but, typically emerge within a few hundred metres of where they last nested. A perfect nesting beach for sea turtles needs to have open-water access, it must be free from the risks of flooding by tide or ground water and the sand must be just the right consistency for egg-laying. Too soft and it is almost impossible for the female to dig a nesting burrow without it

collapsing. Too solid and there is not enough air for the incubating eggs.

Gathering off the rookeries to mate after weeks or even months of migration, the females are sexually receptive for just one week. During this time they may be inseminated by several males, who are sexually active for about a month. At the end of this courtship period, the males return home, but the females will remain for months. Using stored sperm, they fertilize the eggs inside their body, then wait offshore for about two weeks until they are ready to lay. They then haul themselves on to the beach.

Within minutes of leaving their natural habit, the turtles are exhausted by the struggles of returning to land. Their eyes clog with sand and every metre up the beach seems an effort. The final challenge is digging a hole in the sand and laying about 120 eggs within it. Just two weeks later, the ordeal must be repeated to lay another clutch of eggs. This process continues throughout the breeding season, with some turtles laying up to 11 clutches.

★ Leatherbacks range further north than other sea turtles, even reaching British waters.

1

During the long months at the rookeries, the females spend little time feeding, living instead off their reserves of fat stored up before the migration began. They are unlikely to return the following year. It will be between two and eight years before this particular set of females undertake the breeding migration again.

The hatchlings emerge

Incubation of the eggs normally takes about eight weeks, but the temperature of the sand determines the speed with which the embryos develop. As turtles have no sex-determining chromosomes, temperature also determines the sex of the hatchlings. Below 28 °C (82 °F) and almost all the hatchlings will be male. Above 30.5 °C (87 °F) and nearly all the hatchlings will be female.

Once they emerge from the eggs, the baby turtles face a real challenge in getting to the sea. In a blindly co-operative effort, the siblings get to the surface of the nest with a sporadic series of thrashings. This may take several days, and they usually emerge at night or during a rainstorm, as hot daytime sand could be lethal. Watching a clutch of turtles hatching is always a touching moment. The surface of the sands begins to twitch. A little black head appears, then a flipper, another head, and soon a gaggle of tiny clockwork toy-like hatchlings emerges.

With no adults to guide them, the newborns rely on instinct to find the sea. Strongly attracted to light, they scurry towards the dim glow reflected off the ocean's surface. As soon as they reach the surf, the tiny turtles instinctively dive down to the bottom, riding the undertow out to calm water beyond the breakers. Then, for 24 hours or more, the hatchlings swim frenziedly to reach deeper water. Those that survive will drift the ocean currents for several years before eventually finding their way to the traditional feeding grounds on the continental shelf.

2

Meal in a shell

A number of different predators have learnt that breeding turtles provide an easy source of food. Crab Island, off the tip of Australia's remote Cape York Peninsula, seems like a perfect nesting place for the rare flat-backed turtle: it is isolated and free of human disturbance – but it is also the home of massive saltwater crocodiles. These creatures, which can measure 7–8 m (23–26 feet) long, are gruesome foes, but even they find it difficult to crack open the shell of a metre-long turtle. For up to 30 minutes the crocodile thrashes the turtle in the surf. Eventually the carapace shatters and all that is left on the beach the following morning are a few scraps of shell and traces of blood.

Despite this hazard, most of the females make it safely up the beach to lay their eggs, but eight weeks later their hatchlings emerge to a different threat. Hundreds of night herons will suddenly appear and catch most of the hatchlings as they dash for the sea. Pelicans also join in, filling their beaks with sand in their haste to steal the hatchlings before the herons. The few newborns that do make it to the water must then get past the crocodiles, sharks and fish waiting in the shallows. Given this gauntlet of predators it is hardly surprising that probably fewer than one in a thousand hatchlings survive to adulthood.

Pressure from predators may be the reason why many turtles choose to breed on islands. Although birds may pose a problem, there are likely to be fewer ground-based predators. The Olive Ridley, however, is one turtle that often nests on mainland shores. There they face a range of extra predators including ants, vultures, ghost crabs, coatis, racoons and feral pigs, but their response has been to develop a different nesting strategy. Having discovered safety in numbers, the females return to breed in their tens of thousands for just a few nights each year. This synchronized mass nesting is called an *arribada* and probably plays a significant part in diluting the effect of predators.

3

1. A newly emerged green turtle hatchling makes a dash for the sea in the Galápagos Islands.

2. The imprint of a saltwater crocodile on Crab Island, Australia. The crocodiles come to feed on flat-backed turtles.

3. Black vultures in Costa Rica eating the eggs of Olive Ridley turtles that have been washed out of the sand by the returning tide.

OUT OF THEIR ELEMENT

On just a few beaches worldwide, and on just a few nights each year, thousands of animals leave the water and gather at the tideline to participate in some of nature's greatest spectacles. Arriving suddenly, as if from nowhere, they seem to time their arrival with a particular phase of the moon, to ensure the tide is at just the right height to help with their breeding needs. This ritual, which lasts just a few days, attracts a whole variety of predators, who have learnt to exploit these occasional bonanzas of food.

2. For a few nights each May, thousands of horseshoe crabs emerge together to spawn on the beaches of Delaware Bay on the USA's eastern seaboard.

1. Californian grunion writhe in the surf as the females lay their eggs. Once laid, the males will compete to fertilize them.

Fish out of water

There are just two species of fish that will leave the sea to breed on land – the capelin and the grunion. Both look remarkably similar, being thin, silvery fish about 15 cm (6 in) long. During June and July each year certain sandy beaches in Newfoundland are literally covered with thousands and thousands of capelin, which form a writhing silver mass all along the water's edge. A similar spectacle takes place on beaches along southern California and northern Baja California when the grunion return. Males and females arrive together, and once the females have laid their eggs, the males compete to fertilize them.

Grunion spawning in particular is a precision exercise, which always takes place during the three or four days following the high spring tides. This allows the fish to lay their eggs at the very top of the beach and ensures that the lower tides on the following days do not wash them away.

Why grunion and capelin alone of all fish choose to spawn out of the sea is not entirely clear. Possibly they are avoiding intertidal predators on their eggs, or perhaps their eggs may develop faster in the warmer conditions on land.

Fossil out of water

Each year in May thousands of horseshoe crabs appear on the beaches of Delaware Bay on the USA's eastern seaboard. Looking rather like ancient frying pans, horseshoe crabs are the only living relative of the long-extinct trilobites and have remained unchanged since the Cambrian era. These ancient creatures are not in fact crabs: they belong in a group of their own, which is closely related to arachnids (the group of which spiders are members). They come to land to breed and time their return on

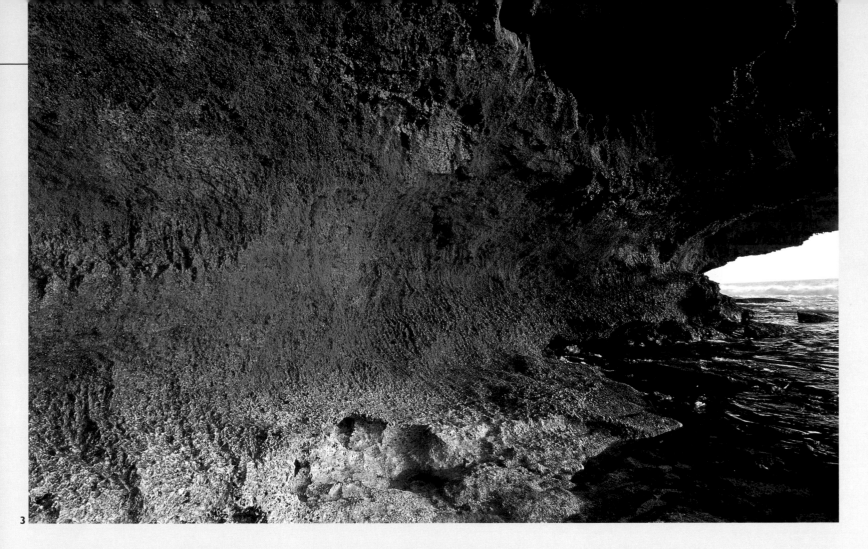

the high spring tides, mostly under cover of darkness. The males, two-thirds the size of their mates, cluster around the water's edge as the females arrive. Each male grabs a mate with the glove-like claws on his front pair of legs and pulls her up to the high tideline. The female then lays as many as 20,000 eggs and the male fertilizes them. With spawning complete, the crabs leave and the waves wash sand over the nest. These eggs provide a valuable source of food for migrant birds, and each year large flocks stop off at Delaware Bay to refuel as they journey north to their Arctic breeding grounds.

Land crabs return

Today's land crabs all evolved from ancestors that lived in the sea. By carefully preserving moisture, they can survive a more parched lifestyle on land, but they still return to the sea to breed. By far the most spectacular example of a breeding migration of land crabs

to the coast occurs each wet season on Christmas Island, in the middle of the Indian Ocean. Around 120 million red crabs, each about 12 cm (5 in) across, wait for the rains to arrive, then march from their forest home down to the coast. They mate in burrows close to a few suitable beaches, and the females then wait for just the right conditions before releasing their eggs into the sea. This always occurs during the last quarter of the moon, when there is the least difference between high and low tides, because it is safer for the females to approach the water's edge at that time. If caught in a rising tide, these land crabs could easily be drowned. At night and precisely on the turn of the high tide, thousands of female crabs head down to the surf to spawn, turning the beach completely red. In three or four nights it is over and the normally blue tropical sea turns brown with crab eggs. The baby crabs will eventually return at exactly the same state of the tide.

3. This cliff on Christmas Island in the Indian Ocean is covered in millions of tiny, baby red crabs that return to land after developing as larvae in the sea.

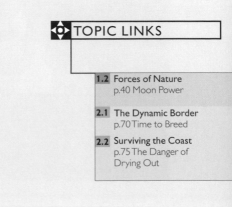

◆ TOPIC LINKS

1.2 Forces of Nature
p.40 Moon Power

2.1 The Dynamic Border
p.70 Time to Breed

2.2 Surviving the Coast
p.75 The Danger of Drying Out

SEA BIRD CITIES

Just like sea turtles, the world's sea birds have no option but to return to land to breed. While the ocean can supply all their day-to-day needs, it cannot provide the dry, hard surfaces on which to raise the next generation. In Antarctica the emperor penguin is unique among birds in its ability to lay its egg on the frozen sea ice that surrounds that continent each winter. All other penguin species – indeed, all the other sea birds – can lay their eggs only on dry land. Some 95 per cent of the world's sea birds nest together in colonies compared with only 15 per cent of the world's other birds, and these huge sea bird cities are spectacular sights.

Steeple Jason, for example, a remote rocky island on the western edge of the Falklands archipelago, is the breeding ground for about half a million black-browed albatross, who normally spend their time scouring for food in vast wastes of the Southern Ocean. Their chosen island is constantly battered by some of the wildest winds anywhere and their closely packed nests stretch in unbroken lines to the horizon. At the start of the breeding season there is a constant cacophony of noise as courting pairs call to each other and clack their bills in display, and the air is heavy with the stench of guano.

This enormous concentration of life can come as something of a surprise to anyone who has spent time at sea. Albatross, and indeed most sea birds, normally live a solitary life, thinly spread over the oceans searching for food. It is only when they come together to breed that it is possible to appreciate the enormous numbers of birds out there.

Although sea birds make up just 3 per cent of the world's 9000 or so species, there can be little doubt they are very numerous. Their life at sea makes them notoriously difficult to count but some species, such as the little auk in the Arctic and the Wilson's storm petrel in Antarctica, must number in their hundreds of millions. In fact, the Wilson's storm petrel may well be the most numerous single species of bird in the world.

1

1. Just part of the world's largest albatross colony. Nearly half a million black-browed albatross breed each year on Steeple Jason.

2. The breeding burrows of thin-billed prions pepper this hillside in the Falkland Islands. The birds only return to them under cover of darkness.

2

Why so many birds?

One of the most striking features of sea bird colonies is their huge variety in size. It is thought that as many as 2 million chinstrap penguins nest together on Zavodovski Island, a remote volcano in the vast Southern Ocean. The warmth from the volcano helps to melt snow and ice from the slopes of this Antarctic island early in the breeding season, providing the bare rock that the penguins need to lay their eggs. Further south, near the Antarctic continent itself, where conditions are considerably harder and the sea is frozen for much of the year, chinstrap colonies are often much smaller, comprising just a few hundred birds.

The key factor in determining the size of any colony seems to be food supply. Birds that can search for their food over a huge distance tend to form large colonies. Sooty terns, for example, forage hundreds of kilometres from their nests on islands in the Tropics, and their colonies can contain several millions of pairs. By contrast, the little terns that nest on shingle banks along the coast of Britain rarely number more than a hundred or so well-dispersed nests. They catch fish locally for their growing chicks and the supply of food is less reliable.

But why do many seabirds choose to nest together in such large colonies? Shortage of suitable nesting space is rarely an important factor. Certainly in the North Atlantic there is a wide choice of empty cliffs that would provide for an expansion in sea bird numbers. One of the possible advantages of nesting together is that birds can share information about the location of good sources of food. But probably the main benefits to be gained from breeding together are the social aspects of colony life. It is social stimulation that encourages gonad development and synchronizes the whole breeding cycle. By laying their eggs together at the same time, the birds reduce the risk of stepping on each other's eggs. When they start to feed their chicks, well-co-ordinated colonies might be better able to exploit the strongly seasonal food supplies typical of the oceans. Finally, by breeding together and ensuring that their chicks all leave the nest at the same time they can substantially reduce the impact of predators.

Safe nesting places

Sea birds have learnt to exploit a wide variety of different coastal habitats to find safe places to nest. In the northern hemisphere many choose to nest on or near steep slopes or cliffs. This is particularly true in the North Atlantic, where the coastline is well endowed with spectacular cliffs, stacks and rocky islands. The remote island of St Kilda, 130 km (80 miles) to the west of the Scottish mainland, is a perfect example of prime nesting territory. Its three rocky stacks – Boreray, Stac Lee and Stac an Armin – emerge almost vertically straight out of the sea. For the 50,000 pairs of gannets that nest there they provide lots of wind and air space, vital for take-off and landing, and safety from ground predators. Avoiding such predators is a key issue for sea birds when they return to land. An agile Arctic fox, for example, can easily steal the eggs from fulmars that nest too close to the top of the cliffs in Iceland, and otters on the west coast of Scotland have learnt to raid the colonies of nesting terns to pick off vulnerable young chicks before they can fly. Antarctica has no ground predators,

1. (opposite) Crested auklets are small sea birds about the size of starlings, that are found in the northern Pacific and nest together in enormous colonies, sometimes hundreds of thousands strong.

2. To reduce pressure from predators, crested auklets gather in swarms out at sea before returning together to their breeding colonies at dusk.

2

so penguins can safely nest on flat ground. By contrast, in the Arctic, polar bears and foxes have driven most of the sea birds up on to the cliffs.

While cliff-nesting eliminates the problem of predators, it presents other hazards. Nests are very exposed to the weather and there is a constant risk that eggs or chicks might fall hundreds of metres to a rocky death. Common guillemots, which nest on tiny rocky ledges on the steepest of cliffs, have developed a specially elongated egg shape that seems to protect the eggs from rolling over the edge. Another adaptation has been noted among kittiwake chicks: when compared with the offspring of similar gull species, kittiwakes are remarkably calm and careful – essential qualities for high-rise survival.

The scree slopes or boulder fields found at the bottom of cliffs can provide more congenial nesting sites than sheer cliff-faces themselves. In Britain black guillemots and razorbills have both taken advantage of the protection offered by holes and crevices in the scree, while the high Arctic swarms with little auks, who nest in crevices among the boulders.

Out in the open

Many sea birds, particularly in the Tropics and Antarctica, have no option but to nest on flat land as there are very few suitable cliffs. Isolated islands, with few or no ground predators, are therefore particularly important nesting sites. Gulls, terns and skuas are typical ground-nesting species of the northern hemisphere. Being agile birds, they can take off quickly when in danger, but they have no hesitation in aggressively attacking any intruder who threatens their eggs or chicks.

In the Tropics and the southern hemisphere boobies and albatrosses can defend themselves by size alone. However, many sea birds, awkward and vulnerable on land, have taken to excavating burrows. In the North Atlantic, the most familiar of these birds is the puffin. Using their colourful bills, puffins excavate tunnels a metre or so into the earth. Finding suitable places to dig, however, is not always easy, so these colonies are often large and very densely packed. Bird Island, off the western tip of South Georgia in the South Atlantic, was so named by Captain Cook

because of the staggering numbers of sea birds he found there. To this day there are many parts of the island where it is impossible to walk without collapsing the burrows of the literally millions of seabirds that honeycomb the hillside. On Nightingale Island, near Tristan da Cunha in the South Atlantic, great shearwaters breed in such numbers – estimated in millions – that the birds run out of burrow space. As a result, nearly 250,000 eggs each year are laid on the surface by birds that have failed to find a burrow.

Predators on the wing

Inevitably, dense colonies of nesting sea birds attract airborne predators, and this is amply illustrated on the island of Talan, just off Russia's far-eastern seaboard, in the Sea of Okhotsk. Just 3 km (1.8 miles) square, Talan is home each summer to over 4 million sea birds of 14 different species. Among the many predators drawn to the island, the most impressive is the Steller's sea eagle, the world's largest eagle, with a wingspan a third as big again as that of the golden eagle.

1

Throughout the breeding season these massive birds patrol the clifftops, riding on the updrafts and looking out for kittiwakes as they come and go from their chicks. When the eagles fold away their giant wings and swoop down the cliffside, the kittiwakes explode from their nests, calling loudly to confuse the predators. Eventually the eagles are successful in snatching a meal from the air, and each summer up to twenty of them and their growing chicks make a very good living out of sea birds alone. But by nesting together and co-ordinating their breeding to ensure that their chicks fledge at roughly the same time: by keeping up numbers, the kittiwakes can ensure that the effect of predation is minimized.

On the other side of Talan massive scree slopes provide nesting sites for another sea bird that has taken the numbers game even further. Every evening during the breeding season, just before sunset, massive swirling clouds appear out low over the ocean. Gradually these clouds build, getting closer and closer, until suddenly the slopes are invaded by thousands and thousands of crested auklets, small black auks just 25 cm (10 in) tall. Their colonies are so large that the numbers are difficult to count, but some are believed to provide nests for half a million pairs. So much potential food attracts many predators, and the slopes are continually patrolled by ravens, peregrine falcons and even sea eagles. But, by returning *en masse* to their nests each evening, the auklets can swamp the predators. For a peregrine falcon, which catches its prey by high-speed dives, a dense flock of swirling auklets provides a challenge. Unplanned air strike could seriously damage a peregrine, so it holds back, and thus for any individual auklet, the chances that it will be taken are greatly reduced by the simple force of numbers.

The ultimate way to avoid airborne predators, though, is to leave and return to nesting sites under cover of darkness. During daylight hours some colonies seem completely deserted, the only evidence of breeding activity being the burrow entrances that pepper the hillside. Nothing starts happening until night falls, and even then overcast or misty conditions are preferred. Suddenly, as if from nowhere, the air is full of fluttering wings and calling birds. Like so many wind-blown snowflakes, hundreds of prions descend on their nesting site. These tiny members of the petrel family spend most of their lives far out to sea, but during the breeding season they come to land *en masse* to lay their eggs or tend their chicks. Frantically busy all night, the majority are gone by dawn, having returned to their natural ocean habitat before first light. Only a few remain to keep the eggs and chicks warm during the day ahead.

MAMMALS RETURN

There can be few stretches of coastline that offer such stunning natural spectacles as St Andrews Bay on the island of South Georgia in the South Atlantic. For a start, the scenery is breathtaking: massive white rollers continually crash onto a 3-km (2-mile) beach left by retreating glaciers. In the distance glaciers are still there, tumbling down the sides of a chain of impressive mountain peaks. Between the sea and mountains the flat glacial plain provides a perfect nursery. All year round, and throughout the worst of the Antarctic winter, 150,000 pairs of king penguins come to this beach to breed.

The activity begins in September and October, with the arrival of 4-tonne bull southern elephant seals. The smaller females follow and soon the whole beach is packed with up to 5000 of the species. For six busy weeks the bay echoes to the roars of males as they battle for access to the females. These bloody, but rarely deadly, contests can last up to 20 minutes.

Lure of the land

Many, but not all, marine mammals need to leave the sea to breed. To understand why it is important to realize that all of today's marine mammals have evolved from ancestors that originally walked the land and continue to share a number of mammalian characteristics: they are warm-blooded, they breathe air with lungs and they give birth to live young who suckle milk secreted by the mother's mammary glands. However, they have also made major adaptations for life at sea.

Life in the water involved two key problems for the ancestors of sea mammals. In the first place, water is far more viscous than air, so marine mammals had to streamline their shape to become efficient swimmers. In addition, water conducts heat much faster than air, so sea mammals had to develop a number of ways to insulate their bodies and reduce heat loss.

Of all marine mammals, the whales and dolphins (cetaceans) are most specialized for life in the water and never need leave it. But pinnipeds (seals, sea lions and walruses) all leave the sea to breed. Seemingly it is simply too energy-sapping to give birth and suckle a warm-blooded pup in such cold water.

There are two different strategies for solving this problem. Many seals live at high latitudes near the poles where they can give birth and suckle their pups on ice floes. Harp seals in the Arctic and Weddell seals in the Antarctic are both examples. While suitable floes are

1. The world's largest eagle, the Steller's sea eagle is a third as big again as a golden eagle.

2. Antarctic fur seals crowd Undine beach on the south coast of South Georgia. Males without a harem can be seen waiting in the shallows.

Southern elephant seals have been recorded diving as deep as 1700 m (5600 feet) in search of food.

abundant and offer easy access back to the sea, ice has distinct disadvantages: it affords little shelter, acts as a heat sink and can easily break up. For these reasons, many seals and all the sea lions choose to breed on land. Although more predictable and providing better shelter, land poses its own problems. Seals and sea lions sacrifice their mobility on leaving the water, and it is not easy to find suitable terrain with easy access to the sea and an absence of predators. Consequently, sea mammals tend to breed on the coast, often forming enormous colonies. On the Pribilof Islands in the Bering Sea, for example, over a million northern fur seals come together in just a few separate colonies.

Why breed together?

Shortage of suitable beaches is not the only reason for these large colonies. Animals used to leading relatively solitary lives searching for food find real social advantages in coming together to breed. All the seals and sea lions that come to land have developed mating systems where one male mates with several females during a breeding season. The exact degree of this polygyny varies from species to species, but a successful bull elephant seal may fertilize up to a hundred females in just one season. As mammals, pinnepeds are predisposed to this breeding system. Because they lactate and the mother's milk is the primary source of energy for raising young, the males are free to spend all their time fighting for females. This activity is fuelled by the thick blubber that keeps them warm in the water, as it also acts as a useful store of energy when they are on land.

The southern and northern elephant seal and the grey seal have a breeding system where males fight to defend females. Pressure

1. Roaring loudly and pulling themselves up to their full height, southern elephant-seal bulls prepare to battle over access to females.

2. A Steller's sea lion bull surrounded by his harem. These males do not fight directly for mates, but defend the space on the beach needed by the females.

3. A grey-seal mother and pup. A white coat is perfect camouflage for ice – evidence that these seals have only recently turned to breeding on land.

to win these battles is so great in elephant seals that the males have grown to an enormous size compared to the females. A southern elephant seal bull weighs 4 tonnes while the female weighs only 1 tonne. This is the largest size differential between the sexes in any mammal.

Once a dominance hierarchy is established through the bloody fights, it is maintained with visual threats and roars. Successful males aim to maintain exclusive access to the females in their group. The females, meanwhile, compete to be in particular groups, choosing central positions that tend to be held by dominant males. This all adds to the cohesion of the colony and encourages elephant seals to breed in dense groups. While a successful male may stay on top for up to four seasons and mate with over 400 females, a female can only bear one pup per season, producing only 12 pups in her

lifetime. However, by sticking with a strong male, she will at least ensure the genetic strength of all of her offspring.

The North Atlantic grey seal, which breeds on isolated beaches on the British coast, has only recently turned to breeding on land. That is known because their pups are white – perfect camouflage if you are born on ice, but less good on rock. The move from ice to land is probably the grey seal's attempt to extend its range further south. Interestingly, grey seal colonies are nowhere near as dense as those of elephant seals, and the size difference between the sexes is far less extreme. However, male grey seals are gradually becoming larger than their mates, and this probably indicates that their colonies will grow denser too. Their breeding system, it seems, is becoming similar to the other two land based species – the northern and southern elephant seals.

All the fur seals and sea lions come to land to breed in colonies. These range from the loosely clustered groups of Galápagos fur seals, with less than a hundred animals, to the extraordinarily dense colonies of Antarctic fur seals, where 150,000 animals will cram on to a beach 1 km (0.6 miles) long. The males do not fight directly for females but try to defend a resource that the females need, such as a safe place to have her pups or a good spot for keeping cool. Animals insulated for life at sea often find the heat on land uncomfortable, particularly if they live near the tropics. In South Georgia, the bull fur seals return first to establish territories, hoping to attract females when they return. At the start of the season, a male may control 60 sq m (650 sq feet), but as more animals return and competition hots up, this may shrink to just 22 sq m (235 sq feet). Females tend to prefer the territories near the top of the beach and the more successful males hold these.

2

3

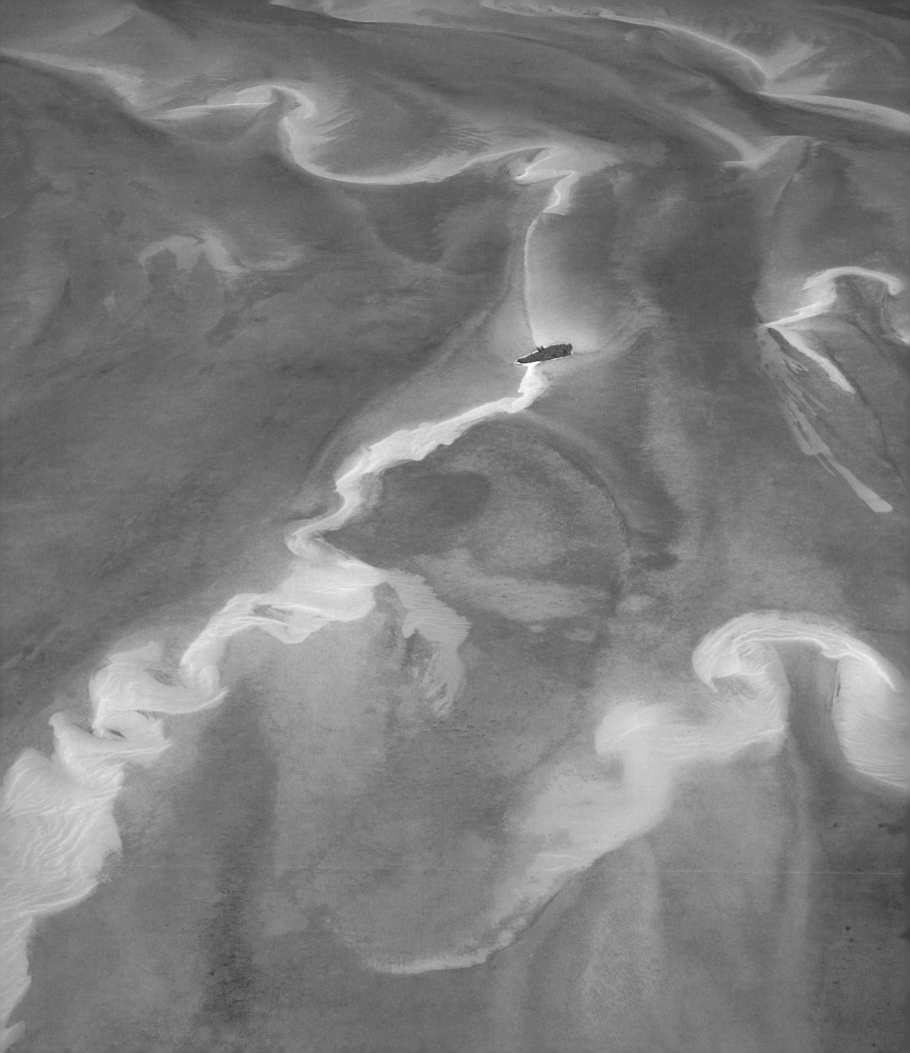

3

TROPICAL SEAS

3.1 CORAL REEFS 102

Built by many millions of tiny, colonial animals, coral reefs are cities of limestone that are simultaneously growing and being destroyed.

3.2 MOUTHS OF THE REEF 114

Diversity is a defining characteristic of the reef and with it comes a variety of feeding techniques and defence strategies unrivalled in the marine world.

SPECIAL FEATURE: Starfish plagues

3.3 SEX ON THE REEF 128

Reproduction in a competitive world is complicated. Most reef animals either change sex or are both male and female at the same time.

3.4 MANGROVES AND SEAGRASS BEDS 138

These important habitats not only protect vulnerable coastlines, but also support an unusual and unique flora and fauna.

SPECIAL FEATURE: Unusual fish – seahorses

CORAL REEFS

Warm seas stretch around the planet in a wide belt either side of the equator. Where land interrupts the open ocean and where the sea floor rises to the surface, a number of different habitats – from apparently lifeless sandy flats to flourishing coral reefs – are found. Seen from the air, isolated coral reefs appear as turquoise jewels in an otherwise empty ocean. Seen underwater, when snorkelling or diving, the profusion of life and the riot of colour and activity are a cause for constant wonder; the eye barely has time to rest on one curiosity or delight before its attention is demanded by another. But coral reefs are far more than visual masterpieces: without the intricate framework that they provide, marine plant and animal diversity in the tropics would be a fraction of what it is. Reefs are places of infinite interest, their richness, beauty and complexity rivalling that of any other habitat on Earth.

Previous page: The sandy shallows of the Bahama Banks are peppered with little islands, some of which support mangroves. Such islands can merely be sandy cays, others are made of limestone.

BUILDING A REEF

Scattered throughout Earth's shallow, sunlit, tropical oceans, coral reefs provide shelter and food for thousands of different fish and invertebrates. Essentially, reefs are like cities, corals themselves being the bricks, and coralline algae the cement. The result is a rampart of consolidated life which can grow so large that it can become a geological feature in its own right. However, reefs do differ in their origin and composition, and consequently in the life that they support.

How do reefs form?

There are several different types of reef, each of which is formed in a different way. How a reef grows and its overall structure depends on the geology of the underlying seabed, the water temperature and the impact of waves.

It was in 1842 that Charles Darwin devised a simple way to classify reefs, which is still broadly used today. He recognized three main types – fringing reefs, barrier reefs and atolls – and noted that one sometimes develops into another. Fringing reefs develop along the

1. The complex physical structure of a coral reef offers both shelter and feeding opportunities to innumerable plants and animals. In the Red Sea anthias feed above the reef, only seeking refuge when danger threatens.

1

coast in the shallow waters lining a tropical island or continent. The corals grow upwards to sea level, or just below, and outwards towards the open ocean. If a lagoon or channel develops between the fringing reef and the land, and the reef continues to grow outwards, the reef becomes further and further offshore – often reaching the edge of the continental shelf – and is called a barrier reef. Barrier reefs can also originate offshore if the depth of the seabed further out is shallow enough to allow corals to grow.

Coral atolls are rings of reef, often encircling an island of sand which is colonized by plants, animals and sometimes by man. They typically have a shallow, sandy, sheltered lagoon in the middle, which has access to the open, deep blue sea beyond through a number of channels. Coral atolls are the tops of submarine mountains. When a volcano erupts and emerges from

the sea, its edge becomes fringed, in time, by coral. This fringing reef may gradually turn into a barrier reef as the coral grows out towards the sea. Over time, as the volcano subsides, the coral continues to grow up, striving to maintain its position in shallow, sun-lit water. When the volcano itself eventually becomes invisible, what remains is a ring of coral reef surrounded by deep ocean.

The most well-known of all reefs is probably the Great Barrier Reef off the north eastern coast of Australia. It is actually a combination of many different types of reef stretched out along 2300 km (1429 miles) of coastline. It includes 2100 reefs, which make up the barrier, along with 540 continental islands which have extensive fringing reefs. Freshwater run-off limits the extent to which corals can grow near the mainland itself, which is one of the

 EARLY SEAS

Before the continents moved to the positions we know today, there was an expanse of tropical water called the Tethys Sea. Bordered by northern Europe and Asia on one side and southern Europe and the Indian continent on the other, it gradually closed up due to continental drift. The animals and plants evolving in the Tethys Sea were squeezed eastwards into what is now the western Pacific. The shallow warm waters and multitudinous islands of that area made it a perfect crucible for marine life, and the greatest diversity of inshore and reef life is still found here. The Indo-Pacific boasts 730 species of coral compared to the Atlantic's 65.

The northward drift of the African continent also meant that the Atlantic Ocean became separated from the Indian Ocean, so Atlantic animals and plants had no opportunity to cross-fertilize with the Indo-Pacific stock. The rise of the Isthmus of Panama about 2 million years ago ensured that no further contact was possible with the eastern Pacific, so the Atlantic became completely isolated. Its animals and plants began to evolve separately and today there are no species common to both regions.

★ The growth rate of coral skeletons varies enormously between species. Some grow only a few millimetres a year, whereas the branching corals can add as much as 15 cm (6 in).

2

principal reasons for coral growth being comparatively luxuriant offshore.

Distribution of reefs

Perhaps surprisingly, coral reefs are not strictly limited to the tropics and they do not necessarily thrive there. Certain physical factors limit their distribution. Corals need warm water, ideally between 18 ° and 30 °C (64 ° and 86 °F). When a cold current runs through an area, as in the Galápagos Islands, the development of reefs is poor to non-existent. Equally, if a warm current persists to the north or south of the tropics, as around Bermuda, which is bathed in the Gulf Stream, reefs can develop.

Corals obviously need a good solid substrate to grow and build a reef upon. They need access to light (for the plants in their tissues), so the water needs to be shallow and clear. Too much sediment in

the water both smothers the coral polyps and cuts down the amount of light that penetrates. Also, too much fresh water kills them. These demands mean that coral reefs do not grow near the mouths of rivers, even where the water temperature and the substrate is suitable. For example, in Brazil, the freshwater and sediment carried down from the forest by the Amazon and other large rivers such as the Sao Francisco prevent substantial coral growth offshore. As a result, Brazil's coast, much of which is tropical, has few well-developed reefs.

Each coral has its own food requirements, its own way of growing, its own way of coping with storms, diseases and predators. Each competes differently for light and space. This gamut of physical and biological factors controls both where reefs grow and the distribution of different types of corals over a reef.

1. Fish of all sizes use the reef as cover. The little blue-striped fang, or mimic blenny, retreats to its hole for safety between bouts of feeding on the skin and scales of other fish.

2. The Great Barrier Reef of Australia is not one long, solid reef, but is made up of thousands of varied offshore reefs, fringing reefs and islands.

WHAT IS CORAL?

Corals belong to a group of animals called Cnidarians. This group encompasses hard and soft corals, sea fans, gorgonians, hydroids, jellyfish and sea anemones. Although the group is remarkably diverse, there are a few features shared by all. They have a free-swimming larval stage and a simple body plan: a central mouth, through which material passes in and out of the body, and a ring of tentacles. The other distinguishing feature of the Cnidarians is the presence of nematocysts (stinging cells) which are used to catch prey.

Colonial life

A coral polyp is a single animal. In isolation it looks very similar to a sea anemone, but unlike sea anemones, many corals have made a huge evolutionary leap – they have evolved to form colonies. A few species remain solitary, but in most cases, new polyps bud off the initial founding polyp and gradually colonies of thousands or even millions of polyps will grow, each connected to its neighbours by living tissue. Freed from the limitations of living alone, colonies can grow to immense sizes and live a very long time.

Corals come in all shapes and sizes, but the basic plan is the same (▷ p. 108); polyps live as a surface layer on some sort of structure, be it hard and inflexible or rubbery. The hard or true corals, for which reefs are most famous, build limestone skeletons beneath the living tissue. Soft corals, as their name implies, do not form solid skeletons; instead they secrete limestone crystal structures called sclerites,

1. Cabbage corals can cope well in the turbid waters of shallow fringing reefs.

2. The colourful soft corals *Dendronephthya* are firm, but flexible.

1

2

which are embedded within a jelly-like matrix beneath the polyps. When they die, little is left of most soft corals as the limestone element of their make-up is so small and easily breaks up.

By contrast, some sea whips and fans and, notably, the black corals have such dense skeletons of limestone, protein and minerals that they are highly durable and are collected and polished for jewellery. The skeleton of black corals is more dense the slower it grows, and it grows more slowly at depth. So it is the very deep, older colonies that are most highly prized.

Building with limestone

Coral reefs would not exist if it were not for the ability of coral polyps to secrete limestone or calcium carbonate. Sea water surrounding a coral is very rich in dissolved calcium carbonate, but the fluid inside the polyp cannnot retain a large quantity of calcium carbonate,

▷ CORAL BLEACHING

Much of the colour we see in corals comes from the pigments of microscopic algae living within coral tissue. Sometimes all the algal cells are expelled from a coral, which then becomes totally white, as in the picture, right. This is called coral bleaching. In large-scale bleaching events, an entire reef can become ghostly white, as if made of ice.

Environmental conditions, such as disease, too much shade and a change in salinity, can induce bleaching, but it seems that the most prevalent cause is a sustained increase in water temperature.

If coral regains some algae, it will probably survive in the long term. However, bleaching can be irreversible, and then the coral will die. When this happens on a large scale a significant change in the reef community follows. Algal turf grows over the dead coral, allowing herbivorous fish and invertebrates, particularly sea urchins, to flourish. Sea urchins graze algae, but in doing so they scrape away the surface layer of rock. By grazing the surface so effectively, they interfere with the recruitment of new coral colonies and perhaps delay the recovery of the reef as a whole.

Being only about 0.01 mm (0.0004 in) across, there may be as many as two million single-celled algae living in each square centimetre of coral tissue, making them the most extensive plant species on coral reefs.

CROSS-SECTION OF A CORAL POLYP

2. (opposite) *Tubastraea* is not a reef-building, colonial coral, but lives in dark, sheltered areas on the reef.

Tentacle

Mouth

Body cavity

Mesentries or gut

Area of limestone growth

Limestone skeleton

1. A simplified diagram to show the basic design and construction of a typical coral polyp.

1

so it is laid down as microscopic needle-shaped crystals beneath and around the polyp. This process occurs in two stages. As the polyp expands to feed with its tentacles at night, it lifts off the skeleton, rather like a glove coming part-way off a hand. At this stage, the calcium carbonate crystals form ridges. During the following day (when the coral polyp is retracted and lying on its new structure), the valleys between the ridges fill in with more calcium carbonate and the skeleton takes on a smoother appearance. Because the skeleton of hard corals is made of limestone or calcium carbonate, it is pure white.

Each coral species lays down its skeleton in a different way. This gives rise to the extraordinary range of shapes and forms that hard corals take. Some form large boulders, where the polyps live in small, isolated depressions or grooves in the skeleton. Some grow in branches, which can be small and stubby,

while others are spreading tree-like structures. Still others grow delicate, leaf-like plates or flat tables. The range is huge, and to complicate the matter further, the same species will grow in a different way depending on the physical characteristics of the place in which it finds itself. Although a coral's genetic blueprint is fundamental in determining what it looks like, its appearance is also affected by waves, currents, light and competition for space on the reef. Such variations in coral form have complicated the matter of identification over the years.

A cosy relationship

None of the hard reef-building corals could lay down their stony skeletons at the rate that they do without help. They simply could not acquire enough food to grow that fast. Help comes from millions of single-celled algae, called zooxanthellae, which live within coral

tissues. It is the relationship between these microscopic cells and their hosts that is the key to reef formation.

Zooxanthellae, like all plants, photosynthesize to produce simple sugars and oxygen, so the coral benefits by having its own in-house supply of food and oxygen. The relationship is symbiotic because the algal cells benefit from the coral's carbon dioxide and nutrients essential for growth. They also have a safe, stable home in which to live.

The importance of zooxanthellae in the building of reefs cannot be overstated. Corals grow up to three times faster because of them, and thus out-compete the slow deterioration of the reef from erosion. However, not all corals house these cells. Most of those living below 40 m (130 feet) do not have zooxanthellae due to the lack of light for photosynthesis. Consequently, such corals grow slowly and are not major contributors to the reef structure.

SHAPING REEFS

Coral reefs the world over conform to the same basic profile in cross-section. Wherever the reef is, be it the Caribbean or the Indo-Pacific, and, therefore, whatever species are responsible for building it, the reef by and large takes on a similar shape. This is because the factors affecting coral growth, namely wave action, currents, sunlight and heat, are the same.

Zonation

The shallowest part of a reef is called the reef flat. Corals here cannot grow above the water level as they would dry out and die, so they grow horizontally, extending the reef flat out towards the sea. Even in shallow water, the heat can be too much for most species of coral, so the variety found on the reef flat is usually quite limited.

On the very outer edge of the flat there is often a narrow crest running along the reef. This is formed partly by boulders or corals that have been thrown up by wave action and then cemented to the reef by a calcareous red alga. The growth of this alga, which does particularly well in this exposed position, adds considerably to the height and breadth of the crest.

1. The Great Barrier Reef has extensive reef areas separated by tidal channels. Water speeds of 10 knots are common in such channels with each change of tide.

On the landward side of the reef flat, there is a lagoon or area of shallow water which typically has a sandy bottom. Depending on the depth of the lagoon, some corals may be able to live here and form patch reefs (literally, a small patch of reef) or the even smaller 'bommies'. The sand may also be colonized by seagrasses, which develop a habitat in their own right.

On the seaward side of the reef is the reef slope. This is where corals reefs are at their most diverse. The majority of corals prefer the slightly less turbulent waters of the reef slope, which receives less battering from waves than the crest. Corals near the top of the slope grow faster as they receive more sunlight than those at depth. This could lead to the slope becoming steeper and steeper, even overhanging, as the shallower corals grow further and further outwards, but corals and chunks of reef break off and tumble down, ensuring that much of the material formed in the shallows lands up in the deeper areas.

Creating sand

Reefs are dynamic structures that change their shape continually, but the change is usually so gradual as to be unnoticeable. None the less, day by day a reef is both growing and eroding in a variety of ways.

The two key factors responsible for the erosion of reefs are waves and boring (tunnelling) animals. Both can cause even the largest coral to break up, turn into rubble and eventually become sand. Clearly, the constant pounding of waves will erode the structure, and a severe storm can wreak serious damage to an entire reef over a very short space of

Slow-growing corals usually leave a dense, longer-lasting rock of skeleton behind them when they die, while the fast-growing corals have light, porous skeletons that break up very easily.

 REEF PLANTS

Algae or seaweeds are non-flowering plants, which are extremely abundant on coral reefs, such as the Great Barrier Reef (right), and are an enormously important part of the ecosystem. The four categories of algae are divided by colour: brown, green, red and the primitive blue-green algae. The colours come from pigments inside the cells, which are responsible for trapping different wavelengths of light for photosynthesis. Algae take on a wide range of forms, from stony encrusting growths to branching plants and solitary bubble-like structures.

Brown algae are present on coral reefs, but they do better in colder water, where they tend to dominate. On coral reefs the growth rate of green algae is particularly fast – an estimated 1–5 kg per square metre per year – but there are so many herbivorous fish and invertebrates living on the reef that these plants are cropped back to mere stubble.

Red algae are most obvious on the reef crest – sometimes called the algal ridge – where they thrive in the area of greatest wave action. Here they consist of 95 per cent limestone rock and only 5 per cent living tissue. Unlike corals, they can withstand the force of big waves because they grow in low-lying encrusting sheets.

⭐ Coral growth varies with the seasons and is indicated by dark and light bands in the skeleton (similar to rings in the trunk of a tree). From these it is possible to tell the age of coral.

1. The appearance and gradual colonization of a sand cay attracts bird life. Sooty terns breed in their thousands on such isolated sanctuaries.

time. More subtle, but no less damaging, is the impact of animals, particularly sponges and bivalve molluscs that come to seek protection. Sponges, which have no means of mechanically drilling into the coral, rely on acids to dissolve away the limestone skeletons. Bivalves, on the other hand, rely mainly on their scraping powers.

Corals are also eaten by parrotfish, particularly the large humphead parrotfish. Whole schools can inflict serious damage on corals as they move across a reef. They bite off sizeable chunks of coral and swallow the skeleton as well as the living tissue. The limestone they consume grinds up both the algae and the organic tissue they have eaten, making it easier to digest. It is then excreted as a curtain of sand as they swim along the reef.

Sand is also produced from other sources. *Halimeda*, a green alga that grows in chains of flat discs, has a large limestone content. When the discs break off or die, they fall to the seabed and in time are eroded into sand. Mollusc shells take longer to break up, once the owner has died, and add larger pieces to the coral sand accumulating on the reef.

The fate of sand

If the waves and currents of a reef are favourable, sand gradually piles up and a coral cay (bank) develops. It may only be temporary and get washed away again, or it may continue growing until the area is well established and ripe for colonization. Initially birds will use it as a resting place, their guano adding nutrients to the sand, so in time plants may colonize it. This encourages more animal life, and gradually the cay will develop into a flourishing island.

Alternatively, as sand settles and becomes compacted in nooks and crannies on the reef, red encrusting algae grow over it, sealing it in. A combination of physical and chemical processes then takes place, which binds the sand particles together to form limestone again. In this way, little by little, perhaps by only 1 mm (0.04 in) per year, the reef grows. While this scale of growth may seem tiny compared to that of corals, the limestone is very dense and hard and does not suffer the same degree of erosion that coral heads experience, making it important in the long-term construction and durability of a reef.

Some sand grains become finer and finer until they dissolve into the sea water again. This calcium carbonate, now in solution, is recycled and deposited by the living corals as delicate limestone skeletons once more. Although the recycling of sand on a reef is complex, it is an indication of how the reef is constantly developing and changing.

1

3.2   MOUTHS OF THE REEF

Diversity is the hallmark of life on the reef, especially when it comes to feeding habits. From animals that unassumingly eat debris off the sea floor, to immobile sponges, to lightning-quick barracuda and sharks, the variety of feeding strategies used is astonishing. It is the evolutionary arms race between predator and prey and the high level of competition for food and space on coral reefs that has led to such specialization. The predators may be equipped with snaring traps, sharp teeth, sucking mouths or harpoons, and they may seek their prey by using sight, smell or electrical senses. They may then use sheer speed or stealth to catch them. Prey, in their turn, have defences, such as camouflage, mimicry, poison, armour and spines. The more vulnerable may simply hide in cracks and crevices on the reef and eke out a living there, but those that venture out must have additional means of escaping the many mouths ready to make a meal of them.

PLANKTON EATERS

One of the best ways in which to understand the complex organization of communities on a coral reef is to look at the feeding structure. Only if you take into account all the primary production of algae on the reef (including the zooxanthellae), the work of billions of bacteria, which break down organic matter, the filter feeders, the detritus feeders, all the animals that come out at night, as well as those seen during the day, does a reef's food web begin to take shape. What emerges is a tightly organized ecosystem where the recycling of nutrients is highly efficient. It has to be because the warm tropical waters that bathe coral reefs are very poor in nutrients. Only by efficiently using and recycling what is already present on the reef and what little comes to it in the way of drifting plankton can the reef ecosystem maintain itself.

Exposed on the reef slope

If you swim along a reef slope when the current is running, the water is filled with little fish lined up, facing the current and busy feeding. Indeed the majority of fish we see on coral reefs are specialized zooplankton feeders. Even those that do not feed on zooplankton as adults usually eat plankton as larvae and young juveniles.

Plankton-eating reef fish rely largely on sight to pick out their food. Their snouts are short, which allows them to focus both eyes

1. Colonial tube worms extend their feather-like feeding tentacles to trap plankton. Sensitive to pressure changes and light, the tentacles are quick to withdraw when disturbed.

on small targets directly ahead. Many species have extendible mouths that are designed to catch prey that is floating by. This is an energy-efficient feeding strategy for fish because they do not have to move to swim towards their prey, instead a quick gulp does the trick. In some species the protrusible mouth creates significant suction which draws the prey into the mouth. Once caught, the plankton cannot escape because the gills have rakers, which are especially long and closely spaced.

To avoid being eaten, daytime plankton living above the reef tend to be transparent – except for pigmented parts, such as the gut – and very small. However, plankton carried on to the reef from the open ocean tend to be more visible and fall victim to the numerous fish which station themselves above the reef slope. These thousands of little fish are vulnerable to predation themselves, from fish such as jacks, so they too have adaptations which reduce their chances of being eaten.

Their best form of defence is to close ranks and dash for the reef, which they do at the slightest provocation. They are also stream-lined and have deeply forked tails for fast swimming. These physical adaptations are more pronounced the further out from the reef the fish go. For instance, damselfishes, which roam only a metre or so from the cover of coral, are less streamlined and have stubbier tails than anthias, which venture further out. Two closely related species that feed in different ways can have very different shapes. Thus herbivorous surgeonfish, which stay on the reef to graze algae, are notably rounder in shape than Thompson's surgeon-fish, which is a planktivore.

There are exceptions to the rule, of course. The pyramid butterflyfish is a plankton feeder, and although it feeds some distance from the reef, it has neither a streamlined body nor a forked tail. Its defence lies in discouraging attack, which its deep body and long spines effectively achieve. The main disadvantage of this body shape for fish is that they might have some difficulty swimming in stronger currents.

1

 CLEANING STATIONS

Like other animals, fishes need to be cleaned, but as they do not have the wherewithal to clean themselves, they get others to do it for them. The appropriately named cleaner wrasse has a distinctive way of swim-ming, lives in one place, a 'cleaning station', and advertises its services by almost dancing in the water. Its clients, ranging from small fishes to large groupers (see right), manta rays and even sharks, adopt a passive pos-ture to assure the cleaner wrasse that it is safe. This little fish will then eat parasites, dead scales, food scraps and fungus from the skin, mouth and gills of its clients and both parties benefit.

Numerous other creatures on the reef also act as cleaners. Herbivo-rous blennies and tangs will clean a turtle's back of fouling algae, butterflyfishes will clean ocean-going sharks that visit the reef, and various shrimps are cleaners too, working on the teeth of moray eels, among other creatures.

VEGETARIANS

Although there are many different plants associated with the reef, algal turf, which predominates on the reef flat, is by far the most productive. Indeed, it is one of the most productive plant communities in the world. Little wonder, then, that an army of fish and invertebrates feed on this bounty.

Who eats plants?

Herbivores come in all shapes and sizes. On Caribbean reefs, invertebrate herbivores, such as the sea urchin *Diadema*, are important, but on Indo-Pacific reefs only fish have a significant role. The dominant plant-eating fishes on all reefs include surgeonfish, damselfish, parrotfish and rabbitfish. There are also smaller fish, such as blennies and gobies, some of which are herbivores, but they play a minor role in harvesting plants. Surprisingly, given the poor nutritional content of reef algae in general, most of these fishes have large populations and fast growth rates. They do well, it seems, on diets that are low in protein. However, they do eat small crustaceans, detritus and bacteria as they graze within the turf. Also, many herbivorous fishes eat planktivore faeces, which are extremely rich in nutrients such as nitrogen.

Herbivorous reef fish have their own set of characteristics, including a small mouth which scrapes the substrate quickly and often, and a body designed more for fine control while grazing than for fast swimming. As they eat they probably take

1. The hawk anthias uses its extendible mouth to catch plankton drifting close-by.

2. The long-spined sea urchin is a voracious herbivore, feeding mostly under the cover of night.

1. Powder blue surgeonfish erect their fins in display to signal territorial ownership.

2. Splendidly adorned harlequin shrimps drag their prey back into the dark recesses of the reef, where they will eat it alive over several days.

in quite a lot of calcareous material, which is of little nutritional benefit to them, so they must eat a lot to ensure they get enough organic material.

Territory defence

Virtually all areas of the reef are fiercely defended by their owners. Boundaries are patrolled, and sometimes the mere presence of a territory owner will deter an intruder. Some herbivores tolerate different species residing within their territory either because they pose little threat to the amount of algae available, or their presence assists in territorial defence.

Some herbivores, such as convict tangs, do not hold territories, but roam over the reef to graze. The only way they can get access to the closely guarded algal turf is to invade a territory in mass numbers. The resident fish, perhaps a pair of powder blue surgeonfish, have little chance against the invading hordes. After a minute or so of frenetic grazing, the swarm of convict tangs moves on, leaving the surgeonfish alone on their territory with a vastly diminished crop of algae.

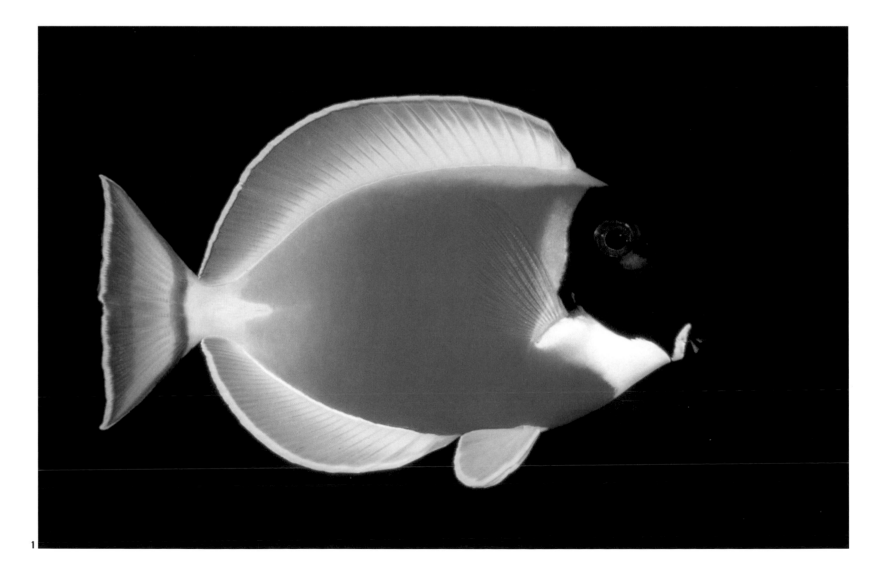

1

MEAT EATERS

With so many planktivores and herbivores living on the reef, there are inevitably many carnivores, including numerous invertebrate predators such as crabs, anemones, cone shells, mantis shrimps and even brittlestars. Brittlestars stand up on their arms and entice small fish into the shelter underneath their central disc. Once a fish has entered, the brittlestar twists its arms and imprisons the fish. The reef is also known for its predatory fish, which range from tiny fish, such as gobies to the largest fish, such as sharks.

Strategies

Predators, particularly piscivores (fish-eaters), use a number of different tactics to catch their mobile and vigilant prey. The open-water species, such as jacks, simply pursue their prey, sometimes hunting in packs if the prey is a schooling species. By simultaneously attacking a mass of small fish, jacks have a better chance of separating individuals from the school. When attacked, small fish, such as silversides, try to stay together to gain some safety in numbers. Also, the visual effect of millions of tiny silver fish acting as one, flashing and shat-

tering like breaking glass, prevents the jacks from being able to home in on one victim.

Lizardfish use a very different hunting strategy; they are ambush predators. Their camouflage is excellent, so they simply lie on the seabed or the reef and keep very still. When an unwary grunt swims by on its way to feed in seagrass beds after dusk, the lizard-fish launches upwards and grabs it.

Groupers are among the largest fish on the reef. They appear docile and hardly move at all, but that is part of their strategy. They place themselves in caves, under overhangs and in holes on the reef, remaining still for so

1. The long-horned cowfish is protected from predators by its box of bony plates.

2. Lionfish use stealth to drift, like weed, within striking distance of their victims. Their own defence is achieved by an array of venomous spines. **1**

long that their prey becomes used to their presence and forgets the danger. Once the victim is within the strike zone, the lunge comes with extraordinary speed.

The trumpet fish has yet another strategy, using non-predatory fish for cover. It swims closely aligned with its innocent partner so that the small fish it hunts cannot see it. When the pair pass close enough to a potential victim, the trumpet fish streaks forward to suck in its prey. Jacks sometimes use the same technique, hiding behind humphead parrotfish.

Defences

The presence of predators has led prey species to develop an extraordinary variety of avoidance mechanisms. Hard exteriors, such as the shells of crustaceans, are commonplace in the invertebrate world, but fishes also use armour of sorts: boxfishes have tough skin and bony plates, scorpionfishes have fin spines they can erect when threatened, and surgeonfishes have scalpel-like spines near their tails. The highly territorial blue-lined surgeonfish goes one step further and has venom within its spines. Other fishes are shaped so that they

are difficult to attack: angelfishes, for example, have deep bodies that are difficult for predators to get their mouths around, and pufferfishes swell up with water at the slightest provocation.

The fantastic array of colours and design seen on a reef is due, in part, to the constant threat of predation. Some colours, such as those seen on nudibranchs (sea slugs), the blue-ringed octopus and certain pufferfishes, indicate that the carrier is poisonous. But colour is more often used as a means of disguise. The harlequin ghost pipefish, for example, is almost indistinguishable from its chosen host, a featherstar. The skin extensions of the pipefish and its coloration match the feeding arms of the featherstar perfectly.

Some prey fish have evolved to resemble predators. For example, the comet hides in a hole head first when threatened, leaving its tail exposed. What remains visible of this small fish – a rounded spotty tail with a large eyespot – resembles a moray eel peering out of a rock. Eyespots are commonly used to trick predators into misdirecting an attack. Many butterflyfishes have eyespots near their tails so that a predator will go for the less vulnerable part of the fish, the tail, rather than its **2**

head. Also, stripes often cover the eyes of butterflyfishes and others so that the precise outline of the body is less discernible.

Defensive behaviour is equally varied. Cowries and hermit crabs withdraw into their shells, while other animals escape into holes on the seabed or on the reef. Some fish school together for protection, whereas others make a quick dash for cover. Despite such strategies predators still win sometimes, not least because they are on the reef in abundance.

Corals as food

Corals cannot move, of course, so most coral polyps spend the daylight hours withdrawn into their protective limestone skeletons where, for the most part, they are safe. As a

second line of defence, they have nematocysts (stinging cells) like barbed harpoons, which contain poison. Primarily, nematocysts are used for catching zooplankton, but they are almost certainly discharged when a fish touches the coral. The venom in stinging cells varies in strength, and some species, such as fire coral and many of the hydroids (small, soft tree-like Cnidarians), can leave a painful weal on your hand.

Despite these deterrents, certain fish remain specialized coral-eaters. Butterflyfishes have delicate snouts, which are perfectly adapted to pick at individual polyps, and some species, such as the chevron butterflyfish, depend entirely on coral for their food. They also fiercely defend their territory, usually a single table coral, from intruders.

Parrotfish are inadvertent coral-eaters; they use their beak-like mouths to scrape algae off the reef and ingest tiny coral colonies while doing so. The humphead parrotfish actually bites large chunks off coral heads, but could well be targeting the zooxanthellae cells within the coral rather than the coral tissue itself, as it is primarily a herbivore.

There is a delicate balance between the herbivores, the coral and the algae. If grazing is too heavy, the newly settled coral larvae, developing polyps and early coral colonies get scraped off before they have become properly established, so no new coral heads will develop. Conversely, if there is too little grazing, the new recruits can become smothered in the faster-growing algal turf and cannot survive.

1. Ghost pipefish are superbly camouflaged against their featherstar hosts. This aids in both hiding from their predators and in approaching their prey.

2. (opposite) Deceptively pretty, fire coral delivers a painful sting when touched. The pain comes from the poison-loaded nematocyst cells that are fired on contact. Divers soon learn to recognize this mustard-yellow coral.

STARFISH PLAGUES

Attractive but deadly, the Crown-of-thorns starfish is notorious for its devastating effect on coral reefs. When these creatures occur in sufficiently large numbers as they did on the Great Barrier Reef in the late 1960s and again in the early 1980s, it was feared that the entire reef would eventually disappear. However, although crown-of-thorns starfish do feed on and kill coral, the plagues always seem to disappear, leaving the reef to recover.

1. Xanthid crabs attack the spines and tube feet of crown-of-thorns starfish to protect their host coral.

2. Crown-of-thorns starfish evert their stomachs and smother living coral tissue before secreting digestive enzymes.

Killing coral

Crown-of-thorns starfish usually measure 25–35 cm (10–14 in) across, but individuals of up to 80 cm (32 in) have been found. As adults they prefer to feed on branching corals, such as staghorn, and plate corals of the genus *Acropora*, but if corals become scarce they will also eat soft corals and algae. Crown-of-thorns pushes its membranous stomach through its central mouth and smothers the coral. Enzymes are secreted which break down the living coral tissue and this is then transported by tiny hairs, called cilia, to the digestive organs. The whole process can take 4–6 hours, and the starfish leaves behind nothing but the white skeleton of the coral. If the coral is large, a starfish might return night after night until the entire colony is dead. In severe crown-of-thorns outbreaks, 90 per cent of the corals can be killed.

Natural or man-made?

Although one starfish eats only about 5 sq m (54 sq feet) of coral per year, the impact of hundreds of starfish is considerable, but an aggregation of starfish is not considered an 'outbreak' unless there are thousands of them. The worst outbreaks recorded have involved several million individuals. Scientists do not yet agree on whether or not outbreaks are natural. The most likely explanation is that they do occur naturally, but that human activities exacerbate the problem.

One possible cause of outbreaks is that starfish predators have been reduced because of the activities of shell-collectors and spear-fishermen. The giant triton in its highly prized shell, is an effective crown-of-thorns predator. This mollusc holds the starfish down with its muscular foot while it cuts through the flesh with its radula (a saw-like cutting organ). It then inserts its long proboscis into the starfish and eats the soft tissues. However, triton numbers have never been very high and it is unlikely ever to have exerted much control over crown-of-thorns populations. Blue-finned and yellowmargin triggerfish also prey on crown-of-thorns. These fishes have hard, plate-like scales and strong, sharp teeth, so they can

3

3. The efficiency with which crown-of-thorns starfish kill coral (making it appear bleached) is remarkable. When starfish numbers build to thousands on one reef, up to 90 per cent of corals can be killed.

handle the venomous starfish with impunity. They pick up the starfish, flip it over and attack it from beneath, where its spines are shorter and less sharp.

Baby boom

Another outbreak theory involves the survival of the starfish larvae. Female crown-of-thorns attract males chemically, then both simultaneously release millions of eggs and sperm into the sea. One female alone can produce about 60 million eggs in a breeding season. Fertilized eggs spend 10–28 days in the plankton as larvae. They feed on phytoplankton, which are very abundant when there are lots of nutrients in the water. Typically, water in the open ocean and on coral reefs is poor in

nutrients, so phytoplankton numbers are limited. But when the nutrient content increases, as a result of high agricultural run-off or sewage and other pollutants entering the system, phtytoplankton will bloom and many more crown-of-thorns larvae will survive. Plankton eaters will consume some of the larvae, but they are present in such huge numbers that many will still manage to settle on the reef. Physical forces, such as favourable currents and winds, will play their part too, and when combined with unlimited food and low predation, the results can be dramatic. Because so many millions of eggs are fertilized, even the slightest percentage increase in larval survival will result in a huge increase in the adult starfish population.

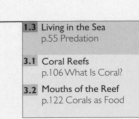

TOPIC LINKS

1.3 Living in the Sea
p.55 Predation

3.1 Coral Reefs
p.106 What Is Coral?

3.2 Mouths of the Reef
p.122 Corals as Food

NIGHT FEEDERS

Catching plankton in the dark

At night everything changes and the adaptations and rules that govern the daytime feeders do not necessarily apply. As the sun goes down, smaller fish seek shelter on the reef first, and gradually, in order of size it seems, all the daytime fish retreat to the shelter of the reef. For about 15–20 minutes there is little visible activity on the reef; the diurnal fish are all hidden and the nocturnal fish have not yet emerged. This is referred to as the 'quiet time'. In fact, certain nocturnal species, such as juvenile cardinal fish, emerge before the quiet time, but as these fish are virtually transparent and less than 3 cm (1.2 in) long, they go unnoticed by the visual hunters patrolling the reef.

After dark, the nocturnal fish swarm out from their daytime resting places – caves and overhangs – where they sought refuge in large groups, and disperse over the reef. Many of them, such as soldierfishes and bigeyes, are planktivores who have evolved exceptionally large eyes in order to find their prey at night. Small zooplankton tend to be overlooked, probably because they cannot be seen. Larger zooplankton, mostly minute crustaceans, who cannot afford to be out on the reef during the daytime, risk emerging at night when the armies of daytime planktivorous fish have retired.

However, it is not just fish that eat plankton at night: all manner of invertebrates emerge to feed under cover of darkness. Brittle stars crawl out from sponges, featherstars make their way to elevated vantage points and basket stars spread their intricate branching arms up into the current to catch plankton. Soft corals, hard corals and sea fans extend their polyps, and sieve the water indiscriminately for plankton of all sizes.

At night then, as the zooplankton rise from the reef to feed, they run the gauntlet of millions of coral polyps and all the other invertebrate traps that are waiting to catch them. Even though the water is full of danger, it seems that the risks of getting caught at night are less than during the day when there are so many fish about.

1. A rarely seen vampire snail extends its proboscis through a sleeping parrotfish's mucus cocoon to suck out and feed on its blood.

2. At night, on some reefs, whitetip reef sharks hunt in packs. Using their extraordinary sense of smell they locate and flush out fish hidden on the reef.

2

Nocturnal hunters

Some daytime fish, such as surgeonfishes, fusiliers and moorish idols, adopt a darker coloration at night, to reduce their chances of being spotted by a nocturnal predator. Their dark hues blend in well with the gloom and help to break up their outline. This adaptation cannot be essential, as many do not appear to change colour at all. Some fish spend the night drifting under a coral, while others tuck themselves right away into holes.

Certain parrotfishes have an unusual form of protection: they hide in a hole and secrete a cocoon of mucus around themselves each night. This is thought to disguise them chemi-

cally from predators such as moray eels, which hunt by smell. But such a cocoon is no defence against vampire snails. These have an extendible mouthpart which acts like a proboscis. When they encounter a sleeping fish, they extend the proboscis into the soft tissue of its mouth and draw blood. Blood is pumped along the tube of the proboscis into the snail.

At night, when there is little light to see by, whitetip reef sharks hunt by homing in on tiny electrical impulses emitted by moving fish. But even inactive fish are not safe because sharks have an acute sense of smell and can detect a fish hidden under a coral. Consequently, many fish tuck themselves away where a shark's ferociously rummaging head cannot reach them.

⭐ Sharks can detect one part of meat or fish skin in one million parts of water, and blood in 100 times that – an equivalent of one teaspoonful in an Olympic-sized swimming pool.

3.3 SEX ON THE REEF

Reproduction on coral reefs, particularly among fish populations, is a complicated business. They do not limit themselves to one male mating with one female, who nurses the developing young. Instead a range of tactics is used, each of which, for the species concerned, enhances the individual's chances of success.

While some, such as butterflyfishes, do form male-female pairs and remain together until either one falls prey to a predator, it is much more common for one male to have a harem of females. To complicate reproductive matters further, many reef fishes change sex, and some are even hermaphrodite: both male and female at the same time. In the invertebrate world where many species, including corals, are immobile, being hermaphrodite is an obvious solution to the problem of not being able to search for mates.

SEX CHANGE

Within the animal kingdom there are some species that can either change sex or act as both male and female at the same time. A significant percentage of the animals that can do this are fishes, and many of them live on coral reefs.

Transsexuals

One of the most problematic aspects of identifying fish is that many of them change sex and colour during their lives. Some parrotfish species, for example, have brightly coloured males and drab females, but to confuse the matter, the same species also have drab juvenile males which look very much like the females.

Hermaphroditism, where a fish has both female and male reproductive tissues, is common among reef fishes. Usually, however, they can reproduce only as one sex at a time. Some fish are protogynous, meaning that they are born as females and develop into males later. Others are protandrous – born male, later changing to females. An exception to this is a group of small fish in the Caribbean whose members are both male and female at the same time (simultaneous hermaphrodites).

Among the wrasses, parrotfishes, groupers, angelfishes and some damselfish and gobies it is usual for the females to change sex. Anthias or fairy basslets, relatives of groupers, are also born as females and later turn into males. Anthias are common throughout the Indo-Pacific, but are nowhere more apparent than in the Red Sea. Indeed, the coral reefs of the Red Sea are renowned for their clouds of orange-coloured scalefin anthias which hover just above the reef, feeding on plankton. The purple males have harems of orange females which remain close to them. These fish swarm above the reef and it is difficult to tell which females belong to which male, except when the fish seek shelter. Then the males and their harems are more clearly defined.

A male anthias stops the females in his harem changing into males by being aggressive to them. This ensures that he is the only male in his group and therefore that his sperm fertilizes any eggs produced. He directs most of his aggression to the largest females, which are next in line for becoming males. It seems that his aggressive behaviour has an impact on the females' hormones and they remain female. However, should he die or be eaten, the largest female in his harem will develop into a male, acquiring longer fins and new colours within a few days.

The black hamlet, a small Caribbean fish, is both male and female at the same time. At spawning time, pairs take it in turns to release their eggs and sperm, swapping roles after each bout.

1. A male anthias has a well-developed dorsal fin, which is raised when he or his authority is threatened. He is considerably more purple in colour than the females that make up his harem.

1

1. Female and male parrotfish rise off the reef together to release their sperm and eggs simultaneously. This increases the chances that the fertilized eggs will escape predation.

2. Spine-cheek anemonefish live in pairs within their anemone, the female being two to three times larger than the male.

Born male

Fish that start life male and later become female include scorpionfish, bream, snapper, bass and some anemone fishes. These last-named fish leave the plankton as tiny males and seek out an anemone. (They are protected from the anemone's sting by a coating of mucus.) If accepted by the resident fish, they join the pecking order at the bottom. The largest fish in an anemone is female, and she prevents the males changing sex by harassing them. Only if she is removed from the anemone will the largest male change sex and assume the dominant role.

Among fishes where the females turn into males later in life, there can also be individuals that are born male and remain so (known as primary males). For example, the primary males amongst blue-barred parrotfish start life being drab, but can later turn out to be the most gaudily coloured fish of all, even more so than the secondary males (males that developed from females).

The primary males among green wrasse retain their dull colours and look like females.

This gives them an advantage at spawning time, when they otherwise could not get into the secondary males' spawning territories without being detected. When the females release their eggs into the water, these clandestine primary males swim up and release their sperm at the same time as the territorial male in the hopes that some of their sperm will be successful.

Why change sex?

All fish want to maximize the number of surviving offspring they have, so here lies the main benefit in changing sex – the ability to reproduce throughout life. Take the protogynous fish which start life as females. They can produce many thousands of small eggs as they are growing up and have them fertilized by a successful male who has proved his worth. When they themselves have grown up and proved that they can survive, they rank high in the pecking order. At this stage they would do better to fertilize the reproductive cells of as many other fish as possible, and to achieve that it is best to be male. Protogyny, therefore, allows fish to maximize their reproductive output throughout their lives, rather than being born male, waiting to become dominant, and reproducing only later in life.

If there are not very many fish of one kind on a reef (as is often true of coral reef fish) and predation is high, then being hermaphroditic makes sense. If individuals of one or other sex are taken by a predator, the chances of reproducing successfully are not diminished at all: if a male is taken, the largest female can turn into a male and all the other females can carry on reproducing. If a female is taken, the male still has other females to mate with, and the other females still have the male. But, if too many of a single sex were to be taken by predators and there was no hermaphroditism, the remaining fish of the opposite sex would be stuck for partners.

2

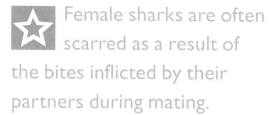 Female sharks are often scarred as a result of the bites inflicted by their partners during mating.

SPAWNING

All coral reef fish try to ensure that their genes continue into the next generation, and they have evolved to do this in a number of ways. Some simply release their eggs and sperm into the open water and hope that at least a few will be fertilized and survive. Others put a little more effort into it and build a nest of sorts. The truly dedicated, however, carry the developing eggs around with them.

Sex in the open

If you dive on a reef in the evening, you can sometimes see thousands of surgeonfish streaming across it. Follow this river of fish and you will probably end up at a prominent coral outcrop on the reef edge. Without warning, a small group of the fish will rise above the reef in perfect synchrony and release a cloud of eggs and sperm into the water. More and more groups will follow suit, returning to the safety of the reef between each bout. This method of reproduction is called broadcast spawning.

Fish that broadcast their spawn produce a great number of small eggs, because there is a high chance that many of them will either remain unfertilized or be eaten by plankton feeders at some stage. Producing lots and lots of eggs improves the chances of a few surviving. Fish enhance their offspring's chances of making it through the drifting planktonic stage and then finding a reef in a number of ways. They spawn at dusk, when most planktivores are retiring to the safety of the coral cover; they spawn at places where the currents take the fertilized eggs away from the hundreds of planktivores that inhabit the reef; they also time their activities to the moon's cycle so that the tides and currents are favourable for taking the developing larvae away from the reef and later delivering them back so they can find a home.

 ## SHARK BABIES

Male sharks have 'claspers', organs which, in some species, function much like a human penis. Before mating, sea water is taken into a pair of muscular sacs which lie along the male's belly, and, when ready, the sacs contract, flushing the sperm into the female. Mating can be a vicious affair: the male bites the female on her flank, back and pectoral fins to maintain his position and, possibly, make her receptive. With a grip on her from behind, the male twists around her and inserts one of his claspers. The picture, right, shows the courtship ritual of a pair of whitetip sharks.

The fertilized egg then develops in different ways, depending on the species. Some, such as bullhead and horn sharks, produce eggs encased in a leathery capsule which is left among weeds or rock. Others give birth to live young, which develop as isolated eggs inside the female. But in some sharks, such as hammerheads, the yolk sac feeds the embryo early on, then develops a placenta that receives nutrients and oxygen from the mother via an umbilical stalk in much the same way as human embryos.

Some methods of broadcast spawning are more haphazard than others. While surgeonfish and groupers may spawn *en masse* in their thousands, green wrasse males establish individual temporary spawning territories into which females are attracted. Angelfishes, butterflyfishes, boxfishes, lionfishes and some wrasses and parrotfishes have one-to-one sex and broadcast their spawn in pairs.

Pair spawning usually involves a degree of courtship. The male may court the female by displaying to her, showing off his colours in some way, and then nuzzling her belly. When she is ready, they will rise high off the reef together, positioning themselves so that the released eggs are immediately covered by sperm. The chances of successful fertilization are higher with this careful approach. Once finished, the pair dive back to the safety of the reef.

Underwater nests

Many fishes prefer not to leave the reef at all to reproduce. Some create a nest of sorts on the sand or on the reef and lay their sticky eggs there. Known as demersal spawners, these fish invest much more in their offspring by producing larger eggs with a larger yolk, and by tending the eggs once they have been fertilized. The survival rate at this stage is much higher than with broadcast spawning, but fewer eggs can be produced at any one time.

Nesting may occur *en masse*, with hundreds of fish clearing small patches of sand cheek by jowl with others. When green chromis spawn, the sandy areas in between shallow reefs begin to look like patchwork quilts from above. The process begins when a male excavates an area, smaller than a saucer, by flicking his tail in the sand. Now in his breeding colour of lemon

1. Trunkfishes release their eggs and sperm high in the water column at dusk when the battalions of daytime planktivorous fish have retreated to the reef for the night.

The red and white starfish, *Linckia multifora*, can reproduce asexually. While four of its five arms hold the substrate, one arm walks off and eventually the tissue tears apart. The lone arm gradually grows into a complete starfish.

yellow, he attracts females to his patch by swimming up and down above his nest, flashing his colours. He also 'chirps', a sound that advertises his readiness to spawn. A blue-green female, attracted by this display, will dive down to his nest, release her eggs on to the sand and swim off again. The male swims alongside her as she deposits her eggs, covering them with sperm. There is no long-term pair bonding, and the female will go and spawn with another male elsewhere on the sand. This frenetic activity lasts throughout the afternoon until dusk, when the fish have to return to the coral for the night.

Large triggerfish also excavate nests in the sand, but these are bigger and require a great deal more work. Large lumps of coral and stone are carried away, and the sand is blown out using their mouths. Usually the female lays her eggs at dawn, leaving the male to tend the nest and defend the developing eggs. Many fish like to feed on the large and nutritious eggs of triggerfish, so the nests are often surrounded by butterflyfishes, wrasses and others waiting for their chance. Any diver who has ventured near a male titan triggerfish on guard duty will testify to its aggression. It will not only scare away other fish, but will also chase and bite divers too.

Broody males

The more time and energy invested in offspring, the better their chances of survival. Bigger eggs have a better start in life, but they need a lot of tending. Among the fish prepared to do this are pipefish, where the male actually broods the eggs.

▷ SOPHISTICATED SHRIMPS

When divers explore a reef, they hear a continual cracking sound. It is produced by thousands of so-called snapping shrimps of many different types and sizes, though most are so tiny that the diver is unlikely to see them. While some snapping shrimps are free-living, others are closely associated with invertebrates such as corals, urchins and sponges. Of those that live in sponges, a few species have incredibly advanced social systems. Like bees, they live in a colony, have only one female producing young and have guards to defend the nest. This is one of the most highly evolved social systems in the animal kingdom and these shrimps are the first marine creatures known to exhibit it.

Synalpheus regalis lives exclusively in the labyrinthine tunnels of sponges, each sponge housing only one colony. Inside each sponge there is a 'queen' shrimp, the only reproductively active female, recognizable by her large, green ovaries. She breeds continuously and all the members of the colony are related to her. The tunnels house numerous young shrimp, but more distinctive are the bigger ones, which all have one large developed claw to fight off intruders. They act as guards for the colony and work together to defend their living space from predators and other shrimp venturing into the sponge.

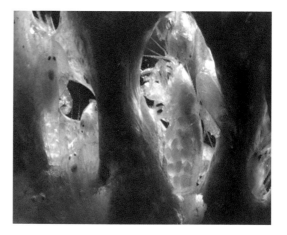

1

Banded pipefish are common on shallow reefs of the Indo-Pacific, particularly in more sheltered waters. They form long-term pairs and although they do not necessarily spend the day feeding together, they do greet each other every morning. At dawn the female swims to the male's home patch and the two swim for a while, gently twisting their bodies together in a simplified version of their courtship dance. On the morning that the female's eggs are ready, the pair dance together, entwining their bodies as they rise up off the coral. In a sudden rush, the female transfers her eggs to the male's sticky pouch. He then carries the developing eggs for about 10 days before they hatch out into the plankton as independent miniature pipefish. During the breeding season, banded pipefish mate every 10 days. It is only because the male takes full responsibility for the fertilized eggs that the female can spend enough time feeding and regaining energy to produce another batch of eggs so soon.

Similar dedication to safeguarding eggs is seen in male cardinalfish. When the female extrudes her eggs in a sticky ball, the male fertilizes them immediately and then keeps them safe in his mouth. He ensures that all the eggs have a good supply of oxygen by turning them around in his mouth at regular intervals, but for the week or so that he carries them, the male appears not to eat at all.

1. Male cardinalfish brood fertilized eggs in their mouth. Far from providing a safe sanctuary, the male eats about 30 per cent of each batch that he carries, whether by accident or by design.

⭐ Giant clams are hermaphrodites, producing both eggs and sperm, but to avoid self-fertilization, they are not released at the same time.

CORAL SEX

Anyone who has dived on the Great Barrier Reef at night a few days after the full moon in November will have witnessed one of the great spectacles of nature: the spawning of corals along the entire 2300 km (1429 miles) of reef. Soon after dark, tiny bundles of eggs and sperm (which look like the small polystyrene balls used in beanbags) float up from the reef to the surface: the water is thick with them.

A question of timing

Being immobile, corals cannot go in search of a mate, so to achieve cross-fertilization between one colony and another of the same species, which may be some distance away, corals have to synchronize their spawning very precisely. Eggs, which take longer to develop than sperm, begin to grow in the coral polyps as early as April. At first they are white, but as winter passes and the spring sun begins to warm the water, development speeds up and eggs become either pink, orange, red, purple, green or even blue. In some corals one polyp will be female and another male, but in most cases the polyps are hermaphrodite, producing both eggs and sperm.

The cue to spawn seems to come from the season, the water temperature and the moon. All three factors must be right for spawning to occur. Along the entire reef, spawning takes place between the second and seventh nights after the full moon, but each species will only spawn on one night during that period. Shortly after dusk the egg-sperm bundles of some species can be seen just under the polyp mouth, ready for release. On cue, each species will release its eggs and sperm at the same time, some early in the evening, some later.

1. The bundles of eggs and sperm rise to the mouth of a coral polyp and are then released.

2. When the time is precisely right, corals release their egg and sperm bundles into the water. As they rise, the bundles break up so that cross-fertilization between different colonies can occur.

The accuracy with which corals spawn is an extraordinary feat, but one that makes absolute sense. By spawning at night they avoid the daytime planktivores, and by spawning all together, they overwhelm the nocturnal planktivores. They also spawn at a time in the month when tidal movement is low. This increases the chances of eggs and sperm meeting rather than being swept away from each other.

Variety of sex cells

Hermaphrodite corals coat their bundles of eggs with sperm only 30 minutes or so before spawning. On reaching the surface, the bundles break up, the sperm swimming off in search of eggs from another coral head of the same species, and the eggs drifting, waiting to be fertilized by sperm from another colony.

Some corals extrude their bundles all at once, almost explosively. For others it happens over a longer period of time, sometimes as long as 30 minutes. Most massive *Porites* coral heads are not hermaphrodite: the females release millions of tiny eggs and the males produce sperm that hangs like a mist, creating an effect very like theatrical dry ice. The sperm of some *Porites* corals actually swim to find another *Porites* coral head with ripe eggs which are then fertilized and brooded internally. Only later are these larvae released into the water.

On a coral spawning night a scum of eggs and sperm forms at the surface. In this soup, eggs are being fertilized and the next generation of corals is developing. Though they can survive adrift in the plankton for longer, most coral larvae settle out on the reef after only a few days.

3. In the aftermath of a mass coral spawning, water currents create great slicks of eggs.

3

MANGROVES AND SEAGRASS BEDS

Dense and usually impenetrable, mangrove swamps are atmospheric places that often fringe shallow tropical seas. They provide an important barrier to the destructive forces of the ocean and they form unique habitats for wildlife. Being less colourful and diverse than coral reefs, they attract less attention, but they are no less important to the diversity of life in the tropics. Seagrass beds, which can stretch for miles along shallow, sandy flats, similarly act as a buffer between ocean and land, protecting vulnerable shorelines against erosion. Both mangrove swamps and seagrass beds not only provide permanent homes to many specialized plants and animals, but also act as nurseries for juveniles that will spend their adult lives out on the reef or in the open sea, and as havens or hunting grounds for passing visitors.

MANGROVES

To visit a mangrove swamp is to step into an unfamiliar world. The occasional shafts of sunlight that penetrate the canopy illuminate a gnarled mass of impenetrable roots below. The air is humid, the water still. Beneath the surface lies a stagnant soup of stinking mud. At first glance, the only signs of animal life are the swarms of mosquitoes ready to plague the visitor. But for those who persevere, mangroves are fascinating places to explore.

Inter-tidal forests

Mangroves are tropical trees that grow in estuaries and on muddy coastlines, where fresh water meets sea water. Here they can form inter-tidal forests. Their most striking difference from typical land forests is that they have no ground vegetation (except the developing young mangrove plants them-selves) and are made up of relatively few species. There are only 40 mangrove species in the most diverse tropical region, the Indo-Pacific, and eight in the Atlantic. Tropical timberlands, by contrast, can boast 100 or more species in a single hectare of forest.

Mangroves are largely tropical, their distribution being governed by sea temperature: they generally avoid water colder than 20 °C (68 °F). Their distribution is therefore not delineated strictly by latitude, but by the presence of cold or warm currents, rather like coral reefs. For example, the cold Humboldt Current running up the west coast of South America results in mangroves having a southern limit of only 30° S (the Peru/Ecuador border), whereas on the east coast, water from the tropical Atlantic moves southwards and mangroves are found as low as 33° S (the Brazil/Uruguay border).

Mangroves are made up of an assortment of unrelated trees and shrubs, which have

1. Exposed at low tide, mangrove roots take in air, which passes down to those roots permanently buried in the mud below.

2. Where the gradient and nature of the coastline is favourable, mangroves can form extensive forests.

⭐ Mangrove trees grow taller where there is more fresh water, but in freshwater habitats they are out-competed by other plants. As a result, they are obliged to eke out a living in the harsh intertidal world.

adapted to the inhospitable habitat between land and sea. They are able to survive in oxygen-starved, waterlogged soil and can also tolerate salty or brackish water. So how have they evolved to cope?

Roots and salt

Like any other plant, mangrove trees have roots that perform the essential functions of absorption, transport and structural support. The living tissue of roots needs air for oxygen, which is found between soil particles on dry land. But in waterlogged mud there is no air, so the roots grow upwards in various ways, or branch off from the trunk high above ground level. These flying buttresses form a network of shallow roots that provides the necessary support and anchorage.

The air passing from the roots above the mud to those lying beneath enters through numerous pores called lenticels, then passes along the root through honeycombed, sponge-like tissue. Most of the air circulates by

diffusion, but as the tide rises and falls, it seems that gas exchange is enhanced. Under water during high tide, the use of oxygen by the root's living tissues creates a negative gas pressure. The lenticels do not allow water in, so the negative pressure is maintained. But when the tide falls and the lenticels are exposed again, they draw in air to equalize the pressure.

Mangroves grow in salty places and have evolved three main ways of dealing with excess salt: they restrict how much gets into the roots in the first place, they have adapted to cope with high salt levels in their tissues; and they get rid of excess salt. Some plants use one method, others two and some all three, depending on the saltiness of the place they are in. They are very good at it, and certain mangroves can keep out 97 per cent of salt. Most mangroves rid themselves of excess salt by excreting it on to the surface of their roots, trunks or more commonly on their leaves. Lick a mangrove leaf and you will find it very salty; you can even see salt crystals lying on its surface.

1

2

1. Above the mud, ribbon-like roots of the cannonball mangrove are flattened to maximize exposure to air when the tide is out.

2. Mangroves excrete unwanted salt on to their leaves.

3. (opposite) The prop roots of this mangrove provide flying-buttress-like support as well as being high enough out of the mud and water to allow gas exchange.

1

ANIMALS OF THE MANGROVE

Hard as it is for mangrove trees to thrive, once established, they do provide a secure home and in some cases food for creatures that live in the canopy, in the water or in the mud beneath. The relationship between the trees and the animals varies, being beneficial to the trees in some cases, but not in others.

Creatures great and small

Mangrove forests provide a home for all manner of land-based creatures. Insects live among the branches and in the canopy, ants colonize the trees, spiders weave webs and these smaller creatures attract larger ones. Birds, either resident or migrant, may depend on food housed in the swamp and may build their nests there. Pigs, deer and antelopes graze in the forest, and monkeys, mongooses, racoons, otters and even tigers use mangroves as hunting grounds. All these animals help with nutrient recycling in the forest, and all leave their droppings, which fertilize the swamp.

The extensive underwater root system provides an excellent hard substrate to live on in a sea of soft mud. The roots of mangroves are often smothered in encrusting animals, such as

1. Ospreys are commonly found in the fish-rich waters of flooded mangrove forests.

2. Scarlet ibis feed and roost in the dense Caroni Swamp of Trinidad. They are rarely seen out in the open like this.

3. Underwater mangrove roots provide an ideal solid substrate for animals and plants that cannot live on unstable mud. The developing roots soon become festooned in algae, sponges, oysters, worms and countless other animals.

2

barnacles, oysters, mussels, anemones, sponges, tunicates, annelid worms, hydroids (sea firs) and bryozoans (sea mats).

Filter-feeding animals, such as barnacles, need the support of a root to keep them up, out of the mud so that they can extract food from the water. But if their growth is unchecked by predators, barnacles can cause problems for the mangrove plant by growing over lenticels and so reducing gas exchange. Conversely, if an underwater root has a good covering of fouling organisms, such as sponges, it is protected from attack by more destructive root-boring or wood-boring animals. Shipworms, piddocks and *Sphaeroma* crustaceans bore into the root systems of mangroves and can seriously inhibit growth.

Crabs

There are two types of crab found universally in mangroves and they come from related families: grapsid crabs and fiddler crabs. The grapsid crabs spend high tide under water in their burrows avoiding predators. When the tide recedes, they emerge to forage on the mud and the exposed roots of mangrove trees. Many of them are herbivores and they occur in extraordinary numbers. Densities of 70 crabs per sq m (11 sq feet) are common, so they can have a significant effect on the mangroves. Luckily for the trees, many of the crabs feed on old, decayed leaves because the tannins of fresh leaves are indigestible. They will, however, carry newer leaves to their burrows and bury them until they become palatable.

Many grapsid crabs feed on the mangrove's unusually large seedlings. In order to ensure successful reproduction in such a testing environment, mangrove trees have to invest more than other plants in their seeds and fruits. The seed does not leave the parent plant, but stays attached and is actually nourished by it, receiving water, nutrients and even food.

3

Male fiddler crabs, like females, feed from particles of sediment, but the one large claw they have for displaying and attracting females is useless for feeding, so they have to work twice as fast as the females with their small claw.

The seed germinates and grows into a seedling called a propagule. During its development, the parent plant regulates the amount of salt the seedling receives, so it can gradually get used to the high concentrations it will experience later on. This high investment in the seedlings gives them a better chance of survival when they drop off into the mud. However, they are also a convenient food source for grapsid crabs.

Crabs are as fussy about the seedlings they eat as about the leaves they select. Those with a high sugar content and low tannin and fibre content are the favourites. If seedling-eating crabs are abundant in one part of the mangrove, fewer of their preferred seedlings will succeed in becoming established as trees, so crabs play a part in determining which type of mangrove trees are found where in the swamp.

Fiddler crabs

Brightly coloured and best known for the males' enlarged claw, used in displaying and fighting, fiddler crabs have burrows all along the shore and can reach densities of 60 crabs per sq m (11 sq feet). They emerge from their burrows as the tide recedes and immediately start foraging on the mud.

Fiddler crabs are deposit feeders. They scoop up sediment from the shore with their claws and sort out particles of food from the grains of sand or mud using specially designed mouthparts, which act like spoons, buckets, sieves and brushes. Different species of crab are adapted to sifting different types of sediment; some species cope better with grains of sand, while others have smaller and finer mouthparts to deal with fine particles of mud.

1. The decorative claw of a male fiddler crab is used to impress, and deter, competing males, as well as to attract potential mates.

2. Mudskippers use burrows in the mud to escape from danger and to spawn. The fertilized eggs are washed away by the flood tide.

Fiddler crabs do not waste their time. If they are not getting enough food for the energy they are expending on feeding, they will move on to a more productive part of the shore. Their foraging hours must be as efficient as possible because as time goes by, the mud dries out and becomes too difficult for them to process. When it does, they begin to socialize.

Males use their enlarged claw to establish and maintain territories by displaying to other males and also, of course, to attract females. Ritualized displays, which involve claw-waving and bobbing up and down, are common between males and probably reduce the necessity to engage in serious fights. Nevertheless, fights do occur from time to time.

Fiddlers cannot roam at random over the mud fighting and looking for food. They require a constant source of water to keep their gills suspended and their bodies supplied with oxygen, so they frequently rush back to their burrows to replenish the water they carry around with them. This is one reason why their burrows are so fiercely guarded. Remarkably, both grapsid and fiddler crabs can cope with very low oxygen levels in the burrows during high tide. They simply build up an oxygen debt, and then, when the tide goes out, they come up into the air so that the water over their gills has a fresh supply of oxygen to absorb.

Crabs running around on the mud or hiding in burrows are clearly vulnerable to predation. During high tide, fiddlers' burrows are closed with a plug of mud, but at low tide, when they constantly dash in and out of their burrows, they are most at risk. Monkeys, kingfishers, herons, snakes, fish and other crabs are just some of the animals on the look-out for tasty fiddlers. One fish in particular, a mudskipper called *Periophthalmus*, is particularly fond of crabs.

Mudskippers

The semi-aquatic mudskipper is an odd-looking fish found in Indo-Pacific mangroves. Some spend the high tide in burrows under water, while others retreat up the shore and even up the mangrove trees to avoid drowning as the tide comes in. As their name implies, they are mostly seen skipping across the mud when disturbed, using their long supple tails as a spring. Their specially adapted pectoral fins vary between species, some using them like crutches, others like suckers to climb trees.

2

1. Mangroves provide a safe nursery for many juvenile fish that spend their later life on the reef.

2. Archerfish squirt water to bring down insects from the canopy above.

Periophthalmus lives on mud among the trees, is carnivorous and highly amphibious. Other mudskippers, such as *Boleophthalmus*, a type of goby, are deposit feeders. They live lower down the shore away from the trees and sweep their heads across the mud scooping up mouthfuls. Like fiddler crabs, they sort food from grains of mud or sand in their mouth, then get rid of the water and sediment they do not want. *Boleophthalmus* does not avoid the rising tide, but spends high tide in a burrow under water and has gills more like that of other gobies.

Like crabs, mudskippers are often seen returning to their burrows, to prevent their skin drying out under the tropical sun. As gills are not very effective in the open air, where many mudskippers spend a great deal of time, it makes sense for them to get oxygen in another way. Mudskippers have skin that is full of blood vessels, particularly at the front of the head. *Periophthalmus*, which spends more time exposed to air than *Boleophthalmus*, depends more on its skin for its oxygen supply.

1

Other mangrove animals

Many marine animals, including catfish, mullet, cardinalfishes and numerous juveniles of reef dwelling or pelagic fish, can invade mangroves only when the tide is high. When the water is out, these creatures can be found concentrated in the creeks and pools that lace the swamp, but, of course, they attract predators. These include the estuarine crocodile, whose distribution ranges from India through Southeast Asia to Fiji and Australia. Where left undisturbed and not hunted, these crocodiles can grow up to 7 m (23 feet) or so in length. However, the saltiness of mangrove water does pose a problem for them. Their largely impermeable skin helps to keep the salt out, and they are careful to drink only fresh water when they can. But inevitably, when they eat, they take in salt water with their food. Along with sea snakes and other reptiles, crocodiles have evolved ways of controlling the salt content of their bodies. In their case, excess salt is excreted through salt glands on their tongue.

2

The most abundant snails in mangroves are periwinkles. They live above the water line, different species being adapted to live in different parts of the tree and in different zones of the forest. Some live on the roots, trunk and branches, grazing the blanket of algae growing there. Others live in the canopy, and prefer to live near land where there is more fresh water. Their shells are coloured and constructed according to where they live. Snails living low on the tree's roots and branches have darker shells, so they are better camouflaged, thicker shells to protect them from predation by crabs, and the entrance to their shell is rounded to fit the curve of the roots. Those living in the canopy can afford thinner shells with a flat opening and they are typically lighter in colour.

Snails eat most of what is available in the mangrove forest. Some get food from the seabed or the mud by scraping the surface of detritus. Herbivorous snails eat dead and fallen leaves or graze on algae. Predatory snails, such as *Thais*, are found in mangroves throughout the world feeding on barnacles.

SEAGRASS BEDS

Seagrass beds occur on shallow, sandy plains that often neighbour coral reefs and mangrove forests. These huge meadows, which carpet the sea floor, house many creatures, most of which are either buried in the sand, or are well camouflaged against the green of the seagrass.

Flowering plants

Most plants in the ocean have no root system and do not produce flowers; they are known as seaweeds or algae. Those that do produce flowers are called seagrasses. There are only 50 plant species that have managed to adapt to a salty, underwater life yet still retain the ability to reproduce using flowers. In some seagrasses, threads of pollen are released by male plants and carried by water currents to a female plant, which is then fertilized. Other seagrasses have flowers that contain both male and female organs, a common occurrence in land plants.

Seagrasses also have an extensive underground network of roots. These are important in anchoring the plant to the ground, as well as for absorbing nutrients from the sediment. But oxygen for the plant is obtained from water absorbed through the leaves.

Seagrass leaves are typically flat and blade-like with a high surface to volume ratio. This maximizes the diffusion of gases and nutrients into the leaf from the water, and also exposes the largest possible surface area of leaf to the sun for photosynthesis. As seagrasses have no stomata (small openings) in the leaf as land plants do, their leaves have a thinner, protective outer layer of cutin, as well as a sponge-like interior to help speed up gas exchange. Despite this, in the afternoon, when photosynthesis and therefore oxygen production is at its peak, the leaves of *Thalassia testudinum* swell up 250 per cent and become oval in shape because they cannot get rid of the oxygen quickly enough.

1

2

3

Seagrass inhabitants

Seagrasses often form extensive beds or meadows, which can be very important to shallow tropical seas of the Caribbean and the Indo-Pacific for a number of reasons. One of the key roles of seagrass beds is in preventing coastal erosion. The root systems stabilize and hold sediments on the sea floor even during hurricanes and storms, and the swaying action of the leaves slows the rate at which water moves over the seabed, thus buffering the effect of wave action and water currents. Seagrass meadows also grow quickly, some plants extending by as much as 5–10 mm (0.2–0.4 in) per shoot per day, so they are a valuable source of food for herbivores, such as sea urchins, fishes, turtles and dugongs. Seagrasses also provide a safe shelter for many small creatures living in the seabed or between the blades of grass. Some live there all their lives, while others are transient and spend time there only to feed, or as a temporary home while they are young. Among the latter are some fishes, lobsters and shrimp, which spend their early days in seagrass beds and their adult life on coral reefs.

Those that come to feed there are often found hiding on nearby reefs during the day. The sea urchin, *Diadema*, is a good example of this. These urchins cannot afford to travel far from their daytime hiding places because of the risk of predation when the sun rises, so they graze a seagrass bed close to their home reef. This can result in a halo effect on the seagrass bed, the plants close to the reef being heavily cropped while those beyond grow taller.

The floor of a seagrass meadow is home to many different types of invertebrates. Worms burrow into the sediment, while starfish and conch live on the surface feeding on detritus and dead blades of seagrass. Sea urchins that do stay in the seagrass beds all day and night usually camouflage themselves with bits of grass and broken shell, or bury themselves in the sediment. Thanks to the stabilizing effect of the plants on the sediment, anemones can dig themselves into the sea floor and be sure

1. Eel grass can form extensive meadows in calm, shallow waters.

2. A ghost pipefish hangs motionless, imitating a drifting blade of seagrass.

3. Caribbean spiny lobsters migrate to deep water annually to avoid winter storms.

they won't become exposed. Their stinging tentacles remain up in the water column to catch food passing by. Seahorses can sometimes be found swaying in the current, their tails wrapped around the blade of a plant, but they are usually extremely well camouflaged and difficult to find.

Sea cows

Perhaps the most exciting animals to be found feeding in seagrass beds are sea cows – the dugong of the Indo-Pacific and the manatee of the Caribbean and West Africa. Manatees, however, spend at least part of their lives in fresh water, so dugongs are the only herbivorous, truly marine mammal. The most obvious difference between these two types of sea cow is the shape of their tails. Dugongs have notched, fish-like tails, whereas manatees have round, paddle-like tails with no notch. The other key difference, though not so visible, is their teeth. Dugongs have tusk-like incisors, while manatees have only molars and premolars, which move forward over

time and are continually replaced by more teeth from the back.

Being slow swimmers, manatees and dugongs are found in the sheltered waters of lagoons and bays, rather than far out at sea. They have a slow metabolic rate, although they are reasonably well insulated, they cannot generate enough heat to tolerate cool water. Thus they are found in the warm water of the tropics and in some subtropical areas.

Dugongs and manatees have dense, massive bones, which help to keep them submerged. Their lungs lie along their back and act like floats, keeping them horizontal in the water. A pair of nostrils, sealed with a flap of skin when under water, is situated near the top of the head so that they can take a breath of air with minimal effort. Their lobed lips, covered with sensory bristles, are prehensile (grasping) and pass seagrass to the mouth.

Dugongs feed voraciously and can eat as much as 40 kg (88 lb) of seagrass a day. But whatever the species, dugongs eat by grubbing up the whole plant, which leaves distinctive troughs in a meadow.

2

1. (opposite) Manatees have distinctive rounded tails, unlike dugongs, which have a notch in their tail.

2. Dugongs eat a lot of seagrass, preferring the soft varieties to the fibrous ones. They root up the nutritious rhizomes growing beneath the sand.

 SEX AMONG SEA COWS

Dugongs are thought to use the 'lek' system whereby males establish and defend courtship territories in traditional areas where females come only to mate. In Australia, when male dugongs encounter one another, they swim in parallel or root around on the seabed facing each other. Only as a last resort will they engage in a serious fight. When the females eventually arrive, sometimes as long as three months later, the males advertise their presence and prowess by thrusting themselves as high out of the water as they can and creating a tremendous splash. A female chooses a partner and mates, and a calf is born approximately one year later.

Manatees have a rather different mating system. The females, who are sexually mature at three years as opposed to the dugong's ten, come into oestrus and are pursued by a herd of males. Up to 20 males can be jostling for access to one female and she may mate with a number of them.

UNUSUAL FISH – SEAHORSES

Seahorses are unusual fish; they move, swim, feed and reproduce unlike any other. Their distinctive snout has a powerful suck and is used to capture tiny crustaceans, fish larvae and plankton. Like chameleons, they have independently moving eyes, which help in spotting their minute prey. A coronet adorns their head, and each is as individual as a human fingerprint. Although seahorses are fish, they have no scales: instead they have skin stretched tight over a frame of interlocking bony plates, which are hinged so that they can bend. They propel themselves through the water by using only their dorsal fin, while their pectoral fins are used for steering and balance.

1. Short-snouted seahorses come belly to belly for the transfer of eggs from female to male.

2. Miniature copies of an adult seahorse are released from the male's pouch two weeks after the eggs are transferred there from the female.

Seahorses at home

There are 35 species of seahorses world-wide, ranging in size from the tiny pygmy seahorse, which is about 2 cm (0.75 in) long, to the eastern Pacific seahorse, which is 36 cm (14 in) long. They usually live in shallow coastal seas, such as seagrass beds, where they can attach themselves to individual blades of grass and mangrove roots. They can change colour within a few seconds to match their background perfectly, grow tendrils which blend in with their surroundings, and allow encrusting organisms and algae to cover their skin, making them incredibly difficult to find.

Reproduction

Seahorses are monogamous, maintaining the bond with their partner by a ritual dance performed every morning just after dawn. The female finds the male in his territory and they greet each other with a brightening in colour. They attach themselves to the same seagrass shoot, using it as a central pivot while they circle around it. Then, swimming closely together with their tails entwined, they move to another place for more circling.

At the beginning of the breeding season it takes some time for the female's eggs to ripen. Only after three days or so of courting, when both change colour dramatically and conspicuously, are the couple ready to mate. On that morning the male indicates his readiness by jack-knifing energetically, bringing his tail up to his body. The female responds by stretching upwards, pointing her snout at the water surface, while keeping the tip of her tail on the seabed. The pair then slowly rise together, belly to belly, the female transferring her string of sticky eggs to the male's pouch.

1

2

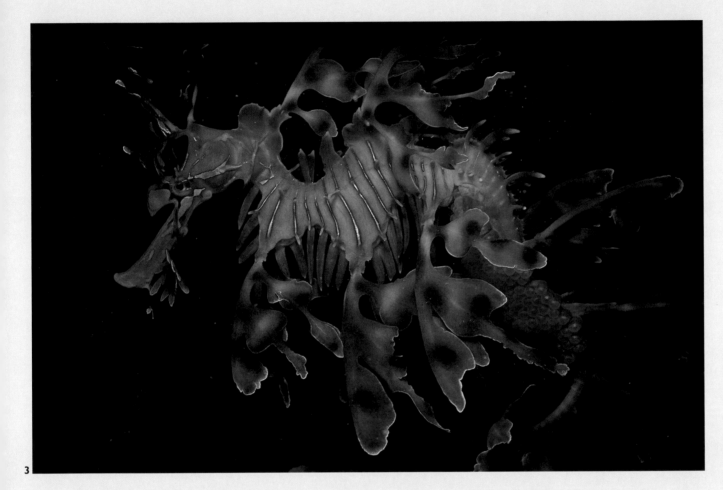

3

3. Found off southern Australia, and well disguised as a floating piece of seaweed, this male leafy seadragon carries a developing clutch of fertilized eggs on the underside of his tail.

Pregnant males

The eggs are fertilized just after they enter the male's pouch and soon become embedded in its wall. The pouch functions very like a mammalian womb: each embryo is supplied with oxygen, housed and nurtured. Male seahorses even release the same hormone (prolactin) as female humans, which helps to nourish the embryos. The fluid in which the embryos are suspended changes during the pregnancy so that it becomes increasingly like sea water. This prepares the young for the shock of being evicted from the pouch.

Pregnancy lasts about two weeks in tropical seahorses, and during this period the female continues to arrive every morning for the greeting ritual. Apart from maintaining the bond between the pair, the ritual reveals when the male has given birth and is ready for the female's next batch of eggs to be transferred

When the young are ready to be born, the male performs his jack-knifing contortions again, expelling the miniature seahorses from his pouch. This can take hours or even days, but from this moment on the young are totally independent. They rise to the surface, take a gulp of air to fill their swim bladders, then sink again, holding on to anything they can find with their prehensile tails. The female mates with him again that same day or the next, so males are pregnant continuously throughout the breeding season.

TOPIC LINKS

3.4 Mangroves and Seagrass Beds
p.149 Seagrass Inhabitants

TEMPERATE SEAS

4.1 THE RICHEST SEAS 156

The annual cycle of the seasons makes the cool temperate seas immensely productive; bounty that attracts migrants from both far and near.

HABITAT ILLUSTRATED SPREAD: Temperate seas

4.2 BLOOMING PLANKTON 168

Microscopic plants and animals blossom to astronomic numbers during the spring and early summer. They are the basic fuel for life in these waters.

SPECIAL FEATURE: Baitball

4.3 OCEAN FORESTS 184

Marine algae, ranging from the microscopic to vast 100 m (330 foot) giants, proliferate in the sunlit shallows. These plants sustain some of the richest habitats on Earth.

SPECIAL FEATURE: Guardians of the forest

4.4 THE LIVING BED 198

In deeper water, where seaweed struggles to survive, lies a world of rocky cliffs and vast plains: the domain of colourful invertebrates and strange predatory fish.

SPECIAL FEATURE: The gray whale

THE RICHEST SEAS

The most consistently productive marine habitats on Earth are found within the temperate zones, which lie between the Tropics and the polar extremes of the globe. Both the northern and southern hemispheres are encircled by a wide band of temperate sea, characterized by a climate that is comparatively mild but intensely seasonal. Summers are warm and winters cold, but not excessively so – there is rarely permanent sea ice in temperate waters. In fact, water temperatures range from a minimum of about 4 °C (39 °F) up to around 20 °C (68 °F). Yet despite this mildness, there is nothing mild about the diversity of the wildlife. Planktonic populations explode to massive annual blooms, which in turn support immense numbers of birds, fish, mammals and invertebrates. Marine plants abound – indeed, most of the world's 10,000 species of seaweed exist in temperate water. But why should such a mild marine habitat be able to support such an immense population?

Previous page: Sunlight cascades through a canopy of giant kelp. These immense seaweed form great forests along temperate coasts, this one is in California.

THE SEASONAL SEA

Think of swimming at the seaside. Most people conjure up an image of warm, blue, crystal clear water, but take a temperate dip and that image is quickly dispelled. Compared to the Tropics, this sea water is cold and dull green rather than crystal blue. It can also be so cloudy that a diver may be able to see only a couple of metres in any direction under water.

To a great extent this cloudy green water hides the clues to the richness of the temperate sea. Tropical waters contain few nutrients, and very little in the way of microscopic plankton, but the temperate sea water can be packed with nutrients, and the green coloration comes, in part, from an immense volume of microscopic plant life swarming in the water. The cloudiness tends to occur in spring and early summer, when microscopic life grows freely; in winter there is far less suspended matter in the water, so the water clarity tends to be better.

The density of microscopic organisms depends on the levels of nutrients and light energy in the water. In the temperate sea, both change constantly, their levels governed by seasonal variations of the weather and day length, but every year there comes a time when the conditions are perfect and the volume of life explodes.

1. Cold surf breaks on a temperate shore. The green colour of the water comes from countless millions of microscopic algae.

THE TEMPERATE SEAS

The temperate zones fall midway between the tropics and the polar regions and are mild in climate. The seas are rich in nutrients and planktonic communities thrive. Between spring and autumn the plankton explode to form massive blooms and, attracted by this bounty, colonies of creatures arrive to feed, many of them undertaking enormous journeys in order to do so (see map, right). While some animals depart as the weather gets cooler, others arrive to escape extreme weather elsewhere. Many inhabitants are therefore visitors, coming and going according to their various needs.

Seas of plenty

Phytoplankton, which form the basis of almost all the food chains of the oceans, require nutrients in order to grow and multiply. These are brought into the oceans through rivers and the bodies of dead oceanic creatures. Temperate waters are particularly rich in these nutrients, but they are not always available in the upper layers of the ocean. In the summer months, when the sea is calm, the dense, nutrient-rich water settles at the bottom of the ocean, but the storms of winter mix the water, distributing the nutrients throughout the ocean and paving the way for the burst of life that will come again in spring (see illustrations, below).

SPRING

SUMMER

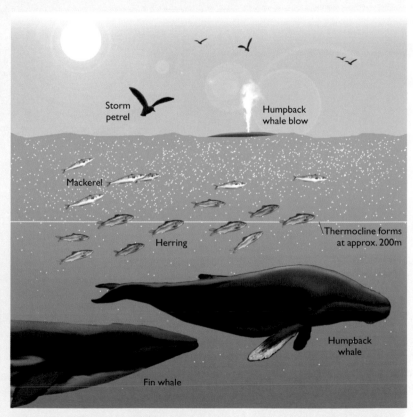

Gannet

Mackerel

Humpback whale

Herring

Fin whale

Storm petrel

Humpback whale blow

Mackerel

Herring

Thermocline forms at approx. 200m

Humpback whale

Fin whale

1. In spring, a massive explosion of plankton growth occurs, owing to increased sunlight and an abundance of nutrients in the water. As a result, many fish arrive to feed (herring from the lee of the land, mackerel from deeper offshore waters), and whales come to feed on the fish. Numerous sea birds arrive at the cliffs to breed.

2. In summer, the sun heats the surface of the water, forming a thermocline. The vast majority of microscopic organisms are trapped at the surface, unable to cross the barrier, and the nutrients are trapped in the depths; as a result, primary growth drops significantly. Many fish and invertebrates migrate to the shallows to feed.

HUMPBACK WHALE MIGRATION ROUTES

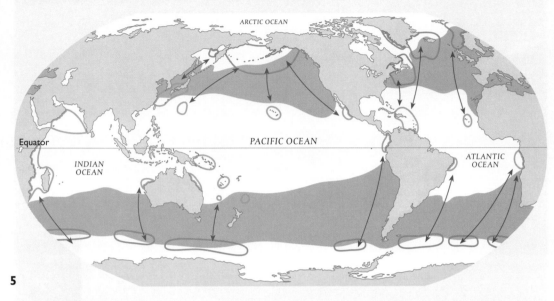

5. Temperate seas are highly changeable according to the season. Consequently, many animals undertake often extensive migrations to benefit from certain conditions at a particular time of year. Humpback whales, for example (see map, left), spend between April and October in nutrient-rich temperate seas, where they feed on vast quantities of fish, increasing their weight by several tonnes. In autumn, they travel thousands of kilometres to warmer areas to breed, surviving without food until the following spring.

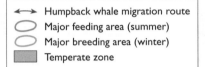

Humpback whale migration route
Major feeding area (summer)
Major breeding area (winter)
Temperate zone

AUTUMN

3. In autumn, if storms occur they can break down the summer thermocline and allow a small amount of nutrient-mixing, sometimes resulting in a second plankton bloom. Mackerel return to deep offshore waters and herring return to the lee of the land, for protection. Whales head to warmer waters to breed.

WINTER

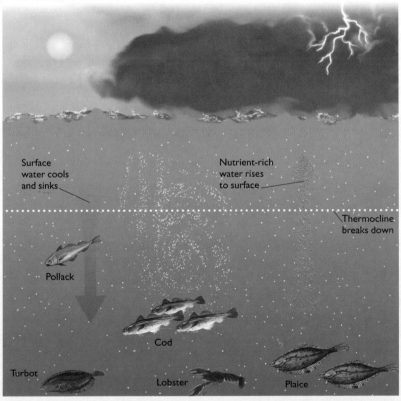

4. In winter, storms break down the thermocline and the nutrients are stirred up by violent wave action. The surface water can chill so much that it becomes dense and sinks, forcing nutrient-rich water up from the depths. Many fish and invertebrates return to deep waters for refuge from the storms.

A sun for all seasons

In temperate regions the hours of daylight change every day of the year, with the shortest days occurring in midwinter and the longest in midsummer. This is because the Earth's polar axis is not perpendicular to the sun, which means that during its annual orbit of the sun the Earth's aspect towards it is constantly changing. Effectively, during the northern hemisphere's summer, the North Pole is inclined towards the sun, and the South Pole away from it. The North Pole therefore sees 24 hours of daylight, while the South Pole endures total darkness and midwinter. The reverse happens during the northern hemisphere's winter – the North Pole being plunged into darkness while the South Pole enjoys 24 hours of daylight. This effect is hardly noticeable at all at the Equator, where every day is roughly the same in length, but it is very noticeable in the temperate areas of both north and south. Temperate oceans will see as little as four hours of sunlight a day in midwinter and up to 20 hours of sunlight in midsummer. This enormous change of light energy has a profound influence on marine life, not least by creating temperature layers in the ocean.

Thermoclines – barriers in the sea

Water has the ability to absorb a great deal of heat, but it takes a lot of energy to raise the temperature of the sea. For this reason the summer sun, powerful as it is, heats only the uppermost 50 m (160 feet) or so. Water also conducts heat rather inefficiently, so this surface-warming effect creates a sharp temperature boundary between the warm upper water and the underlying cooler layers. This boundary is called a thermocline and it has a profound influence on marine life in temperate seas.

1

A seasonal thermocline exists only when the sun is at its most powerful and the ocean calm enough to prevent the layers from mixing up. During winter, the thermocline quickly breaks down, but in summer the boundary of the thermocline can see a marked variation of from 22 °C (72 °F) in the upper water to a mere 12 °C (54 °F) below. In the ocean this constitutes a massive change, so once the thermocline has stabilized it is very difficult for small creatures or nutrients to pass through it in either direction. A thermocline represents a major barrier and exerts a powerful control over the productivity of the sea.

Nutrients – the ocean's fertilizers

The vast majority of life in the ocean is absolutely dependent upon the presence of nutrients, particularly nitrates and phosphates, and temperate waters can have unusually high levels of these minerals. As many of the world's temperate seas lie on the shallow coastal plains, called continental shelves, that fringe the edges of the major continents, rain-swollen rivers pour nutrients from the land into the sea.

Other major sources of nutrients are detritus and decomposed bodies of dead marine organisms, but these generally sink down into the abyss, taking the vital nutrients far from the surface water. Deep oceanic water often contains a high level of nutrients, but under normal circumstances this cold, dense water cannot intermingle with the less dense surface water, so the nutrients are trapped in the depths.

Winter at sea, as on the land, is a time of fertilizing – mixing minerals in preparation for next year's growth. During the winter months, temperate seas are cold, and violent storms are commonplace. If it gets cold enough, the surface water chills so much that it becomes dense and sinks, forcing nutrient-rich water up from the depths in its place. In shallower water the violent wave action during storms is quite sufficient to stir up nutrients from the

HOURS OF DAYLIGHT

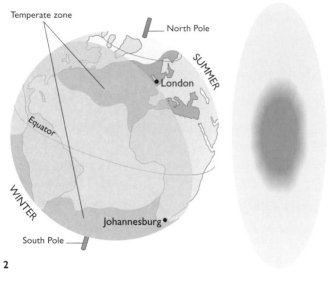

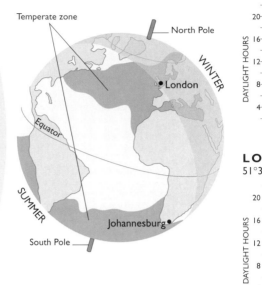

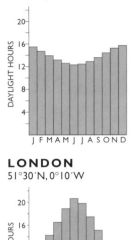

JOHANNESBURG
26°10′N, 28°02′E

LONDON
51°30′N, 0°10′W

1. In the Bay of Fundy, on the Atlantic coast of Canada, tidal currents pour past a rock island, mixing nutrients from the seabed to the surface.

2. Earth's axis is not perpendicular to its solar orbit, so the hours of daylight change through the year, creating seasons. In winter the days are shortest, in summer they are longest.

---

seabed over 100 m (320 feet) below. It is this process of mixing up water and spreading nutrients throughout the water column that makes temperate seas so extraordinarily rich. Each spring the sea water, as carefully tilled as any farmer's field and packed with nitrates, phosphates and other minerals, allows an abundance of life to grow, as long as it is sufficiently shallow for sunlight to penetrate.

The cycle of life

The seasonal climate of the temperate world governs both the supply of nutrients and sunlight, thereby controlling the annual cycle of life in its seas.

Winter has short days and little sunlight, so there is insufficient energy for the growth of microscopic plant life (phytoplankton). Storms break up any thermoclines in the water, rivers pour nutrients into the sea, and cold weather causes surface water cooling to displace deep water. All three events ensure

thorough mixing of nutrients from the deep to the surface.

Spring sees daylight increase and the sun's power strengthen. The water is full of nutrients, but the warming effect of the sun has not yet had a chance to form thermoclines. This combination of abundant nutrients and increased sunlight causes a dramatic explosion of primary growth of microscopic life.

Summer brings maximum daylight and power from the sun. Seasonal thermoclines form, preventing the free passage of nutrients between the surface water and deeper water. The growth of microscopic life uses up most available nutrients in the sunlit shallow water above the thermocline. Small organisms trapped above the thermocline are unable to reach the nutrient-rich water below. With the mineral supply exhausted, primary growth drops significantly.

Autumn sees daylight hours shorten and the sun's power start to reduce. If autumnal storms occur, they break up the summer

thermocline and allow a small amount of nutrient mixing. More nutrients are available to microscopic life in the shallows, and a second, smaller bloom of primary growth can occur. Within a few weeks the hours of sunlight decrease further, and the supply of energy is insufficient to sustain primary life.

Mixed up with the tide

In coastal areas, tidal currents may also act as agents of nutrient recycling. Such currents can reach speeds of up to 30 kph (15 knots), creating white water, whirlpools and giant standing waves. These manifestations of water power are found in places such as the Bay of Fundy in Nova Scotia, the west coast of Scotland, Norway and British Columbia. Their effect is to create tremendous local mixing of nutrients and to prevent thermoclines from forming at all, so the nutrient supply is unabated during the summer. This ensures that tidal areas have a localized abundance of wildlife.

⭐ A Manx shearwater took only 12 days to fly 4828 km (3000 miles) from Boston to its nest in Wales.

MIGRATIONS

The pronounced seasonal nature of the temperate sea creates a wealth of changing opportunities, and a number of animals carefully time their movements according to the seasons and their needs. Some come to feed, others to breed; some leave to avoid the wildness of winter and yet others, paradoxically, arrive to escape the vicious winters of the polar regions. In fact, most forms of life in the temperate sea seem constantly on the move, trying to find the best conditions to suit their lifestyle.

Winter storms turn the top 100 m (328 feet) of the temperate oceans into a cauldron of wave-whipped violence: 20-m (65-foot) waves are not uncommon, and winds can scream by at speeds of over 150 kph (93 mph). With storms occurring far more regularly in the extreme latitudes of the planet than anywhere else, the open expanses of the temperate oceans are best avoided in winter, but there is more than one way of escaping bad weather.

Winter havens

During summer, water below 100–200 m (328–650 feet) is much cooler than the surface layer above the seasonal thermocline. The growing warmth of the surface layer provides far more energy for the processes of life, so many creatures migrate from deep water to the shallows. When winter arrives, the thermocline breaks down once more and there is a far smaller temperature difference between the depths and the surface – in fact, it can even be coldest in the topmost few metres. The shallows also become extremely violent, whipped up by frequent storms that can stir the sea down to depths of 100 m (328 feet). By contrast, the cool water below 150 m (490 feet) or so is hardly

1. North-Atlantic gannets squabble for fish. During summer they breed on rocky pinnacles in fish-rich temperate waters, but in winter they disperse far out into the ocean.

2. During the winter season a southern right whale nurtures her calf in sheltered water off the coast of Argentina. By the time summer comes in the southern hemisphere, they may have travelled thousands of miles to feed near Antarctica.

2

affected by storm movement at all. In winter, therefore, deep water becomes a sanctuary and many fish and invertebrates take refuge there. The ideal strategy is then to lay low, use little energy and just wait for spring before heading towards the action-packed shallows once more.

Countless fish display this behaviour during their annual migration routes – from their spawning grounds to their summer feeding grounds and then back to their over-wintering grounds.

Seeking shelter

Another way of finding shelter in a storm is to head for the lee of the land – which is exactly what 8 billion herring do every year, swimming far into the narrow fjords of Norway in late September. The water is protected on all sides by massive mountains and can be as much as 500 m (1600 feet) deep, so the herring spend the four months until January gently cruising about in total shelter from wild winter weather.

Some migrants travel to the polar areas in summer, but at the approach of winter have to head towards the temperate seas where conditions are relatively mild in comparison to the Arctic or Antarctic. A number of marine mammals even use their temperate overwintering as an opportunity to breed. Right whales heading north from their feeding grounds in the Antarctic breed in sheltered bays in Argentina, Auckland Island near New Zealand, South Africa and Australia. The females have sufficient energy stored in their blubber to allow them to suckle their calves, despite the fact that they will not feed again until they head south for the Antarctic summer.

If the going is too tough, there is always the final option – leave the temperate sea altogether and head for warmer tropical waters, which is exactly what a number of pelagic fish do. Bluefin tuna, for example, spend the summer feeding off the coast of New England, then head south towards the Atlantic tropics (▷ p. 296).

Travelling to dinner

Winter in temperate areas is wild with comparatively little food about, but spring and summer are a different story. Then, the productivity of the shallow shelf areas is among the highest in the world, and fish, birds and mammals all beat a path to these richest of feeding grounds.

The Bay of Fundy in Nova Scotia, for example, attracts a wealth of fairweather visitors. The area has very strong tides – in fact it has the world's highest tidal range, with the sea level changing by up to 14 m (46 feet) on big tides. The massive water movements create an extremely rich nutrient supply that supports a vast influx of life in early spring: herring, capelin and sand eel populations all soar as the fish congregate in the area to feed on plankton. On their tail come sea birds and marine mammals ready for a summer feast. The most dramatic of these annual visitors is the finback whale. At up to 20 m (65 feet) in length and nearly 80 tonnes in weight, it is the second largest whale in the ocean. It is also a highspeed killing machine that specializes in eating small fish: a single whale can consume up to 2 tonnes of herring a day and has a cruising speed of up to 10 kph (6 mph). During the summer months, they travel on a constant search for the best feeding conditions and as many as 500 finback whales may visit the Bay of Fundy, attracted by concentrations of schooling fish. They either hunt in the Bay or far offshore in the Atlantic, wherever the pickings are best.

1. Fin whales erupt through the water surface in the Bay of Fundy in Canada. Their herring prey leap skywards in a desperate, final bid for survival.

▷ OCEAN CRUISERS

Mackerel, close relatives of tuna, are among the fastest and most beautiful fish in the sea (see picture, right). Stunning as any is the Atlantic mackerel, a fairly small fish less than a kilo in weight. It is elegantly marked with a pattern of black and irridescent blue-green bands across its back and a creamy white belly below. Mackerel are fast and efficient swimmers and can easily reach speeds of 50 kph (31 mph). Perhaps surprisingly, they are skilled nomads, following distinct migratory routes every year.

One population of Atlantic mackerel spends its summers feeding around the coasts of Norway, but as winter approaches, the fish gather into tight schools and set off to find warmer water, covering about 25 km (15.5 miles) a day. They swim south along the edge of the continental shelf, skirting around the northwest of Scotland until they find a slow-moving current of warmer water. There they rest in the comparatively comfortable temperature of about 8 °C (46 °F), safe below the worst of the storms. Whenever the water cools too much, they simply head south again. By April the mackerel reach their spawning grounds to the southwest of Ireland, where the females lay half a million floating eggs apiece. Then, as spring returns once more, the fish head north towards Norway again, where their prey (crustaceans, herring and sand eels) will be busy chasing plankton.

⭐ An astonishing 99 per cent of fish die in their first 10 months of life. As few as one in a million live to become adults.

Summer breeding bonanza

The strongest impetus for long migrations is the need to breed. Each spring and summer sea birds in their millions congregate on the rocky cliffs and islands around the temperate landmasses. Their main need is to find areas where there is sufficient prey to feed both the adults and their chicks. Manx shearwaters, for example, spend the winter feeding in the Atlantic Ocean around Brazil, then make a journey of some 9000 km (5590 miles) up the coast of North America before reaching their nesting sites on the west coast of Britain in May. As many as 100,000 pairs nest on Skomer Island, southwest Wales, alone.

In just a few weeks the graceful shearwater will have completed a journey of many thousands of kilometres, crossing oceans and the Equator to visit distant corners of both the northern and southern hemispheres. All this to find the best meal at the best time in the best place, before going back home to raise a new generation.

Fish also make desperately difficult journeys in their attempts to breed. Salmon in both the Pacific and the Atlantic spend several years feeding in open ocean before venturing back to the coastal rivers of their birth, in some cases a journey of more than 5000 km (3100 miles). The fish then travel in fresh water, swimming up rapids and waterfalls, until finally breeding in gravel beds far upstream and, more often than not, dying in the process, very few surviving to make the return journey back to their oceanic feeding grounds. Two years later their offspring take the traumatic step of leaving their quietly sheltered river existence and head out to sea, retracing their parents' route several thousand kilometres out into the ocean. It is a remarkable life cycle that twice calls for a complete body transition as the fish adjust back and forth from life in fresh water to life in salt water. It is also an indication of the lengths that animals will go to in order to find the very best conditions in a seasonal world. The biggest draw of all for migrants to the temperate sea is the annual plankton bloom.

1. North Atlantic salmon feed at sea for several years before a marathon return journey to their breeding grounds in fresh-water rivers.

2. Returning from the sea, under cover of darkness, a manx shearwater rests outside its nesting burrow on Skomer Island in Wales.

CLAWS ON THE MARCH

With their thickly armoured blue external skeletons, four pairs of walking legs and massive claws held out in front of their heads, lobsters are powerful creatures. They are active mainly at night, ponderously hunting for invertebrates.

Female Atlantic lobsters can reach such immense sizes – 15 kg (33 lb) is not uncommon – that they have little to fear from natural predators. Perhaps because of their size they have difficulty finding suitable shelter in the coastal shallows during the winter, preferring instead the safety of the deep below 250 m (820 feet).

They mate in late October or November and can hold more than 20,000 fertilized eggs below their long tails. Come the summer, they must return to the warmth of the shallows so that their eggs can develop properly. This journey, which can be over 150 km (93 miles) up a gradually shelving sea floor, may take the slowly marching lobsters a month to complete. By late July, nine months after the females mated, the tiny baby lobsters are ready to hatch, and spend their first few weeks of life in the plankton. The females spend the rest of the summer feeding in fairly shallow water before moving back down to the depths to wait out another winter, safe beneath the storms.

BLOOMING PLANKTON

Temperate waters are green, partly because they are full of minute plants that are slightly green themselves. They belong to the planktonic community, which is the single most important source of food in the marine system. Being poor swimmers, the plankton drift about in open water more or less at the mercy of the ocean's currents. They range in size from minute picoplankton of less than a hair's width to large megaplankton, which can be a couple of metres in diameter and weigh up to a tonne. The entire community is a vital food source, but without doubt the most important members of it are the planktonic plants – the phytoplankton. Almost uniquely in open water, they have the ability to transform the sun's energy into living tissue, which makes them the first and most fundamental part of the ocean's food chain. So each spring the phytoplankton bloom is the single most important event in the temperate seas.

PHYTOPLANKTON

There are several different groups of phytoplankton, varying greatly in both size and design: their glittering array of beautifully sculpted shapes range from perfect gleaming spheres to glinting 'pill boxes' and incredible glass-spiked balls. Some literally are made of glass, others from cellulose, while some have more in common with animals than plants. Their variety of form is endless, but they all contain coloured pigments which allow them to transform the sun's energy into the basic chemicals of living matter through the process of photosynthesis.

Cyanobacteria

The smallest of all the phytoplankton, cyanobacteria, are minute, single-celled organisms which have both green and blue pigments. They also have the very handy trick of being able to produce nitrogen-based compounds from gaseous nitrogen, so they are a vital source of nutrients for other more complex creatures. In some areas they can account for a staggering 80 per cent of the total production in the ocean.

Diatoms

There are at least 6000 marine species of minute single-celled algae called diatoms. They are extremely beautiful, with two tightly fitting, glass-like halves, which often have spines and ribs radiating out from them. Oil droplets inside the skeleton help to keep the diatoms afloat in the surface waters, where the sunlight can blaze through their transparent casings to the golden brown photosynthesizing pigments within. They are often the most numerous phytoplankton in temperate water.

⭐ Diatomaceous earth, a sedimentary material that originates from the skeletons of microscopic diatoms, is used to help clarify beer.

1. Each year, six billion tonnes of microscopic algae, such as these diatoms, grow in the world's oceans, producing nearly 50 per cent of the world's oxygen.

1. A small sea gooseberry, a type of ctenophore, unfurls its sticky tentacles to trap herbivorous zooplankton that are grazing on minute algae.

Dinoflagellates

The second major group of single-celled organisms are the dinoflagellates, which have a plant's ability to use the sun's energy for photosynthesis; but these phytoplankton also have animal-like qualities and move actively, powered by two whip-like appendages or flagellae. Their bodies are made of armoured cellulose and they have the ability to produce bioluminescent light. If you venture out at night and stir up water that has a high concentration of dinoflagellates, they will glow a ghostly green-blue colour, and everything the water touches will glow eerily in the dark. Even footsteps on a damp beach will glow for several minutes before the magic finally subsides.

Protozoans

The protozoans are single-celled animals, but some contain symbiotic algae that can photosynthesize. Their shells are made either of calcium carbonate, as in the case of foraminiferans, or silica, like the radiolarians. Many have needle-like spines, and actively catch food with thin radiating strands of streaming filopodia. Both can become dominant in the planktonic community when the right seasonal conditions allow.

Seasonal bloom

Phytoplankton need lots of sunlight and nutrients to flourish. They also need to grow rapidly because they are endlessly grazed by a vast and growing population of zooplankton (▷ p. 172). By the end of winter, a lavish supply of nutrients has been forced into the surface water by storm mixing. At this stage few zooplankton are active. Once the sun's energy increases, the phytoplankton can start their annual production of carbon-based living matter. To do this in the temperate world, they are forced to remain in the top 50 m (160 feet) or so, where the sun's light can penetrate.

Spring comes earlier than on land in temperate waters, so in the northern hemisphere by February or March, the hours of sunlight are sufficient for the phytoplankton to start photosynthesizing, growing and reproducing. This is the beginning of a bloom,

SEASONAL DISTRIBUTION OF PHYTOPLANKTON

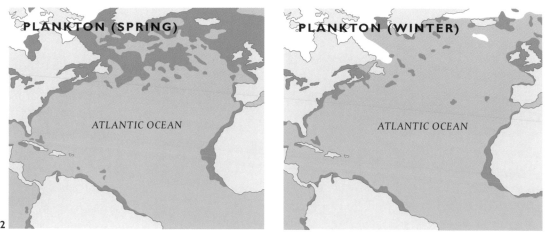

PLANKTON (SPRING)

ATLANTIC OCEAN

PLANKTON (WINTER)

ATLANTIC OCEAN

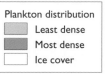

Plankton distribution
- Least dense
- Most dense
- Ice cover

2. Map showing seasonal changes in phytoplankton density. The increase in sunlight during the spring causes a phytoplankton bloom that covers the entire North Atlantic.

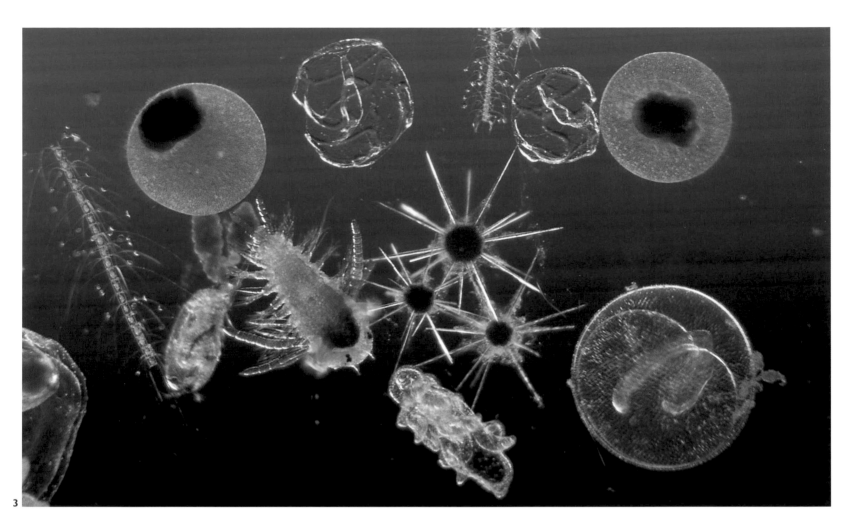

3

which, by May, can result in a staggering 425 million individuals existing in a cubic metre (35 cubic feet) of water.

Initially it is the minute picoplankton and flagellate protozoans that get off to a head start, being the fastest growers. But the burgeoning bloom of micro-zooplanktonic grazers soon cut their numbers down. By mid-spring it is the second-fastest growers, the diatoms, that take over the lead role, but they require a plentiful supply of silica to make their glassy cases and the diatom population increases so fast that, by the end of May, the supply of silica dissolved in the surface water is exhausted. The developing thermocline (▷ p. 160) prevents the arrival of fresh nutrients from deeper water, so the

diatom bloom starts to die back. Picoplankton have a brief resurgence before, finally, the slow-growing dinoflagellates have their moment. By late summer the supply of nutrients is running out; even the nitrates are used up and the whole phytoplankton bloom starts to die back, still being grazed ferociously by an expanding population of herbivorous zooplankton. Only if bad weather arrives early in the autumn will there be a further phytoplankton bloom: the gales can quickly break down the thermocline, making nutrients available to the primary producers once more. In many temperate seas this enables a late and highly productive burst of life before the sun's energy finally becomes too weak for photosynthesis to continue.

3. Plankton consists of both animals and plants. It varies in size from the microscopic, such as spiky radiolarians, fish eggs and foraminifera, to huge jellyfish.

ZOOPLANKTON

In early spring the water teems with a new group of plankton, a vast population of free-swimming animals – the zooplankton. Their population is slower to expand than the phytoplankton, partly because many of them feed on phytoplankton and have to wait for the bloom to develop, and partly because they grow more slowly anyway. They can be either herbivores that specialize in grazing phytoplankton, or carnivores that hunt other zooplankton and small fish, using bizarre hunting techniques and weaponry that owes more to the world of science fiction than natural history. Their variety of size is staggering – from a few microns to a couple of metres across.

Grazing for picoplankton

Few animals can graze the picoplankton because they are unbelievably tiny and that makes them very difficult to trap. Those that can include the gelatinous salps, strange relatives of sea squirts that look rather like transparent jet engines. Salps stream water through their hollow bodies and pump it through a mucus net to extract tiny food particles. Other specialist grazers of picoplankton include some microscopic protozoans, which are enormously important in ensuring that energy from the immense populations of picoplankton does not go to waste. Unfortunately for the protozoans this means being consumed by other zooplankton.

Copepod invasion

The chief adversaries of larger phytoplankton, are small crustaceans that appear rather like tiny, elongated shrimps, with antennae spreading sideways from their heads to create a T-shaped animal. These are the copepods, and shortly after the phytoplankton bloom starts, they arrive to feed and breed until they themselves form immense plankton blooms. They are probably the most numerous animals on the planet, forming 70 per cent of the total zooplankton. They are also incredibly efficient at catching phytoplankton.

Being just a couple of millimetres long, copepods find water heavy, viscous and resistant to every twitch. In fact, every move

1. Copepods like the Calanoid, Candacia are miniature crustaceans that occur in astronomic numbers. Their two long antennae are covered with sensory cells for detecting food, mates and enemies.

2. Despite their small size, copepods are sophisticated animals. This one, the predatory female Sapphirinid, Copilia, has complex eyes that give it stereoscopic vision.

1

they make leaves a trace behind them, forming a wake that remains in the water column for many seconds, rather like a jet's vapour trail in the sky. They use these trails to help locate breeding mates but they may also advertise their whereabouts to passing predators. However, it's the viscosity of water that makes a copepod such a good grazer. When it beats its tiny leg appendages (swimmerets), it creates a powerful current of 'viscous' water sweeping towards its head. Every microscopic phytoplankton in that current is helplessly carried towards the basket-like appendages on the copepod's feeding legs. It can trap diatoms and dinoflagellates from the sea in huge numbers. But grazing copepods are very high on the menu for other, larger zooplankton, so they must be alert to predators.

Most copepods can see quite effectively, but they also test the water for chemicals and movements that might spell danger ahead. However, the turbulence created by the manic beating of their legs while feeding interferes with this process, so they have evolved long antennae with sensory cells which penetrate beyond the disturbance. In fact the drawing of water towards the small crustaceans enables the sensors to test fresh water all the time, optimizing their vigilance.

Meroplankton – just passing through

Not all plankton are destined to remain in the dog-eat-dog world of open water. Meroplankton is the collective name for the tiny eggs and larvae that spend part of their life in the plankton before growing into much larger and more sophisticated animals or plants. At the right time of the summer the sea will be full of floating eggs, paddling larvae and weakly swimming baby invertebrates. The young of crabs, lobsters, sea urchins, molluscs, barnacles and even fish are

2

⭐ Some jellyfish have simple eyes and organs of balance called statocysts, so they know which way up they are.

among the huge variety of creatures who spend their first weeks of life among the plankton.

Many of the meroplankton are herbivores but some start out in life as minute predators. In time they all change drastically in appearance – either becoming large fish in open water, or settling for a life on the seabed. If the larvae are fortunate, the ocean currents will sweep them to a suitable environment in which to progress from juvenile to adult form, but before that happens they have to survive weeks in open water, feeding on other tiny plankton, while some of the most successful predators on the planet hunt them down.

Hunting copepods

Many large copepods are carnivores. Some have legs that end in vicious hooks and blades, designed for trapping and dismembering unwary creatures. Just like the herbivorous copepods, these hunters have sensory cells on their antennae, but they are tuned to finding prey, so rather than flee from a 'jet' trail in the viscous sea, they are likely to head towards it, sensing their next meal.

Spineless hunters

As the spring months pass by the temperate sea becomes full of jelly-like zooplankton,

1. The battle of the medusas! A small, voracious lion's mane jellyfish (*Cyanea lamarckii*) overpowers two moon jellyfish (*Aurelia aurita*) which it will slowly consume.

2. At the height of the summer, *Aurelia aurita* gather in increasing numbers, forming swarms so dense that they create a solid pink wall of jelly.

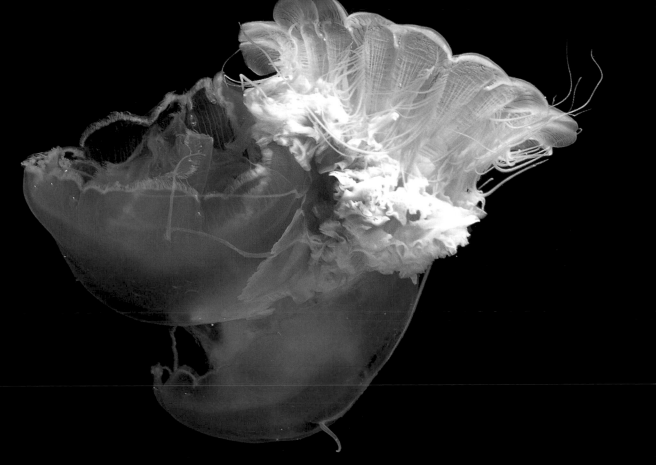

1

which have no skeleton at all. These include ctenophores (▷ p. 320) and free-swimming cnidarian medusae, which are the true jelly-fish. Among these are scyphozoans, which at the height of summer can plague bathing beaches, painfully stinging unwary swimmers, and oozing stinging slime over the sand as they rot after stranding.

Out in open water, jellyfish are among the most beautiful animals in the ocean – diaphanous floating creatures, trailing nets of delicately shaded tentacles behind lacy plumes and gently pulsating swimming bells. However, their painful stings can be dangerous, even to humans, proving that jellyfish are powerful hunters.

Related to coral polyps and sea anemones, jellyfish share the same bizarre lifestyle, having both a bottom-living polyp phase and a free-swimming, planktonic stage, known as a medusa and which has the bell shape so characteristic of jellyfish. For corals and sea anemones the free-swimming medusa stage is very short-lived, but for jellyfish it is the most important part of their life cycle.

Jellyfish could be imagined as floating, highly organized bunches of sticky fly-traps, where the prey is plankton rather than flies. Their immense masses of lacy plumes are in fact highly convoluted extensions to their mouths, which, along with the tentacles, are covered in lethal harpoon cells called nematocysts. It's likely that one of the main functions of the tentacle net is to slow the jellyfish down, acting as a sea anchor when the hunting is good. The large pulsing bell is extremely inefficient at pulling the body through the water, but it's a great feeding mechanism, forcing a stream of plankton-rich water over the mouth frills and past the base of the tentacles. Feeding like this, the lion's mane jellyfish can grow to more than a tonne, with tentacles stretching to 50 m (160 feet) in length and covering an area larger than a soccer pitch.

Jellyfish can kill and consume thousands of copepods a day. Their numbers are seldom **2**

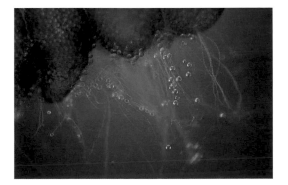

▷ STINGERS

Fragile as they are, jellyfish have evolved an effective method of immobi-lizing prey quickly so that they can drag it back to their mouths. Every tentacle has hundreds of special cells called nematocysts, each of which contains poison and a tightly coiled harpoon. The length and complexity of the harpoon varies with the species, as does the power of the poison.

When the hair-like trigger at the edge of the nematocyst touches pro-teins, such as skin, the harpoon fires (illustrated, opposite), punching through the body wall of the target like a hypodermic syringe. Poison from the nematocyst oozes along inside the harpoon into the victim. Depending on the size of the prey, hundreds, thousands, even hundreds of thousands of nematocysts will fire. The venom is formed from proteins that attack both the blood cells and nervous systems of their prey. Jelly-fish stings leave weal-like scars, and even when the jellyfish have died and the tentacles are dry, they can still inflict a sting if they contact soft wet skin. The most virulent of all, box jellyfish, can kill a human in minutes.

1

1. The tentacles of the compass jellyfish, *Chrysaora hysoscella*, have millions of stinging cells, but juvenile fish still hide amongst them because few predators dare come close.

2. A basking shark powers forward, straining plankton through its gills. Each hour it sieves enough water to fill two Olympic-sized pools.

constant from one year to the next, but they can reach almost plague proportions, and, just like phytoplankton, different species reach their zenith at different times in the season. The common moon jellyfish, for example, feeds mostly on copepods, so it reaches its peak during the main spring bloom, when the copepod numbers are at a maximum. Swarms of this jellyfish are so dense that they turn the water a pinkish-white and can be seen clearly from the air. However, the numbers start to fall when the summer decline of the plankton bloom sets in.

The giant lion's mane is a late summer jellyfish, which reaches its peak in September and October because it feeds on fish, mero-plankton and other jellyfish, as well as copepods. It tends not to form dense swarms, but individual jellyfish are very large, commonly more than a metre across the bell. The tentacles from all the lion's manes will sometimes interlace, effectively turning the sea into a giant stinging fishing net.

So, as the plankton-rich months pass by, different species of jellyfish blossom into immense swarms and then disappear, depending on the availability of their prey.

BIG HUNTERS

Although zooplankton is a complex web of feeding organisms all dependent upon phyto-plankton for primary production, they are not the only animals to consume plankton.

School diners

Many fish are, to a greater or lesser degree, plankton feeders. The most obvious examples are the giant schools of herring, sardine and anchovy that historically provided key fish catches to fishing fleets in temperate waters.

Planktonic feeding fish tend either to sieve plankton from the water by swimming open-mouthed, or by visually spotting and swallowing individual plankton. Those using the latter method have forward-focusing eyes so that they can effectively judge the distance to their prey.

Sievers have fine rakers on their gills specially designed to entrap plankton as the water streams past. Often they can distend their head to huge proportions to ensure the maximum amount of water can be swept through their mouth. The sight of a shoal of shimmering sardine suddenly turning into blunt-headed megamouths with gaping jaws and flared gill cases is extraordinary.

Nearly all planktivorous fish have long annual migration routes, which means they reach rich plankton sites in time for the late spring bloom. They will then follow the vagaries of the plankton population through-out the summer months, ensuring that they remain in water containing significant amounts of planktonic food. The herring population that spawns in the coastal fjords of Norway heads far out to the east of Iceland in early May. When June arrives, they head north, reaching the northern Norwegian Sea some time in July or August. Although their route varies from year to year, it seems remarkable that comparatively simple fish are constantly on the move, tracking down the richest plankton populations throughout the months of bloom.

▷ 'BLOOMING JAWS'

Basking sharks, which weigh up to 5 tonnes and reach over 9 m (30 feet) in length, need to consume vast quantities of plankton, so they have adapted to track down and catch the maximum amount of food from the water.

As they are extremely sensitive to both chemical and electrical changes in the ocean, it is likely that they can measure differences between water layers, ensuring that they swim along boundaries, such as thermoclines, where the plankton is thickest. It is also probable that they can sense areas of intense planktonic activity by picking up chemical traces in the water, literally tasting swarming microscopic life. Once they reach an area with plenty of plankton, they open their massive mouths and plough through the water, forcing it out of five pairs of metre-long gill slits. Each gill opening is screened by pink, closely dovetailed gill rakers, which simply trap and direct plankton down the shark's throat, while the water streams through the gills back into the sea. Feeding like this, 1000 tonnes of water pass through a shark's mouth every hour.

In winter, when the bloom dies away, the sharks shed their gill rakers and retreat to the ocean depths. There they grow a new set of gill rakers in preparation for the next year's spring plankton bloom.

2

BAITBALL

The prime targets of many animals hunting in temperate water are immense schools of small plankton-eating fish, such as herring. Once a school is under attack, it responds instantly by closing its ranks into a dense, swirling ball of fish. The spinning mass of hundreds or thousands of bodies shifts and changes shape in an attempt to confuse predators. This decreases the odds of any individual fish being picked out and eaten. All the while the predators harass the ball of fish, intent on panicking the herring to such an extent that they scatter. Once the ball breaks down, it is much easier to pick off single victims. This desperate wheeling carousel is one of the most spectacular and beautiful sights in the natural world, a ruthless battle between hunter and prey.

1

1. At the first hint of danger, schooling herring form up into a ball. When their predators close, the ball becomes a solid swirling mass.

2. The baitball explodes through the surface as the fish make a last ditch attempt to avoid predators attacking from below.

Life in the shoal
Among the most highly sought-after bait fish in the sea, herring have two main strategies for avoiding predators: schooling and daily migration from deep to shallow water. Their main diet is small zooplankton, which concentrate near the surface. But there is a problem: herring are easy to spot if they swim in brightly lit water, and as most of their predators hunt by sight during the daytime, the herring prefer to stay hidden in deep water during the day. Under cover of darkness, they swim up to the surface to feed. On dark nights they form loose swarms rather than tight-knit schools, swimming gently along with mouths agape sieving plankton. As soon as the daylight returns, they form into spectacularly controlled schools of thousands of fish swimming in perfect unison and head for the safety of the depths.

2

Controlling the school

From an early age herring perfect the art of synchronized swimming because they depend upon it for their survival. They can co-ordinate the school in two main ways: by seeing their immediate neighbours and (being very sensitive to both vibrations and sound) by hearing. When the fish move, they create vibrations from their quivering bodies and sharp noises if they accelerate very suddenly. As herring shy away from danger, pulses of sound radiate across the school, prompting individuals into action. They react extraordinarily quickly to the flashes of light reflecting off their mirrored silver scales when they turn. The effect is of the whole school moving almost as one, but despite their skill, the forces ranged against them are overpowering.

Facing predators

Although herring retire to the depths during the day, they are not necessarily safe. Many predators can detect their presence, either sensing the fish themselves or picking up the trail of proteins and oil that drifts in the wake of the school. The predators – such as dolphins, humpback whales or dogfish – simply dive below the herring, then soar upwards towards the fish. Even birds such as auks may reach the school, diving down to depths of 70 m (230 feet). Whoever the aggressor, the herring always respond in the same way, gathering instantly into a tight school and heading as fast as they can away from danger, up towards the surface. Once there, they form into a giant swarming ball. The commotion of their movements attracts more and more predators to the scene, until the herring are surrounded by a terrible and unrelenting battery of attacking mouths and beaks from above and below. The feeding

3

will continue remorselessly until all the herring are consumed, unless they can outmanoeuvre their attackers for long enough to escape into the depths again, perhaps this time getting lost in the darkness below 100 m (328 feet).

3. In Norway, adult herring manoeuvre at such speed that killer whales have to club the herring with their tails, stunning them and making them easy to catch.

◆ TOPIC LINKS

4.1 The Richest Seas
p.163 Seeking Shelter

4.2 Blooming Plankton
p.177 School Diners
p.181 The Web of Life

6.2 Ocean Drifters
p.283 Sieving Schools

6.3 Ocean Hunters
p.296 Mammal Pack

Planktivorous giants

The bigger the creature, the more effectively it can sieve large amounts of water to extract a maximum quantity of plankton. Sieving is a very efficient form of feeding, involving none of the excessive energy loss of several types of animals feeding on each other before finally being eaten by a major predator. A big planktivore gets the most energy possible by feeding directly on plankton and it is a technique that produces giants.

The 11 species of baleen whale are specialized for feeding on small fish and plankton, and vary in weight from 20 tonnes to over 100 tonnes. Instead of teeth they have long plates fringed in a fibrous mesh of bristles, which are called baleen, and which act as planktonic sieves. Gulping huge mouthfuls of plankton-rich water, they expel it through the baleen with their giant tongues and swallow the trapped plankton.

Baleen whales are also extraordinarily adept at locating plankton, probably by using low wavelength sonar to distinguish water temperature and salinity boundaries where the plankton are likely to concentrate. Every year the Bay of Fundy sees the arrival of small numbers of northern right whales, which feed mostly by swimming along with their mouths agape, allowing water to stream through their fine baleen. The whales remain in the area from April until September, stopping where the conditions are most likely to allow dense plankton swarms.

Aerial attack

Sea birds can also be skilled plankton hunters. Most gulls will sit on the water and dip their beaks into any dense concentrations of large plankton. Shearwaters will do the same, or actually skim plankton from the water as they fly. Perhaps most entrancing of all is the feeding dance of the Wilson's storm petrel, which can be seen fluttering delicately on top of the water, dabbling at the surface with its feet. In all probability the petrel uses its feet as sea anchors, dipping them in the water to prevent itself being blown backwards by the wind, and so it can continually search in water with fresh plankton that it hasn't seen before. The petrel simply plucks any suitable plankton from the water as soon as they appear beneath its toes.

1. A southern right whale skims plankton from the water's surface. Just the tip of its upper jaw shows, with the pale sieve-like baleen plates clearly visible.

2. Adult kittiwakes guard chicks perched precariously, far above the sea. Their nest sites neighbour plankton-rich waters where there is a good supply of food.

Overleaf: A humpback whale lunge-feeds in Southeast Alaska, its throat pleats hugely distended by the weight of water and herring. The plankton-rich water supports such vast numbers of herring that the whales can feed continuously for months on end.

2

THE WEB OF LIFE

In temperate seas, as in any other open water, plankton form the base of the food chain. Although not everything feeds directly off plankton, ultimately many animals depend upon it in one way or another. Copepods may be eaten by planktivorous herring, but those herring may be consumed by larger fish or by diving sea birds, dolphin, whales or seals. In turn, all the animals that feed on herring can themselves be hunted down by bigger predators. Many of the larger animals to visit the temperate world time their visits to coincide with the peak of the plankton blooms for just this reason: even if they do not feed on plankton themselves, something they eat is sure to.

Hatching the chicks

Sea birds time their breeding season to match the spring plankton bloom. Gannets, puffins, guillemots, auklets and others all arrive at their nesting cliffs in early spring. It is essential for the success of their colony that there is sufficient food to fuel both the adults and the chicks, once they hatch. As many sea birds feed on planktivorous fish, such as sand eels, or herring, most nesting sites are selected for their proximity to areas where the plankton is likely to be most dense.

Getting fat fast

The peak of the plankton season is comparatively short and for many fish and marine mammals it is the only source of food for some time to come. As a result, they pile on the fat as quickly as possible, hoping that it will sustain them through the long winter months of fasting. Humpback whales in Alaska do precisely this, feeding on large schools of Pacific herring between April to October, and increasing their weight by several tonnes. Most of this is stored as fatty blubber up to half a metre thick. When they leave in the autumn they swim 4000 km (2500 miles) to Hawaii to breed, but have no suitable source of food for up to five months.

OCEAN FORESTS

Walk at low tide along any rocky headland in temperate latitudes and it is likely to be coated in a mass of slippery, leather-like weeds, endangering the balance of even the most surefooted. Return at high tide to swim by those same rocks and the leathery tangle will have been transformed by the water into a magical world of gently undulating seaweed. The profusion of shapes and colours will include delicate purple frills, hard encrusted pinks, translucent green laces and tufted yellow-brown clumps held aloft by plump, gas-filled bladders. Bustling around this swaying forest will be a horde of fish and invertebrates all dependent upon the plants for sanctuary. Seaweed are marine algae, and although they occur more or less worldwide, nowhere are they as abundant as in the temperate sea, where most of their 10,000 species are to be found. They create some of the most productive marine habitats in the ocean.

OCEAN GARDEN

Like all plants, seaweed need nutrients, sunlight and a suitable spot in which to grow. As long as the water is sufficiently shallow and clear to allow light to penetrate, algae of some sort will be able to photosynthesize and survive. Just like land plants, it is their ability to manufacture living tissue from the sun's energy, using the pigment chlorophyll, that makes them so important: they are the beginning of the food chain, the ocean's primary producer of life. The smallest algae can be free-swimming in the plankton or exist between grains of sand while some live inside the shells and bodies of animals. Many grow on other seaweed or even within their tissues, but the most familiar are the large plants that festoon our coastal waters.

Large seaweed need a firm footing, so they are rarely found on a sandy sea floor where the shifting sand grains do not allow a secure anchoring point. They are plants of the rocky coasts. At the base of each plant is a clump of entwined, tube-like growths called a holdfast, which anchors the plant securely to the rock. Stretching up from the holdfast is a long, trunk-like stipe, which is simply a stem to support the leaf-like fronds in which most of the photosynthesis occurs. In the largest seaweed the fronds are buoyed in the sun-bathed surface water by gas-filled bladders called pneumatocysts. Despite their comparatively simple form, seaweed are far from uniform in either design or colour. Their shape depends on the different demands of their preferred habitats and their colour varies according to their natural pigments and chlorophyll content.

1. Below the high tide mark, seaweed can grow in such profusion that it forms a dense mat of brown, red and green plants.

Sea greens

Like land plants, green algae get their colour from the green pigment chlorophyll and contain no other pigments to obscure its rich hues. Comparatively few of the 6000 species of green algae are marine, but those that are make a common sight around temperate rock-pools. They are generally quite small, and many are filamentous, like fine green hair. The most common are the sea lettuces, whose paper-thin, fresh green blades crowd out rock-pools and spread around the bases of other larger seaweed. Sea lettuces are a popular food for small invertebrates, and rock-pool life is a war of attrition between the grazers and the green plants: as soon as the algae get a footing, they are cropped by a ravenous horde of snails, baby crabs and urchins.

The reds

With about 4000 species, red algae are the most numerous of all the marine algae. They do contain chlorophyll, but the green colour is usually masked by a red pigment called phycobilin. Some very small red algae even lose their chlorophyll altogether, so they become parasites obtaining their nourishment from within the tissues of a host seaweed. Even the larger branched forms are seldom more than 2 m (6.5 feet) long, and generally their structure is simple. They are commonly small, tissue-like plants that fringe rock-pools or grow like minute banners up the 'mast' of bigger brown seaweed's long stipe. But they make up for their simplicity and size by appearing in a beautiful range of colours – pinks, reds and metallic purples – which can vary

1. *Ulva lactuca* is a bright green alga called the sea lettuce. It is a common sight in rock pools, with sparkling bubbles of oxygen trickling from its blades.

2. Red algae, such as this one, *Erythrymenia minuta*, commonly have short, hard frond designs that can resist the rough wave action on rocky shores.

SEAWEED CUISINE

About 500 species of seaweed are eaten around the world, and at least 160 are commercially important as food. The Japanese are the main consumers and have honed seaweed preparation to an art form. Kelp, sea lettuces and red algae are dried, steamed, sautéd and boiled in an array of dishes, and the ubiquitous sushi bars owe their success to a humble red alga called Porphyra. Rolled into thin black sheets, Porphyra is the sushi's outer wrapping, and so popular that Japan farms it on 101,000 hectares (250,000 acres) of its coast.

Even if you don't fancy eating seaweed, you've probably consumed it unknowingly. Alginates from brown seaweed are used to give ice cream its smooth and creamy texture. Agar, taken from red seaweed, is used in cake icings and is a useful clarifying agent for beer. Carrageenans are perfect thickeners, appearing in a wide variety of creams, puddings and dairy products.

Seaweed even penetrates your car, as crude oils and natural gases are effectively the pressure-cooked remains of immense algal plankton blooms from millions of years ago.

⭐ A kelp holdfast is home to more than 175 marine species, including sea anemones, brittle stars crabs and juvenile molluscs.

according to the way in which the light strikes them.

Some red algae deposit thick calcium carbonate around their cell walls – exactly the same mineral that coral is made from. These coralline red algae grow in dense short branched or disc-like forms and are sufficiently tough to endure the extreme forces of the rocky surf zone.

Forest browns

There are approximately 1500 species of brown seaweed, whose colours vary from yellowish to rich brown. They are the dominant primary producers of temperate coasts and range from simple filamentous algae to the largest seaweed of all, giant kelp, stretching up to 100 m (330 feet) in length.

The most familiar are the fucoids or wracks – leathery brown algae that live on the rocky foreshores where they are exposed by the tides. Many of these plants have hordes of conspicuous small bladders to buoy their blades near the surface when the tide returns. They are a vital refuge for animals both when covered by the sea and when the falling tide leaves them high and dry. Astonishingly, they can withstand the loss of almost 90 per cent of their liquid while drying in the sun: when the tide returns, they simply re-hydrate.

The most impressive of all brown algae are the kelp – large-bladed seaweed with representatives in all coastal temperate seas of the world. Some are annuals, completing their life cycle within a year, but their greatest representatives live for several years. These plants possess a truly remarkable ability to grow and when conditions allow, do so so profusely that they make giant underwater forests, which are unique to the temperate sea.

1. A forest of 30-m (98-foot) bull kelp streams in a tidal current off western Canada. The heavy mass of fronds is supported by a single, almost ridiculously thin, stipe.

2. Numerous small gas bladders help clumps of knotted wrack, a brown fucoid alga, float at the surface where there is plenty of energy-giving sunlight.

HANGING ON

The vast majority of large seaweed need a firm, rocky seabed on which to anchor, but competition for free rock is fierce, a constant battle between seaweed and animals. In places the power of the waves or currents is simply too much for the seaweed to cope with. At such spots the rock is stripped bare.

Wild water

Crashing surf on exposed rock faces and strong tidal currents can exert incredible pressure on seaweed fixed to the sea floor. The seaweed's best defence is their extreme flexibility. Lacking any woody structures in their stipes and fronds, they can bend back and forth with the waves. The best example of this must surely be the palm weed, a kelp that appears almost to explode, such is the violence of the Pacific swells that strike against it on the rocky coasts of northwest America where it grows. After each crashing wave, the kelp simply flicks back upright, its rubbery body more than a match for the pounding water.

Many large kelp are less exposed to severe wave action, tending to grow slightly further off shore, but even there, flowing currents can subject them to a battering. Under water, 30-metre-long kelp fronds stream horizontally from the pressure of the speeding water, while whirlpools and down currents make them whip around crazily, like sinuous palm trees straining before a hurricane.

Finding the right space

Where algae grow depends largely upon the visibility of the water. In areas such as river estuaries, where the water is full of sediments and organic detritus, little light can penetrate, so few algae can grow. In clearer water, light can penetrate more deeply, although rarely much below 50 or 60 m (c 90 feet) in the temperate sea. Competition for the light is fierce between the different species of algae. There are also countless bottom-living invertebrates that use rock faces as an anchoring point and intensify the competition for space. If a fresh area of rock suddenly becomes exposed, whatever larvae or plant spores happen to be passing by in the plankton at the time will be the successful colonizers. Even if an alga arrives first, it may soon be eaten. If there are insufficient predators about, grazers, such as urchins or whelk snails, go unchecked and any tender sprouting algae will be cropped. For algae to flourish they need not only clear rock space in light conditions but sufficient active predators to keep the grazing hordes at bay long enough for the plants to establish a dense algal forest.

3. Sea palms are unusual among kelp plants because they can thrive on shallow rocky slopes, which the waves batter with daunting power.

FORESTS OF KELP

Kelp are the most dramatic of all seaweed. There are about 100 species worldwide, but they are restricted to cool temperate coasts in both the northern and southern hemispheres. They grow further towards the Equator on the eastern side of the major oceans since the cold ocean currents of the ocean gyres head towards the Equator along the east coasts, ensuring that suitable cool water conditions occur in lower latitudes.

Generally, kelp plants establish themselves below the lowest tide line, typically preferring rocky habitats beyond the worst of the surf zone. When conditions are perfect, they grow to an immense size and cover vast areas with towering underwater forests. California alone has 44,000 acres of the giant kelp (macrocystis) growing along its coast. Here the water can be so clear that the sea floor 35 m (115 feet) below is plainly visible from the surface.

These underwater forests have the same cathedral-like calm as ancient land forests. Great banners of yellow-green puckered fronds waft lightly in the current, sometimes glowing gold as shafts of sunlight stream through them. Every centimetre of the forest moves with life. Weird animal clicks and grunts echo up from the sea floor, and large schools of fish flit back and forth on feeding forays, for all the world like rushing commuters in a big city. Kelp forests are special places and sustain an extraordinary amount of life.

1. A square kilometre of kelp forest can contain 67,000 animals and even the smooth, trunk-like kelp stipes are covered in invertebrates and red and brown algae.

2. A giant kelp has round floats, known as pneumatocysts, full of carbon monoxide, which buoy the heavy fronds at the water surface.

Growing power

The attractive bull kelp from British Columbia and Alaska is an annual, dying away completely at the end of each autumn. Like most kelp, it has a dual life cycle, with both a sexual and asexual stage. Microscopic spores form minute male and female gametophytes, which produce sperm and eggs as early as January or February. The fertilized eggs settle on the sea floor and grow into tiny plants called sporophytes, which each quickly start to produce a long, thin stipe. By late summer the bull kelp will be 20 or 30 m (c 80 feet) long, each plant a giant clump of streaming fronds all radiating from one gas-filled float. The plant is tethered to the bottom by a single, extraordinarily thin, whip-like stipe, which despite its slender appearance, is sufficiently robust to endure powerful tidal currents. During the summer the adult sporophyte produces many millions of microscopic spores. By autumn it starts to disintegrate, but even as it dies, its spores will be starting the cycle over again. ▷▷ **2**

 RIDING THE WAVES

To escape the worst effects of bad weather, big algae grow off shore beyond the line of breaking waves, but even the toughest are vulnerable to wave damage. Severe storms can destroy entire forests, covering long stretches of beach in hundreds of tonnes of shredded giant kelp.

At sea the torn and twisted fronds become compressed by the action of the waves to form floating mats called kelp paddies. These algal life rafts, such as the one illustrated, right, can extend hundreds of metres and support a variety of life, but they are rotting and doomed to sink. In the meantime, schools of juvenile fish, and a variety of invertebrates usually found in shallow water, congregate beneath them, playing a deadly game of hide and seek with passing pelagic predators. Will the currents sweep the weed mat towards the shore and the haven of the coastal shallows, or will it remain in open water, doomed to sink? If it is the latter, many small marine creatures will perish. Only time, wind and the currents can decide their fate.

⭐ The world's biggest slug, the Californian sea hare, can weigh 15 kg (33 lb) and be nearly 1 m (3 feet) long. It feeds high in the kelp forests.

Previous Page: A lone blue shark cruises gently past a kelp paddy, sensing the water ahead for any traces of injured or unwary prey.

Kelp plants in general grow fast, but none more so than the giant kelp, the world's largest seaweed. This perennial, which lasts up to six years, can grow over 30 m (98 feet) a year, putting on 60 cm (24 in) a day in ideal conditions. This high-speed growth produces an enormous, expanding surface that can stretch up to 100 m (330 feet) in length, and on which other seaweed and animals can find refuge.

Living on a kelp plant

The holdfast provides a secure interwoven basket of tubes, which makes a perfect habitat for small invertebrates, such as the enchanting sea anemone.

The stipe and fronds of the sporophyte itself are covered in other seaweed and invertebrates. Snails, sea slugs, crustaceans and fish all spend their life in snug proximity to the plant, and some are unique to the kelp forests. The yellow-green kelp fish, for example, is almost indistinguishable from the plant itself, so it can hide among the fronds, waiting to ambush its prey.

Kelp grows continuously, with pieces constantly breaking off the ends of the fronds. Animals such as the delicate bryozoans (moss animals) that are permanently fixed to the fronds therefore have to complete their life cycle in a hurry before their piece of frond becomes detached. When they are cast adrift, they might float for months if their piece has a pneumatocyst on it, but eventually they are doomed to sink along with their host frond.

Small crustaceans, such as isopods and kelp curler amphipods, depend on kelp for both sanctuary and food. These shrimp-like animals of less than 3 cm (1 in) are both popular food for fish. The kelp curler, however, has developed an extraordinary means of hiding: it weaves a web of silk between two ends of a piece of kelp, making a secure tent in which to hide from predators.

Several species of fish living in the kelp beds are active predators, targeting specific

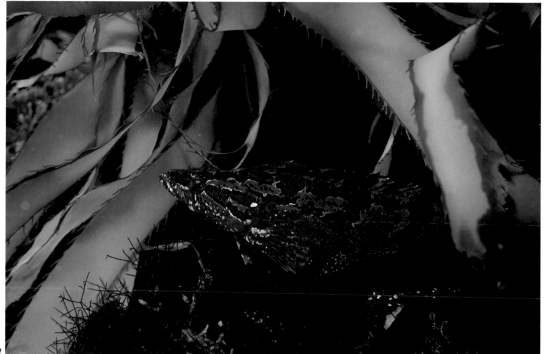

1. Kelp holdfasts both secure the plant to the sea bed and provide a home for animals. Here, hidden brittle stars poke their arms out of the holdfast to trap food.

2. Some animals, like the kelp fishes, have evolved specifically to live in seaweed forests. These fish can change colour to blend in with their surroundings.

3. The world's largest damsel fish, the garibaldi fish, is a famously garish sight in Pacific kelp forests. It feeds on small invertebrates that live in the kelp.

prey and protecting the forest from overgrazing. These include the great sheephead wrasse, which feeds on urchins, and the vibrant orange garibaldi fish, which targets amphipods. When there are too few predators, the grazers feast unchecked and become so numerous that they destroy their forest home.

Life in the forest

Kelp forests are giant refuges offering sanctuary from many of the large predatory fish, birds and dolphins that are active in open water. Residents include great schools of plankton-feeding fish, such as the blacksmiths, who feed during the daylight hours. The best feeding is to be had out in open water, where the plankton is thickest, but at the first hint of danger they head back to the shelter of the forest.

Different types of fish target different plankton, and since their target prey are active at different times of the day, the fish can take shifts. All through the day and night great shoals of fish move back and forth from their preferred feeding spots to their resting berths in the forest. Senoritas, blacksmiths, rockfish and others sweep past each other in a complex riot of motion and colour.

Other creatures that shelter in the forest include sea birds, which use the floating fronds as both a roost and a staging post from which to launch their next hunting foray. Sea lions and harbour seals skim through the kelp, secure in the knowledge that great white sharks prefer to hunt in open water than among the entangling plants. Even giant 40-tonne gray whales will cruise through the kelp as they migrate up and down the North American coastline, snacking on amphipods and other small crustaceans as they strip kelp through their mouths. Perhaps most celebrated of all kelp forest inhabitants are the Californian sea otters, which play, sleep and feed among the life-giving seaweed.

3

GUARDIANS OF THE FOREST

The most appealing animal in the ocean is, without any doubt, the sea otter. As large as a medium-sized dog, an otter snoozes half a kilometre off shore, floating gently on its back and anchored firmly in place by wrapping itself in the fronds of a kelp plant. Sun-bleached fur forms a fuzzy blond halo around the otter's face, which it softly massages, even in half-sleep, to perfect cleanliness. The sea otter's beautiful fur and exquisite looks have been a very mixed blessing. During the nineteenth century, such was the cosmetic value of its coat that it was hunted to virtual extinction. Now, in the twenty-first century, the otter's endearing appearance has made it one of the most fiercely protected animals in the USA.

1

1. A Californian sea otter dives in search of food. Despite a rather ungainly swimming style the otters can remain underwater for several minutes at a time.

2. A resting otter meticulously grooms its coat to protect itself against the cold Pacific water.

3. Red sea urchins creep relentlessly towards kelp holdfasts. Voracious grazers, these relatives of starfish can raise whole forests if their numbers are unchecked.

Grooming for life

Life is hard work for sea otters. They have such a high energy consumption that they need to consume 25 per cent of their body weight daily – a considerable target when their prey lies on the sea floor up to 30 m (98 feet) below them. Their energy is also spent in energetically grooming their fur for nearly half their waking hours, an essential task as it is their only protection against the cold water of the temperate Pacific. Lacking any blubber, they rub natural oils into their fur and fluff it up to trap air bubbles. The fur is an effective insulator because of its extraordinary density – up to 150,000 hairs per square centimetre!

Otter recovery

In their heyday as many as 20,000 Californian sea otters lived along the Pacific coast of the USA. Today a paltry 2000 live along a 400-km (250-mile) strip of Californian coast. The closely related and more northerly sea otters have fared better: there are now 20,000 Russian sea otters and 120,000 Alaskan sea otters. The fluctuations in the otter population has had a devastating effect on the northern Pacific coastlines: vast areas of kelp forest disappeared because there were no otters to protect them.

Protecting the forests

The voracious appetite of all sea otters is satisfied mainly by invertebrates, many of which

graze kelp, most significantly sea urchins. Otters pluck the urchins from the sea floor along with a small rock. On reaching the surface, the otter uses the rock as an anvil on which to smash the urchin. This high-protein snack is perfect for an otter with a high calorie demand, and urchin populations drop where otters abound. A consequence of this is that the kelp forests bloom again to full size within a few years. The loss of the forest reduces the diversity of the coast, but the proliferation of urchins is popular with fishermen for whom they are a lucrative catch. So despite the sea otters' public appeal and their role in conserving kelp forests, they are still persecuted and many fishermen would prefer to see their recovery forcibly restricted.

3

⬥ TOPIC LINKS

1.3 Living in the Sea
p.54 Grazing

4.3 Ocean Forests
p.187 Seaweed Cuisine
p.188 Forest Browns
p.190 Forests of Kelp
p.195 Life in the Forest

4.4 THE LIVING BED

In the cold gloom, beyond the reach of bright sunlight, dwells the 'benthos' of the temperate sea: these are the creatures that colonize both the rocky reefs and flat sedimentary expanses of the sea floor.

The gently shelving seabed forms a broad plain stretching out from the coast towards the deep ocean for up to 400 km (250 miles). Then, at a depth of about 200 m (650 feet) the gradient increases abruptly, as the continental slope is reached and the sea floor sinks towards the abyssal plains. Most of the sea floor of the temperate continental shelves is a world in near-darkness: there is so much sediment and plankton suspended in the temperate sea that little light penetrates beyond 30 or 40 m (about 100 feet). While the gloom prevents the growth of algae, the sea floor teems with life, supporting a bizarre community that feeds on detritus – dead plants and animals raining from the sea above. There is so much detritus that this habitat is among the most productive in the ocean.

ROCK WALLS

The coastal margins of land can end in steep wave-cut cliffs that drop sheer into the sea, their rocky ledges fading into the greeny blackness of the depths. Algal forests cluster near the surface in a shallow fringe where the light is best, but rocks in the gloomy water below are also festooned with life. During the summer, water sliding past these underwater cliffs is laden with plankton and organic material washed from the land. For invertebrates the rocky walls are ideal places from which to grab the passing food – they simply have to find an empty space, hang on and trap their meal.

Drift with the tide past a submerged cliff in temperate water and it seems a sombre place, but turn on a powerful underwater torch and the sullen crags transform. As the beam plays across the cliff face, a riot of colour and shapes explodes into view. Colonies of orange, blue and white anemones, pink or purple gorgonians and crimson or bright yellow sponges all vie for attention. The profusion of life is amazing: tube worms, barnacles, hydroids, amphipods, urchins, sea slugs, multicoloured starfish, brittlestars, snails, bryozoans and translucent tunicates cover every centimetre. Crabs, brightly coloured shrimp and lobster hunt from the security of rocky ledges, and a variety of fish pick at the encrusting invertebrates. At their best, temperate cliffs are as rich and colourful as many coral reefs.

1. Rock faces in temperate waters can be vibrant with life – starfish, sea urchins, anemones, tunicates, and molluscs, among others, all vie for prime space.

⭐ **Barnacles cement their backs to a suitable surface, which can vary from a rock to a whale. They then build a hard protective shell and feed by waving their feet in the water.**

Adapted for grazing

Depending on the depth, a great variety of animals live by grazing algae or detritus from the rock surface. Large seaweed disappear a few metres below the surface, unable to survive without light. Descend deeper and only small red algae grow, but before long there is so little light that no plants remain at all. Instead, detritus becomes the primary source of food. This underwater rain of decomposing organisms falls from above and coats the rock bed with a soft sediment. Both algae and sediment fuel a horde of fish and invertebrates.

Sea urchins, with their hard external skeletons and heavily armoured spines, move slowly across the rock, grazing algae as they go. They are pulled along by thousands of hydrostatically powered extendible tube feet with sucker-like endings. Competing for the grazing rights are numerous herbivorous snails, which rasp algae with a sharp band of small teeth hidden inside their mouths. Large sea cucumbers, resembling long, leathery sacks, creep over the rocks on tube feet that look exactly like those of their sea urchin cousins, but sea cucumbers have modified some of their feet for a special purpose. A group of tube feet around their mouths have evolved into thick tentacles that end in floret-like suckers. These are spread out on the rock face to collect detritus, each feeding foot in turn being plunged into their mouths to suck off the food.

Other invertebrates have evolved to graze the vast arrays of filter-feeding life forms that crowd the rock surfaces, a necessary adaptation given the absence of algae.

▷ A SEA OF SLUGS

Unlike their dull-coloured, ugly land cousins, sea slugs – known scientifically as nudibranchs – are among the most beautiful animals in the ocean. They come in an extraordinary variety of sizes and colours, and frill-like gills and pointed tentacles adorn their backs. Their translucent bodies are tinted with every colour of the rainbow in patterns of stripes and swirls. (The picture, left, shows an alabaster nudibranch searching for food on the seabed.) But sea slugs are far more than pretty creatures – they are efficient hunters with clever defence techniques, and a few, even, are elegant swimmers.

Like all slugs, they have razor-sharp belts of rasping teeth, called radulas, which in some cases can be driven forward like the jaws of the monster in *Alien*. Each species has a preferred prey that it is specially adapted to hunt. This can be plankton, fixed tunicates, bryozoans, sea anemones, jellyfish polyps or other sea slugs ... the list is endless. Most sea slugs have a remarkable ability to absorb the toxins and nematocysts of their prey and pass them harmlessly to the tips of their own tentacles. These assimilated poisons and 'harpoons' are then used to defend the sea slug from its own predators. That is why many slugs are so brightly coloured: it is a warning that they are armed and dangerous – unsafe to eat.

Filter-feeders

Close examination of a rock face reveals that it is entirely covered by a great variety of minute filter-feeding invertebrates, each with a different technique of trapping food. The simplest are the colourful sponges that pump water into the pores riddling their outer surface. Special cells trap any small food particles before the water is expelled from large openings at the top of the sponge. Minute hydroid polyps snare individual plankton with their tentacles. Transparent tunicates siphon water through their hollow cylindrical bodies. Bryozoans flower into feathery white colonies of particle-catching polyps. Barnacles extend their modified legs into the water, enmeshing detritus as it drifts past. Tube worms waft whorls of modified appendages in a feathery fan around their mouths. Even certain sea cucumbers are filter feeders, burrowing into cracks in the rock face, then lifting their branched tube-feet up into the water so the sticky plumes can grab the detritus. Perhaps most unusually, the porcelain crab holds aloft a pair of modified legs, each of which is shaped rather like a baseball catcher's mitt: an intricate mesh of fine, hair-like appendages that efficiently trap passing plankton.

But in temperate waters the sea anemones and soft corals are the dominant cliff-dwelling filter-feeders. Both can sting prey with harpoon-like nematocysts ($\triangleright$ p. 122), but they are outwardly very different. Sea anemones are large, solitary polyps, which can reach 50 cm (20 in) in height, while soft corals are colonial animals, living in groups within a protein-toughened 'skeleton'. Both anemones and soft coral occur in a wide profusion of colours and shapes. Their ability to reproduce

1. A burrowing sea cucumber protrudes feathery modified tube legs in a detritus-trapping whorl around its mouth.

2. A colony of sea squirts gleams with transparent brilliance. These simple animals filter plankton from the water.

by budding tiny perfect clones from the larger 'adult', leads to vast colonies of them spreading across the rock-face, creating great patches of colour. All these colonies grab plankton and detritus from the water with a web of waving tentacles. More than any other creatures, it is these soft-bodied animals that give temperate cliffs their stunning colour.

Cliffside predators

Wherever there is a rich population of animals growing in the sea, predators will arrive to feed on them and temperate cliffs attract hunters aplenty. Fish, ranging from tiny gobies, which can be as small as a few millimetres and spend their whole life on a single sponge, to 20-kg (44-lb) predatory rockfish, regularly cruise the rock walls. Some are herbivorous, but most feed either on the numerous invertebrates crowding the cliffs or by ambushing smaller fish.

Inevitably, larger predators, such as seals and dolphins, will pass through from time to time, picking up any crustacean or fish that fails to spot their approach.

The most unlikely and ubiquitous hunters are the starfish, which occur in all sizes and colours. The largest (and most aggressive) is the bright orange or blue sunstar, which has numerous arms and can measure up to a metre across. They move fast, for starfish, and, as they cruise across the seabed on thousands of marching tube feet, any invertebrates in their path attempt to flee: urchins let go of the rocks and roll away; sea cucumbers try to swim by writhing awkwardly; cockles actually run by lunging their massive foot sideways; but most bizarre of all, scallops swim off by frantically flapping their shell halves together, looking for all the world like gnashing false teeth. These aggressive sunstars will even dig for their dinner. If they sense bivalves beneath the sand they will drill a leg downwards, passing sand grains out of the hole with wave-like movements of their tube feet. The buried mollusc has little chance of escape.

1. At over 50 cm (20 in) in diameter the sunstar is not to be trifled with. It may appear benign, but this is one of the most feared predators of temperate rock faces.

2. Two colonies of jewel anemones compete for space. These colonies come in a multitude of dazzling colours – blues, mauves, yellows, creams and reds.

1

2

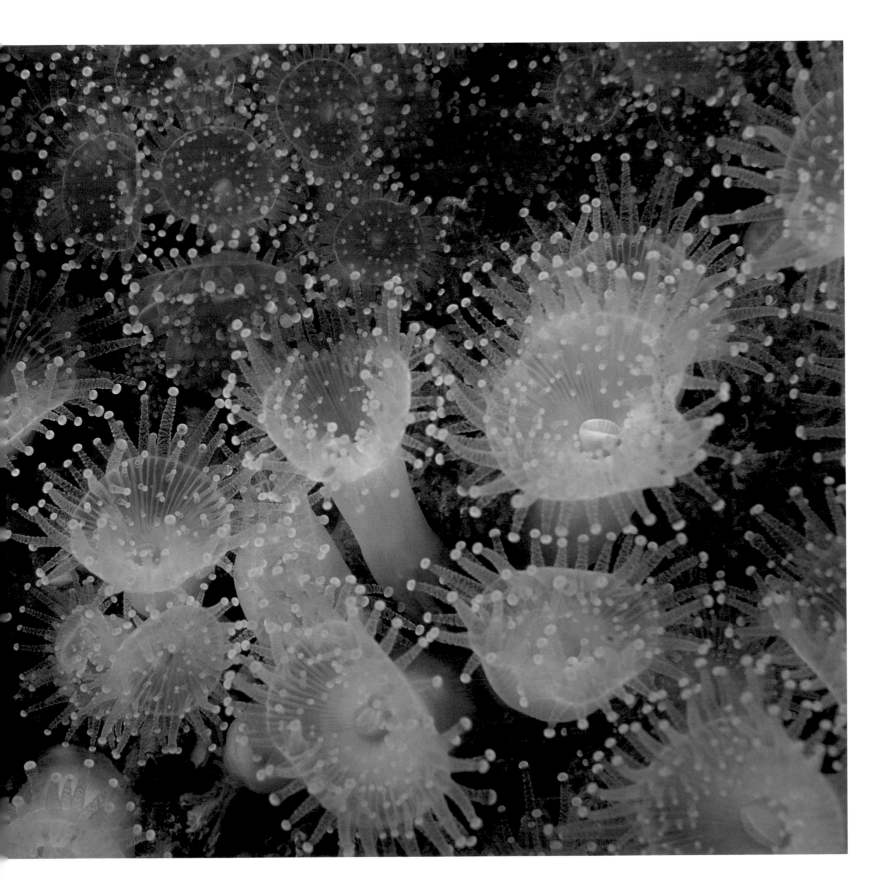

THE SEABED

1. The crown of a tubeworm forms a bright swirl. Its tentacle-like radioles trap plankton from the water, but retract into a buried tube if threatened.

2. Another worm, the sea mouse, is rarely seen in the open. It is an expert excavator feeding mainly on buried detritus.

3. Sea pens are skilful filter feeders: water passes through leaf-like branches and the plume of polyps traps food particles.

Eventually the rock meets the sea floor, a plain of sediment ranging from coarse pebbles to fine oozing mud. There is no obvious shelter. The only place to hide is on the open seabed or buried under its surface. This is the habitat where, more than any other, detritus is the key to survival. The bodies of large organisms, dead plankton and decomposing mats of seaweed all drift across the sea floor, where they are broken down by bacteria and become part of a whole new chain of life. Suspension feeders sift for bacteria and decaying bodies and they themselves are hunted down by other invertebrates and specially adapted predatory fish.

Suspension-feeders

Coarse sediment allows water to flow between the grains more easily so it is much

richer in oxygen, enabling more animals to survive in the sand. Bivalve molluscs such as cockles build tunnels and then push a siphon through to the surface: one tube draws in food-laden water, and another pumps out waste. This simple and efficient feeding technique allows the creatures to remain securely buried while they feed.

Many shrimp are suspension-feeders, and several species are expert excavators, building large tunnel homes. Ghost shrimp and Dublin Bay prawns riddle the sea floor with holes, so the top layers of silt have the consistency of Emmenthal cheese.

Large mantis shrimp use burrows as a launch pad for ambushing. They live in sandy silt but are active predators, launching lightning forays from the safety of their underground lairs. Their sharp stabbing claws can punch through the armour of other crustaceans, but despite this fierce weaponry,

the mantis needs to be careful – other predators cruise the sea floor.

Infauna

All these animals that burrow into the sand and mud are called infauna. Perhaps the most bizarre infauna of all are the meiofauna – microscopic worms, protozoans and rotifers. Some are herbivores, grazing any microscopic algae that can be found. Others are minute predators which hide in ambush behind sand grains, waiting to pounce on other less wary meiofauna as they blunder by.

Deposit-feeders

Not just microscopic life exists in the sea floor. Fine mud plains contain more decomposing matter and the small silty particles do not allow free passage of water, so there is little oxygen in the sediment and only a few animals can survive. Just the top layer of mud contains animals, and most are deposit-feeding worms.

Among the other creatures that survive on the muddy seabed are specially adapted sea urchins. The oddly flattened sand dollar and wiry bristled sea mouse are both urchins that feed under the surface. Amphipods also consume detritus in the mud, building great communities of tube dwellings. In the Bering Sea, south of the Arctic Circle, amphipods can become incredibly numerous, covering the sea floor in great mats of orange tubes. They are the favourite food of gray whales.

Demersal hunters

The continental shelf is home to a great variety of fish adapted for life on the sea floor. These are the so-called demersal fish, whose once-huge numbers have been seriously depleted by commercial fisheries. ▷▷

3

THE GRAY WHALE

Weighing up to 40 tonnes, the gray whale is the largest animal to plunder a living from the seabed, having perfected an extraordinary feeding technique that involves grabbing huge mouthfuls of mud and sifting out a snack of hidden worms and amphipods. Somehow this lifestyle of tilling the mud has earned the gray whale a less than glamorous image, yet it is a spectacular animal. The population of eastern Pacific gray whales has bounced back from near extinction to a healthy population of 20,000. This amazing recovery is all the more remarkable considering that this is a nomadic whale, whose chosen route takes it the entire length of the North American Pacific coastline on an annual round journey of 20,000 km (12,400 miles) through some of the busiest waters on Earth.

1. A feeding gray whale begins its ascent to the surface, after completing a mud-grabbing forage across the seabed.

Friendly giants

Perhaps the success of the gray whale is partly due to its popularity as a tourist attraction. From the early 1970s gray whales in their Mexican breeding grounds have sought out the company of humans in the most intimate fashion. Thousands of tourists venture to these salt-encrusted desert waterways to warm their hearts in the cold of winter. The whale-watchers set off in small open boats to drift slowly around, hoping for a magical encounter. An erupting high-pressure blast followed by a roaring sucking of air announces the arrival of a friendly whale surfacing ponderously to breathe. When a 30-tonne back erupts alongside a boat, it is impossible not to be awed. As the whale's barnacled chin scrapes on to the gunwale, awe turns to a mixture of delight and terror. There is stench of fish – whale's breath. The beautiful mottled skin of grey and black is strangely soft and yielding, but there is no need for caution – the whale is here for a scratching. People can rub as hard as they like, even stretch their hands into the gaping mouth and tickling the sensitive tongue. It seems that the whales genuinely enjoy the experience, and when they have had enough, they simply leave.

Breeding and feeding

Gray whales breed in shallow lagoons and the coastal waters of the peninsula of Baja California from late December until March. The warm water of the subtropics is ideal for incubating newborn calves, which start out in life with only a thin layer of blubber. But this coast has insufficient food for the thousands of breeding adult grays, so they are forced to fast until they leave for their northern feeding grounds. From as early as February the first wave of migrants sets off at a steady 4 knots (7 kph/ 4 mph), hugging the coast and covering about 80 km (50 miles) a day. Most of them head for the Bering Sea, where the seabed is covered in huge mats of their favoured diet – amphipods.

Living in the shallows

Grays are whales of the shallow seas, seldom venturing further than a few kilometres off shore during their migration, and even when they reach the open water of the Bering Sea, the seabed is little more than 40 m (130 feet) deep. They have evolved to harvest coastal invertebrates and appear to work almost like farmers, picking the best crops at the best time of year. They also have a wide range of feeding techniques. Using their short brushy baleen, they can sieve plankton from the water, targeting swarms of mysid shrimp, crab larvae and fish eggs as and when they are available.

They can lunge into schooling fish to grab a snack, and they even strip grazing invertebrates from kelp running the long fronds delicately through their jaws. But it is on the seabed that they reveal their true colours.

Ploughing the sea floor

The Bering Sea is full of whales cruising along the surface, leaving long plumes of mud that they have dredged from the bottom streaming behind them. Just like tractors in a field, their progress is followed by hordes of screaming gulls, snatching at fragments spilling from the whales' jaws. They excavate hundreds of thousands of tonnes every summer, diving gracefully to the sea floor, turning on their sides to glide across the mud and powerfully gouging deep 2- or 3-m (c 7 feet) long furrows from the bottom. Their tongues expel the silt through their baleen, allowing them to swallow a rich wriggling mass of amphipods and worms. It is a remarkable method of feeding and it is certainly true that it helps enrich the sea itself, dragging nutrients from the seabed up into the water and thus ensuring that the pickings will be good the following year, when they return once more from their marathon 20,000-km (12,400-mile) swim.

2. A gray whale blows for air at the surface. When they travel, the whales take three or four breaths before swimming underwater for at least ten minutes.

3. Gray whales are remarkably adaptive feeders. This one is stripping invertebrates from giant kelp fronds by dragging the seaweed through its stubby baleen.

TOPIC LINKS

4.2 Blooming Plankton
p.180 Planktivorous Giants

4.3 Ocean Forests
p.195 Life in the Forest

4.4 The Living Bed
p.205 Deposit-feeders

6.4 Ocean Birth
p.308 Baleen Whales

The most successful of the seabed fish are flat and camouflaged so that they can't be seen by predators or prey. The monkfish works on exactly this principle. Living in the Atlantic and weighing up to 80 kg (175 lb), it is compressed into a large disc-shape and has an enormous upward-facing mouth. Being well camouflaged, it simply sits on the bottom waiting for prey to come along, then launches a sudden lunging attack. Some sharks and rays feed like this too. The beautiful guitar fish, a 2-metre-long (6.5-foot-long) shark found in the Pacific, is so flattened that it manages to bury itself completely in the sand, where it will wait for hours in the hope of prey passing nearby.

The most compressed demersal fish of all are the flat fish. Extraordinarily, they start out in life looking like regular fish larvae, with one eye on either side of their heads. As they develop, however, they turn slowly sideways so that the tail becomes horizontal, the body flattens and the eye facing the seabed migrates up through the head to join the other eye on one side of the body. They spend the rest of their lives swimming on their sides generally with both eyes protruding above the head as though on stalks, in order to see above the sea floor. This technique helps the flatfishes to see even when they are buried in the sand waiting for food.

While many bottom-living fish, particularly daytime hunters such as Atlantic plaice, have large, efficient eyes, night-time hunters such as Dover sole do not. Their bead-like eyes are virtually useless since there is little chance of seeing food in the dark. So how does the sole find its prey? The answer is by the numerous chemical sensors arranged around its mouth and underside. As it swims along, the sensors react to any trace of protein or other chemicals that wash from hidden prey, causing the fish to double back and intensify its search. These sensors are so efficient that in pitch darkness Dover sole can locate small prey, such as shrimp or prawns buried in the sand with almost unerring accuracy.

★ The blue whale is the largest animal ever to have lived on Earth. Normally around 80 tonnes in weight, it has been recorded at over 170 tonnes.

3. (opposite) Despite its sluggish swimming skills, the torpedo ray has little to fear: its ability to emit electricity keeps even the most determined predators at bay.

1. A larval plaice shows the characteristic flatfish's appearance with both eyes appearing on one side of the head, but when they hatch their eyes are in the same position as a tiny conventional fish.

2. A far cry from *Jaws*, horn sharks feed mainly on invertebrates that live on or in the sea floor.

1

1. Cod have an ultra-sensitive chin: their barbels are packed with sensory cells that help them to detect prey on the sea floor.

2. A giant Pacific octopus glides from its lair. At least 5 m (16 feet) across, these animals are fiercely intelligent hunters of rocky habitats, but only live for two or three years.

In fact, most demersal fish have a complex system of sensors to help locate hidden prey. Atlantic cod have sensor pits all around their head and a great concentration of sensors in their barbels. When hunting hidden prey, they draw their barbels over the silt, retracing their tracks if they get the slightest scent of food.

Rays and sharks go one step further – they use electrical signals to locate prey. Even the tiniest movement creates a minute electrical impulse, which can be picked up by the strong electromagnetic sensory system of a cruising ray, for example. The ray can pinpoint its meal and then dig it out.

Rays also have the ability to excavate deep into the sand in their search for food. Water is drawn into openings on the upper side of the head, then pumped strongly out of exhalent gills on the underside of the body. When this is done while lunging the head

 SHOCKING FISH

As they move, all animals discharge minute amounts of electricity from their muscles, which comes in handy for predators, such as sharks and rays, who have special sense organs in their head to detect it. Rays can locate even small worms and shells buried deep under the sand, so they know exactly where to dig to unearth their next meal. Many sharks sense for electrical impulses in open water, but if the signal they pursue happens to be a torpedo ray, even a large shark would turn tail and flee.

Torpedo rays don't just sense for electricity – they manufacture it. Two large organs that occupy up to a third of their body volume can contain 1 million electricity-producing cells, a powerhouse capable of delivering a 1000-watt shock, sufficient to stun a man. Torpedo rays have none of the gliding elegance of other ocean rays. In fact, they are so slow that it is very difficult for them to outmanoeuvre prey. However, well camouflaged, they either ambush from the seabed or edge up on a target fish and zap it with a blue-sparking electrical discharge that lasts a fraction of a second. The energy bolt kills the faster prey stone dead, and the slow-moving ray can feed at its leisure.

2

into the seabed, the rays can literally jet-blast sand aside with a stream of exhaled water. This works so well that the sea floor can be covered in deep pits, sometimes a couple of metres in diameter, where rays have been digging for tube worms or bivalves.

Fish and rays are so successful at adapting themselves to feeding on sea floor infauna that they can grow to immense sizes. Cod have been known to weigh over 80 kg (175 lb), while rays, such as skate, can reach 90 kg (196 lb). Perhaps most impressive of all, the giant Atlantic halibut has been netted in shelf water off the coast of Iceland, weighing in at a stag-

gering 300 kg (660 lb). Most of these giants have long since been fished to extinction; only much smaller examples of their kind are caught today. It is intriguing, none the less, to consider what life must have been like for a several hundred kilogram halibut. Imagine almost complete darkness over 50 m (160 feet) below the surface. The giant flatfish, nearly 3 m (10 feet) in length, cruises gently across a gloomy grey-black plain where little light and no colour ever reaches. Although its chemosensors pick up the scent of worms and shells hidden in the sand below, these are small fry – not big enough for this hunter. Its great

tail beats rhythmically up and down, driving its bulk further into the murk. At last it senses significant electrical movements ahead. Slowing to cloak its approach, the predator eases in, waiting for a first glimpse of its prey. Suddenly there is a hint of movement ahead. Ghost-like forms speed back and forth across the sea floor. The giant halibut has found a shoal of 10-kg (22-lb) cod working a school of sand eels. The huge toothed mouth drops open, protruding forward, and 200 kg (440 lb) of muscle drives it onwards. Moments later, 30 kg (66 lb) of cod are shuddering to the touch of acid inside the giant halibut's stomach.

FROZEN SEAS

5.1 THE POLAR REGIONS 214

Bitter cold, grinding ice and months of winter darkness are common to both the Arctic and the Antarctic, but for animals the two polar regions differ significantly.

SPECIAL FEATURE: Nature's ice machines

5.2 ANTARCTIC WILDLIFE 228

The 'frozen continent' is surrounded by a nutrient-rich, turbulent ocean, which provides boundless feeding opportunities for Antarctic wildlife.

SPECIAL FEATURE: South Georgia

SPECIAL FEATURE: Emperor penguins

5.3 ARCTIC WILDLIFE 246

The lives of Arctic animals are not only governed by the unpredictable nature of sea ice, but also by the presence of land predators, particularly polar bears.

SPECIAL FEATURE: People of the Arctic

THE POLAR REGIONS

We think of the polar regions as cold, icy wastelands, blasted by winds and devoid of life. In certain places that is not far from the truth. But both the Antarctic in the south and the Arctic to the north are regions of extraordinary variety. At their centres the cold is intense, but at their margins the climate can feel almost temperate. They contain magnificent mountain ranges, sheltered coves, glaciers and even a desert. The sculpted ice can be hauntingly beautiful: its colour ranging from white to an intense turquoise, its texture from silk to crystal blades. It can tower as icebergs, or carpet the sea from shore to shore. The winds do blow, often at speed, and create mountainous waves. There are also periods of calm, when the water lies still. In summer, the poles are blessed with 24 hours of daylight; in winter they endure months of darkness. Despite the extremes of cold and dark, life does exist in the polar regions – and it is life in surprising abundance.

Previous page: Imposing cliffs of ice tower over a still backwater. All life in the polar seas is up against a cold, changing and unforgiving environment.

ROCK AND ICE

Viewed from space, the poles stand out as areas of glaring white; the ice reflects back the sun's rays and dazzles the eye. Ice is the key feature uniting the two poles, but in most other respects the Arctic and Antarctic are surprisingly different.

Poles apart

The boundaries of the polar regions are defined differently by different disciplines: biologists use ecological limits, oceanographers use water masses, and geographers use the polar circles. However, a generally agreed delineation of the Antarctic is the line in the Southern Ocean where cold Antarctic waters meet and sink below warmer northern waters; this is called the Antarctic Convergence. The Arctic is more complicated to delineate because it includes landmasses that stretch into temperate latitudes. Consensus about its boundaries is therefore less widespread, but a working guide is that Arctic life does not exist above a mean upper limit of 10 °C (50 °F). So a meandering line has been drawn around the Arctic, reaching as far south as 50° N in the Bering Sea and as high as 70° N near Norway.

The Arctic and Antarctic circles themselves are defined by the sun and the tilt of the Earth. On 21 June in the northern summer, the sun's rays hit the Earth at right angles to the Tropic of Cancer (23° 30′ N). On that day, the area due north of the Arctic Circle (latitude 66° 33′ N) sees the midnight sun. On the circle itself, the midnight sun is seen for that one night only. On the same day, the entire area due south of the Antarctic Circle (latitude 66° 33′ S) receives no direct sunlight. The opposite happens on 21 December, when the sun favours the southern hemisphere and is over the Tropic of Capricorn.

As you move towards the poles, the summer daylight lengthens and in winter the days are correspondingly shorter. At the North and South Poles, this reaches its maximum: once risen in spring, the sun spirals around the sky for six months without setting. When autumn arrives, it sets, once only, and a six-month-long period of darkness, or near darkness, begins.

Taken over a whole year, the poles receive a similar number of hours of solar radiation as

1. The key seasonal factor that governs the behaviour of animals in the polar regions is the growth and melt of the sea ice. It prevents or allows them access to their feeding grounds and, in some cases, their breeding grounds.

the Equator, but the effects in these locations are widely different. When the sun's radiation hits Earth's atmosphere, some of it is absorbed by atmospheric gases and some of it is reflected back by clouds. At the poles, where the sun is never directly overhead, the radiation that does pass through has little warming effect because 85 per cent of the short-wave radiation, or heat, is reflected back straight away by the snow and ice. This compares to 5 per cent reflection in ice-free oceans. In addition, the snow radiates long wavelengths out into space, further cooling the surface. Thus, in the Antarctic, except for two months in midsummer, more radiation is lost than is gained by the sun.

Arctic sea

Despite sharing dark winters, midnight sun, ice and a frigid climate, the Arctic and the Antarctic are very different. Antarctica is a continent of rock in its own right, but as it is covered with an ice-cap, which blankets the land and obscures the mountains, little is seen of the rock itself. The surrounding Southern Ocean is small by world standards, but far larger than the Arctic Ocean. It is also warmer because it is contiguous with the Pacific, Atlantic and Indian oceans: ice covers a mere 2.6 per cent of it. By contrast, the centre of the Arctic is a small ocean almost entirely covered by a layer of ice, several metres thick.

The Arctic also includes the northern fringes of the great landmasses of North America, Greenland and Eurasia. This land is crucial in shaping the nature of the Arctic Ocean, not least because it has an ameliorating effect on the climate. Land absorbs much more of the sun's radiation than ice, warming the rock, the fresh water and the air itself.

This heat filters down to the sea via rivers, particularly those in Siberia, and warm winds make it less cold than it might otherwise be. Temperatures of 10 °C (50 °F) can be reached in summer, and in winter only a few places, such as Siberia, experience the numbing cold of -50 °C (-60 °F) or below.

The prehistory of the Arctic basin is barely known, but it is believed to have changed little for aeons: it was and still is a sea surrounded by land. But a more recent series of events – the Pleistocene ice ages, which occurred between approximately 1.6 million and 10,000 years ago – have had a great influence on the Arctic. The northern ice-caps were the largest in the world. In North America the sheets were almost continuous from Canada down to New York, and stretched west across the continent. In Europe the sheets were broken by corridors

LIGHTS IN THE SKY

Both polar skies are blessed with unearthly displays of coloured light, which gently roll, fold on fold, fading and glowing through the night. Known as the aurora borealis (northern lights) in the Arctic and aurora australis (southern lights) in the Antarctic (illustrated, left) they entrance anyone lucky enough to see them.

These displays are born from ionized gases blasted out of the sun. They travel through space at 400 km (250 miles) per second. This solar wind hits the Earth's magnetic field and is channelled by it. The ionized particles penetrate into Earth's upper atmosphere down magnetic field lines at the poles, colliding with atoms and molecules in the thermosphere. The collisions create colours as light particles are released. Nitrogen produces a violet colour, but the most commonly seen colours are red and green, created by oxygen.

The lights are best seen within auroral zones, which have their centres on the magnetic poles. Here the aurora, be it northern or southern, can be seen almost every night of the year – given no cloud cover and a dark night. The auroras, present all the time, are synchronous and the same at each end of the Earth at any given moment.

of land, which allowed the migration of animals to continue. There was so much water bound up in the ice-sheets that the sea level was about 100 m (350 feet) lower than it is today. Land that had previously been under water was exposed and formed 'bridges', which enabled animals to move freely from island to island or continent to continent: Asia and Alaska, for example, were linked by the Beringia land-bridge.

As the ice began to melt, land-bridges disappeared, local conditions changed and animals, such as mammoths and woolly rhinoceroses, became extinct. Others, which had survived the advancing ice by moving south, now spread north and some adapted to the new conditions, becoming true Arctic specialists.

Splendid isolation

Antarctica has not always been the frozen, isolated continent it is today. At one time it was the centre of the supercontinent Gondwanaland, with South America, Africa, Australasia and India grouped around its perimeter. About 290 million years ago, Gondwanaland sat over the South Pole, with Antarctica in very much the same place as it is today, but then the supercontinent began to move northwards and became subtropical. Fossils from this period are shared by most of the landmasses – evidence that they were once connected. Some 170 million years ago, after a period of considerable volcanic activity, Gondwanaland began to break up: first a rift appeared between Africa and Antarctica (still joined to Madagascar, India and Australasia), then South America and Africa separated, which created the South Atlantic Ocean. Madagascar stopped moving and India drifted north, leaving Antarctica and Australasia still connected and moving south. About 100 million years ago, Australasia

began to break away from Antarctica, and 40 million years later the continents had become truly isolated.

Antarctica's isolation meant that a strong, circumpolar current developed in the surrounding ocean and the cooling process began. Having been subtropical, the climate turned temperate, but still supported a lush growth of forest and fern with their accompanying prehistoric animals. As the continent moved further south, the cooling accelerated, and 25 million years ago the forests vanished. Antarctica became covered with ice.

The geographic isolation of Antarctica remains complete. The effects of this isolation are compounded by a recurring barrier of sea ice, which grows out from the continent each autumn, and the roughest seas in the world – those of the Southern Ocean. As the ocean is not interrupted by landmasses of any significance, the winds blow unimpeded and the seas can become mountainous. This creates an effective barrier, which no land animals, even good swimmers, could hope to cross.

Due to its isolation, Antarctica is also significantly colder than the Arctic. It does not enjoy the warming effects of other continents: South America, the closest, lies 1000 km (620 miles) away, Australia is now 2500 km (1550 miles) distant, and Africa lies 4000 km (2500 miles) off. Antarctica is also colder because it is so high. For every 100 m (330 feet) gained in height, the air temperature drops by 1 °C (1.8 °F). The average height of the continent is 2500 m (8200 feet) compared with North America at 720 m (2360 feet), and as a result, it is the coldest place on Earth. While the Arctic's winter temperatures plummet to -50 °C (-60 °F) for periods, the Antarctic's can remain a steady, stupefying -70 °C (-95 °F) in places. However, it is only in the middle of the Antarctic continent, where the warming effects of the sea cannot be felt, that temperatures fall so low.

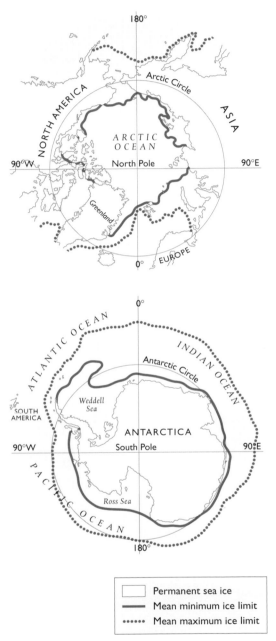

1

OUT IN THE COLD

Most people fortunate enough to visit the Arctic and the Antarctic have their expectations fulfilled. They see a lot of ice and they experience subzero temperatures, but they usually visit during the summer, and even then, they are well wrapped against the cold. Few endure the winters, and if they do, they rarely venture out of superheated buildings.

Temperatures

During a polar summer, air temperatures can change dramatically with the daily rising and setting sun, but the sun has little impact on the temperature of the polar seas. In temperate and even tropical climes the summer sun will gradually heat up a body of water, leaving it significantly warmer at the beginning of autumn than it was in spring. But in the polar seas, the little radiation that is not reflected back by the glaring whiteness first melts the ice. By the time the blanketing sea ice has dissolved, the season has progressed and there is scant time or warmth left for heating up such a cold body of water. Certainly, the sea surface freezes over in autumn and melts again in spring, but the change in the actual temperature of the water is minimal.

Antarctica is not uniformly cold. The plateau, having a higher latitude and elevation above sea level, is unrelentingly bitter, with mean temperatures of -40 °C (-40 °F) in summer and -70 °C (-95 °F) in winter. This ice-cap receives precious little rain or snow, and because of the extreme cold, there is no moisture in the air. It is an icy desert, where virtually no life survives. Move northward and down to the perimeter of the continent and it becomes almost tropical by comparison. The coast enjoys balmy summers, when mean temperatures are 0 °C (-32 °F), with the occasional day of +5 °C (40 °F) or more, and endures winters where -30 °C (-20 °F) is normal. There is more rain here and the winds are stronger. Cold, dense air rolling off the plateau pours down the glaciers as katabatic or gravity-driven winds, accelerating as they go. These winds are not gentle; they arrive suddenly and at terrific speeds, scouring the ice beneath them. As this air meets the coast, it mixes with warm air from the ocean, creating a storm belt that rings the continent. This belt brings clouds, blinding blizzards and, on stiller days, fog.

The Arctic has a wider variety of both climates and habitats, encompassing a frozen sea, the ice-cap of Greenland, the forests of Scandinavia and the tundra of Siberia. Greenland is the Arctic's answer to the Antarctic plateau. It is high and cold, and has glaciers streaming down to the sea, but it covers only one-tenth of the area and thus has less impact. The Arctic Ocean, the frozen sea itself, is generally warmer than its neighbouring landmasses in winter, and colder than them in summer, but the water temperature changes hardly at all. Just as the coldest place in Antarctica is high on the plateau, far from the sea, the coldest places in the Arctic are on the Greenland ice-cap and in Siberia, both a long way from the warming effects of the ocean.

Frozen sea

The temperature of the water in both the Arctic and the Antarctic hovers just below 0 °C (-32 °F). It freezes at -1.8 °C (29 °F), leaving most of its salt dissolved in the water below. First, hexagonal crystals form in the water and drift near the surface as frazil ice. When

The coldest air temperature ever recorded on Earth was at a Russian Antarctic Station called Vostok: one winter the thermometer dropped to -89.2 °C (-129 °F).

1. Polar bears are so well insulated against the cold by their fur, tough hide and layer of blubber, that for much of the time they are obliged to move at a steady plod to avoid overheating.

2. Both polar regions have glaciers that pour ice into the sea, but those of the Arctic are much shorter and narrower than those of the Antarctic.

1. (opposite) The geometric mosaic of Arctic pack ice offers a refuge to some species of breeding seals, as polar bears find travel across such terrain laborious.

2. The solid sea ice of Cape Washington, Antarctica provides a stable and secure platform on which emperor penguins lay their eggs and rear their chicks.

conditions are calm, the crystals congeal to create an oily textured slick called grease ice. The combination of grease ice on the surface and frazil ice below forms a thick, soupy texture. On further cooling, the ice coalesces into a more solid layer of flat ice, which breaks and moves with the swell to create small plates, called pancake ice. The constant motion of the water causes these plates to bump and jostle against one another, their edges are pushed up into little ridges and they begin to look like lily-pads. Gradually, the soup between these plates freezes and the sea becomes solid. Below the thin ice layer, more freezing occurs and more frazil ice continues to form, resting against the solid ceiling. In a prolonged cold spell, the sea ice can be 20 cm (8 in) thick after just 24 hours: a week later it is double that. As winter progresses, layer upon layer of snow covers the ice, insulating it from the air above. Thus air temperatures may plummet, but beneath the ice the sea water continues to freeze only slowly. By the end of winter, the annual sea ice is usually 1–2 m (3–6 feet) thick.

Large swells, which develop as the winds continue to blow, break the solid sea ice into large pieces called ice floes, which collectively form pack ice. In some places the pack ice is refrozen solid; in others, where ocean currents are on the move, it forms a shifting, unpredictable platform. To some animals, pack ice is a haven, a place where they are safe from predators: to man it presents a treacherous hazard, where unprotected boats can be crushed between the moving floes.

Ice on the move

In both polar oceans, the seasonal formation and melt of the sea ice is one of the great driving forces behind the lives of all animals. As the colder temperatures of March start to grip the Antarctic, the sea begins to freeze over – first in the coastal bays, then marching steadily north. The advance of the sea ice is relentless – freezing an impressive 4 km (2.5 miles) per day through the winter, it extends 600–3000 km (315–1900 miles) from the coastline by September, when it is at its maximum. By then the new area of sea covered by ice is 22 million sq km (8 million sq miles), more than twice the size of the Antarctic continent itself. During the spring and summer the sea ice decays, breaks up and melts away, leaving only 4 million sq km (1.5 million sq miles) of ice covering the most southern backwaters and bays.

The growth of sea ice in the Arctic Ocean is also dramatic, covering a total area of 14 million sq km (5.5 million sq miles) at its peak. The Arctic Ocean is characterized by a large area of sea ice, some 6.6 million sq km (2.5 million sq miles) or 47 per cent of the ocean, that remains solid year on year. This is called multi-year ice. (The Antarctic also has multi-year ice, but it occurs mostly in the Weddell Sea, where it moves endlessly in a large circle.) Multi-year ice melts a little and grows a little in each year. The thaw occurs in summer, as the snow and top layer of ice melt in the sun; the freezing occurs in winter under the ice. When the climate is in balance, the multi-year ice remains up to 8 m (25 feet) thick. Currently, there is real concern that global warming is changing this balance, and that multi-year ice is melting altogether in some places.

The ice covering the Arctic Ocean is not fixed in position: it is moved by both local currents and by a surface ocean current – the Transpolar Drift – that moves in a south-westerly direction. The water travels from Siberia to eastern Greenland, where some water is directed south out of the Arctic Ocean, carrying with it 4 million megatonnes of drifting ice. The main current continues around past Greenland, the archipelago of northern Canada, Alaska and back to Siberia. This ice movement was first discovered in 1893, when the Norwegian polar explorer Fridtjof Nansen set off in his specially designed boat, the *Fram*, to drift in the ice to the North Pole. After a year of being locked in the sea ice, the boat began travelling west rather than north, the first evidence that the Transpolar Drift existed.

NATURE'S ICE MACHINES

The Antarctic ice-cap dwarfs all others on Earth. It contains 30 million cubic km, or nearly 70 per cent of the world's fresh water, covers 98 per cent of the continent and is nearly 5 km (3 miles) thick in places. The Greenland ice-cap, by comparison, contains a mere 2.5 million cubic km of water. Despite the amount of water contained in these ice caps, the rate at which they accrue snow and ice is very slow.

2. Vast chunks of ice break off the front of glaciers creating icebergs. Here, a section of the Mertz glacier has broken free, forming a flat-topped 'tabular' berg.

1. Ice that has collected on the Antarctic plateau spills down in giant glaciers towards the sea. The Reeves glacier, Victoria Land, is highly crevassed near its mouth.

Making ice

Water evaporates from the oceans and is transported high into the atmosphere. Here, in the cooler temperatures, tiny crystals of ice form around dust particles. As more water molecules are added and the crystals join together, they form snowflakes. Snow falls through the lower atmosphere and settles on the ground only when the temperature is cold enough.

Antarctica is so cold that it is dry; the air simply cannot carry water in any form. Overall the continent receives an average 12–15 cm (5–6 in) of precipitation (mostly snow) each year, but the interior is much colder and in some places only 20 mm (0.75 in) of snow falls. Once fallen, the flakes are blown by the wind. Their delicate arms are broken off and they become rounded. With less surface area to act on, winds become unable to carry the crystals and they remain on the ground, gradually cementing themselves to each other.

As snow piles on snow, the weight of the top layers presses down and the density increases. So while at the surface the snow seems soft, 10 m (30 feet) down it is packed hard. At 100 m

(325 feet) air bubbles are sealed between the crystals and the ice appears bubbly. Further down still, at 1200 m (4000 feet) or more, the air has been squeezed into the crystals and the ice is solid.

On the move

Ice near the bottom of the Antarctic ice-cap is estimated to be 250,000 years old. Even this ice is on the move, if only a little. Unlike glaciers, which slide as blocks, ice sheets move by internal deformation. The bottom layer of ice is frozen to the bedrock, preventing the sheet above it sliding, so, under its own weight, the ice moves layer by layer. Like a pack of cards being spread across a table, each layer within the ice moves at a different rate, the upper ones faster than those lower down. Ice flows downhill from high points on the continent to the margins, accelerating from a paltry few centimetres per year to 200 m (650 foot). In the form of glaciers and ice sheets, its perimeters can reach speeds of 2 km (1 mile) per year.

Glaciers, often called rivers of ice, move fast. The speed is greatest at the surface, and internal deformation still occurs, but glaciers

3

also move by sliding over the bedrock. Under the immense pressure of the ice and with heat generated by so much friction against the rock, the layer of ice in contact with the land melts, forming streams. The running water provides lubrication and the whole body of the glacier can slide downhill as one.

Icebergs

Where the ice sheet and glaciers meet the sea, they shed ice. Indeed, about 1450 cubic km of Antarctic ice breaks away as icebergs each year – the equivalent of half the human world's annual freshwater usage. The largest – tabular bergs – are great chunks of the ice sheet that break off and float away. These can be 200–300 m (600–1000 feet) deep and many kilometres across. As they drift north, they begin to disintegrate, cracking first along lines of

weakness, such as old crevasses. As their centre of gravity shifts, they become unstable and begin a painfully slow roll, which can finish with the berg upside-down. In time, the berg splinters further and is eroded by sun, wind and waves. The official term for bergs that are 2–5 m (5–15 feet) across is 'bergy bits'; smaller pieces are known as brash ice.

The huge quantity of fresh water trapped in large, tabular icebergs has resulted in people researching the possibility of harvesting bergs. With modern technology it now would be feasible to tow a berg a great distance, but given the time it would take, even to reach southern hemisphere destinations, at least half the berg would have melted away. Furthermore, the difficulty of actually extracting the fresh water has not been resolved: the deep draft of icebergs makes them difficult to bring close inshore.

3. As icebergs drift at sea they are exposed to the vagaries of wind, weather and currents; the gradual erosion can create magnificent shapes.

TOPIC LINKS

5.1 The Polar Regions
p.215 Rock and Ice
p.218 Out in the Cold

1

1. Walruses are so well insulated by their hides and blubber that they are happy to remain amidst the ice all year. In winter they remain in polynyas (areas of open water) so that they have access to air.

2. Female polar bears give birth to 30-cm (12-inch) long cubs in winter-dens under the snow. Both the insulating layer of snow above and the mother's warmth, keep the temperature of the den some 10–20 °C (18–35 °F) higher than outside.

LIVING WITH ICE

The polar regions have a lower diversity of animals and plants than most other habitats, which is perhaps why we think of them as wastelands. The tough regime of a life dominated by cold and sea ice has allowed only some of the plant and animal groups to colonize the regions successfully. There are no reptiles, for example, and no amphibians on land. In addition, Antarctica has no land mammals, no freshwater fishes and very few plants. Indeed, only 4 per cent of Antarctica supports life, which mostly consists of small things, such as microbes, spiders, insects, lichens and mosses. However, as the sea ice melts back in spring, there is a huge burst of productivity, attracting huge numbers of migratory birds, seals and whales, which spend the summer feeding on the waters' bounty.

Staying warm

All the animals that endure the ice, either throughout the year or for only part of it, have to cope with the cold. They achieve this by adapting in a number of ways. Morphological adaptations are the easiest to see. Large body size and a bulky shape decrease an animal's surface to volume ratio, reducing heat loss through the skin. The rotund figure of a walrus

or a Weddell seal are obvious examples. Good insulation by fur and blubber also helps keep out the cold. Whales rely wholly on blubber, while some seals use both. The Weddell seal, which overwinters in the deep south of the Antarctic, is particularly fat and well insulated. In the north, polar bears have large, furry feet, both to keep them from losing too much heat to the snow, and to spread their weight as they walk across snow and ice that would not otherwise support them.

Other adaptations occur within the bodies of organisms. Enzymes typically function best within a limited temperature range, and some that are activated at unusually low temperatures have been found in Antarctic crustaceans. Also, animals and plants can use a biological antifreeze in their tissues to stop them freezing. All Antarctic fishes use antifreezes, whereas they are used less universally by Arctic fishes, and of those, some use them only in winter.

One significant way in which animals deal with the cold is behaviourally. Newborn walrus pups would not be able to survive life on the sea ice if their mothers did not shield them from the worst of the weather. Similarly, male emperor penguins cannot endure the searing winds and -50 °C (-60 °F) temperatures of winter unless they form tight huddles and share body warmth. In the Arctic, female polar bears spend the winter in dens, where they

2

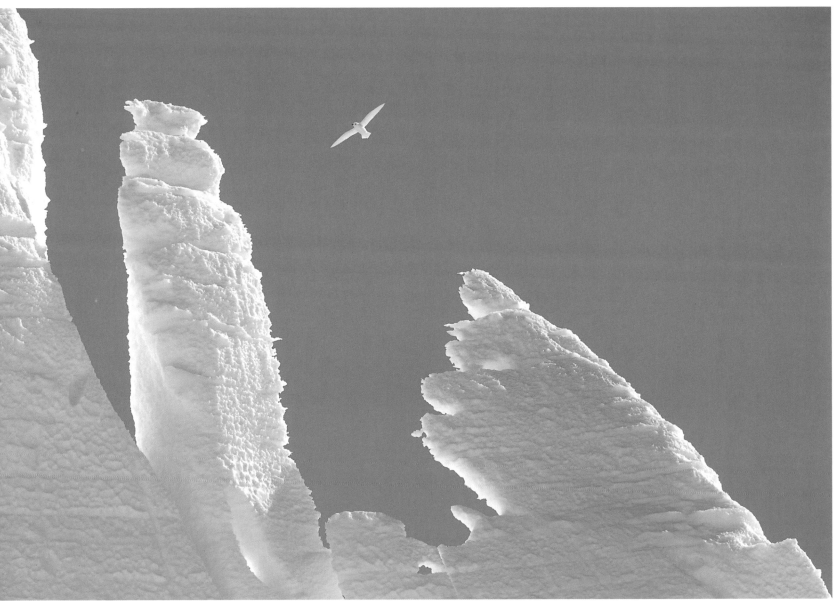

3

give birth to their tiny cubs. The den acts like a womb, keeping the cub insulated against the savage winter outside.

But by far the most common way animals escape the extremes of the cold is to avoid it altogether. Many birds and whales migrate north from Antarctica to escape the winter. Similarly, a massive migration occurs to and from the Arctic each year. The migrants spend the summer months replenishing their spent reserves, and stocking up for the winter

to come when they will be in the less productive waters of the tropics.

Living with sea ice

It would be easy to imagine that with the sea covered with ice for much of the year, polar ocean productivity would be very low. Not so. The Arctic Ocean is bordered by shallow continental shelves, fed by rivers and mixed by currents. In spring the phytoplankton blooms

3. Snow petrels, usually seen flying over pack ice or near icebergs, breed on rocky ledges. Some fly as far as 180 km (110 miles) inland from the coast to find a suitable ledge.

⭐ Algae living within the Antarctic sea ice use antifreezes to survive the winter. They also become dormant, slowing their metabolism to barely measurable levels.

over these shallow areas with extraordinary speed, though it does not last long. Productivity in the Southern Ocean is even greater.

But it is not just when the ice has melted away that all this growth occurs. Even in the middle of Antarctic sea ice there is life. In tiny, salty channels between the crystals of ice, bacteria, fungi, protozoans, small crustaceans, flatworms and, most crucially, microscopic plants called diatoms survive the winter. Diatoms are brown, and when they occur in good numbers, the bottom of the ice changes colour. They can photosynthesize and grow at very low light levels so that even in late winter and early spring, diatoms can start their annual bloom. Using nutrients from the water, they can reproduce so rapidly that they cover the underside of the sea ice, blocking

out any light filtering through, and making the water beneath an inky black.

Throughout the winter, diatoms sustain the invertebrates that live in the briny channels within the sea ice. By the time the sun returns, the system has been kick-started into growth. As the ice melts, sea-ice algae seed the bloom that occurs in water at the edge of floes. Thus diatoms are important in the productivity of the Southern Ocean as they significantly lengthen the period of growth.

Other animals live on top of the ice. The frozen sea creates a solid platform, similar to land, on which polar bears can hunt seals, walruses can haul out and have their pups, and penguins can rest. In the Arctic the sea ice extends the range of many animals away from land that they would otherwise rely on.

1. Crabeater seals use the ice as a resting and breeding platform. These are the most abundant seals in the world, with a total population estimated at 30 million.

2. Anchor ice forms on the seabed when the temperature there is below freezing. Being buoyant, it will eventually break free and float up, carrying with it any plant or animal attached to it.

2

Most truly polar seals are now dependent on the sea ice as a place to rest, warm up in summer and give birth to their pups.

Living beneath ice

Ice is an unforgiving bedfellow. When the sea freezes at the end of autumn, and the hard, rock-like sheet butts up against the shore, marine animals living there do not survive long. The sea ice moves with each tide, scraping and scouring the shoreline to a depth of 10 m (30 feet) or more, dislodging kelp and crushing animals, such as barnacles, which cannot escape. Icebergs go deeper, their keels gouging the sea floor down to a depth of 300 m (1000 feet) in the Antarctic. It is not surprising, then, that polar shorelines are bereft of the clusters of mussels, barnacles, seaweed and limpets that are found on temperate shores.

Limpets are common in the Antarctic, but they are careful not to be caught by the freeze. In summer they inch their way up to the shallows to feed on fast-growing algae. In winter they migrate down below the sea ice and hide in crevices and overhangs, out of harm's way. They then cloak themselves in an antifreeze mucus to prevent their tissues from freezing solid. Similarly, in the Arctic, periwinkles move away from the sea ice. They avoid ice crystals forming in their tissues by becoming dehydrated for the winter, and then can survive down to -15 °C (5 °F) for the duration.

Beneath the shoreline, life becomes less hazardous, and the number of species living there correspondingly more diverse. The Arctic is characterized by shallow, silty or gravelly continental shelves, which in places are extremely rich in invertebrates. Indeed, these are the largest and some of the most productive seabed habitats on Earth. Bivalves

are the most numerous, with amphipods, crabs and starfish among others found in great abundance. These life forms support the migratory predators: in fact, some 100 million tonnes of pelagic and benthic animals are consumed in the Bering Sea each year by marine mammals.

Overall, the Southern Ocean seabed community is far richer than the Arctic's. Where the Arctic's animals are closely related to those of the Atlantic and Pacific, those of the Antarctic are endemic because the continent has been isolated for so long. Safe below a ceiling of ice, productivity may not be high, but animals are diverse and numerous. Starfish, ribbon worms, crustaceans and fish feed off the sea floor. Below that, a zone of soft corals, hydroids and anemones dominate, and deeper still are the sponges, some of which can be many centuries old.

ANTARCTIC WILDLIFE

Of those who travel south to experience the harshness, beauty and isolation of Antarctica, few are disappointed. The towering icebergs, the sweeping glaciers and the sheer scale of the frozen wilderness overawe most human visitors. But for many, the attraction lies also in the chance to see the creatures that live there; penguins feeding their chicks and whales surfacing between ice floes, are particular favourites. But the charm of seals, albatrosses and other birds also wins admiration in time. No visitor can fail to be surprised by the abundance of wildlife in Antarctica, even if it is concentrated in small, coastal pockets, or perched high on the cliffs that emerge from the smothering ice. However they live, the animals of Antarctica earn our respect for their ability to survive, indeed thrive, in such a punishing climate. Not only do they endure the cold, but they must also devise strategies to cope with two major annual changes in their environment: the melt and freeze of the sea ice.

STRATEGIES FOR SPRING

Surviving the dark, bitter winter and being ready to exploit the burst of life in spring and through the short summer requires special adaptations. Animals must change their behaviour and their metabolism in order to endure the lean months and to take full advantage of the good ones. Even krill, the cornerstone of the Antarctic food web on which so many animals depend, has to achieve this annual transition.

Krill – staple diet

Krill is the name given to a group of shrimp-like crustaceans of which there are 85 species worldwide. In Antarctic waters there are 11 species, but only one – *Euphausia superba* – is absolutely key to the marine ecosystem. This animal, 4–6 cm (2–3 in) long, is the one link in a simple food chain from tiny phytoplankton to most of Antarctica's whales, seals and birds, including penguins. Owing to its complicated life history, its tendency to occur in patches and the difficulties of studying a small animal that divides its time between the winter sea ice, the open ocean and the deep sea, estimates of its population size vary a great deal. The most recent figures based on acoustic surveys puts the weight of krill within the Southern Ocean at 100–500 million tonnes.

Some krill spend the winter under the sea ice. For the juveniles it acts like a nursery, where they can feed on the diatoms living in little pockets in the ice. Adults can also spend the winter dispersed under the ice, but they go through a series of changes to survive. They rely on fatty reserves built up over the summer, and feed at only 5 per cent of their usual rate, lowering their metabolism to about a half or a third of its summer level. Incredibly, they regress physically to resemble juveniles. Most crustaceans have to moult to

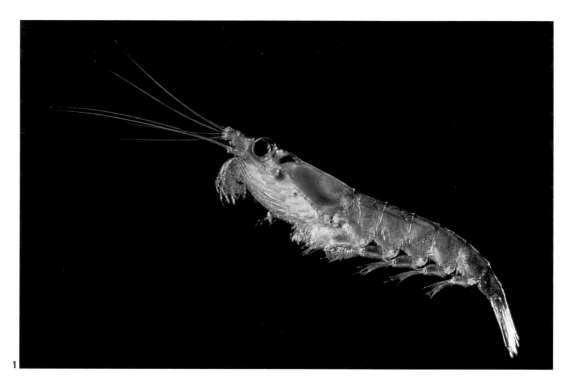

increase in size because their shell restricts growth, but krill seem to moult in winter to reduce their size; they actually shrink. They even eat their own shells, though these probably give little nourishment.

As spring returns and the light available for photosynthesis increases, diatoms flourish and krill can feed properly once more. Phytoplankton blooms and clouds the open water. Krill use their modified limbs to gather food, sort it and ingest it. Six pairs of limbs are thrown out, forming a basket-shape, to encompass a small body of water, which is then squeezed out through small flaps in the basket. Fine bristles on the limbs trap food, which is passed to the mouth. Largely dependent on phytoplankton, especially in spring and summer when the first blooms occur, krill are now thought to feed on zooplankton as well, managing to get enough energy even when phytoplankton is less abundant.

When the sea ice vanishes completely in the warmer weather, krill congregate into massive

1. Krill is the foundation of the Antarctic food web. In summer it forms vast swarms that can colour the surface of the ocean red from horizon to horizon.

Crabeater seals eat krill rather than crabs. They have special interlocking teeth that strain krill out of the water as it is squeezed through their mouths.

swarms that can be many kilometres across. These swarms seem to have a diurnal pattern, staying deep during the day, where the krill are less likely to be eaten by surface-diving birds, and rising to the surface at night. Despite these anti-predator tactics, krill are eaten in their millions during both day and night.

Breeding on the ice

One of the main predators of krill are crabeater seals. Once thought to be uncommon, these seals are in fact not only the most numerous seal in Antarctica, but the most numerous seal in the world, and probably the most abundant large mammal in the world – apart from man. It is hard to estimate their numbers accurately because they live on the drifting pack ice, a hazardous place for boats to work, but there are thought to be 30 million of them. They are social animals for much of the year, foraging in groups of ten to hundreds

of individuals, but when they breed in spring they spread out over the pack.

The female will give birth to her pup in early October on an ice floe. The pup, weighing 20 kg (45 lb) at birth, lives off its mother's milk for four weeks and gains around 100 kg (220 lb) in that time. The transfer of energy takes its toll on the mother, who loses 50 per cent of her own body weight. During this time, each mother-pup pair is closely watched by a male on a nearby floe. He is waiting for the pup to be weaned. Males defend breeding territories that are about 50 m (150 feet) in diameter around their chosen females, hence the even spread of crabeater seals over the ice. Males defend their territories vigorously and engage in serious fights with neighbouring or challenging males. Sometimes, impatient to mate, they will even fight with their chosen female, but she will mate only once her pup is ready to be weaned. Usually the pup is driven off by

the male and the pair copulate on the ice, possibly a precaution against predatory leopard seals.

Seals time their breeding so that the newly independent pup can feed on the developing krill swarms. But young crabeater seals are easy prey for two large marine predators that patrol these waters: killer whales and leopard seals. The pack ice is a hard place for killer whales to hunt, but it does not deter the more agile leopard seal. Almost all crabeater seals, young and adults alike, have scars on their bodies, typically two parallel lines spaced at exactly the width of a leopard seal's canines. It is during their first year that they acquire their lifelong scars, or fall victim to these predators.

Unable to fly

Penguins, perhaps the most popular face of Antarctica, are also vulnerable to leopard seals. Given there are only seven species of

1. Chinstrap penguins are often obliged to brave mountainous waves to gain access to their breeding sites on sub-Antarctic islands, such as Zavodovski.

Overleaf: As icebergs erode, their centre of gravity changes and sometimes they overturn, revealing entirely new, often exquisite shapes.

ICE FISH

Of the 20,000 or so known species of fish in the world, only 120 live in Antarctic waters. In order to cope with the cold, they live in a 'super-cooled' state, where their body temperature is below that at which freezing occurs. To achieve this they use eight different types of antifreeze, called glycopeptides. These molecules attach easily to developing ice crystals, preventing the further growth and spread of ice through the body.

Ice fish, which appear a ghostly white colour (see picture, right), have evolved other features appropriate to life in an oxygen-rich, cold environment. They have no haemoglobin (the oxygen-carrying pigment that colours blood red), so their blood is translucent, and their gills – typically scarlet in fish – are white. As a result, the oxygen capacity of their blood is only 10 per cent that of other Antarctic fish. To compensate, they have a higher volume of blood, their heart is twice as big and it beats faster. Nevertheless, they have a lower metabolic rate than all other Antarctic fish, especially at rest. Not surprisingly, therefore, ice fish, along with other Antarctic fish, are not fast movers; they might even be called sluggish.

polar penguin and that their numbers are relatively low, they receive more than their fair share of popular attention.

Most Antarctic penguins, apart from male emperors, spend the winter at sea. Some of those that live on sub-Antarctic islands can be found on the beaches during the winter, but even so, the majority of the colony will be at sea. Chinstrap penguins breed on islands near the outer reaches of the continent, while Adélie penguins breed even further south. For these two species in particular (along with the emperor penguin), the sea ice is critical. During winter and early spring their main food source, krill, is scarce and they need to conserve energy; the sea ice and, in more open water, the occasional iceberg provide vital resting platforms.

Penguins are well adapted to life in the cold, but on the sea ice temperatures rarely drop below -20 °C (-4 °F) because of the warming effect of the water. Both under water and on the ice they are insulated from the cold by their feathers and a layer of fat under the skin. Their feathers are short and flattened, and overlap like tiles on a roof, trapping air in the soft down beneath them. A light coating of oil ensures they are waterproof and windproof.

Squat and ungainly on land, penguins turn into mini-torpedoes under water, using their flippers for propulsion and their legs and short tails as rudders. To maintain speed when swimming at the surface they 'porpoise' like dolphins, breathing on the move and gaining the extra advantage of reduced friction – a layer of air bubbles coats them each time they surface and allows them to slide more easily through the water.

Penguins can live without the ability to fly because Antarctica has no land predators. If there were a southern equivalent of polar bears, or even wolves, flightlessness would not be an option. But free from such threat, penguins can nest with impunity on the shore. **1**

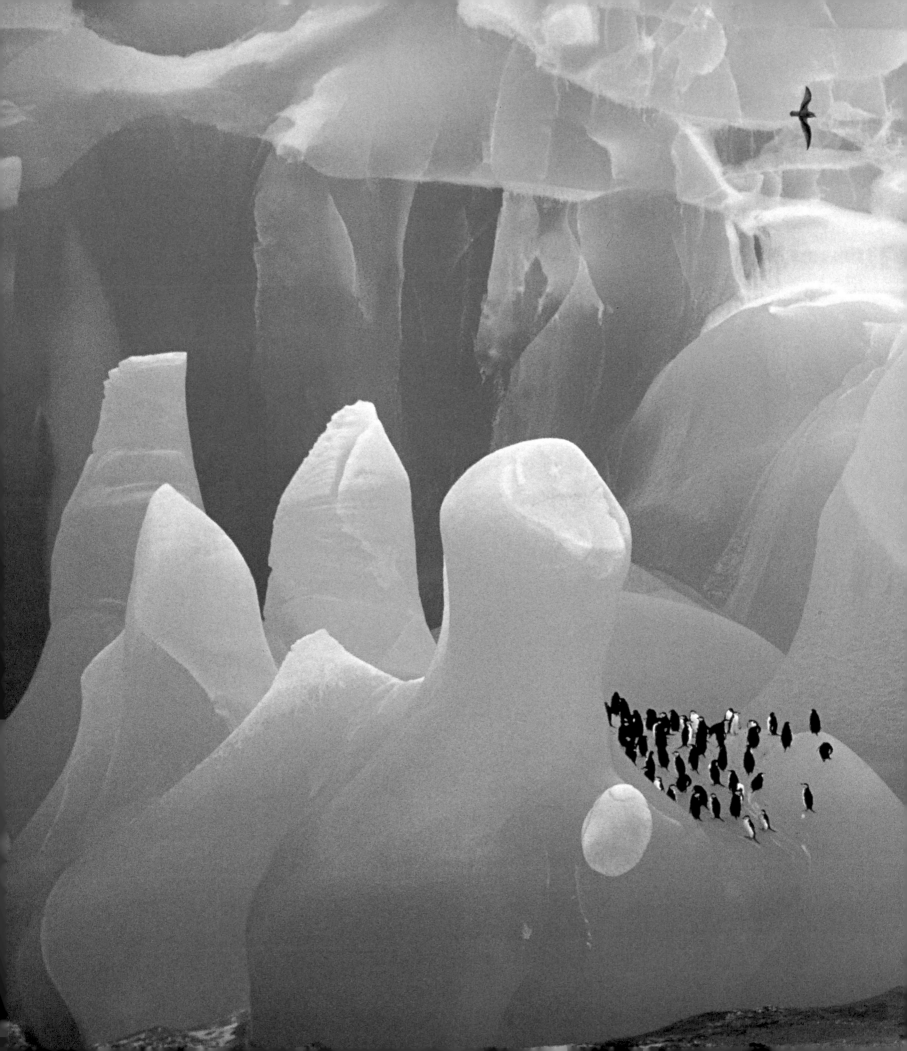

SUMMER BEGINS

It takes a while for the sun's rays to penetrate the cold of Antarctica, but when they do and the ice gives way, the waters surrounding the continent come alive with terns and petrels diving for food, the explosive blow of whales as they surface to breathe, and bands of penguins 'porpoising' as they travel in search of krill.

Nests of rock

Emperors apart, all penguins need bare ground for a nest. For the Adélie penguins, which nest on the continent, as far south as 77° 33′ S at Cape Royds on Ross Island, this is quite a tall order. Two-thirds of the Antarctic coast is blocked by glaciers or ice cliffs, and what little exposed rock exists is often precipitous. The gentler sloping rocks and beaches often retain an impenetrable covering of winter snow well

into spring. It is not surprising, then, that Adélie colonies are well spread out around the continent's perimeter – some small, some large, depending on the amount of space available to them and the sea conditions nearby. For apart from bare rock, they also need easy access to open water where there is a reliable supply of krill and, to a lesser extent, larval fish for when they are rearing their chicks.

Adélie penguins arrive at their nesting sites at the end of October. For some it is an easy climb out of the sea on to a rocky island; those that nest further south have to undertake a long trek across the still-frozen sea, where they are faced with considerably colder temperatures and a shorter summer. Adélie pairs are mostly faithful to one another, returning year after year to breed with the same partner at the same nest.

Courtship among penguins involves both a visual and a vocal display, making Adélie

colonies extremely noisy places during the first two weeks of November. Each pair gathers a few pebbles to create a nest and then fiercely defends it against raids by others. During the courtship and mating period, neither male nor female return to sea to feed. Two eggs are laid in the last two weeks of November and a five-week incubation begins, the male taking the first turn. The female feeds at sea for two weeks, so by the time she returns to the nest ready to take over from her partner, he will not have eaten for a month or more. Thereafter, the swap-over time decreases and each adult spends only two or three days away. Despite biting winds and cold snaps, the eggs are well protected and their temperature remains within a couple of degrees of the adult's body.

On hatching, the chicks are very small and vulnerable to the cold, but by the end of the second week, they are able to maintain their body temperature, so they begin to wander.

 HEATED NEST

One of the difficulties that faces chinstrap, gentoo and Adélie penguins is the availability of ice- and snow-free ground for nesting sites. The summer in Antarctica is short and these birds have to court, mate, lay and incubate their eggs, and feed their growing chicks, while the ocean remains ice-free and krill is abundant. Furthermore, the chicks themselves need time to fledge and feed themselves up before winter sets in.

The bulk of chinstrap penguins breed on the South Sandwich, South Shetland and South Orkney islands, as well as on the arm of the Antarctic Peninsula. The largest colony of all is on Zavodovski, one of the South Sandwich Islands, shown right, where an estimated 1 million pairs of chinstraps breed. The reason for the popularity of this island is two-fold. First, the surrounding waters are particularly rich in krill. Second, the island is an active volcano and the heat from the crater and the fumaroles keeps the slopes free of snow. That means that chinstraps can start breeding early in the season and that their chicks will fledge sooner and have longer to fatten up before the dark days of winter. Clearly, the benefits of breeding on this active volcano must outweigh the considerable risks.

In the third week after hatching they congregate into groups while the parents are away feeding, and by the end of the fourth week they are developing their adult plumage. In early February, after a growth period of nearly eight weeks, Adélie chicks are ready to fledge.

Large visitors

The need for open water and access to krill is as important for whales as it is for penguins. Six different species of whale – humpback, right, blue, fin, sei and minke – visit the Antarctic to eat krill. They are all baleen whales, and use their hanging plates of baleen – a horny material made of keratin – to sieve krill out of the water. Most of them spend the winter in tropical waters, where they give birth to their calves before mating again. Being nutrient-poor and warm, the tropics are not good feeding grounds, so whales do not eat and they lose weight. The return to colder waters, especially the Southern Ocean where krill abounds, marks the start of their feeding season.

Humpbacks are probably the most commonly seen whale along the Antarctic Peninsula. Here they can be found resting quietly ('logging') at the surface or feeding. When the krill is in dense swarms at the surface, humpbacks simply open their cavernous mouths and lunge at them, taking in vast quantities of water as well as krill. Water spills out through the top of their mouths, while the krill remain trapped by the baleen's bristles.

If krill is less concentrated, the whales have to work harder for their food. Usually in pairs, they dive down steeply, lifting their tail flukes skyward and disappearing for a minute or two. Deep below the surface the whales swim together in a spiral, releasing bubbles from their blow-holes as they do so. This rising curtain or net of bubbles concentrates krill into the centre of the spiral, then the whales appear through the middle, mouths agape. Water is squeezed out of their mouths by the contraction of the extended throat pleats and by raising the muscular tongue, and a mouthful of krill is swallowed.

Right whales are sometimes seen 'skim feeding', but only when krill is at the surface. They swim along with their mouths open and their heads raised slightly out of the water. Krill is caught on the baleen, and water simply passes through. When enough krill has accumulated, the whale closes its mouth and swallows. Right whales have been seen using their tails as makeshift sails, holding them up to catch the wind and thus being propelled through the water. After an intensive feeding season lasting 3–4 months during the Antarctic summer, the whales head north again.

1. Killer whales exploit the channels and gaps in breaking pack ice to hunt for penguins and seals.

SOUTH GEORGIA

Scattered around the Southern Ocean are a number of isolated islands. Some lie close to the Antarctic continent and are under its icy influence for at least part of the year; others are well beyond its reach and are virtually temperate, having no permanent ice-caps or significant glaciers; in between lie the sub-Antarctic islands. Although only tiny dots in a great expanse of ocean, these islands are vital to the animals that live in the area. Because there is so little exposed land in the Southern Ocean, and because its waters are so rich, sub-Antarctic islands are crammed with life. Their climates (-10 °C/15 °F in winter, rising to +20 °C/70 °F in summer) allow year-round occupation by those that need it.

2. Black-browed albatrosses nest high on the cliffs of sub-Antarctic islands.

They build perfectly round nests of mud where they raise one chick.

1. Macaroni penguins lay two eggs, the first of which rarely hatches; this is possibly an evolutionary shift towards laying one egg.

Abundant bird life

The beaches, grassy slopes and cliffs of South Georgia are alive with birds. Penguins, petrels, prions, shearwaters and albatrosses each find their own preferred place to nest. In an ocean where land is at such a premium, birds cannot be choosy about nesting close to each other, so they form enormous colonies. While most birds choose sheltered spots out of the wind, albatrosses opt for grassy cliffs exposed to the prevailing winds, which they need in order to fly. Most impressive among these birds is the wandering albatross, the largest flying bird in the world. With a wing span of 3.5 m (12 feet), it quarters the entire Southern Ocean looking for food. All albatrosses use the updrafts of waves to fly, but none so spectacularly as the wanderer. This bird glides over the tempestuous ocean with ease, reaching speeds of nearly 90 kph (55 mph), and travelling for weeks at a time without expending precious energy. Only the Southern Ocean, with its uninterrupted swathe of open water providing consistent winds and an abundance of food, can support these magnificent birds.

Shoreline occupants

The shores of South Georgia are dominated by seals and penguins. Smaller penguins, such as the macaronis, nest in vast, deafening colonies on rocky slopes. In fact, South Georgia boasts by far the largest population, with about 5.5 million breeding pairs. Their dependence on krill as a source of food is proof that the waters surrounding this outpost are extremely rich: macaronis do not travel far in search of food, and they waste little energy in finding it. They typically venture out on overnight foraging trips, feeding when the krill is nearer the surface. While their occasional daytime dives are to depths of 20–80 m (65–250 feet), their night dives rarely go below 20 m (65 feet).

King penguins are strictly sub-Antarctic, or warmer, penguins. These large, distinguished-looking birds, standing nearly a metre (3 feet) tall, closely resemble emperor penguins.

3

However, they weigh only 10–15 kg (20–30 lb), less than half the weight of their more southerly counterpart. King penguins rely on squid and, to a lesser extent, fish to rear their brown, fluffy, bear-like chicks. They are found only on islands free of sea ice because their chicks take over 12 months to rear, so year-round access to their breeding beaches is essential.

Summer visitors

During the summer months many of South Georgia's beaches are virtually impassable – they are covered and defended by seals. Elephant and fur seals return to the protected bays and breed in their thousands on the beaches. Where elephant seals are simply intimidating because of their immense size,

fur seals are downright aggressive and will bite or even chase intruders. They are, of course, simply defending a harem of breeding females or protecting a young pup, depending on which sex launches the attack.

Fur seals, like macaroni penguins, eat krill and usually save their energy by foraging for it between dusk and dawn when it is nearer the surface. During the extended nursing period of almost four months, the females leave their pups and go to sea to feed for 3–4 days at a time. Left on their own, the pups are vulnera-ble, with over 10 per cent getting crushed in crowded colonies. As they grow, the pups play in groups and splash around in pools, where it is safer to learn to swim than the sea, where the occasional predatory leopard seal lurks.

3. King penguins tend to live in massive colonies. The breeding cycle takes 14–16 months to complete, so within a colony there are chicks at different stages of development.

◆ TOPIC LINKS

2.3 The Need to Breed
p.92 Sea Bird Cities
p.95 Out in the Open
p.97 Mammals Return

5.1 The Polar Regions
p.227 Living Beneath Ice

6.1 Ocean Wide, Ocean Blue
p.270 Airborne Divisions

Finite bounty

This annual migration has been shadowed by man in the last two centuries. Captain James Cook's voyages in the 1770s explored parts of the Southern Ocean and he wrote about the abundance of seals and whales to be found there. His reports came at a time when the stocks of northern seals had been exhausted by British and American sealers, and they were looking for new opportunities. Quick to capitalize on the information, the sealers moved south. First the southern fur seals were taken, and by 1822 were all but extinct. The elephant seals were then targeted, as their skin made strong leather and their blubber produced an oil as clear and valuable as whale oil. Finally, the penguins were butchered for their oil. By the late nineteenth century, most of the sub-Antarctic islands had been stripped of their seals and penguins.

Then came the turn of the whalers. When North Atlantic stocks became depleted, the whalers moved south and there was an explosive growth in the Southern Ocean whaling industry. Numerous whaling stations were built to handle the catch, and in the 1912–13 season alone nearly 11,000 whales were caught and processed. The peak of the whaling boom was the 1937–8 season, when 46,000 whales were taken. By 1965, a grand total of 175,000 blue, humpback, right, fin, sei and sperm whales had gone and all these species were considered commercially extinct.

The extraordinary depletion in whale numbers has affected other animals in the Southern Ocean. With the removal of the whales, a surplus of krill, estimated at 70–150 million tonnes, became free for exploitation by others. Fur seals, once thought to be biologically extinct, recovered their numbers, and now over 3 million are living on the beaches

of South Georgia alone. Adélie, chinstrap and gentoo penguins have all benefitted as have crabeater seals. Even minke whales, considered too small to be commercially viable in the heyday of whaling, managed to maintain a stable population, despite being targeted since.

By the end of commercial whaling, only 1 per cent of the original population of blue, right and humpback whales was left. It was hoped, however, that the extra krill available would soon allow whale numbers to recover. The process will be inevitably slow because whales breed only every 2–3 years. Moreover, if other species that rely on krill have done so well, perhaps the increased competition for krill will also slow the process. On the other hand, the whales that did survive have responded positively to the abundance of food. The age of maturity – when individuals start to breed – in blue, fin, sei and minke whales is significantly lower than it used to be.

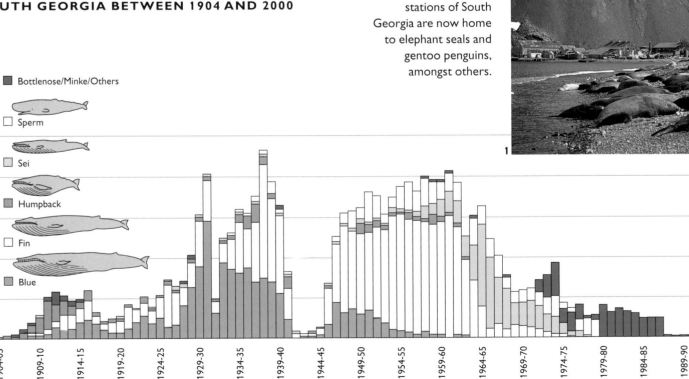

GRAPH TO SHOW THE NUMBER OF WHALES CAUGHT IN SOUTH GEORGIA BETWEEN 1904 AND 2000

1. The disused whaling stations of South Georgia are now home to elephant seals and gentoo penguins, amongst others.

Number of whales caught (thousands)

■ Bottlenose/Minke/Others
□ Sperm
□ Sei
■ Humpback
□ Fin
■ Blue

Year

DARK DAYS OF AUTUMN

In March, as summer turns to autumn, the sea ice is at its minimum. The nights become noticeably darker, the days a little colder. Snow, when it lands, settles rather than melts away, and the sea begins to freeze. The mood of the Antarctic changes as it begins to shut down for winter.

Sinuous predators

Leopard seals are probably the most feared of all seals. About 3 m (10 feet) long with disproportionately large heads, they have a massive lower jaw and a wide gape, which they display when threatened. Combined with their sinuous bodies they can be intimidating, although they rarely bite humans.

For other animals diving in Antarctic waters it is very different. Leopard seals are opportunists, taking whatever prey they can, so penguins, young seals, birds, fish and krill all fall victim to their impressive array of teeth. For such a well-armed predator, a surprising 40–45 per cent of their diet is krill, which they catch by using their interlocking lobed teeth, similar to those of crabeater seals.

Leopard seals live mostly on the edge of the pack ice, though some prowl the waters near penguin rookeries, hoping to catch an adult in the shallows. But adult penguins are wise to leopard seals and either wait on the shore or, if coming back to land from a feeding trip, swim around offshore until there is no sign of them. Nevertheless, during the summer, when both penguin parents must go to and from the rookery frequently in order to feed their growing chick, adults are taken. The leopard seal will wait in hiding until the penguins build their confidence and swim for it. Then, suddenly, with extraordinary acceleration, it appears through the murky water and grabs an unsuspecting bird. Penguin skin

is tough, so leopard seals skin their prey before eating it. This is a grisly affair, with the penguin being thrashed back and forth at the surface until its flesh is clean of skin.

The aftermath

In late summer and early autumn leopard seals gather near penguin rookeries and wait for the chicks to fledge. The adult penguins begin to feed their chicks closer to the shore and even guide them to the water's edge. Some adults stop returning to feed them altogether, so that the urge to leave the rookery and venture into the sea to feed for themselves overtakes the hungry chicks. They stack up at the water's edge, uncertain about what to do next. Gliding patiently beneath are the leopard seals. As the penguin chicks enter the water for the first time, some dive underneath and swim away confidently; others become easy prey for the seals.

2. Leopard seals prowl the waters around penguin colonies, waiting to pick off inexperienced chicks as they take to the water for the first time.

3. Adélie penguin chicks that are weak, or stray from the crèche, may fall victim to giant petrels.

The death toll is not as large as it might be. In one Adélie colony of 200, 000 pairs, an estimated 1200 chicks were lost to leopard seals in one season. However, in the same year 4800 adults had already been taken, so perhaps the leopard seals were sated by the time the chicks fledged. As the days go by, and more and more fledglings leave the rookery, leopard seals, no longer hungry, play with their prey like cat and mouse. They catch a penguin, and then let it go, half-drowning it before catching it again. Eventually the young penguin dies of exhaustion or drowns.

Stripped of its meat, a penguin carcass sinks. Before long, the chemicals released by the carcass attract scavengers. The first to arrive might be a giant, alien-like crustacean called *Glyptonotus antarcticus*. This weird-looking, well-armoured creature grows to about 20 cm (8 in) long and occupies the niche dominated by crabs elsewhere in the world. The low temperatures and scant supplies of food can lead to slow growth and gigantism in invertebrates, and some of these creatures can be extremely large. Moving slowly, they crawl across the seabed in search of food.

Emerging more slowly, but in far greater numbers, come nemertine or 'ribbon' worms.

These metre-long worms 'smell' the carcass and follow the gradient of the chemicals until they are upon it. Within a few days of falling to the sea floor, all that can be seen of the penguin carcass is a knotted mass of worms.

Overwintering species

While other seals gradually move north with the open pack ice, remaining ahead of the solid autumn freeze, Weddell seals stay put. These are the most southerly occurring mammals, except man, and they are the only ones to live, year round in areas of fast-ice that remain in some bays. To avoid the worst of the cold and storms, and to be able to feed, Weddell seals spend a large part of the winter under water. Like all mammals they need air to breathe, so when the sea begins to freeze over, they seek out cracks in the ice. But as days go by and the temperature drops further even these cracks threaten to freeze over, so Weddells must keep the breathing holes open themselves. Using their large incisor and canine teeth, they scrape away at the ice, but this punishing necessity takes its toll over the years: their teeth wear down, their gums become abscessed and they die young.

Weddell seals are built for life under the ice. They have small heads, rotund, blubber-lined bodies about 3 m (10 feet) long, and large eyes to compensate for the low light levels they experience both in winter and at depth where they feed. They eat fish and squid, which they find by diving 200–400 m (650–1300 feet), though some dive as deep as 700 m (2300 feet). These feeding dives are short, lasting only 5–25 minutes, whereas exploratory dives, which are shallow, can last over an hour.

Females are pregnant during the winter, giving birth on the sea ice in spring. Free from the threat of land predators, Weddell seals can leave newborn pups alone while they return to the water to feed. At birth the pups weigh 25–30 kg (50–60 lb), but after 6–8 weeks of being fed on fat-rich milk, they quadruple their weight.

Like crabeater seals, the male Weddell seals wait for the females to come back into oestrus. The best place to gain access to the females is near the breathing holes, and males set up territories under the ice. They advertise their presence to other competing males by vocalizing: the trilling, groaning and hooting form a slow, haunting call that penetrates far into the Antarctic waters still blanketed by ice.

1. (opposite) Weddell seals give birth to pups that weigh 25–30 kg (50–60 lb). But after only 6–8 weeks of being suckled on extremely fat-rich milk, the pups quadruple their weight.

2. Nemertine worms and starfish feed on the sea floor. Attracted to decaying matter, these scavengers seek out penguin carcasses, seal faeces and other available food.

Overleaf: When their parents are feeding at sea, emperor chicks congregate in crèches and huddle together tightly to conserve heat when it is cold.

2

EMPEROR PENGUINS

At over a metre high and weighing between 30 and 40 kg (65 and 90 lb), emperor penguins are most impressive birds. But it is not just their size that earns them such respect; they are the only birds to overwinter in the Antarctic. As the sea begins to freeze in the autumn, all the other birds, having completed the year's breeding, head north to escape the winter. Emperor penguins, however, go against the flow and head south, emerging from the sea as soon as the ice is strong enough to bear their weight.

1. Colonies are usually sited far enough from open water to ensure that, in summer, the receding ice edge does not reach the colony before the chicks are ready to fledge. In some places that is only a few miles, in others it may be over 160 km (100 miles).

Icy nests

In April and May emperor penguins make their way across the newly frozen sea ice to their traditional breeding colonies, which are sheltered from the worst of the prevailing winds and where the ice is stable. Easy access to open water is clearly an advantage.

On arriving at the colony, emperors find partners and have a noisy courtship that lasts 3–5 weeks, during which time the pair learn to recognize each other's call. One large egg, about 12 cm (5 in) long, is laid in late May or early June and the male quickly secretes it under a feathered fold of his abdominal skin to keep it warm in the months to come.

1

Without further ado, the female heads back to sea to resume feeding and does not see her partner again for two months.

Enduring the worst

Male emperor penguins, having already lost 25 per cent of their body weight during the courtship period, now endure a further 65 days without food. Their feathers and underlying layer of fat are designed to maintain their body heat, when temperatures fall below -20° C (-4 °F) and winds blow at 200 kph (125 mph). To save energy, the penguins huddle together for warmth, taking it in turns to bear the brunt of the storms. By doing this they expose only one-sixth of their body to the winds and thus save a substantial amount of energy.

The female returns to the colony just as the chick hatches. The timing is critical because the male can give the chick only one or two measly mouthfuls of a secretion from the wall of his crop. If the female is late, he has no choice but to abandon the chick and head to the sea to feed himself. Having not eaten for three months, he has lost 40 per cent of his body weight and cannot afford to wait longer.

Out to sea

On arriving at the colony, the female calls, finds her partner and takes the tiny chick from him, snuggling it under her feathers. The male then heads out to sea, where he feeds up, restoring his condition. During the 3–5 weeks that he is away, the female has sole charge of the chick, feeding it regurgitated food on demand. As spring arrives and the ice begins to melt back, getting to and from the ice edge becomes easier and the parents alternate chick duty more frequently. After only 5–6 weeks the chicks form crèches and huddle together for warmth. This increasing independence allows both adults to go foraging at sea at the same time. By late December or early January, although the chicks retain much of their grey down and weigh less than a third of an adult, they are ready to fledge. Some wait for the ice to break up around them, while others march to the ice edge and boldly take the plunge.

2. Emperor penguin chicks are fed and kept warm in their parents' brood pouch for the first two months after hatching.

3. Being most vulnerable at the ice edge, where leopard seals lurk, emperor penguins take it at a flying leap.

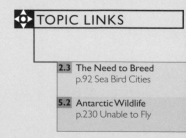

◆ TOPIC LINKS

2.3 The Need to Breed
p.92 Sea Bird Cities

5.2 Antarctic Wildlife
p.230 Unable to Fly

ARCTIC WILDLIFE

Like Antarctica, the Arctic Ocean is an ice machine; it endlessly spawns bergs and floes that drift away into neighbouring seas. But, in contrast to Antarctica, the Arctic is not an isolated continent in a massive ocean: it is a frozen ocean encircled by continents. This geographical fact has shaped the biology of the animals that live there. The surrounding land-masses have been places from where predators have had easy access to the shore in summer for many thousands of years. Many of these hunters have learnt to treat the frozen sea of winter and spring as an extension of their hunting platform. As a result, much of the behaviour of the Arctic's wildlife is governed by the presence of a handful of predators. All likely prey animals are vigilant, wary and easily scared. Only the giant bowhead whales are immune from the threat of the Arctic's dominant predator, the polar bear. But if man is included in the list of top predators living in the Arctic, then even bowhead whales have to be on their guard.

SEA-ICE PREDATORS

While the main predator of the Arctic sea ice is the polar bear, other animals also exert an impact. Wolves occasionally venture out from land to hunt for young seal pups, but they never travel far, preferring to remain on terra firma. Arctic foxes also pose a threat. In spring they sniff out newly born ringed seal pups, but can penetrate their lairs only if the snow covering is not too thick. In some parts of the Arctic, such as the Beaufort Sea, the foxes have more success because of the milder climatic conditions. Here as many as 26 per cent of pups fall prey to foxes in spring. Throughout the Arctic, foxes trail bears, following their footprints and moving in on the remains of a kill when the bear has finished.

Pupping in safety

Polar bears are indiscriminate predators, so Arctic animals have evolved various ways of avoiding them. Harp seals – best known, perhaps, for their pretty, white-coated pups, which were once harvested in thousands for

1. Arctic foxes shadow polar bears on the sea ice in the hope of scavenging a meal from the remains of a bear kill.

their pelts – give birth, or whelp, on unstable pack ice on the Atlantic side of the Arctic. Out on the shifting ice, these seals are less likely to encounter hunting bears in early spring. The pups' white coats act as camouflage in the snow; another anti-predator strategy. In addition, harp seals have a very short breeding season. They suckle their pups with milk that contains 45 per cent fat (compared to 4 per cent in cow's milk), and in only 12 days the pup is fully independent, having tripled its weight since birth to 35 kg (77lb). This brief nursing period means that mother and pup are obliged to stay on the unstable pack ice for a very short time.

All true Arctic seal pups have white natal fur, or lanugo, at some stage in their development. Most are born with it and retain it for a few days or weeks before moulting, but lanugo insulates the pups only when it is dry. As seal pups learn to swim very young, they have to rely on other means of staying warm. By they time they graduate to the water, most pups have already acquired enough blubber to insulate them against the cold. The hooded seal pup pre-empts this process. It moults while still inside its mother's womb and there develops an embryonic layer of blubber to keep warm.

Hooded seals also breed on the precarious pack ice to avoid polar bears, but they are even faster than harp seals at producing independent pups. After only four days of nursing on milk that is over 60 per cent fat, a hooded seal pup has doubled its weight and is abandoned by its mother. This is the shortest lactation period known for any mammal.

During this brief nursing period, male hooded seals haul out on the ice and guard their chosen mates against rivals. When a male is challenged, he inflates a skin sac on top of his head into a two-humped 'hood'. More impressively, to woo the female he wants to mate with, or to ward off a rival, he inflates his nasal septum until it emerges as a large, red balloon. This he shakes up and down to produce a knocking sound. With such a repertoire of displays and threats, actual fights between rival males are rare. When the female has abandoned her pup, she mates with the attendant male, before swimming off to resume feeding.

1. Harp seal pups are born with white coats to camouflage them against the snow. This, and the fact that they are born on drifting pack ice, reduces the chances of predation by bears, foxes and wolves.

2. Ringed seals, so named because of the markings on their coats, are the favoured prey of polar bears. The bears have greater success hunting inexperienced young pups rather than adults such as this one.

1

Ringed seals

Further north, where in spring the sea ice is solid and locked fast to the land, ringed seals give birth. Since they are free from the dangers of losing the pup in moving or crushing ice, these small seals, have a much longer weaning period of 6–7 weeks. The problem with living in the solid sea-ice zone is that polar bears and foxes pose a threat to newborn pups. To reduce the risk of predation, ringed seals give birth to their pups in lairs, little caves under the snow, which can be found along pressure ridges. These ridges form early in winter, when moving sheets of sea ice collide with each other and buckle up under the impact. They become covered with snow and by spring can be seen as meandering ridges that stretch across the solid sea ice for miles. The small size of ringed seals (4–5 kg/9–11 lb at birth and only 65 kg/150 lb as adults) is unusual for cold-climate animals, but it allows them to make use of the natural 'caves' under the snow. Inside the temperature remains between 0 and 2 °C (32 and 36 °F), while outside it can drop to -30 °C (-22 °F).

Ringed seals are the Arctic equivalent of Antarctic Weddell seals: both breed on the solid sea ice, but many aspects of their biology are different because one species is free from the threat of polar bears and the other is not. For example, ringed seals use a number of breathing-holes spread over a wide area because they cannot risk continually returning to one hole where a bear might be waiting. Also, ringed seal pups learn to swim while they are still lactating, and spend about half their time in the water. Although they tend to stay close to the surface, seal pups have been known to dive to 90 m (300 feet) and stay under water for 12 minutes. Their innate skill allows them to move confidently from one breathing-hole to another and their white coats provide camouflage when they haul out in the sun.

2

PEOPLE OF THE ARCTIC

There are 23 different major ethnic groups living around the Arctic from Alaska to Greenland and through northern Europe to the Chukchi Sea. Some are primarily land-based, relying on herds of reindeer or caribou for food and clothing, while others live on the coast, and depend on the sea for their needs. All these people, properly known as Inuit rather than Eskimos (a nineteenth-century term, meaning 'eaters of raw flesh'), are noted for their adaptation to the harsh Arctic environment.

1

Origins

There have been three significant waves of people and culture across the Arctic. The first were the Palaeoeskimos, who crossed the land-bridge of Beringia to reach the North American continent 20,000 years ago. These people slowly spread eastwards to Greenland. The second wave, about 3000–2500 years ago, led to the emergence of the so-called Dorset culture, whose people clustered on the coast, perhaps retreating from Native Americans moving up from the south. New tools were developed, including the first stone lamps, and large winter homes were dug into the ground. Their move to the coast meant that they looked increasingly to the sea for survival. Dorset people were probably the first to build snow houses or igloos, and perfected the art of harpooning seals at their breathing holes.

While the Dorset people remained isolated in Canada and Greenland, a third wave of Inuit were fast evolving in Alaska. The Thule Inuit, as they became known, had good canoes and

developed the use of sewn animal skins for floats, which allowed them to hunt large marine mammals, particularly whales, in the open sea. The reason behind their great migration east across Canada and into Greenland is not known; possibly it was a result of a warming climate, which melted the ice and allowed whales to spread further afield, with the Thule people in pursuit. However, by 1000 years ago they had replaced the Dorset people right

2

across the Arctic. They lived well, had large villages, stocked up with food in summer and spent winters snug in their houses of whale-bone, earth sods and skins. Then, during the sixteenth century, the Thule culture died out, possibly through a combination of climate change, disease and European whaling activities. The Inuit who descended from them were less sophisticated and returned to eking out a hard-won existence from the sea and the land.

1. The ability to build an igloo quickly, for protection against the elements, is still valued in the high Arctic, though today most hunters use tents.

2. In a summer camp, Inuit cut up and dry the skin, blubber and meat of beluga whales for use in the winter months.

3

Survival

The Inuit were totally self-sufficient and had little long-term impact on the ecosystem: when food became scarce, they moved on, loading their few possessions on to a sledge partly made of frozen fish and drawn by dogs. They travelled on the sea in open, skin-covered canoes, called umiaks, which were also useful for transporting goods and hunting whales. Their readiness to travel meant that the Inuit culture spread right across the Arctic. In winter they built igloos, which could be erected in less than an hour and warmed to a cosy 10 °C (50 °F) by a seal oil stove.

Hunting was the Inuit means of survival. On open water, hunters used a kayak, a light and durable canoe having a frame of bones and driftwood bound together with walrus hide thonging and covered with sealskin. This craft allowed hunters to approach seals

sleeping on ice floes without being heard. When the sea was frozen, dogs would be used to sniff out the seals' snow-covered breathing holes or to chase down polar bears. Every part of the animals they caught was used for food, heat and light, shelter, clothing, tools and weapons. Even today, Inuit use sealskin boots rather than modern synthetic ones, as they are considerably warmer.

Although they no longer depend on seals, whales, polar bears and caribou, the Inuit still hunt them, but their methods have changed. Dogs have been universally replaced by skidoos, kayaks by small boats with outboard engines, and harpoons by high-powered rifles. Without doubt, the success rate of hunters using modern gear is far greater, and with a human population that is expanding fast, there is an increasing and, to some, a worrying, impact on marine life.

3. Dog teams are still kept by some communities, though they are mostly used to take white hunters out on polar bear shoots. Skidoos have superseded dogs as a means of transport.

TOPIC LINKS

5.1 The Polar Regions
p.216 Arctic Sea
p.218 Out in the Cold

HUNTING

Despite ringed seals strategically reducing the risks, they are the main prey of polar bears from April to July. During that time the bears acquire enough energy to last them through the leaner summer months, and almost invariably it is seal pups that provide it. At the beginning of the season, when the pups are still hidden in their lairs, polar bears spend many of their waking hours walking the pressure ridges in search of them.

Insatiable appetites

Polar bears have a hard time on the sea ice in winter, particularly during December and January, when the weather is appalling. If conditions get really intolerable, bears dig a rough pit to escape the wind, or simply lie down behind a shelter of some kind. Only the pregnant females remain buried in winter dens for about four months. They do not feed at all during that time, emerging from their dens in March and early April when their cubs are about three months old. By this time the mothers have lost one-third or more of their body weight and are near starvation. For two weeks or so they remain near their dens, allowing their cubs, usually twins, to become accustomed to the outside world and to gain strength and coordination by playing. Eventually, the families venture down from their mountain retreats and out on to the sea ice, driven by the mothers' desperate need for food.

Their timing is perfect. Just when the females begin to hunt, ringed seal pups are starting to acquire a nourishing layer of blubber. Despite all the precautions ringed seals take in order to avoid predation, they cannot evade the bears' astonishingly acute sense of smell: a polar bear can smell a seal hidden under the snow at a distance of 2 km (1.5 miles). As it nears the exact location, it slows almost to a halt, all the while sniffing and listening for the tell-tale signs of a seal pup. Alert and tense, the bear creeps forward, carefully placing its huge paws on the snow so as not to make the slightest sound. Suddenly, it makes an almighty leap and throws its full weight on to its front paws, crashing through the snow into the lair beneath. If, on the first lunge, the bear does not break through into the lair, it rears up on its hind legs and pounds the snow again and again. The seal pup beneath has only one escape hole to the sea; if that is blocked by the

1. Ringed seal pups are hidden in lairs under the snow. Polar bears need stealth to catch them; if alarmed, a pup will escape to the sea below.

2. A female bear with cubs needs to be a successful huntress; if she fails, she stops producing milk and her cubs will die. Yearling cubs also depend on their mothers' kills for meat.

1

2

first pounce the pup is unlikely to survive. But if it hears the bear, or manages to reach its hole, it can dive into the sea beneath unharmed.

The success rate of bears hunting for ringed seal pups varies according to the snow conditions. Where it is soft and the bear easily breaks through into the lair, one in every three attempts can be successful. In less favourable conditions the rate is more like one in every 20 attempts. As spring progresses and ringed seal pups convert milk into fat, they become increasingly valuable as a source of food. Polar bears will continue feeding on inexperienced pups whose bodies are 50–75 per cent fat, until the ice breaks up in summer. By then the female bears, who lost so much body weight over

the winter, will have replenished their reserves and be ready for the leaner months ahead.

Summer melt

In June there is a tangible change in the Arctic: the ice begins to melt back in earnest. Where, throughout April and May, the sea ice seemed a stable platform, albeit only a metre or two thick, in June it begins to lose its solidity. Strong winds can break off great floes, which drift into open water and disintegrate quickly. The heat of the midday sun produces melt-pools, which grow and merge until the entire sheet of ice becomes merely a series of isolated lumps.

The northern equivalent of krill – the animals that dominate the zooplankton – are copepods. They, too, are small crustaceans that appear in their millions as the summer sun triggers a phytoplankton bloom upon which they feed. There are four main species of copepod, but the most important in the food chain is called *Calanus hyperboreus*. Its three-year life cycle includes a year for development from egg to a juvenile form, another year to reach near-adulthood and a third year to mature and spawn. During the winter, copepods stay below 300 m (1000 feet), rising to spend the summer between the surface and 100 m (330 feet), where light penetrates far enough for phytoplankton to photosynthesize.

⭐ Belugas, bowheads and narwhals have no dorsal fin, so they can dive and feed under ice without fear of damaging themselves.

The distribution of copepods is patchy, but where they are found in significant numbers, their predators will also find them. Birds, such as northern fulmars, migrate north to feed on the zooplankton during the summer and also to raise their chicks. Other Arctic birds that remain in the high latitudes all year round tend to rely on other sources of food. Brünnich's guillemot, or the thick-billed murre, is a hardy northern bird which specializes in feeding on Arctic cod during the summer, when it can get access to them beneath the retreating ice. At other times of year these guillemots have a more varied diet, which includes squid, crustaceans and bottom-dwelling fish. In total there are 50 species of Arctic sea bird, which include terns, fulmars and cormorants, as well as 14 species of auk, guillemot and razorbill, and 10 species of gull and skua. These birds breed in June and July on the towering cliffs surrounding the Arctic Ocean, high above the menace of hungry bears.

Migration north

As in the Antarctic, there is a huge migration of animals into the areas of retreating Arctic ice. Some feed exclusively on copepods, others on fish. Belugas, sometimes called white whales, and narwhals spend the winter in areas of open water, then follow the retreating ice edge in spring and through the summer, gaining access to feeding grounds untouched throughout the winter. They use leads (cracks in the ice), which open up as the ice gives way, to penetrate further into frozen inlets.

There are at least five different, separate stocks of beluga, whose migration patterns and diets vary according to location. One population, which overwinters near the Chukchi Peninsula and follows the ice up through the Beaufort Sea, spends the month of July moulting in the Mackenzie Delta. The males then travel 1000 km (600 miles) eastwards to spend August feeding in a deep

1. Brünnich's guillemots nest on ledges high on sea cliffs. Here, they and their developing chicks remain out of the reach of predators, such as polar bears and foxes.

2. Beluga whales use 'leads', natural channels in the ice, to migrate towards their summer feeding grounds.

1

trench in the Canadian archipelago. Here they dive to 550 m (1800 feet) to catch either Arctic cod or Greenland halibut. Female and young belugas, which are smaller and therefore have a smaller lung capacity, use other feeding grounds, where the seabed is only 200–450 m (650–1500 feet) deep.

The only baleen whale that remains north and is a true Arctic whale is the bowhead. Although bowheads spend the winter in areas where the sea ice is broken, they are on the move as early as April and May. Even before the ice begins to fracture, they begin their noisy migration back to their summer feeding grounds, breaking a trail through the still-frozen sea ice. Bowheads move in loose groups, maintaining contact by low moans and screeches and working as a team to find the best route through the ice. These massive whales, some 80–100 tonnes in weight, feed on the tiny copepods and other zooplankton in the water column.

2

GIANT TOOTH

All male narwhals (and the occasional female) have a single, spirally fluted tusk, which grows out through the upper lip. It is extremely rare to see a narwhal with two tusks, but they do exist and are prized by Inuit hunters.

The tusk first shows as a small, finger-sized tooth when the narwhal is a year old, and it grows slowly until the whale reaches sexual maturity around eight or nine years later. Then a spurt occurs and the tusk grows up to 2 m (6.5 feet) long and weighs some 6–9 kg (13–19 lb).

The role of the tusk has not yet been determined. In summer, the males can be seen gently crossing tusks (see picture, right), but no serious combat has been observed. It is possible that this 'tusking' is used as a way of testing the relative strengths of potential rivals so that during the spring mating season a whale does not waste his energy and risk injury fighting with a stronger opponent. Certainly, one third of males have broken tusks and many have scars around their heads – testimony to battles of some sort. However, the ivory at the end of the tusk is invariably smooth and well worn, which suggests that it has another role.

⭐ Female polar bears give birth in winter dens. The cubs weigh a little over 500 g (18 oz) and are blind for 30 days.

HALCYON DAYS

By July the ice is rotten, and in some places only remnants of ice floes litter the open water. Sea birds, ringed seals, harp seals, bearded seals, walrus, beluga, narwhal, bowheads and others all benefit from the open water and the access to feeding grounds. Copepods and other zooplankton are eaten by bowhead whales and Arctic cod, which in turn feed the seals and other whales. But at this time of year, when all the other Arctic residents are doing so well, polar bears, the top predator, lose their edge.

Ice-free summer

Ringed seals are less vulnerable to bears during the summer, as they have the freedom of open water. Nevertheless, bears continue to stay on what little ice remains as it is cooler than land and they are more likely to encounter seals basking in the sun. When the ice platform is riddled with melt channels and holes, bears hunt their prey using the water. Aquatic stalking, as it is called, requires stealth. Bears spot their prey at a distance and begin the long, slow approach. Keeping their heads out of sight below the ice, they negotiate the maze of channels to creep up on unsuspecting seals. When the bear is close enough it makes a grab for the seal. At this time of year, bears catch seals about once every five days by both still hunting (waiting at breathing-holes) and aquatic stalking, but the return on the hours invested slowly diminishes as the ice continues to dissolve.

1. As their icy hunting platform melts away in summer, polar bears may have to swim many miles to find land. They are excellent swimmers, using their massive front paws as paddles.

2. In late summer, when there is little ice, Pacific walruses can be found in huge herds on land. They haul out to rest on islands close to their shallow feeding grounds.

1

When floes become too small for hunting, bears are forced to swim for land. They are strong swimmers, using their large front paws for paddling, while their rear legs trail behind. They can swim for many hours and have been seen more than 100 km (62 miles) from shore, a testimony to their ease in the water. Sometimes they dive beneath the surface after a seal or a guillemot, but their chances of success are slim. Near the shore, they have been seen to dive for kelp, which can offer them little energy but is perhaps a source of nutrients.

The more southerly bears, which are forced to spend the summer on land, now enter a period of near-starvation. Some move inland to eat what berries they can find, some scavenge along the shoreline looking for anything edible, and others patrol the bottom of guillemot colonies, feeding on the meagre remains of dead birds. Until the sea ice begins to refreeze in early November, these bears suffer from the heat and the lack of food. With their heavy coats they are ill-equipped to keep cool, so inactivity serves them best, both to avoid over-heating and to save precious energy.

Walruses living further south can also be stranded by a hot summer. In August they can be found in small numbers, lying about on sandy shores in a communal, grunting heap. At this time of year they are moulting, but being well protected by a thick layer of blubber, they do not rely on their hair for insulation, and can continue feeding. Walruses eat mainly soft-shelled clams and sometimes cockles, using their bewhiskered snouts to root around on the seabed and suck them out of their shells. At other times of year Pacific walruses sometimes eat ringed seals.

The freeze

Sea birds, seals and whales all enjoy the ice-free months because there is such an abundance **2**

1

1. Arctic terns breed in the Arctic during summer, then fly over 12,000 km (7500 miles) south to spend the southern summer feeding in Antarctic waters.

2. Trapped in the ice, a young bowhead whale rises to breathe in a hole that is kept open by strong tidal currents.

3. Beluga whales, encircled by sea ice, keep their breathing hole ice-free by their continuous movement. Crowded together in such a small hole, they are vulnerable to polar bears.

of food, but the halcyon days do not last, and in September the first autumnal storms begin to blow. Then young guillemots teeter on their airy perches, ready to make a headlong plunge to the sea below. In an extraordinary display of fearlessness, they launch themselves off the cliff and, still unable to fly properly, plummet hundreds of feet with their wings outstretched. Some manage to glide to the sea, but others hit rocks, where they bounce in an unlikely manner, apparently unharmed. Accompanied by a parent bird, they head for the open water and prepare for the migration to wintering grounds.

With the bird colonies empty and the air now increasingly cold, the mood of the Arctic changes fast. The skies fill with snow-laden clouds and the days become short. Bears that have spent the late summer and autumn on land now gather near the shore and wait for the sea to freeze. In Churchill, the most southerly population of bears congregates on a headland where the sea breeze is cooler. Males play in mock fights to perfect their skills, test their strength and establish some sort of hierarchy. By getting to know their rivals' abilities now, they save themselves the danger of having to engage in serious fights the following spring when competition for receptive females is high.

When the sea eventually freezes over, the bears walk off to hunt for seals once more. As the ice freezes in a different way each year and moves with the ocean currents, bears cannot predict where seals will be found, so they are not territorial: they roam thousands of kilometres in their hunt for food. Ringed seals, however, have to breathe, so they can be found along cracks in the ice, such as near the shoreline, or areas where the sea does not freeze over completely. Thus, bears do not wander at random over the sea ice, but follow such cracks for days on end, in their hunt for food.

Polynyas

Areas of open water surrounded by ice are known as polynyas. By and large they are reliable, remaining open year after year, though in exceptionally cold years the water in small polynyas may freeze over for a few months. By March or April, however, the water will usually be ice-free again.

Polynyas are created by local conditions: tidal currents, localized winds or upwellings (▷ p. 33) can all contribute to the maintenance of open water. Their importance is far-reaching, and not only are they used by birds and mammals overwintering in the north, they are also associated with a high rate of productivity which extends down the food chain. The benefits of remaining in a patch of water surrounded by ice are clear: calmer water makes resting at the surface easier, and there is a platform nearby to haul out or sit on. There is also access to air when diving under the ice for food, and, perhaps most significantly, the algae living within the thin ice surrounding the polynya form the basis for a localized but very rich food web.

The Arctic has a number of recurring polynyas of varying shapes and sizes. The largest, called Northwater, lies in Baffin Bay, between Greenland and the eastern side of the Canadian archipelago. Proof of its importance to marine life comes from the tens of millions of sea birds that nest on nearby cliffs. Other polynyas dotted around the Arctic support bird colonies too, but none in such fantastic numbers. As sea birds are totally dependent on open water to feed, they must be within easy flying distance of a polynya so that, in summer particularly, they can make daily excursions to collect enough food for their growing chicks.

But it is not only sea birds that demonstrate the importance of polynyas. When whalers reached the high Arctic in the early

⭐ Belugas of the western Arctic leave the Beaufort Sea as it begins to freeze in autumn, and travel over 1200 km (7500 miles) to spend the winter in the Bering Sea.

nineteenth century, they targeted polynyas, such as Northwater, where bowhead whales overwintered. More recently it has been discovered that ringed seal densities near Northwater are double that of areas where there are no polynyas. And where there are ringed seals, there are polar bears. Moreover, the lower productivity in areas without significant polynyas, such as the Beaufort Sea side of the Arctic, results in animals maturing later. The consequent lower pup production, has a knock-on effect on female polar bears, who breed for the first time at five years old, a year later than bears further east.

The Arctic Ocean, though having low productivity in its very centre, where the sea is permanently frozen and thick multi-year ice reduces the amount of light penetrating to the diatoms living there, does have patches where productivity is high. The richest areas are found over the continental shelf, where nutrient input is higher and nutrient mixing is aided by currents. Here, especially in polynyas that never freeze over, marine life can be extraordinarily abundant.

THE OPEN OCEAN

6.1 OCEAN WIDE, OCEAN BLUE 262

The seemingly featureless oceans contain an invisible 'topography' of sudden changes in temperature, salinity and currents. These are perimeters that control ocean life productivity.

HABITAT ILLUSTRATED SPREAD: The open ocean

SPECIAL FEATURE: Airborne divisions

6.2 OCEAN DRIFTERS 276

There is nowhere to hide in the open ocean, so plankton engage in a constant battle to remain undetected by predators in a deadly three-dimensional game of hide and seek.

SPECIAL FEATURE: Fish that fly

6.3 OCEAN HUNTERS 288

The high seas are home to the most atheletic of all marine predators – swimming machines that are capable of blistering speed, and that can pursue prey hundreds of metres down.

SPECIAL FEATURE: Sound hunters

6.4 OCEAN BIRTH 300

All organisms must successfully reproduce, but in the ocean this is not simple: finding a mate can be difficult and the odds are heavily against surviving to adulthood.

SPECIAL FEATURE: Dolphin friendly

OCEAN WIDE, OCEAN BLUE

The open ocean is immense, stretching far beyond the narrow continental shelves that border the land. It covers an area of 361 million sq km (139 million sq miles) – more than 70 per cent of the world's surface. The Pacific Ocean alone is over 17,000 km (10,500 miles) wide and contains 50 per cent of all the world's water. The Indian, Atlantic and Pacific oceans combined have a volume of 1340 million cubic km and an average depth of 3730 m (12,230 feet). Even the warm surface layer of sea water, the uppermost 200 m (656 feet) where much of the marine life exists, has a volume of over 72 million cubic km (2540 million cubic feet). Much of this water lies in the tropical and subtropical areas of the world, and contains few nutrients and comparatively little plankton. Yet these vast tracts of blue water are home to some of the most extraordinary creatures on the planet, many of which are capable of travelling thousands of kilometres in just a matter of weeks to track down food or find mates.

Previous page: Spinner dolphin travel in 'superpods', which may number more than 1000 individuals. The noise of their chattering makes an incredible cacophony of sound.

HORIZONS IN THE OCEAN

Fly over the Pacific Ocean on a clear day and you will get some idea of its immense scale. At an altitude of 10,000 m (32,800 feet), the water appears smooth and shimmering in the reflected glare of the sun. For hour after hour, it slides beneath the plane, apparently unchanging, with only the distant speck of an occasional island to break the otherwise featureless expanse. From such a height, the horizon appears as a curved arc, disappearing into a smoky haze, and no major land mass appears over that horizon for a staggering 12 hours. The most noticeable changes come from the passage of day and night across the seascape, and the build-up of clouds as weather systems develop and sweep across the ocean.

Beneath the waves

Under the water itself the visibility may stretch to 30 m (98 feet) or more. Once below the sunlit shadows, everything appears in grey or silver because all red light has been filtered out. Deeper still the water is blue-black, with no topography and no obvious signs of life. The surface is the only feature

The biggest accurately recorded wave was 34 m (112 feet) high and travelled at 102 kph (63 mph).

1. The unbroken horizon of the open ocean. A virtual wilderness by day, most marine life has long since retreated to shelter hundreds of metres below the surface.

that changes discernibly: it is a constantly moving, shimmering interface with the air beyond. But look again more closely, for the ocean has hidden layers within: an invisible topography all its own.

The ocean's skin

The immense world of the open ocean is known as the pelagic realm. It contains many horizontal and vertical layers, the boundaries of which serve as barriers where nutrients and plankton become concentrated, creating patches of dense feeding opportunities for pelagic hunters. The most ubiquitous of these barriers is the surface of the sea itself.

The topmost metre of the ocean is quite different biologically and chemically from the rest of the water mass. Known as the neuston layer, it is comparatively rich in nutrients because many of the waste chemicals excreted by plankton in deeper water float up to the surface and concentrate there. Even larger organisms contribute to the surface chemistry when they die, because the oils and chemicals released from their decaying bodies on the seabed float upwards to collect in the neuston layer. This chemically enriched environment provides an ideal habitat for bacteria, unicellular protozoans and microscopic algae.

In the right weather and current conditions this enriched surface layer can be further concentrated into large, oily slicks, which serve as magnets for wandering oceanic life. The abundance of food attracts swarms of plankton and other larger animals.

Ocean layers

Beneath the neuston layer the ocean has several other divisions, each with significantly different water properties. The top 100–200 m (328–656 feet) of water, known as the surface layer, is warm, highly mixed and effectively floats upon the colder, denser water below. It is the sunlit zone of the ocean, where, in clear conditions, the sun's light and warmth can penetrate down to 200 m (656 feet).

Below this surface layer lies the colder and denser intermediate layer, which, at a depth of approximately 1000 m (3300 feet), gives way to the deep layer of extremely heavy, cold water. Few animals are free to journey at will between these different layers because their physical and chemical differences pose formidable physiological barriers.

Physical barriers

The water of the oceans' different layers is separated by distinct thermoclines (▷ p. 160). In tropical oceans the surface layer may be as warm as 25 °C (77 °F), while the top of the

 DEEP-DIVING BLUBBER

Around 5 m (16 feet) long and 4 tonnes in weight, the bull elephant seal (illustrated, right) is no beauty, but it is the champion of marine mammal divers. It comes to shore twice each year, once to breed and once to moult its fur. The remaining 250 days of the year are spent at sea, and in that time it migrates 21,000 km (13,000 miles) back and forth between its preferred Pacific feeding grounds and its breeding sites. Remarkable though this achievement is, it pales into insignificance when set beside the elephant seal's diving performance. This denizen of the open ocean has little time for cruising in the surface layer; instead, it heads for the deep, diving to depths of 1500 m (5000 feet) and remaining under water for up to two hours at a time. At 40 m (130 feet) down, the seal's lungs are crushed flat, so its oxygen supply comes from its huge quantity of blood, which contains special pigments to increase its oxygen-carrying capacity. Even so, the seal has to reduce its metabolism to near-dormancy, slowing its heart-rate to as little as six beats per minute. Despite the torpor that this induces, it manages to trap prey far below the minimum oxygen layer. Diving like this, it remains underwater for 90 per cent of each 24 hour day, apparently never even sleeping!

1

underlying intermediate zone may be a mere 11 °C (52 °F). The main ocean thermocline lies within the intermediate zone. Below it, the water becomes very much colder, about 5 °C (41 °F) or less. This thermocline is a permanent feature that is rarely broken down, and it proves an impenetrable barrier to most marine life in the open ocean, because it cannot cope with the sudden changes of temperature. By and large, the thermocline separates the ocean's upper-water organisms from those in the deep. Any that venture through it must develop special adaptations.

Another boundary exists within the intermediate zone. Known as the oxygen minimum layer, it marks the level below which dissolved oxygen in the water is at its minimum. Few organisms from the warm, oxygen-rich surface waters above can survive in these oxygen-depleted conditions. They are effectively trapped in the surface layer by physical and chemical boundaries.

Sinking life force

Anything that is heavier than water sinks under the influence of gravity, so many dying organisms and nutrients fall through the thermocline into the deep zone below. If the ocean were static, these sources of food would be lost for ever to life forms within the surface layer. Fortunately, oceanic water is far from static. In the polar and temperate oceans, in a process called overturn, winter chilling causes the surface water to become so dense that it sinks into the deep ocean, forcing nutrient-rich water up from the bottom. Winter storms further mix the water layers, ensuring that oceans in the far north and south of the world have high nutrient levels and can support massive plankton populations in the summer months. Subtropical and tropical oceans do not experience sufficient cooling to allow overturn to happen, so here the stable surface zone contains vastly fewer nutrients than the deep zone.

1. Sailfish are predators of the surface layer in tropical oceans. They can erect their dorsal fin to form a broad fluttering sail, which helps them to corral their prey.

THE OPEN OCEAN

To the human eye the vast tracts of open ocean stretching across our planet seem featureless and unchanging. As much of this water is found in tropical regions, the waters are relatively poor in nutrients and would not be expected to sustain a large amount of life. Nevertheless, beneath the surface live a variety of creatures, many of which are designed to travel long distances in search of food (see diagram, below). While the open ocean has its share of beautiful creatures, it also contains some of the ocean's most ferocious hunters, such as blue sharks and makos.

DAY TIME

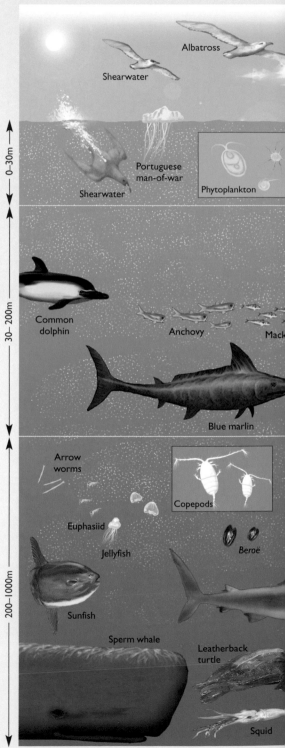

Vertical hunters

While the open ocean can be a relatively barren landscape in places, food can be found in abundance if you know how and where to seek it out.

Winds and currents are significant throughout the whole of the ocean realm, but in the open ocean, where food is sparse, they can be a lifeline. While warm-water currents are low in nutrients and plankton, they can provide safe passage for tropical species to penetrate cooler waters where food is more abundant. Cold currents, on the other hand, are rich in nutrients and attract large numbers of hungry creatures.

Some of the most efficient hunters can be found in the open water and, as there is very little cover, potential prey has had to adapt in a variety of ways. Many fish are camouflaged (see illustration, right), but perhaps the most significant way in which marine life avoids predators is to wait until darkness falls before migrating to the surface to feed. Scientists are still discovering more about this process, called vertical migration, but it is one of the largest mass movements of creatures on the planet. (The main illustration is an approximate representation of how far different creatures migrate.)

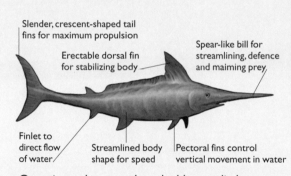

Slender, crescent-shaped tail fins for maximum propulsion

Erectable dorsal fin for stabilizing body

Spear-like bill for streamlining, defence and maiming prey

Finlet to direct flow of water

Streamlined body shape for speed

Pectoral fins control vertical movement in water

Oceanic predators such as the blue marlin have to cover vast distances, often thousands of kilometres, in search of prey. As a result, their bodies are designed to be extremely hydrodynamically efficient.

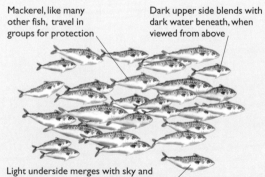

Mackerel, like many other fish, travel in groups for protection

Dark upper side blends with dark water beneath, when viewed from above

Light underside merges with sky and surface waters, when viewed from below

Most fish that live in brightly lit, open water have dark backs shading to silvery underparts for camouflage. This protects them from surface predators, as well as those that swim beneath them.

NIGHT TIME

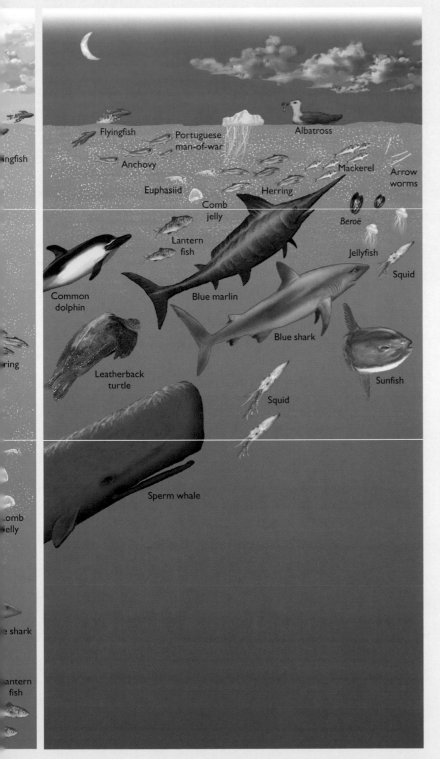

Every night, millions of tonnes of animals undertake the largest mass migration on Earth, journeying up from the twilight zone (approximately 200–1000 m/650–3200 feet down) to the richer, sunlit waters of the surface (photic zone) in search of food. In the middle of the night, the top 30 m (98 feet) of the ocean teems with plankton. At dawn, the same animals will return to the twilight zone, to avoid the attention of visual predators.

The extent of vertical migration varies between species. The smallest plankton probably travel up only 10–20 m (33–66 feet) each night, while larger animals may travel up to 1000 m (3200 feet). Lantern fish are exceptional: they travel from 1700 m (5570 feet) down, rising to within 100 m (328 feet) of the surface, and return to the depths at daybreak.

DISTRIBUTION OF MARINE LIFE

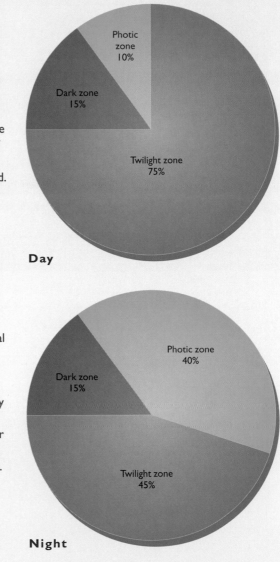

Day

Night

During the day, the photic zone contains only about 10 per cent of marine life; most creatures prefer to stay in the twilight zone, where they will not be spotted by surface predators. At night, however, the amount of life at the surface quadruples as a result of mass vertical migrations.

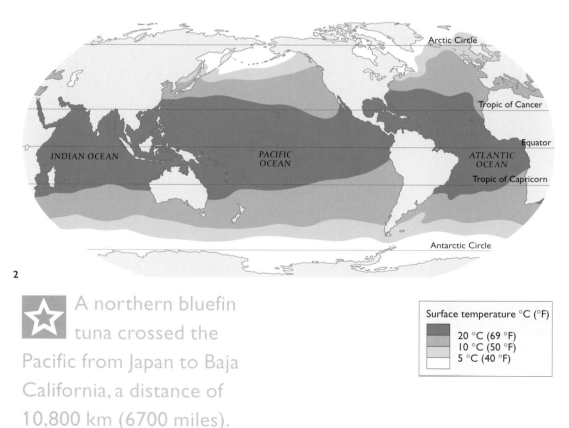

1

THE AVERAGE SEA-SURFACE TEMPERATURES OF THE OCEANS

2

A northern bluefin tuna crossed the Pacific from Japan to Baja California, a distance of 10,800 km (6700 miles).

Surface temperature °C (°F)		
	20 °C (69 °F)	
	10 °C (50 °F)	
	5 °C (40 °F)	

OCEANIC RIVERS

Global wind systems and the Coriolis effect create immense gyres in the surface water layer (▷ p. 36). Their effects produce vast currents of warm or cold water that sweep through the oceans in both the northern and southern hemispheres. These currents circulate both water and nutrients around the oceans, and their boundaries, marked by abrupt changes in the physical and chemical properties of the water, are zones that can afford opportunities to marine life.

Warm-water currents

Formed from tropical water that is driven from the Equatorial regions by the trade winds, warm currents have clear blue water, with little nutrient content and a low plankton count. One such current is the Gulf Stream, which flows from the Caribbean along the east coast of the USA and then eastwards across the North Atlantic towards northern Europe. The current is fast, moving at 6.5 kph (4 mph), and large, shifting 150 million cubic metres (5300 million cubic feet) of water per second. It is also up to 11 °C (19 °F) warmer than the surrounding ocean.

This warm water is a highway that tropical and subtropical surface-layer species can follow northwards into temperate seas. Although there is comparatively little food within the main current itself, highly adapted hunters, such as tuna, are able to make forays out into the colder, temperate water, where food is much more plentiful. Some of the densest feeding areas are found within the colder water at the borders of the current itself. Here the plankton become concentrated, attracting planktivores and their hunters. As the current moves through the ocean, small eddies are ripped from its edge, making 'islands' of warm water. These can create small, local feeding zones that attract surface-layer hunters.

3

Cold-water currents

Parts of the ocean gyres flow from the polar extremes towards the Equator. These cold-water currents are distinctive for their high nutrient concentrations. Their water is dense and slow-moving, travelling a mere 1.8 kph (1.1 mph). A classic example, the Humboldt Current, flows north from the Antarctic along the Pacific coast of Chile, carrying nutrient-rich water far into the subtropics, where the sunlight is intense and the phyto-plankton can therefore bloom to great densities. For upper-layer hunters, these

currents present immense feeding opportu-nities: the only limiting factor is the ability of the hunter to survive in cooler water, but at the Equatorial edges of the cold currents, even tropical fish are able to benefit from the nutrient-fuelled riches. The effects of the Humboldt Current are felt as far north as Panama in Central America. Here elegant sailfish are able to congregate and feed on immense schools of anchovetta, which have followed the plankton northwards. At times the Humboldt currents' nutrients fuel such dense plankton blooms here, that the tropical ocean turns a bright green or even livid red.

1. Bluefin tuna are well adapted for a migratory ocean lifestyle. They can hunt below the thermocline, to depths of over 1000 m (3280 feet), and travel thousands of miles between the tropics and temperate seas.

2. The pattern of sea surface-temperatures

is not just affected by climate: the oceans' current gyres push tongues of warm and cold water to the north and south.

3. The biggest fish in the ocean, the whale shark, travels endlessly to locate areas where the plankton supply is thickest.

AIRBORNE DIVISIONS

Albatrosses are among the top predators of the ocean. The secret to their success lies within their elegant wings, which make them the most efficient fliers in the world. They are capable of covering immense distances at speed, travelling from one feeding spot to another with consummate ease. Day or night they glide above the waves, searching for any sign of prey or carrion. Some can even swim under water, diving down to 7 m (23 feet), and all are heavily armed; their thick, curved beak is a powerful hunting tool.

2. Wandering albatrosses returning to South Georgia to breed. They take turns to leave the nest and fly as far as the coast of Brazil on feeding sorties.

1. A grey-headed albatross picks prey from the ocean surface.

Albatrosses will feed like this by night as well as day.

Wave riders

Albatrosses are large birds with a wingspan of 2–3 m (7–10 feet). The wings themselves are extremely thin, designed to create minimal drag and therefore perfect for gliding. The birds are powered by the wind, gliding across the air that is pushed in front of a wave and gradually dropping towards the water. At a critical point, they pull up to the maximum height of their flight path, some 10–15 m (33– 49 feet) above the sea, then glide back down towards the water once more. It is such an efficient form of flight that the wings are seldom flapped at all: wandering albatrosses glide for over 90 per cent of the time.

The travel statistics of wandering albatrosses defy belief. They fly at an average speed of 55 kph (34 mph), but for short periods can reach 90 kph (56 mph). They fly both by day and night, sometimes for up to 11 hours without a break, but they do rest by spending time on the sea surface at night. The distances covered are huge: one bird has been recorded as travelling 33,000 km (20,500 miles) in just 71 days. The spur to all this activity is food: if there is prey to be found, they will track it down.

Aerial attack

All the albatross species specialize in open ocean hunting. By far the major constituent of their diet is squid, which is why several species continue to hunt by night, chasing the squid that migrate near to the surface in darkness.

When a major feeding opportunity arises, such as schooling fish forced to the surface by dolphins, the albatrosses join in the surface mêlée of sea birds, running across the water with half-open wings and muscling their way to the heart of the action. Their size and weight – up to 8.5 kg (19 lb) in the case of wandering albatrosses – allows them to

3

dominate the feeding frenzy. Once above the squirming ball of fish, they simply thrust their beaks into it and take their pick.

Albatrosses can also attack prey while remaining airborne, travelling close to the surface and simply plucking victims from the water. When feeding on krill, they sit on the water and pick at them sedately.

Vulnerable giants

The albatrosses' habit of plunge-diving for squid and carrion can be dangerous, particularly where commercial fishing fleets are active. The boats, in pursuit of valuable fish such as bluefin tuna, throw out lines up to 20 km (12 miles) long, which are set with large hooks every few metres. Unfortunately, the hooks are totally indiscriminate and kill anything that bites the bait. Albatrosses fall victim to these hooks because they are simply too good at locating food.

4

3. With the largest wingspan of any sea bird, the wandering albatross glides for 90 per cent of its time in the air, searching hundreds of kilometres of ocean in a day.

4. Thousands of albatross die each year by attempting to grab bait from long-line hooks. They become hooked on the lines and drown.

◆ TOPIC LINKS

2.3 The Need to Breed
p.92 Sea Bird Cities

4.2 Blooming Plankton
p.178 Baitball

5.2 Antarctic Wildlife
p.236 South Georgia

1

1. A blue shark hunts a dense shoal of anchovies near the ocean surface. These sharks often feed on squid, diving repeatedly to depths of more than 500 m (1640 feet) to do so.

Upwelling effects

Trade winds blow to the southwest above the Equator and to the northwest below it. These winds power the North and South Equatorial Currents. The direction of the Coriolis effect changes from right to left at the Equator, so the North Equatorial Current moves surface water to the right (north), while the South Equatorial Current moves surface water to the left (south). As this happens cold, nutrient-rich water from the deep wells up in the middle to replace the surface layers. This process increases the productivity of the upper water layers in Equatorial regions, particularly in the Pacific.

Along coasts, where the prevailing wind is parallel to the land, the Coriolis effect can cause an offshore displacement of warm surface water, which is replaced by the upwelling of nutrient-rich cold water from the depths (▷ p. 33). Just such an upwelling occurs along the coast of Namibia in southern Africa, where the prevailing wind runs north. It fuels a remarkable boost in plankton productivity, attracting a staggering abundance of planktivorous fish, such as sardines. Pelagic hunters, such as dolphins, whales, fur seals, sea birds and sharks, all migrate to feed on the dense populations of prey.

MOUNTAINS IN THE OCEAN

Predators will travel huge distances to find food in the surface layers of the ocean where the current effects enrich the water. But there are other, more local influences on oceanic productivity. The Pacific Ocean alone has upwards of 25,000 islands sprinkled across its immense floor, and, like all oceans, has a varied topography. From the edges of the continental shelves to the remotest mid-ocean reaches, the sea floor is littered with canyons, mountain ranges, volcanoes and plateaux. These features can have a profound influence on the biological richness of the surface layer of the ocean, even when they remain many hundreds of metres below the surface.

Seamounts

Both the underwater flanks of islands and the submerged volcanoes known as seamounts create vortices in the flow of passing oceanic currents. These 'teeth' of rock, rising abruptly from the sea floor, force the upwelling of deep, nutrient-rich water to the surface and create a circular current effect around the island or volcano. This phenomenon helps to support localized abundances of phytoplanktonic growth. In addition, the sudden depth reduction concentrates the amount of plankton in the water: instead of being spread vertically over several hundred metres of sea water, the plankton may be compressed into mere tens of metres as it sweeps past the rocky outcrop.

Even sudden changes in the topography of the sea floor several hundred metres below the surface, can be sufficient to affect the current flow and raise productivity in the surface layer. For animals hunting in the open ocean, such underwater pinnacles, islands and topographical changes become vital oases, where the planktonic abundance can support vast schools of fish and the migratory predators will journey from one oasis to the next.

 Unlike ships, fish do not slow down to turn around. They have a turning radius of only 10 to 30 per cent of their body length, while ships require 10 times their body length.

▷ FLEXIBLE REPTILES

Leatherback turtles are cold-blooded reptiles which breathe air, yet still dive to depths in excess of 1300 m (4265 feet). Weighing up to 1000 kg (2200 lb), these giant creatures are superbly adapted navigators and divers, with a preferred diet of jellyfish. They migrate thousands of kilometres to reach their temperate feeding grounds, where immense concentrations of plankton are found in the deep scattering layer (▷ p. 328). During the night, this layer is at depths of as little as 100 m (330 feet), but by day it migrates to over 500 m (1640 feet) down. The turtles follow with ease, their bodies being coated in smooth skin to improve their hydrodynamic performance. Unlike other sea turtles, leatherbacks have a flexible shell made of ribs set in a thick, oily cartilage and covered with a pattern of bony plates. This helps them to cope with the pressures of deep diving. Most staggering of all is the speed of their dives: in as little as 10 minutes they can plummet vertically downwards for 500 m (1640 feet), feed and return to the surface, repeating the performance five times each hour.

⭐ Tuna must swim to breathe. To improve streamlining they do not pump their gill covers; instead they swim with their mouths open, forcing water past their gills.

CLIMATE CRITICAL

Most marine organisms are extremely intolerant of rapid changes in either temperature or water chemistry, so the effects of climate can be profound, forcing massed exoduses or even killing animals that become marooned in water of the wrong quality. The secret of success is to move with the conditions, leaving areas that become inhospitable and heading for new places, where climatic changes could have turned the barren into the bountiful.

Nowhere is this more marked than in polar and temperate regions. Here winter cooling and storms force nutrients into the surface water and, once the sunlight of spring and summer returns, the phytoplankton can bloom to immense proportions, attracting hordes of planktivores and predators.

Climate effects are less extreme in tropical and subtropical oceans, where the seasons are far less marked. None the less, they still profoundly influence the pelagic system.

Flood

Storm conditions can produce beneficial effects for ocean life: flood water rushing from the land may raise the nutrient level of water at the ocean margins, leading to a rapid increase in plankton density. When this occurs, both planktivores and pelagic hunters arrive *en masse*, taking advantage of the localized feast.

Winter chill

As winter arrives, the surface layer starts to cool. Although this effect is most profound in polar

1. A striped marlin makes a feeding pass through a bait school off the coast of Mexico. Warm-water predators, when these seas cool in winter marlin head south towards the equator.

2. A school of skipjack tuna gathers to hunt on the up-current side of a seamount, where upwelling often concentrates small fish and plankton.

and temperate regions, it still has an influence in the subtropics, as demonstrated by the California Current. This cold-water current travels south along the Pacific Coast of North America, where it has traditionally supported large populations of tunas, mackerel and sardine. During the summer, the surface layer warms sufficiently to allow subtropical species, such as the striped marlin, to head north into Californian waters to feed on the localized abundance of schooling planktivores. When the chill of winter sets in, the water cools to such an extent that the marlin, which prefer temperatures of 20–25 °C (68–77 °F), are forced to head south, even if the prey density is lower there.

Climatic currents

The ocean's current systems are driven by the wind, so any major change in the weather will effect the currents themselves, even altering their direction of flow. No long-term weather pattern has a more profound effect than that of El Niño (▷ p. 39).

In the western Pacific Ocean there is a large area of extremely warm, and barren water called the warm pool. Perversely it supports one of the largest skipjack tuna populations in the world, but these fish feed most actively on the western edge of the warm pool, where two current systems of quite different water qualities meet, creating a convergence zone: a boundary in the water around which nutrients, plankton and tuna all congregate.

This convergence zone moves back and forth with the ENSO cycle. In El Niño years it moves in an easterly direction, whereas in the succeeding La Niña year it moves back towards the west. This movement of the convergence zone sweeps across a staggering 4000 kilometres (2500 miles) of ocean, during a period of as little as six months. The schools of marauding skipjack tuna simply follow the food, migrating with the currents.

2

Phytoplankton and zooplankton, the tiny plants and animals that form such an important part of the ocean food chain, must remain near to the ocean surface to survive. A mere 500 m (1640 feet) down there is so little oxygen in the water that many plankton would perish. The plants are even more restricted: they need light, so they cannot survive in depths below 200 m (656 feet) where sunlight cannot penetrate. Since the sea floor may be under 7000 m (23,000 feet) of water, or more, the planktonic community uses a variety of adaptations to remain nearer to the surface: buoyancy bubbles, weirdly bristling body shapes, fat stores, or just concerted swimming efforts. Survival is not a simple task. Predators from above and below patrol the surface water and intermediate layer, in endless pursuit of the plankton. By night, life becomes more dangerous still, as countless millions more predators travel upwards from the depths, to feed on plankton near the surface under cover of darkness.

OCEAN PRODUCTION

Every organism that lives in the surface layer of the ocean depends upon phytoplankton for its survival. There is no secure seabed to provide alternative sources of plant life. Indeed, there is nowhere else at all to search for food. However, opportunities for the successful growth of plankton vary enormously. Although the upper layer of water can be among the richest habitats on Earth, there are also huge areas where it can be a virtual desert.

All marine life in the open ocean is drawn to areas where phytoplankton grows, but even the most productive of these are ephemeral, changing over time with the fickle oceanographic conditions.

Nutrient supply

Nitrates and phosphates are the most fundamental mineral requirements for phytoplanktonic growth. In the ocean, the main source of nutrients is through recycling. Dissolved nutrients are transformed into living tissue by the phytoplankton. They are consumed by zooplankton, and they in turn by nekton. In time, all these organisms die and are decomposed by bacteria, which release the nutrients once more. Neat though this system is, it does have a problem: much of the decomposing matter and detritus simply sinks through the thermoclines, lost into the abyss below. Most plankton production is therefore concentrated in those parts of the oceans where nutrients can be recovered from the oceanic depths. For example, in polar regions significant nutrient recycling occurs through cold-water overturn, so plankton production is high in those areas. In temperate seas the nutrient recovery is driven principally by storm water mixing (▷ p. 160).

In subtropical and tropical oceans the water layers are much more stable, so the main sources of nutrients are either from upwellings (▷ p. 33) or from currents sweeping from more enriched areas. But in the centre of tropical oceans there is no force to drive nutrients back up into the system, so plankton struggle to survive here and most pelagic animals simply pass through these areas *en route* to better feeding grounds.

1. Living-chain diatoms are microscopic algae that grow in the sunlit surface layers of the ocean. They will only develop if the water contains sufficient nutrients.

⭐ The sea slug *Glaucus* feeds on one of the most venomous creatures in the ocean – the Portuguese man-of-war – even stealing the poisonous nematocysts to use for its own defence.

SURFACE TENSIONS

The first place most marine animals look for food is the neuston layer – the zone of enriched oils, minerals and metal ions in the very top metre of the ocean. This zone has obvious attractions: intense sunlight and some nutrients, so phytoplankton and cyanobacteria can all photosynthesize here. Wherever these photosynthetic organisms gather, zooplankton will follow, but there are significant dangers in life at the top of the ocean.

Zooplankton hiding

Feeding at the surface in daylight leaves large plankton, such as copepods, exposed to predators that can see clearly in the bright light. All copepods that try to remain within the comparative riches of the neuston layer therefore have totally transparent bodies. They also have high lipid levels, which increase their buoyancy and minimize the need for them to swim. This helps them to avoid detection, but life at the surface still has it drawbacks: during inclement weather the ocean surface is whipped into a positive maelstrom.

Surface nursery

Although the ocean's surface is extremely volatile and explored endlessly by predators, it is a highly attractive place for eggs and larvae to grow up in, given its high concentration of

1. The spectacular sea slug, *Glaucus*, feeds on a siphonophore, *Vellela*. These slugs swallow air to help them float on the ocean surface and voraciously attack floating plankton.

2. A deadly Portuguese man-of-war trails stinging tentacles to trap prey, but small gnomious fish risk living below it; most predators give the siphonophore a wide berth.

1

planktonic food and oxygen. Furthermore, the undulating movements of the surface give small animals some shelter. Many eggs are therefore buoyant, containing droplets of oil that hold them at the surface, and larvae of both coastal animals and true pelagics congregate in the surface layer, hunting copepods and each other.

Even large hunters, such as 50-kg (110-lb) sailfish start out life in the surface layer. Their larvae are just millimetres in length, but they voraciously hunt copepods and other plankton. In time they may become some of the most feared predators in the sea, but first they must avoid the hunters that drift on the ocean surface.

Floating killers

A few highly specialized cnidarian relatives of the jellyfish have adapted to a life on the ocean waves. One such is *Vellela*, the by-the-wind sailor, which is 5–6 cm (2–2.4 in) long, camouflaged blue and has a radiating fringe of tentacles surrounding an oval body, which floats on the surface. Uniquely, it has a pyra-mid-shaped glassy plate that runs diagonally across the top of its floating disc, its function being to act as a sail and catch the breeze. As the wind pushes it along, its tentacles sweep below the surface in search of food, firing nematocysts at any small plankton they touch.

Another floating hunter is the flagship of the fleet, a siphonophore called the Portuguese man-of-war. It is supported on the water surface by a translucent gas-filled float, coloured in exquisite shades of lilac and blue. The top of its sail has a comb-like fringe, which it pumps up or deflates according to how fast it wishes to sail. Exposed to the full force of the tropical sun, it also needs to capsize its body, periodically, in order to wet the surfaces of the float and protect it from drying out.

However remarkable its sailing abilities, the Portuguese man-of-war reveals its true force under water. Its bright purple tentacles, which stretch down into the water below for over 20 m (66 feet), are coated in millions of extremely venomous nematocysts that are deadly to small fish.

2

SNAKE ATTACK

Sixty species of snake have adapted to life in salt water. Most hunt the coastal sea bed, but the yellow-bellied sea snake has opted for a more pelagic lifestyle. This animal has the widest distribution of all sea snakes, ranging from the east coast of Africa to the west coast of Central America. It is highly venomous and has distinctive yellow and black bands, which serve to warn other predators not to come too close. Even if they are not bitten, digesting a yellow-bellied sea snake would almost certainly be fatal. Although it could kill a human, it has a generally benign nature, and its 1.5-mm (0.06-in) fangs would not penetrate even the thinnest of diving suits. This snake uses its venom for an entirely different purpose: it is an ambush hunter, waiting for prey in surface slicks where plankton is thickest. Rather than using eyesight, it relies on its sensitivity to sudden movements, vibrations and chemical scents in the water, to strike at small larval fish in the neuston by day and by night.

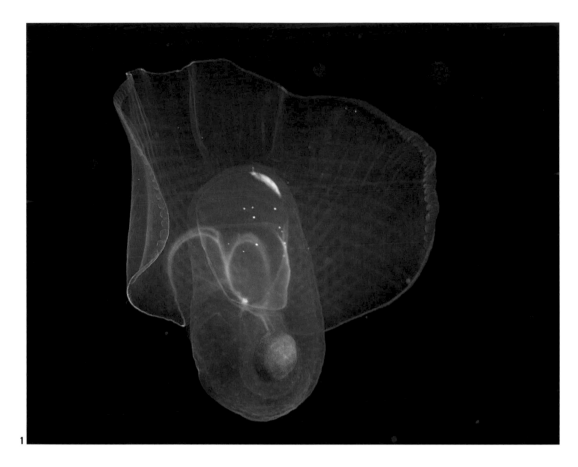

1

PLANKTONIC NOMADS

Most zooplankton feed near to the surface of the ocean, as this is where phytoplankton are most numerous. But, while food may be plentiful, there is a problem: the surface can be a dangerous place as larger predators cruise up and down, looking for prey, including grazing plankton.

Dark journeys

Transparent organisms are even more difficult to spot in darkness, so vast numbers of plankton travel up to feed near the surface at night time, returning to depths of 150 m (492 feet) or more during the day. This daily journey is known as vertical migration (▷ p. 327), and is the largest mass movement of creatures on this planet.

By late afternoon, with the sun low in the sky, more and more sunlight reflects off the ocean's surface, and little penetrates the water below. Eager to reach phytoplankton that are

 THE DEVIL FISH

With its gigantic, black-backed, winged form and two horn-shaped appendages protruding from its head, it is easy to see how the manta ray came to be named the devil fish. The largest manta can measure 5 m (16 feet) from one wing tip to the other and weigh over 2 tonnes, but these immense rays are quite harmless to humans, feeding only on plankton and small fish. Living in warm oceanic water, manta specialize in feeding where plankton concentrations are high, and are commonly found patrolling close to seamounts. Although they do feed by daylight, they remain active at night because that is when plankton migrate to the surface. If the plankton are not sufficiently dense, the manta swim in a tight loop, creating their own circular water current, which may help to concentrate their prey. The elegant, sweeping movements of their giant wings are almost balletic in their gracefulness. To feed, they open their long, oval mouths, training a current of water through their gills and fil-tering out a steady stream of plankton (see illustration, right).

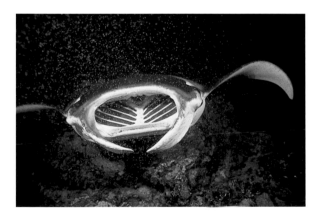

still photosynthesizing in the fading light near the surface, a great wave of herbivorous zoo-plankton, including many copepods, sets off towards them. They are not alone.

Where the herbivores lead, other predators follow: carnivorous copepods, siphonophores, krill, larval invertebrates and fish, arrow worms, pteropods and ctenophores all trek upwards. In the darkest part of the night the top 30 m (98 feet) of the ocean will be seething with plankton. At first light, the whole immense assemblage will silently fade back into the gloom 150 m (492 feet) below.

Waste not, want not

Nutrients are the key to the abundance of oceanic life, so most plants and animals use them as efficiently as possible. Sadly, however, phytoplankton leak. Dissolved organic matter seeps through their cell walls and out into the ocean. Even the excretions of larger zooplank-ton contain precious nutrients that are lost in

the water. Fortunately, the surface layers of the ocean are full of incredibly small bacteria, which can utilize this dissolved organic matter, and they, in turn, are consumed by slightly larger protozoans. These creatures are so small that many zooplankton cannot eat them, but there are specialist hunters that can.

Larvaceans

These small relatives of the sea squirts have an extraordinary constructional talent: they can build a transparent, mucus 'house' in a matter of minutes. By beating its tail, the larvacean draws a jet of water through a complex mucus mesh in the open-ended house, and sieves out minute protozoans and bacteria. When the mesh becomes clogged, the larvacean abandons it and builds another house. In the last hours of daylight, the ocean's surface can be littered with gleaming mucus shapes, some of which are 2 m (6 feet) in diameter. Both larvaceans and their mucus houses fall victim to other zooplankton,

Plankton a mere 2 mm (0.08 in) long make a daily journey of 400 m (1300 feet) to and from the surface — the equivalent of a 400-km (250-mile) swim for a human being.

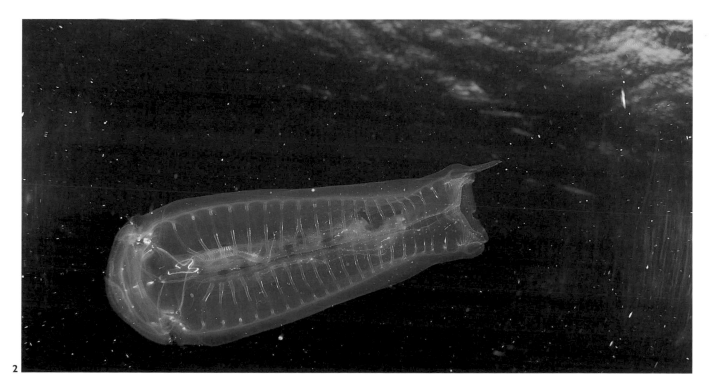

1. A pteropod drifts in open water 50 m (164 feet) down. This planktonic snail has no hard shell and relies on its transparency to dodge predators.

2. A solitary salp heads towards the ocean surface as the evening draws near, siphoning the water for phytoplankton and protozoans.

2

★ Ctenophores are the largest animals on earth that use only cilia for locomotion.

so the dissolved organic matter finds its way back into the planktonic feeding cycle after all.

Beautiful grazer

The jellied life forms of open ocean plankton include some of the most beautiful creatures on Earth. Even more elegant than the larvacean is its relative the salp. Looking rather like jet engines, these creatures stream water through their hollow bodies and pump it through a mucus net to extract phytoplankton from the water. They can be many centimetres long, and some species form colonies – great chains of pulsing cylinders that can be several metres in length. To help slow down their descent into the depths, these linked colonies coordinate a remarkable transformation: careful manoeuvring twists the chain into a giant gleaming disc, presenting the biggest surface area to slow down their free fall.

Jewelled hunters

Other beautiful creatures of the open ocean include the predatory ctenophores or comb jellies. They look not unlike jellyfish, but their gelatinous bodies gleam with lines of iridescence: eight rows of beating paddles called ciliary combs flicker with all the colours of the spectrum. Unlike jellyfish, they do not possess stinging cells, but even so, they are fierce predators with varied hunting techniques.

The small, oval sea gooseberry spins with elegant grace, setting out two long sets of sticky nets to trap copepods. *Mnemiopsis* opt for a different trapping style: if they sense a copepod below them, they move gently closer with subtle beats of their ciliary combs. When near enough, they simply swing shut four lobe-like appendages, engulfing their unfortunate prey. So stealthy are their movements that even the hypersensitive copepods have difficulty in detecting their approach. Some ctenophores, such as the voracious *Beroe*, hunt down and consume much larger prey, including other ctenophores. Whatever their diet, nearly all these beautiful, transparent predators follow the planktonic migration and appear in numbers at the surface only as the sunlight starts to fade.

1. In the world of plankton, the comb jelly, *Beroe*, is a voracious predator. Radial lines of beating cilia drive it forwards on the hunt. (Its slot-like mouth is on the left of the picture.)

2. Bigeye jacks circle in a resting pattern. These predatory fish congregate near seamounts and ridges, feeding on anything from zooplankton to other smaller, schooling fish.

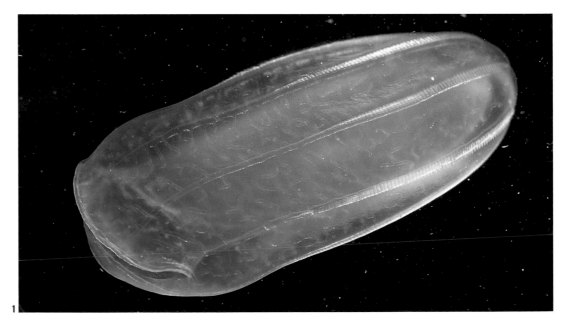

1

2

PURSUIT OF THE PLANKTON

The surface layer of the oceans contains over 70 million cubic km of water, and much of that is barren, having little or no plankton within it. Animals wishing to feed on plankton need to be able to find it, then they must feed quickly and efficiently so that they can move on before they too become prey. Different species use different methods of achieving this.

Sieving schools

The first task – perhaps the hardest – is to find sufficient quantities of plankton. Fish schools tend to accumulate where there is a nutrient upwelling, or where oceanic current systems converge to create zones of nutrient and planktonic enrichment. Many species of schooling fish use gill rakers to sieve plankton from the water, just as herring do in temperate seas (▷ p. 177). Even when they find a suitable place, the fish still have to modify their behaviour to fit in with the pattern of vertical migration.

Many schooling fish feed most actively in the late evening and early morning, when the plankton are nearer the surface. During the peak hours of daylight, the fish themselves are more likely to be seen by predators, so they too head for the gloomy depths. As they are active and need plenty of oxygen, they may have difficulty finding a suitable retreat in some areas of the tropics, and may be forced to stay in more brightly lit water above 100 m (328 feet), where the risks of being found are much greater.

To minimize these difficulties, several species of planktivore have evolved to feed at night. The most effective of these are lantern fish – the myctophids. These small fish follow the plankton's vertical migration and have sufficiently sensitive eyesight to be able to feed effectively near the ocean surface, even in the middle of the darkest night. On nights when the moon is brightest, fewer lantern fish risk being at the surface, because of the possibility that predators with less sensitive eyes, will be able to see and hunt them.

FISH THAT FLY

Flyingfish are planktivores that feed near the surface, remaining there day and night. Although opportunities for locating plankton in the neuston layer are high, it is a habitat fraught with dangers: throughout the day predators cruise above and below the water, searching for any sign of movement. It is a world where prey can be in short supply, as many species seek safety in deeper water during the daylight hours. Unsurprisingly, then, flyingfish are among the most sought-after prey in the ocean, but they have developed a remarkable escape technique.

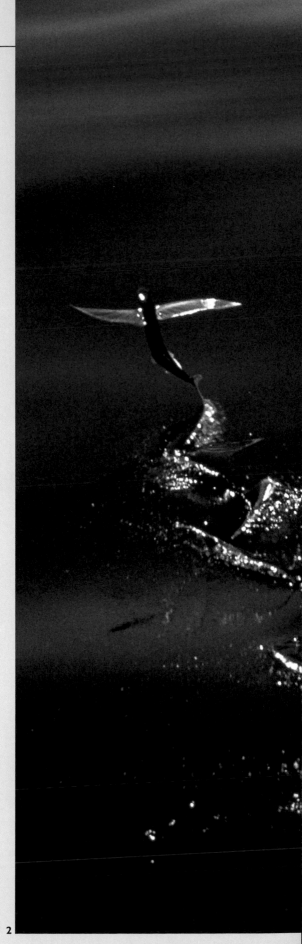

Ghostly presence
At 30 cm (12 in) long, the four-winged flying-fish is among the largest species of flyingfish, and one of the most numerous, a common resident of tropical Atlantic waters. Moving in small, loosely grouped schools, these fish travel within 50 cm (20 in) of the ocean's surface, but even in broad daylight they are hard to see, being perfectly counter-shaded: their bellies are pure white, so they disappear against the bright sky when viewed from below, and their backs are grey, merging into the dark water when viewed from above. Seen from the side, they are silver with an exquisite hint of blue, just enough to match the layer of dark blue seen when looking directly parallel to the surface. What makes them even harder to pick out is the swell of the ocean itself: by travelling so close to the surface, the flyingfish vanish behind small waves.

Spotting plankton
As long as they remain undetected, flyingfish are free to search for plankton. Their large eyes are placed in such a way that they command a field of view right around their bodies. But the eyes slightly favour a forward and upward view to help them spot plankton silhouetted against the surface. Although they are active during the day, flyingfish have sufficiently large eyes to see at night, particularly when the moon is bright, so their hunting and feeding can continue in darkness, after the bounty of the vertical migration has neared the surface.

The great escape
Despite their best efforts, flyingfish are spotted regularly, and by the fastest, most voracious predators in the ocean: dorado (dolphin fish), wahoo, tuna and sailfish. The flyingfish respond immediately, accelerating at an oblique angle straight at the surface. As their bodies burst into the air, they snap forward massively

1

2

3

elongated pectoral fins, locking them open. The fins form two sets of shimmering, gossamer wings. Immediately on leaving the water, the flyingfish rapidly beat their tails, the lower half of which are specially elongated so that they still reach the water, giving them a final thrust into flight. From that initial burst of speed, and with a good breeze following them, the fish can travel for at least 100 m (330 feet), and they may even give the water another kick if they fall close enough to a wave, to further extend their flight. With luck they will finally land beyond reach of the predators and make good their escape.

Even so, tuna are capable of explosive bursts into the air to cut the flyingfish off at the start of their flight, and frigate birds can snatch them from the sky. Life for the flying-fish is spent on a knife edge between air and water, and therefore life, and death.

1. Flyingfish fold their enormously extended pectoral fins back against their bodies when they swim.

2. Its pectoral fins widespread, a flyingfish uses the elongated lower half of its tail to give it a final thrust into the air to perform its gliding flight.

3. The spectacularly coloured dolphin fish cruises near the sea's surface. This fearless and dynamic predator favours flyingfish and is fast enough to run them down.

◈ TOPIC LINKS

6.4 Ocean Birth
p.302 Floating Nurseries

1. (opposite) A sunfish waits patiently while half-moon fish clean its sides, pecking away any parasites from its tough skin.

2. A dwarf minke whale cruises near the Barrier Reef. This small baleen whale hunts schooling fish and swarms of large plankton, such as euphasids.

2

The biggest mouths

Feeding directly on plankton is an energy-efficient feeding technique, which has led to gigantism in certain species. Despite the difficulties of locating plankton in warm oceans, the world's biggest sharks and rays are to be found there. At up to 14 m (46 feet) long and 14 tonnes in weight, the whale shark is the ocean's biggest fish, while the massive 5-m (16-foot) wingspan of the manta ray dwarfs all other rays. These impressive dimensions are not confined to fish: whales that specialize in sieving plankton and small nekton also reach vast sizes, with fin whales reaching weights of 80 tonnes and blue whales more than 100 tonnes.

In tropical oceans the plankton supply is much more ephemeral than in temperate and polar seas. Perhaps a wind-induced shift of currents, a sudden influx of flood water, a powerful circulation current around a seamount or a major change in atmospheric pressure can suddenly switch part of the ocean into an ideal plankton nursery, perhaps for a month, maybe even less. The point is that for planktivores to succeed in the warm ocean, they must be able to locate plankton hotspots across hundreds of kilometres and to swim very efficiently to reach them.

Baleen whales are among the more streamlined, elegant swimmers, and the sei whale is a prime example. Comparatively small at up to 14 m (46 feet), it is the fastest, most sinuous swimmer of all, capable of covering long distances in the most energy-saving way.

Picky feeders

Sieving is not the only successful feeding technique, for those keen on plankton. Many sea birds, including petrels, shearwaters and albatrosses, cruise over the waves seeking out aggregations of larger plankton, such as krill. In fact, some of them continue to feed at night when the moon is bright in the sky. Generally they land on the water and pick plankton from the surface with their bills.

However, grabbing individual plankton is not the sole preserve of avian hunters. The massive leatherback turtle pursues plankton far down in the deep scattering layer, but perhaps the most bizarre planktivore of all is the giant sunfish. At upwards of 2000 kg (4400 lb) and over 3 m (10 feet) long, this is the biggest bony fish of all (as distinct from cartilaginous sharks and rays). Its weird, angular body is covered in a tough, white and grey blotched skin, which is coated in mucus. It doesn't even swim like a normal oceanic fish: it simply uses its stumpy tail for steerage and slowly paddles along with its long dorsal and pectoral fins. Despite its odd appearance, the giant sunfish is an efficient hunter, pursuing gelatinous plankton to depths far below the reach of sunlight, then returning to the warmer surface waters, where the heat helps it to digest its food more easily.

As much of the open ocean is characterized by limited amounts of food often dispersed over immense areas, it simply does not pay to be too choosy. Even tuna, among the most dynamic hunters in the sea, will feed on plankton. During daylight, bigeye tuna will even swim below the thermocline to find plankton at depth. To survive the open ocean requires incessant opportunism. If an animal becomes too specialized in its tastes, it risks starvation.

OCEAN HUNTERS

The predators of the open ocean include the most advanced swimming machines on Earth, their exquisitely streamlined shapes gliding through the water on a constant search for food. Both mammals and fish have evolved extraordinary physiological adaptations to give them the advantage over their prey. Tails can be scimitar-thin or fluted at the edges for maximum propulsive efficiency. Fins are perfectly hydrodynamic, giving as much lift and manoeuvrability as do wings in the air. Some fish even fold their fins back into slotted grooves on their flanks to increase their streamlining still further, snapping them open when they turn or slow down. These predators have evolved anything that will help in the chase, from superheated blood systems to rapier-sharp swords. Their sensory systems are so finely tuned that many can hunt by day or night and chase prey to depths of several hundred metres. They are the ocean hunters: perhaps the most impressive hunters on the planet.

KILLER DESIGNS

In the open ocean there is virtually no place to hide, but that does not make it easy for predators to track down prey. Animals can escape detection simply because the ocean is so immense. Vision is severely limited under water, because conditions are so variable. Even in clear water, animals with good sight cannot see much more than 30 m (98 feet) in any direction. So using vision alone to catch prey is simply not an option. In addition, many of the conditions that allow the build-up of plankton – so vital for attracting prey – are short-lived: winds wax and wane, current fronts shift across tens or even thousands of kilometres, upwellings develop and fade away, seasons change. As a result, the locations of suitable prey move unpredictably through the oceans.

Even the physical and chemical conditions of the water itself impose severe restrictions upon predators. Most cannot operate for long in deep water because the oxygen levels are very low, and many are intolerant of a sudden drop in temperature or salinity of the water.

To further compound these problems, competition between predators is high. There is only so much food available, even if it can be found, and there are many mouths to feed. Hunting is a difficult game, where tactics and design determine the difference between life and death.

Sensory warfare

The key to locating prey in an immense space is to develop a battery of different sensory systems. All fish are acutely sensitive to

Sharks are sensitive to noises of exactly the low-wavelength sound that moving muscles make.

2

1. A shortfin mako glides effortlessly towards the surface. This fearsome predator hunts fast-moving fish and will tackle both tuna and billfish.

2. The dagger-like dentistry of a shortfin mako. Teeth break off at the outer edge of the jaw, but are constantly replaced by rows of new teeth growing inside the mouth.

1

chemicals in the water, having well-developed olfactory glands that open to a pair of nostrils, and taste buds peppering their mouth, skin and fins. As prey swim through the water, they leave a long trail of proteins, faecal pellets and mucus behind them. To detect it, predators have to be down current of the prey or they will miss the scent.

Swimming fish also create water vibrations as they move. Predators can detect these with their lateral line systems – a network of thin canals in the skin that run along the full length of the body and are lined with sensory cells sensitive to changes of water pressure. Fast-swimming prey also make sounds as they move, and predators pick these up, both with their lateral lines and simple inner ears set behind their eyes.

Sharks and rays have yet another sensory system, which is capable of extreme accuracy. Organs called ampullae of Lorenzini detect weak electrical signals in the water, which are generated by muscle movements in their prey.

Once close enough, predators can switch to vision for their final approach. The degree to which they use it depends upon the depth and time at which they hunt.

Picking targets

Predatory success requires the ability to find prey, to get to them first and, once there, to outmanoeuvre them. Predators either become highly specialized – the best at catching a particular group of animals – or they become generalists, being fairly good at dealing with a variety of prey and thereby increasing their chances of success.

Another major choice faced by predators is whether to hunt in the light or the dark. Most visual hunters of planktivorous fish choose to hunt in surface waters by day. Those who prefer to feed by night or in deep water often concentrate on hunting squid, which follow the deeper layers of vertical migration.

An additional key to hunting success is the ability to remain unseen by the quarry. In the open ocean the background colour depends on the direction of view. Overhead is the white, mirror-like surface, below is the blue-black of the deep, and to the sides are rich blues or greens. Counter-shading helps predators to blend in: their dark backs merge into the gloom when viewed from above, and their pale bellies vanish against the bright surface when viewed from below.

Need for speed

Feeding opportunities may be separated by vast distances, and prey are constantly on the move, often executing high-speed escape manoeuvres. Predators need to be extremely

COOL BLUES

Blue sharks have no counter-current system (▷ p. 295) to regulate their blood temperature but, by preference, they chase squid and pelagic octopus, which move with the vertical migration, into the cold waters far below the thermocline. Somehow these sinuous hunters of temperate and tropical oceans can dive over 600 m (1970 feet) down, enduring water as cold as 7 °C (45 °F), but they cannot stay at such depths. They would chill to such an extent that they would be far slower than their prey. Instead, they swim back and forth between the surface and the depths, spending up to two hours in the cold, before heading back for 30 minutes of warming up in shallow waters. By keeping their muscles warmer than the surrounding ocean, blue sharks remain alert and active, highly capable of snatching large squid.

The diving challenge is less onerous at night than by day because the vertical migration brings their prey to within 100 m (330 feet) of the surface. Even so, the sharks continue to dive to and from the surface. As they hunt mainly by smell, their vertical journey increases their chances of picking up horizontal scent trails that may lead to the glow of bioluminescent squid.

1

efficient swimmers, able to cover thousands of kilometres at a low energy rate, yet produce blistering turns of speed to run down their prey. One group of fish that includes many such predators is the billfish, the group of 11 species of pelagic fish whose upper jaws are elongated into a bony spear. The group includes sailfish – which can reach at least 130 kph (80 mph) – spearfish and the giant blue marlin. Tuna can also attain similar speeds.

Most oceanic predators are hydrodynamically efficient. The big fish generally have torpedo-shaped bodies with smooth skin and thin, stiff fins, which tuck up neatly into grooves for maximum streamlining. Small keels and finlets near the tail direct the flow of water past them, reducing resistance to a minimum. The tails are narrow and sickle-shaped, producing maximum power with minimum effort. These fish sense the water flow as it slides past their bodies. They actually time their tail strokes to achieve a slipstreaming effect from small turbulence eddies, gaining additional speed, rather like a racing car in an overtaking manoeuvre.

1. The javelin-like bill of a blue marlin is an impressive weapon. It almost certainly helps to maximize streamlining, helping the predator to achieve its extreme acceleration.

STAKE-OUT

The easiest way to hunt is to set an ambush and wait for prey to come close. In the open ocean, this can be an extremely effective technique: the trick is knowing where to wait.

Volcanic attraction

Since seamounts tend to have an enriching effect on local plankton populations, they can be a tremendous draw for planktivorous animals. Where they are situated in the path of a major current, they can both force nutrient upwelling and reduce the depth of water through which the plankton must pass. As a result, the plankton becomes far more concentrated as it is swept over the rocky summit.

Large schools of planktivorous fish congregate on the up-current side of the seamount, working the enriched plankton layer. Flitting schools of creole wrasse drift upwards from the protection of the rock-faces, while higher in the water, schools of scad mackerel streak back and forth. Further out still, tight-knit schools of bonito cruise tirelessly back and forth, waiting for dusk and the beginning of the vertical migration.

All these fish attract bigger predators. Schools of juvenile yellowfin tuna spend many months working the area for easy prey, such as anchovetta. Black marlin periodically close up on the seamount, looking for unwary reef fish. Even dolphin pause on their wide-ranging journeys: concentrations of fish, such as those around seamounts, will always provide a feeding opportunity sooner or later.

Life-rafts

In the clear ocean, away from the seamounts, finding a concentrated source of food can be a great deal harder. However the water is rarely clear: fallen trees are swept out from land, seaweed is ripped from the coast and carried out to sea, and all sorts of man-made rubbish – tyres, fishing nets, barrels, packing cases, metal containers, bitumen and worse – clutters the water.

Perversely, there is a positive benefit from some of this rubbish. Whatever the object, if it floats, it will become a shelter for larvae and juvenile fish growing up in the ocean. If nothing else, it offers protection from sea birds, who are unable to see directly beneath the flotsam.

What lives under the raft of debris depends upon the temperature of the water through which it is floating. In the tropics common residents are young triggerfish, jacks, sardine and rainbow chub. All these fish are fair game, so predators drop by for a closer look. In fact, several hunting species

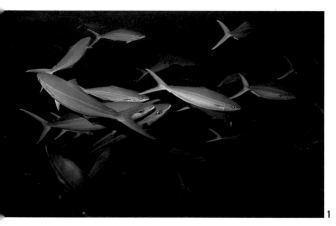

1

2

will travel with a particular piece of debris for many kilometres, effectively staking out a territory. A single piece of flotsam can be the focal point for several hundred tonnes of fish including young tuna and major predators such as shark. The elegant silver wahoo, which looks not unlike a barracuda and weighs up to 50 kg (110 lb), is a master flotsam hunter, as is the magnificently coloured dolphin fish. Both will make forays into the blue, perhaps on the look-out for flyingfish, but they will always glide back to the debris, making use of their counter-shading to sneak up from below or to glide unseen just below the surface. They attack only at the plankti-vores' feeding time – usually at dawn or dusk – when they are most likely to be caught unawares. Then, both wahoo and dolphin fish can strike with extreme speed and violence.

Hitch-hikers

Possibly the most cunning technique is to allow another, larger animal to do the work of track-ing down prey. The banded pilot fish does this, travelling in the slipstream of creatures such as sharks and turtles. Pilot fish wait for their host to feed, then dodge out of formation to grab scraps.

Even finer exponents of this art are the remoras. They have a specially adapted sucker on top of their heads with which they attach themselves to a host and hang on for the ride. Different species of remora favour different hosts: huge white remoras travel on manta rays, small white or spearfish remora abound on billfish, and elegant striped species often ride with sharks. None is permanently attached and can let go to feed if necessary. Spearfish remora go one step further, swimming inside the gill chambers of their billfish hosts, a perfect place for feeding on food scraps in safety.

The biggest great white shark ever measured was 6 m (20 foot) long and 3 tonnes in weight.

1. Rainbow runners, medium-sized pelagic fish, commonly hunt near flotsam. They hunt with such ferocity that shark will follow them, picking off the damaged victims in their wake.

2. Oceanic triggers hover below a discarded rope-trawl that has become their floating home. Flotsam like this can attract literally hundreds of tonnes of fish.

3. Two remora fish ride shotgun on a gliding manta. They do not cause their host any harm.

1

SOLITARY PATROL

Debris and seamounts are mere pinpricks in the ocean, which stretches out across thousands of kilometres, revealing few solid surfaces of any sort. The main features that attract life in the open ocean are the different boundaries in the water itself: the thermocline at depth, the fronts between currents and the surrounding ocean, convergences between currents and zones of upwelling. These are features that giant solitary hunters target because they are the areas where food is most likely to be found.

Billfish

These powerful fish are famed for their extra-ordinary pointed snouts, which can be well over a metre long. There are 11 related species of billfish, the biggest being the blue marlin, which can weigh over 900 kg (2000 lb).

 STRIPED MUSKETEERS

Striped Marlin, the most glamorous-looking of fish (see illustration, right), reach weights of over 200 kg (440 lb), and hunt in the upper layers of tropical to sub-temperate waters. Unusually among billfish, they do not always hunt alone, working in packs of 30 or so to trap prey more effectively. Dull grey against the ocean, a loose-knit group of striped marlin glide at a steady 3 kph (2 mph), pursuing a fleeing shoal of mackerel towards the surface. The trapped prey form up into a defensive baitball (▷ p. 178) and are prevented from diving to safety by the big marlin circling lazily below. The marlin do not attack at once: almost certainly because 30 needle-sharp swords slashing in a confined space would lead to some of the marlin being injured. Instead, a few at a time make high-speed runs at the baitball, suddenly lighting up with fluorescent stripes and patches of ultraviolet blue as they do so. These distinctive colours may help the marlin to see each other and avoid potentially fatal collisions. But the colours have a more sinister use: mackerel eyes are especially sensitive to ultraviolet, so the fast moving bands of colour confuse them, making their movements more desperate and the fish easier to catch.

This is a massively powerful fish found mainly in tropical surface water above the thermocline, although it occasionally ventures down to colder water. Being mainly a visual hunter, the marlin is most active in the early and late hours of daylight but it can also hunt at night near the surface. Its diet is varied, consisting of squid, fish and even large planktonic crustaceans. Debate rages about the purpose of its spear-like bill. It probably serves equally well for defence, streamlining and predation. There are certainly eyewitness accounts of it being used to stun tightly packed prey, such as swarms of paper nautilus.

The heaviest bill of all belongs to a predator unrelated to the other billfish. This is the so-called broadbill, or swordfish, which can reach weights of up to 500 kg (1100 lb) and is adapted specifically for hunting in deep water. Swordfish do use their broad bills for defence, and it is likely that they also use them to dig into the seabed and flush out prey. Their immense eyes are sensitive to very low light levels, and they endure the cold below the thermocline by having a high fat concentration and body diameter. Like many species of pelagic fish, they further conserve heat by having their blood vessels arranged in a so-called counter-current system: cold veins returning to the heart from the skin run parallel and close to warm arteries, so venous blood is progressively warmed as it flows back to the heart. Swordfish even have a specially warmed muscle behind the eye and brain, to keep these vital organs as warm and active as possible. The factor that limits them most is the amount of oxygen in the water. They cannot penetrate below the minimum oxygen layer, but when there is sufficient oxygen they can swim down to depths of several hundred metres, where they hunt squid during the day.

Open-ocean sharks

Like swordfish, hammerhead sharks also feed on squid, but they have a remarkable way of finding them. The sharks are almost certainly sensitive to faint magnetic fields, and the sea floor is banded with layers of weak magnetism. As their ampullae of Lorenzini (▷ p. 290) are widely spaced, it is probable that they can form a stereo map of the magnetic field, allowing them to follow 'roads' of magnetism directly to their prey.

The Mako can weigh more than 600 kg (1300 lb) and is probably the fastest shark in the ocean. It has dagger-like teeth that make easy prey even of swordfish. Driving upwards, the mako is unseen against the dark water and its speed prevents its target from accelerating to safety. On the first pass the mako removes the swordfish's tail, on the second its bill. The massive meal is then safe to eat.

1. The swordfish is an extremely powerful deep-water predator that probably uses its bill to dig out prey from the sea floor.

2. A school of scalloped hammerhead gather around the edge of a seamount. By night they will split up and travel far out into the ocean to hunt squid.

2

1

2

PACK HUNTERS

Hunting solo has a major drawback: with only one individual searching for prey, the chances of detecting a suitable target are comparatively low. As a result, many oceanic predators work as teams: the sensory abilities of a large group of animals dramatically increases the area searched at any one time. As long as there is enough food to go round, working in a pack can greatly increase the efficiency of the hunters.

Tuna squadrons

Certain species of tuna can attain immense sizes, yellowfin reaching weights of over 150 kg (331 lb) and bluefin more than 500 kg (1100 lb). Such giants have relatively few predators, but despite this, all tuna are schooling fish.

Yellowfin tuna increase their efficiency with a swim-and-glide system of hunting. The school swims gently upwards until it nears the surface, then the individuals glide downwards with open pectoral fins for several minutes, dropping towards 150 m (490 feet). This technique ensures that they search not just a wide area, but also a significant depth band. The gliding freefall also conserves energy.

All tuna possess the counter-current blood system that allows their body temperature to remain above that of the surrounding water (▷ p. 295). This allows the yellowfin to keep their muscles operating at maximum efficiency so that they can outperform their prey and extend their hunting into cooler water below 150 m (490 feet). The giant bluefin tuna has the most advanced counter-current system and is the only tuna that can hunt far into the cool temperate ocean, where productivity is highest.

Mammal pack

The marine mammals hold most of the answers to successful pelagic hunting. With

3

1. Yellowfin tuna are perfectly streamlined. Even their gill cases are immoveable in order to reduce drag, so they swim with their mouths constantly agape to force water over their gills.

2. A large school of tuna chase small baitfish so fast that they simply burst through the surface, creating a spectacle known as a 'tuna foamer'.

3. A giant herd of common dolphin on the move. If there is insufficient food to feed such numbers in one place, they will split into smaller groups to hunt.

sufficient insulation, and the advantage of warm blood, they can dive deep below the thermocline. Although they have to breathe air, they are immune to the effects of the oxygen minimum layer, since they are carrying an on-board and renewable oxygen supply. Dolphins also have the most advanced detection system in the ocean – extremely high-resolution sonar that can pinpoint minute echoes of sounds at distance. By working in groups, they further increase the efficiency of the hunt: several dolphins swimming beside each other vastly increase the effective width of the sonar search beam. In addition, they are capable of carefully coordinated attack patterns, which ensure that their prey is captured with the greatest ease.

The dolphins work as a team, driving their prey up towards the surface. They keep the prey penned there by making fast sorties around the bottom of the fish school, forcing them into an ever-more dense ball by emitting loud clicks and blowing both bursts and walls of bubbles around the fringes of the school. It is then an easy task to pick off individual fish.

Dolphins are such efficient locators of prey that they are sought out by other predators, who simply shadow their progress. It is not difficult to follow a large dolphin school: the sound of their incessant whistling travels far and wide. Sharks, tuna, and bonito follow them under water, while shearwaters and other oceanic birds, follow them above. Once prey has been located, the profusion of hunters increases the kill rate: the bait fish become so confused that numbers of them are actually blasted out of the baitball. As soon as they are separated from their school, the lone fish are devoured in seconds.

Bluefin tuna conserve body heat so efficiently that these 'cold-blooded' fish can maintain their core temperature at 25 °C (77 °F) even in water as cold as 7 °C (45 °F).

SOUND HUNTERS

Everyone likes dolphins. These toothed whales have highly developed social behaviours and communicate with complex clicks and squeaks extending far beyond the range of human hearing. Their 32 species are to be found worldwide from the polar seas to the tropics and their numbers include truly ocean-going animals that spend their whole lives far from land. Although many dolphins are curious and some even play with humans, this belies their true character: these animals are voracious predators of the utmost efficiency. Their weapons are sonar, speed, intelligence and co-operation.

Extravagant lifestyle

Dolphins are possibly the most exuberant animals in the ocean. Most are highly social and gather in groups numbering anything from a few individuals to vast herds several thousand strong. Like all mammals, they have a high metabolism, but this is particularly important in the ocean since keeping blood temperatures raised can be an energy-sapping process. Despite this, virtually any encounter with dolphins reveals that they have time and energy for play. A passing ship is an ideal excuse for a spot of surfing in the bow wave, while a stray piece of seaweed is a chance to show off their relay abilities by passing it from one individual to another.

Whenever the urge takes them, these acrobats of the ocean will leap several metres into the air, often appearing to synchronize their jumps with others. None is more exuberant in its display than the tropical spinner dolphin.

Most dolphins are also polygamous, so socializing groups nearly always have energetic

sexual activities breaking out somewhere in the pack. The question is: how do dolphins find enough food to support such large groups in such extravagant behaviour?

Crowd control

The size of toothed whales' social groups depends largely on diet. Most of the whales that primarily hunt squid live in fairly small groups. Squid are not the most nutritious of prey, and their density in the ocean can be comparatively low, even at the depths where they concentrate. Pilot whales, false killer whales and Risso's dolphins all consume a good deal of squid and therefore tend to live

1. A spinner dolphin makes a trademark twisting leap. It is not clear whether these dolphin are just exuberant, or if the acrobatics have a more serious role.

2. Atlantic spotted dolphin gather into huge social groups, but more normally hunt in small herds.

3. A spotted dolphin cuts through the surface at speed, showing off the streamlining shared by all the pelagic dolphin.

in smaller groups. However, dolphins that pursue schooling fish are quite a different story, even though most will still eat squid and other cephalopods when the opportunity arises. Fish are highly nutritious and in the right conditions can occur in vast, tight-packed schools. These are food supplies that produce enough energy to support much bigger groupings. Consequently, the open ocean is home to immense herds of common dolphins, spotted dolphins and spinners.

Commuting hunters

Although a social gathering may consist of hundreds or even thousands of dolphins, they do not necessarily stay together permanently. Within the large population are numbers of smaller, rather volatile family groupings, and up to 100 peel off to go on a hunting foray. Able to communicate over considerable distances, they have no difficulty in re-establishing contact with the large social group at a later stage. Indeed, joining up with the big group can be a useful defence against larger predators, including sharks and false killer whales. Dolphin life is therefore divided into periods of intense hunting activity, often in smaller groups, and huge social gatherings that last many hours, and allow the dolphins to rest, play and breed in relative safety.

◆ TOPIC LINKS

6.3 Ocean Hunters
    p.296 Mammal Pack

6.4 Ocean Birth
    p.306 Dolphin Friendly
    p.309 Toothed Whales

OCEAN BIRTH

In the ocean the cycle of life and death is constant. From the moment of birth, animals enter a high-risk world where they will constantly be preyed upon. For a species to survive, its final challenge is to reproduce successfully, and in the huge expanses of open water that is not easy. There are many different strategies that pelagic animals use to safeguard their offspring. The most sophisticated give birth to a single baby and then lavish it with parental care for several months. At the other extreme are the numerous fish that shed many millions of eggs in their lifetime: casting them unattended into the wilderness of the seas. But even the simplest of breeding programmes requires care in its execution if any offspring are to survive to an adulthood in the open ocean. Fish may travel thousands of kilometres to find water of exactly the right quality to nurture their young. From the moment of hatching, the fish larvae embark on a ferocious struggle for survival in the plankton.

MASS SPAWNING

The mating ritual of fish like the yellowfin tuna is brief and frantic. As the females release clouds of microscopic eggs into the water, the males are hot on their tails, covering the eggs with sperm. The commotion is over in minutes, leaving millions of fertilized eggs to drift in the water. The frenetic activity is typical of the way in which many pelagic fish spawn. They do not expend energy in direct parental care, opting instead to cast their offspring adrift in an ocean where food is limited and eggs are potential targets for feeding plankton and planktivores. Fewer than one egg in a million will survive to adulthood, so mass spawners produce immense amounts of eggs to maximize the chances of survival.

This spectacularly wasteful style of breeding is called broadcast spawning.

Abandoned at sea

It is not as though adult fish make no effort, however, to ensure their offspring's success. Although knowledge of exactly where pelagic fish spawn remains extremely sketchy, it is abundantly clear that the adults sometimes travel many thousands of kilometres from rich feeding areas to reach waters that are suitable for spawning. Tagged giant bluefin tuna, for example, are known to have crossed the Pacific Ocean. In the Atlantic, bluefin tuna, which feed as far north as Nova Scotia in Canada, are commonly believed to travel back to the Gulf of Mexico to breed, although increasing evidence suggests that many head far out into the open Atlantic, along the southern edge of the Gulf Stream. Like most fish that abandon their eggs, they need to spawn in water where the conditions are perfect for their young's development. They seek warm, tropical water with a high salinity, in areas where there are strong current boundaries. The boundary currents ensure sufficient planktonic life for their larvae to feed on once they hatch.

Initially, tuna larvae are minute and, like the eggs from which they hatch, contain small oil droplets to help them float in the saline water. From the start, they are voracious hunters, feeding on copepods in the early morning and late evening when the plankton densities increase.

1. Fish eggs with different stages of embryo development. The gleaming spheres inside the eggs are oil droplets that keep them afloat near the surface.

If they avoid being eaten, the larvae grow with astonishing speed, reaching weights of several kilograms within a year. In fact, a medium-sized adult weighing well over 100 kg (220 lb) can be a mere three years old. Despite this, tuna populations suffer heavily from predation while they grow to adolescence. On reaching the apparent safety of adulthood, they face another problem – this time from the fishing industry, which catches millions of tonnes a year, outstripping even the tuna's remarkable ability to propagate.

Floating nurseries

The four-winged flyingfish is another highly fertile, mass-spawning fish, and is common in the Atlantic and the Caribbean. Like tuna, these fish congregate in carefully selected breeding sites, but take more care over the dispersal of their eggs than the giant broadcast breeders. They gather a few miles off the coast of the Caribbean islands, arriving *en masse* at the same time as the plankton population soars, in order to ensure an abundance of food when their larvae hatch. The adults lay their eggs on flotsam, such as sargassum weed.

This seaweed supports a unique community in the Sargasso Sea, an area of warm water within the North Atlantic Gyre. The currents sweep patches of the weed past the Caribbean, and early in the year, when they start breeding, flyingfish congregate in their thousands around the weed or any other floating debris.

As the flyingfish court, they display to one another by opening one pectoral fin, turning it pale pink and fluttering it gently. At spawning time, the females lay strings of bright orange eggs, twining them around the weed in a dense web, and males pour out clouds of sperm nearby. The activity can be so frenzied that the weed becomes clogged with eggs, sometimes even sinking into the abyss. Where the weed-raft stays afloat, however, the eggs develop in comparative safety.

1. Flyingfish eggs developing in sargassum weed; the black eyes of the babies are clearly visible. Tough fibres fix the eggs to their weedy sanctuary.

2. (opposite) The sargassum fish is perfectly camouflaged to hide in floating sargassum weed. It has evolved especially to live amongst the weeds.

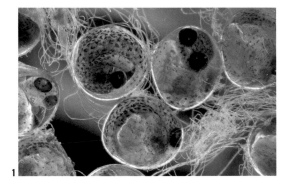

1

 SLIPPERY CONCEPTION

The European eel has one of the most extraordinary life cycles on Earth. Between the ages of 4 and 18 years old, it lives far from the sea in freshwater rivers and lakes, and leads a celibate life. When it reaches adulthood, it heads downstream towards the ocean, even slithering across land if necessary. On reaching the sea, it makes a remarkably quick transition to saltwater life and heads into the open ocean. Heading south and west, it swims 6000 km (3700 miles) using the flow of the Equatorial Current to take it to the Sargasso Sea. Here, at a depth of 700 m (2300 feet), it meets up with thousands of other eels and spawns in the deep cold below the thermocline. The effort is terminal, and the adult eels all die. Their microscopic larvae spend three years slowly growing up in the plankton and following the Gulf Stream past the Caribbean and gradually back across the Atlantic. By their fourth year, thousands of juvenile elvers, such as those illustrated, right, wriggle and slip their way up the rocky slopes of European rivers to spend their celibate years in fresh water.

> Most squid live for only 1–3 years, and die as soon as they have reproduced.

CASTAWAYS

The risk of predators eating eggs and newly hatched offspring can be marginally reduced by laying smaller numbers of eggs in yet more carefully selected nurseries. Although they are still abandoned by the parents, the young will have an even greater chance of survival.

The death dance

Squid take great care with their egg-laying. Although different species lay in different water depths and locations, they all display similar breeding behaviour.

Large numbers of breeding squid congregate in a chosen site and indulge in elaborate courtship displays. They pair up and swim together while flashing sudden, dramatic skin colour changes. In deeper water, some species use bioluminescence, to glow in the darkness.

Females are copulated with almost surgical precision by the males, which use their long arms to pass a packet of sperm to their partners. The tough, rubbery eggs are then laid as clumps or strings on the sea floor. Immediately after this, many adults die, their brief lives spent. In some cases, the males remain on guard with their eggs, protecting them from predation while they develop. They, too, die once the eggs hatch. This system ensures that a high proportion will hatch unharmed, but then they are at the mercy of numerous predators. Many will perish long before they reach even young adulthood.

1. Breeding market squid lay clusters of white egg cases on a shallow sea floor. The tentacles of the male squid flush red as they mate with the females.

2. A swell shark slips from its tough egg case. Many shark and rays incubate like this and upon hatching are fully capable of hunting small prey.

LIVE BIRTH

To increase the chance of successfully starting a new generation, a number of open-ocean creatures give birth to live young. This ensures that the embryos develop within the comparative safety of a fully grown female and that, by the time they are born, they will be well developed and better able to cope with the rigours of ocean life.

Abandoning the babies

Parental care is extremely hard work. For most animals, life in the open ocean is too precarious for them to expend additional energy on parenting. Instead, they give their offspring the best chance of survival at the time of birth, then move on to ensure their own survival.

Many sea snakes (▷ p. 279) bear live young, which are comparatively large. The brood size averages seven individuals, fully venomous and independent from the moment of birth. They need to be, since from the moment they leave their mother's womb, they are on their own.

Certain cartilaginous fish have also devised ways to avoid laying eggs in the open ocean. Most pelagic sharks, including the mako, and all rays, develop the eggs within their body. Often the mother continues to produce infertile eggs which the developing embryos eat inside her womb. In some cases, they go one step further and actually consume their siblings. This can mean that only two huge young are born. ▷▷

2

 DESPERATELY SEEKING FISH

Humans like to eat fish, particularly pelagic giants, such as swordfish, tuna, dolphin fish and even shark. (The picture, right, shows bluefin tuna being hauled onto a reefer boat.) Worldwide around 90 million tonnes of fish are caught every year as fishing fleets attempt to meet estimated fishing quotas called the maximum sustainable yield (MSY). The MSY is the highest predicted number of fish that can be caught while still allowing natural reproduction to replenish stocks. Marine biologists, however, are only just beginning to understand how any of these fish live, migrate and breed, and how their populations are affected by oceanographic conditions. The MSY is therefore little more than an educated guess, and often it is wrong.

Unfortunately, the oceans are now fast running out of fish. To match demand, new ways of harvesting the open ocean must be found. Improved knowledge and greater accuracy of population assessments will help, but research is also being conducted into how to raise large pelagic fish in captivity. It is not easy: at their planktonic stages they are so fragile that bumping into a tank wall is fatal. None the less, the superb dolphin fish is already being farmed in Florida, and yellowfin tuna are now bred in captivity and may yet be economically viable. It is just possible that people will be able to consume pelagic fish without driving them to extinction.

DOLPHIN FRIENDLY

Both sharks and dolphins are unintended victims of commercial fishing for the world's favourite sandwich filler, the yellowfin tuna. They are by-catch, an age-old fishing problem in which unwanted species are landed alongside the true targets. The by-catch are simply thrown back into the sea dead. It is a significant problem in the tuna fisheries of the eastern Pacific and for many years the chief victims have been beautiful pelagic dolphin. Their demise caused an immense public outcry, with a growing determination to halt the slaughter, whatever the cost. 'Dolphin-friendly' tuna was born, but how friendly is it really?

2

1

1. A purse-seine net is set into a perfect circular wall around the targeted animals. Steel cables then draw the net floor together, trapping the tuna inside.

2. A fishing-boat crewman dives to hand-release a dolphin after a net has been set around a dolphin herd in order to capture the adult tuna associated with the dolphin.

Tuna tendencies

Yellowfin tuna have three quite distinct lifestyles. Juveniles of less than half a metre long congregate near surface-floating debris during the night, heading into deeper water during the day. Slightly larger tuna spend their time in free-ranging schools away from flotsam, but also make a small vertical migration. The biggest tuna swim with large schools of spotted, spinner and common dolphins, probably following them to increase the chances of finding food.

Outcry and outcome

Big tuna are the most valuable, and the easiest way to catch them is to look for herds of dolphin. Once found, the dolphins are chased by high-speed boats to cut off their escape, meanwhile a fishing vessel encircles the school. A 1.5 km (1 mile) long net is quickly pulled over the stern of the vessel and within minutes a perfect circle of net 200 m (656 feet) deep is set around the school. The bottom of the net is closed, trapping both the dolphin and the tuna that are following them. If care is not taken to let the dolphins out they become enmeshed in the netting and drown. This technique is called purse-seine fishing, and in 1986 it was responsible for killing about 133,000 dolphin in the eastern Pacific. Video footage of bleeding and dying dolphin being thrown overboard, created such an outcry that the US government eventually introduced a moratorium on this form of fishing, and tuna-canning companies conceived the idea of 'Dolphin-friendly' tuna, caught without purse-seining around dolphin herds.

3

Dilemma

Thanks to the changes, dolphin deaths plummeted, but many thousands of other pelagic animals have become by-catch instead. Literally tens of thousands of sharks, wahoo, dorado (dolphin fish) and many others are needlessly killed. Even worse, the smaller tuna being caught are sexually immature, so they are removed from the sea before they can breed.

The moratorium on purse-seining around dolphin schools has now been lifted because improvements to the technique mean that fewer than 2500 dolphins are killed per year. That is only 1 dolphin killed for every three settings of the net. Whereas many fish species, other than tuna, die on non-dolphin sets of the net.

Populations

Annually, an estimated 0.1 per cent of the eastern Pacific dolphin population now dies during purse-seine fishing around dolphin herds. As dolphin reproduce by a level of at least 2 per cent each year, the losses are almost negligible. No one knows exactly what losses are suffered by other species in the huge by-catches of 'dolphin-friendly' tuna, but they are undoubtedly higher than the dolphins', particularly among sharks. The extremely slow reproduction rates of the sharks means that losses of hundreds of thousands a year will ultimately lead to extinction.

For humans with a taste for tuna, this is a quandary. Does our affection for dolphin make it acceptable for fishermen to kill thousands of other 'less appealing' animals each year? How much is a tuna sandwich really worth?

3. Bycatch of shark trapped in a 'dolphin friendly' net set around flotsam. Only the fins are kept, the bodies are simply thrown overboard to die; waste of an important pelagic predator on a scale we can ill afford.

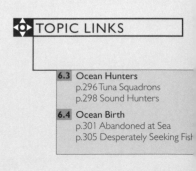

TOPIC LINKS

6.3 Ocean Hunters
p.296 Tuna Squadrons
p.298 Sound Hunters

6.4 Ocean Birth
p.301 Abandoned at Sea
p.305 Desperately Seeking Fish

★ Shark jaws bite with a force of 3 tonnes per square centimetre – the equivalent of stacking 3 Rolls Royce cars on your thumbnail.

1

2

1. Dried shark fins collect a high price to supply the demand for shark-fin soup.

2. A lemon shark gives birth to a live pup that was nourished through an umbilicus inside her womb.

3. A humpback whale protects her calf and, like all mammals, she suckles her young with rich milk.

Overleaf: A bottlenose dolphin mother and calf. Even new-borns have to be able to keep up with their fast-swimming mothers.

A few sharks, rather like mammals, nourish their young through a placenta. Blue sharks reproduce like this, giving birth to as many as 50 sharklets after 12 months of gestation. This is, perhaps, the most advanced breeding behaviour of any fish, and it ensures that the young, from the very beginning, are fully developed miniature predators, starting life near the top of the food chain.

The system, however, has two serious flaws. Compared to the egg-laying of bony fish, it offers a very low reproduction rate, and the young grow extremely slowly: a shark may be one or two decades old before it is sexually mature. Yet as many as 1 million sharks die each year, supplying the demand for shark-fin soup. At the rate that sharks are being hauled out of the ocean by human fishing fleets, they will not be able to reproduce fast enough to survive.

Babycare

To give the next generation the very best chance of success, active parenting, however brief, is essential. Mammals do this particularly well and maximize their effectiveness by raising a single baby. Cetaceans, such as whales, dolphins and porpoises, manage this difficult task in often inhospitable oceanic conditions.

Baleen whales

Many baleen whales migrate thousands of kilometres between their preferred feeding grounds and breeding grounds. Perhaps they do this simply because their chosen territories have drifted further apart as the oceans have spread and grown under the control of plate tectonics (▷ p. 24). Or perhaps there are behavioural reasons for doing so.

3

The gray whale travels back and forth from the Bering Sea to breeding grounds in the warm coastal waters of Baja California – a round journey of 18,000 km (11,000 miles), the entire route hugging the coastline. Many other species, including the blue whale, travel further out in the open ocean on their annual travels.

Humpback whales feed in the rich waters of the temperate and polar seas, where there is an abundance of plankton and small fish, but such large appetites are best satisfied in small groups. If too many whales were to hunt in a small area, the food supplies would prove inadequate, so the animals are spread out over many thousands of kilometres.

Come the breeding season – January to March in the northern hemisphere, and July to October in the southern hemisphere – the humpback whales travel to focal points in the Tropics, such as Hawaii and Tonga, a distance of several thousand kilometres. They gather in huge numbers and the concentration of animals increases the strength of the gene pool.

By this point, pregnant females will have been gestating their embryos for 12 months and are ready to give birth. There are several advantages to doing so in tropical areas. Calves do not have much blubber at birth, so the warm water compensates for their poor insulation, and the salinity of the mid-ocean helps them to stay afloat. They also find it is easier to breathe in the sheltered waters of tropical islands.

As for nourishment, that is supplied by the mother's rich milk, and so effectively that the newborns may increase their weight eight-fold in the first 12 months of life. The mother is unlikely to have another calf for two years, as she puts all her energy into successfully nurturing her baby.

Toothed whales

Like their baleen relatives, toothed whales and dolphins display a great deal of care towards their offspring. They gestate their young for 10 – 16 months, depending on the species, and the mothers suckle their young for up to two years. Most do not make such massive migrations between feeding and breeding areas as the baleen whales because their energy stores are not sufficiently high. They therefore remain in food-rich areas to breed.

Being born in the ocean, the young must swim with the pack from the start. While they have no active involvement in hunting duties, they still need to keep up, and do this by hugging into their mother's bodies. The slipstream of the adult's path helps to draw the youngster through the water, allowing it to keep up while using minimal energy.

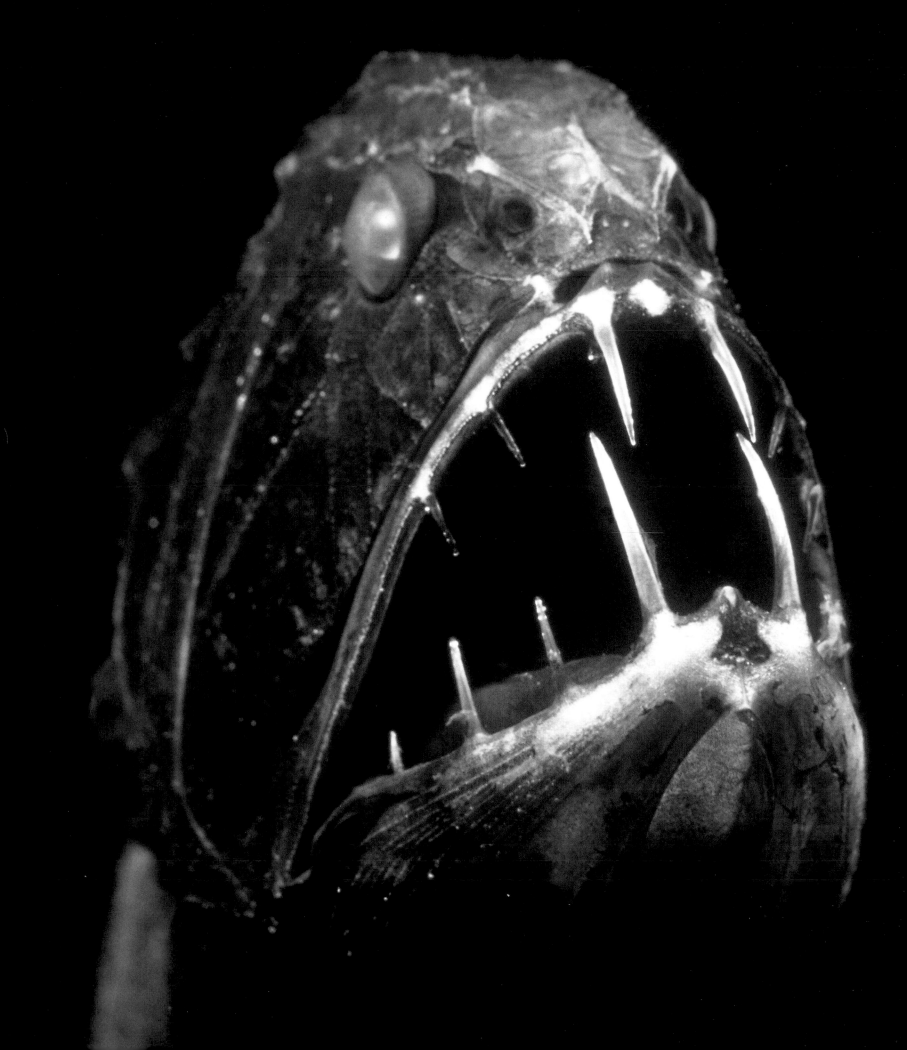

7

THE DEEP

7.1 THE TWILIGHT ZONE 314

At the top of the deep ocean there is a thin, horizontal strip which is penetrated by the last remnants of sunlight. This is a world of gloom where animals play a constant game of hide and seek.

HABITAT ILLUSTRATED SPREAD: The deep

7.2 THE DARK ZONE 330

Journey below 1000 m (3200 feet) and you enter a mid-water world of perpetual darkness where not even the faintest glimmer of sunlight penetrates.

SPECIAL FEATURE: Extraordinary deep-sea cephalopods

7.3 THE DEEP-SEA FLOOR 344

Life on the deep-sea floor relies almost entirely on food from the surface. With over 80 per cent of the ocean being more than 3000 m (9,840 feet) deep, these supply lines can be very long.

SPECIAL FEATURE: The shape of the deep-sea floor

7.4 LIFE WITHOUT THE SUN 360

At the bottom of the deep sea there are two remarkable communities of life that exist independently of energy from the sun – the hot vents and the cold seeps.

SPECIAL FEATURE: Exploring the abyss

THE TWILIGHT ZONE

The deep sea is by far the largest habitat for life on Earth. By volume, it makes up almost 80 per cent of the available space, while the land represents just 0.5 per cent, and yet it remains the least-known part of our world. More people have travelled into space than have journeyed down to the depths of the abyss. The enormous pressures make exploration extremely difficult, and until very recently the deep ocean was thought to be almost completely barren. How could there be life in the total darkness of the deepest seas? Today we are just beginning to understand the enormous variety and quantity of life down there, having as yet explored less than 1 per cent of it. The deep sea is the last true frontier on Earth. Our journey down into the deep ocean starts 150 m (492 feet) below the surface where there is no longer enough sunlight for photosynthesis. This is the beginning of the twilight zone – a world of gloom where animals play a constant game of hide and seek.

Previous page: The fangtooth is an aggressive deep-sea predator with some of the largest teeth, relative to body size, in the ocean.

INTO THE GLOOM

A sperm whale takes its last breath of air for over an hour. It is about to leave the warm, sunlit surface waters and dive down a thousand metres into the deep ocean in search of squid to eat. Only sperm whales and a few other toothed whales dive this deep. Even with scuba gear, most people rarely go below 30 m (98 feet). The only way that we can follow the whales is in specially designed submarines, which can carry just two or three observers and a pilot. Only a handful of these craft worldwide can reach 1000 m (3280 feet), and none at all can get to the bottom of the Marianas Trench, which at 11,022 m (36,161 feet) is the deepest part of the ocean.

The problem is pressure. When a whale leaves the surface of the water, the pressure is just 1 atmosphere, the equivalent of 1 kg per sq cm (2 lb per sq in). By the time it reaches 1000 m (3280 feet) the pressure will have increased 100 times and the whale's lungs will have been crushed flat, containing just 1 per cent of the volume of air they had at the surface. If the whale were able to dive down to 10,000 m (32,808 feet) the pressure would be 1000 times that at the surface – just over 1 tonne per sq cm – enough to quickly kill the whale.

1. Sperm whales are among the deepest diving mammals, reaching at least 1000 m (3280 feet) in dives that last for over an hour.

It is not just the change in pressure, however, that the sperm whale would experience as it descended, it would also notice a change in temperature. At the surface, water temperatures vary a great deal, depending on location. The water at the poles, for example, is considerably colder than water in the Tropics, but the deeper you go, the more uniform the temperature becomes. The biggest change occurs in the first 1000 m (3280 feet): in fact, tropical waters can drop from 20 °C (68 °F) to around 5 °C (41 °F) in just a few hundred metres. Below 1000 m (3280 feet), temperatures are remarkably similar throughout the ocean and range from 4 °C (39 °F) to -1 °C (30 °F).

Safe inside a submarine, the external changes in pressure and temperature are unnoticeable. However, the decrease in light becomes apparent very quickly. Even in the clearest tropical seas, little useful sunlight penetrates much beyond 150 m (492 feet). For many years, therefore, it was thought that only animals would be found below this depth because there was simply not enough light for plants to photosynthesize – a process vital to their survival. However, small red algae have been seen growing at almost 300 m (984 feet) – a depth record for plants. This, though, is very much the exception, and the vast majority of life in the ocean is restricted to the top 100–200 m (328–656 feet), the so-called photic zone, where photosynthesis is possible.

In the clearest seas tiny quantities of light can penetrate as deep as 1000 m (3280 feet). Below that depth is a dark world untouched by sunlight. Between this dark zone and the photic zone way above is an in-between world known as the twilight zone.

Life in the twilight zone

As the submarine gently descends into the increasing gloom of the twilight zone, you have to look hard to spot any life at all. Occasionally there will be a quick flash of

1. The deep-sea amphipod *Cystisoma* is almost totally transparent. Its head is filled with two enormous eyes that search for prey in the twilight.

2. *Phronima* is a deep-sea amphipod that hijacks the body of a salp, in which it lays its pink eggs.

Overleaf: The leptocephalus larvae of European eels hatch out in the Sargasso Sea and spend two or three years drifting in the Gulf Stream, eventually reaching rivers throughout western Europe.

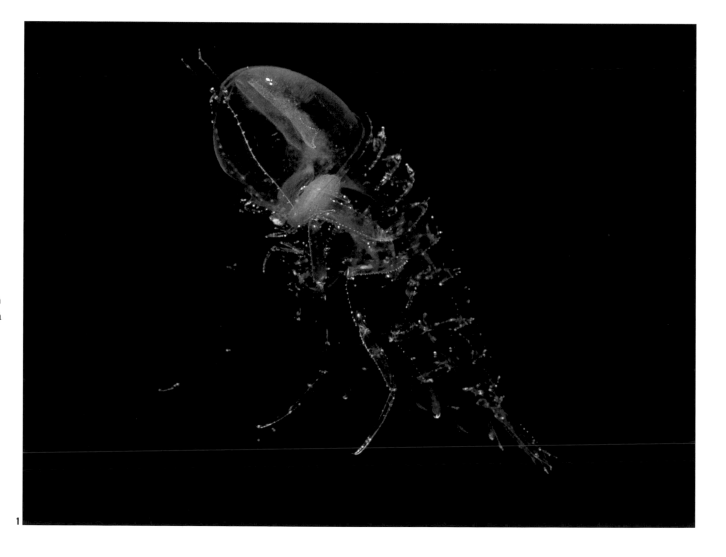

silver as a tiny fish dashes into the darkness, or a beautiful jellyfish will twinkle in the submarine lights, but for the most part it seems empty of life. This first impression is not entirely wrong because on average the twilight zone has only 10 per cent of the life found in the photic zone above.

In recent years, submarines and remote cameras have begun to explore the mid-water and discovered more about the extraordinary animals that live in this world of endless gloom. Many are difficult to see because they go to great lengths not to be seen – a good way of avoiding predators. The beautiful amphipod *Cystisoma*, for example, is 15 cm

(6 in) long and perfectly transparent, like a beautiful glass sculpture. Every organ in its body is completely see-through, and its whole head consists of two massive transparent eyes designed to make maximum use of the tiny amounts of light that reach this depth. Another completely see-through life form from the twilight zone is the monstrous crustacean *Phronima*, which looks so terrifying that it was the inspiration for the creature in the 1979 film *Alien*. Like its Hollywood offspring, *Phronima* is a parasite: it takes over the body of a salp, a member of the jellyfish family, living and bringing up its young inside it. Quite different in looks from a normal ▷▷

▷ SURVIVING THE PRESSURE

As a memento of their deep-sea dives, biologists tie polystyrene drinking cups to the outside of the submersible before they embark on their trip. By the time they reach the surface again, the cups are crushed into tiny rigid thimbles just a couple of centimetres tall. How, then, can deep-sea animals survive such crushing pressures? In fact, an animal that normally lives at the bottom of the ocean is no more aware of the pressure upon it than human beings on land are aware of several tonnes of atmosphere bearing down. In both cases, the internal and external pressures are the same. We notice a problem only if the pressure changes — when going up in a plane, for instance, or doing some scuba diving. Most deep-sea animals are full of water, and since liquids are almost incompressible, they can survive enormous pressures. Fish, though, can experience difficulties with their swim-bladders. To trim their buoyancy, fish inflate or deflate these gas-filled organs as necessary, but changes in external pressure can have a dramatic effect on the size of swim-bladders which would double in volume if the outside pressure were halved. As every diver knows, this is a particular problem near the surface. Dive from the surface down to 10 m (33 feet) and the pressure doubles. But dive down from 5000 m (16,404 feet) a further 10 m (33 feet) and the pressure goes up from 500 times that at the surface to 501 times. The change in pressure is therefore far more gradual in the deep sea and even fish with swim-bladders can journey quite freely between the depths in the deep ocean.

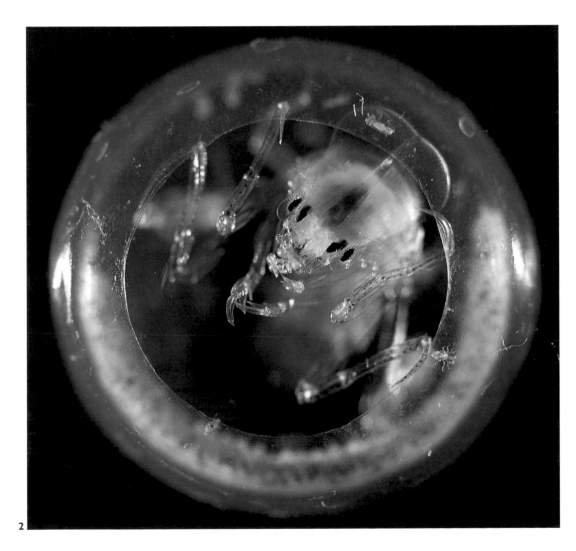

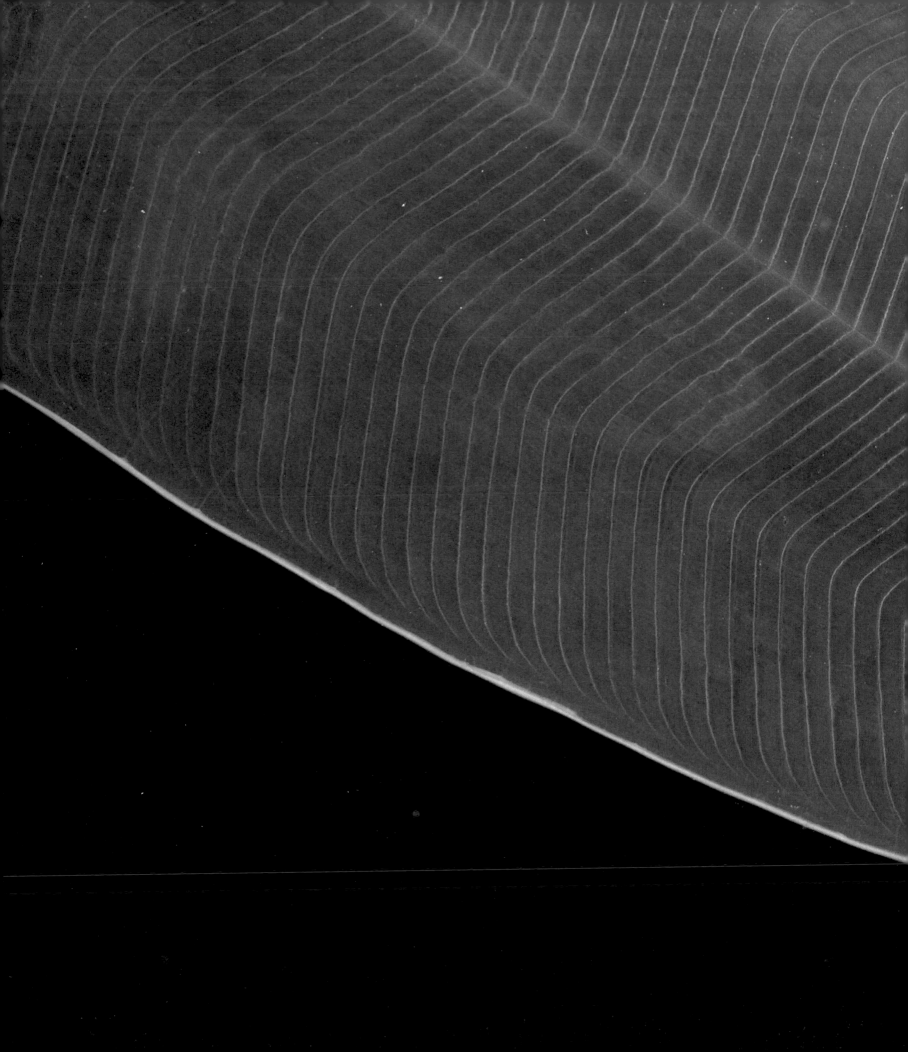

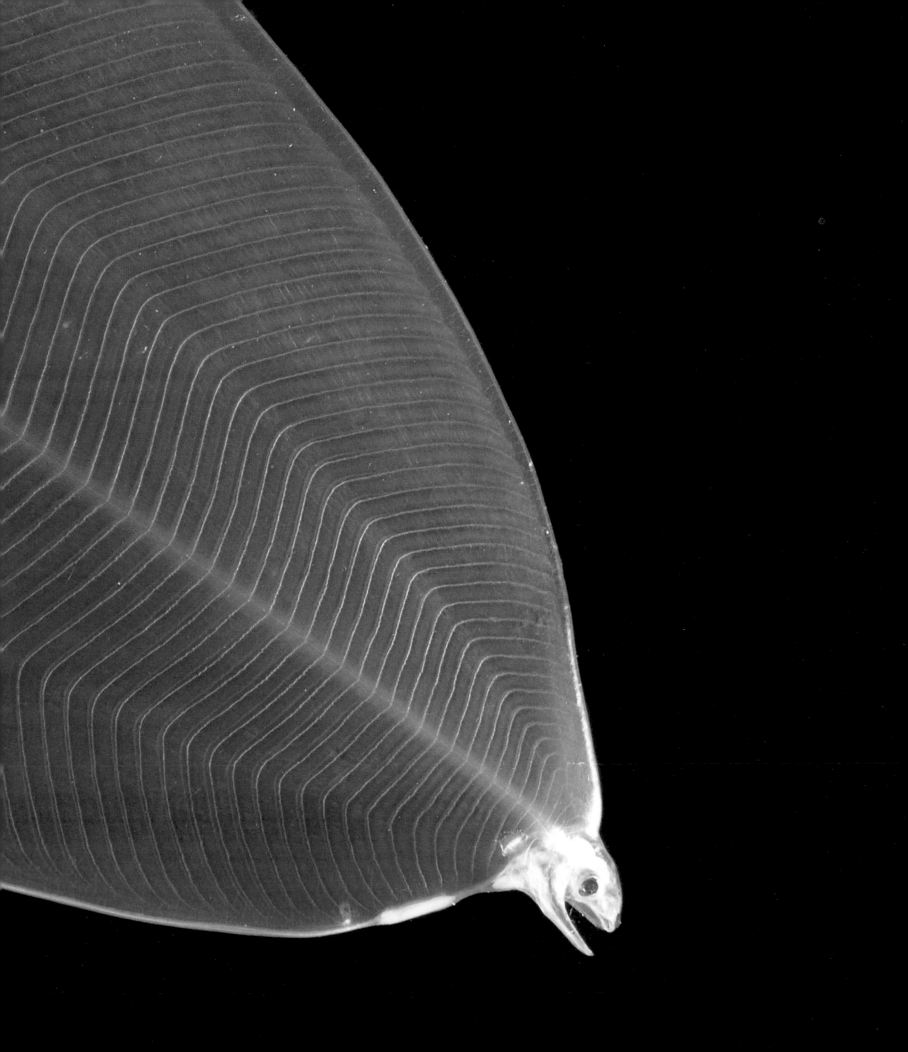

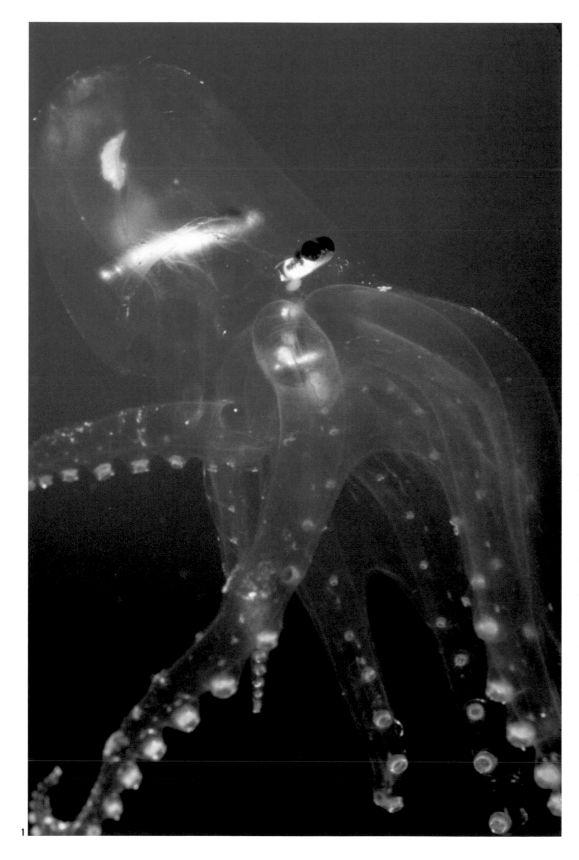

crustacean, it has two giant eyes on a hammer-shaped head and an array of weapons to attack its prey, giving it the appearance of a transparent Swiss Army penknife.

But the most terrifying weapons in the twilight zone must surely be the rotating sets of razor-sharp teeth belonging to the heteropods. Although these animals are from the same family as the snails, they have managed to make themselves almost invisible in the gloom. Even their external shell is transparent. The teeth of these predators are carried on a long, mobile proboscis, rather like an elephant's trunk.

Even the most sophisticated of invertebrates – the squid and octopus – have managed to make themselves practically invisible in the gloom. Where complex organs, such as the eyes, are impossible to make transparent, the animals will break up their outline with a reflective layer of silver. These mid-water cephalopods can achieve transparency in a way that their shallow-water cousins never could, because their bodies do not need to be as physically strong. Throughout their lives, they will never meet a hard surface as they float through the endless gloom of this world without walls.

The jelly net

Now and again, the mid-water darkness is lit up by a colourful firework display when a comb jelly or jellyfish floats gently through the lights of the submarine. The jellies – as comb jellies, jellyfish and siphonophores are collectively known – are an important part of the twilight zone ecosystem, making up a complex food web in which predators and prey interact.

Comb jellies or ctenophores get their name from the comb-like rows of ctenes that occur along the length of their bodies. These consist

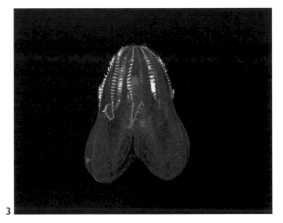

The largest siphonophores reach 40 m (131 feet) in length, making them one of the longest animals on Earth.

of fused groups of short fibres called cilia, which beat in synchronous waves and transport the jellies through the water. In the glare of the submarine headlights, it is these rows of beating cilia that create interference patterns in the light to produce an explosion of rainbow colours.

The gentle movements and great beauty of the jellies belie their aggressive nature. In fact, most of them are extremely efficient predators, feeding on shrimps, fish and other jellies. Many ctenophores let out a delicate net of sticky tentacles in which they trap their prey. Another species, called *Beroë*, specializes in feeding on other gelatinous animals, which it sucks up with the wide mouth that spreads right across the front of its body. But the most impressive of all the jelly predators are the siphonophores. They drag the ocean with a net of literally hundreds of slender tentacles covered in

deadly stinging cells. In this way they can capture fish, shrimps and a wide variety of other jellies.

What is fascinating about siphonophores is that they are not a single animal but a linear colony made up of many individuals attached to a common stem. Just as in a colony of bees, different individuals have different roles. Some are at the top of the colony, forming a pulsating bell that propels the siphonophore through the water. Others are involved in reproduction or in capturing prey. Unlike bees, however, the individuals in a siphonophore are linked together and nobody is sure whether they should be considered as a complex colony of individuals that are joined together, or some sort of 'super organism'. The complex feeding behaviour that has recently been observed in some siphonophores, seems to support the idea of 'super organisms' with complex shared nervous systems.

1. The deep-sea squid *Vitronella* has an almost totally transparent body that makes it practically invisible in the gloom of the twilight zone.

2. Siphonophores are colonial jellyfish that can reach up to 40 m (131 foot) long. They drag the ocean with hundreds of tentacles covered in deadly stinging cells.

3. Caught in the lights of a submersible, the beating cilia on this deep-sea comb jelly produce a firework-like display of interference colours.

THE DEEP

The deep ocean is one of the most fascinating of all the ocean habitats. Stretching from roughly 200 m (656 feet) below the surface the deep ocean extends through the twilight and dark zones to the sea floor itself. It is a world of darkness inhabited by ferocious-looking creatures that have adapted to survive in this inhospitable environment. Man has only explored a fraction of this habitat, but what has been discovered goes some way towards revealing the unique conditions under which the creatures of the deep ocean eke out an existence.

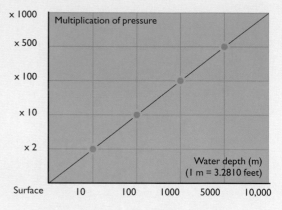

The change of pressure is considerably greater at the water surface (doubling from the surface down to 10 m/33 feet) than in the deep sea.

Life under pressure

At 1000 m (3280 feet) below the surface of the oceans the pressure increases to 100 times that at the surface. A human being would be crushed, but the creatures that live here are designed to cope with pressure. Many are filled with water and, since liquids are almost incompressible, they can survive without difficulty.

Creatures of the deep sea must be efficient predators as food is hard to come by. Some nutrients from decaying organisms fall from the shallower waters as marine snow, but this is not enough to meet demands. Many of the fish have large teeth and gaping jaws enabling them to eat prey of many times their own size. A large percentage also exhibit bioluminescence. Here, photophores on the creatures' bodies light up, serving a range of functions including illuminating prey and confusing predators.

While most of the deep-sea floor is featureless, the edges of the oceanic plates are much more varied, with deep trenches and mountainous ridges. As new sea floor is produced at underwater volcanoes, heated sea water gushes out as hydrothermal vents. Full of minerals, these vents are unique oases of life, existing independently of the sun's energy.

3

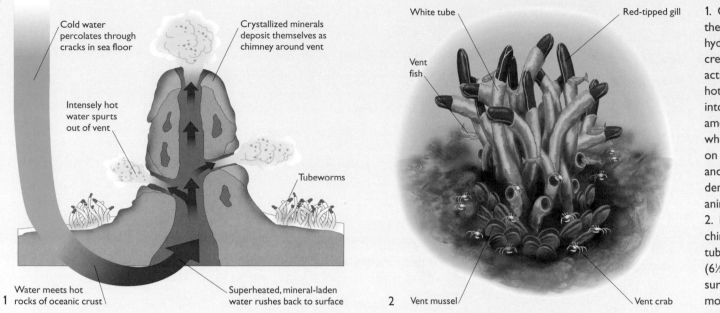

Cold water percolates through cracks in sea floor

Crystallized minerals deposit themselves as chimney around vent

Intensely hot water spurts out of vent

Tubeworms

Water meets hot rocks of oceanic crust

Superheated, mineral-laden water rushes back to surface

1

White tube

Red-tipped gill

Vent fish

2 Vent mussel

Vent crab

1. Characterized by their tall black chimneys, hydrothermal vents are created by volcanic activity releasing very hot, mineral-laden water into the ocean. They are among the few habitats where life does not rely on energy from the sun, and they sustain a vast density and variety of animal life.

2. Packed around the chimneys are amazing tubeworms, up to 2 m (6½ feet) long, surrounded by molluscs, crabs and fish.

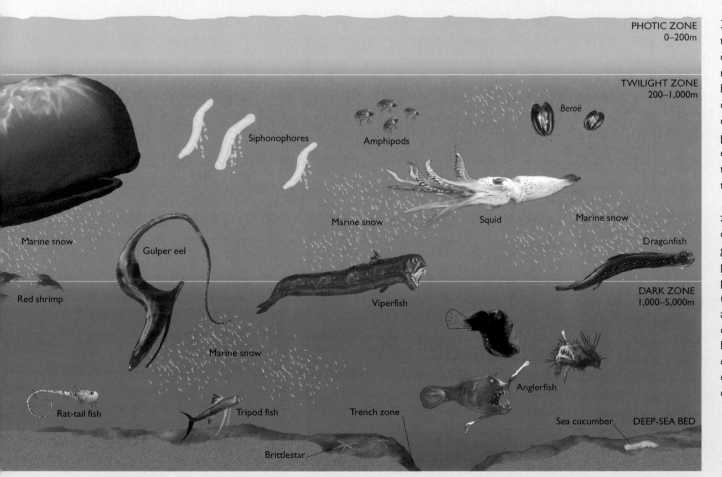

PHOTIC ZONE
0–200m

TWILIGHT ZONE
200–1,000m

Siphonophores

Amphipods

Beroë

Marine snow

Marine snow

Squid

Marine snow

Gulper eel

Dragonfish

Red shrimp

Viperfish

DARK ZONE
1,000–5,000m

Marine snow

Anglerfish

Rat-tail fish

Tripod fish

Trench zone

Sea cucumber   DEEP-SEA BED

Brittlestar

3. Creatures in the twilight zone are often transparent or reflective silver, blending in with the dim light to avoid detection from predators. Many have excellent vision to help them search out prey in the gloomy depths.

Creatures in the dark zone are usually black or dark red, frequently grotesque and with poor vision. Most produce their own light (bioluminescence) to attract prey, to alarm or confuse predators, as a headlight, or as a means of communication with other animals of their own species.

⭐ Over 90 per cent of the animals that live in the mid-water of the deep sea are bioluminescent.

1. *Winteria* has extraordinary tubular eyes, designed to look up at the surface and spot the silhouettes of potential prey.

2. Hatchetfish have flattened bodies to reduce their silhouette, and silvered sides that act like mirrors, reflecting back the remnants of light from the surface.

3. Along their bellies hatchetfish have light-producing cells called photophores that break up their silhouette from below by exactly matching the colour of light from the surface.

HIDE AND SEEK

Survival in the twilight zone is very much a case of see or be seen. A constant battle is waged between predators and their prey, a game of hide and seek, where every predator knows there is always a bigger fish out there ready to eat it. With so little light penetrating these gloomy depths, animals need powerful senses to search out their prey. Good eyesight is particularly important, and many animals in the twilight zone have very impressive eyes. Among the most spectacular are those protruding from the head of *Winteria*, a fish with the appearance of an underwater bush-baby. These tubular eyes concentrate the light from one particular direction and produce very acute vision.

Many fish in the twilight zone have tubular eyes that are designed to look upwards at the surface where they hope the remnants of light will outline the silhouettes of their prey. The problem with tubular eyes is that they are not so good for lateral (side-to-side) vision. To compensate for this, some of these fish have very large retinas that allow them to see to the sides and below. Adaptations very similar to tubular eyes have been found in at least one octopus and even some shrimps. The deep-sea squid *Histioteuthis* has taken a different strategy and has one eye much larger than the other. It is thought that the squid hangs in the water column with its large eye looking up at the surface and its small eye checking out below.

Hiding in the gloom

In an attempt to escape the powerful eyes of predators, animals in the twilight zone have made many adaptations of their own. As already noted, transparency can be very useful but it is not possible with all body designs. Those who cannot achieve it have had to resort to other tricks. The eelpout, for example, which looks rather like a pink eel, responds to threats from predators by bringing its tail round to its mouth and forming a bagel shape. In this position, it will float completely motionless through the water for many minutes before suddenly darting away when the predator has gone. It is thought that the eelpout's bagel pose makes it resemble a jelly-fish that the predator would prefer to avoid.

A completely different trick is used by hatchetfish. They have tubular eyes to spot

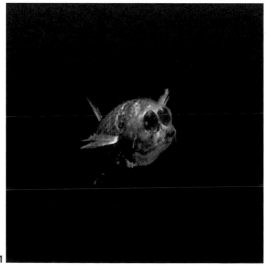

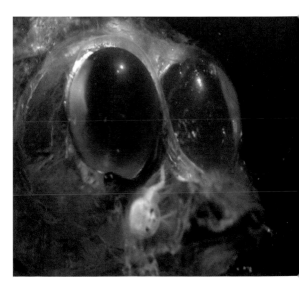

1

their own prey, but go to great lengths to avoid being eaten themselves. In the first place, their bodies are completely flattened to make them wafer-thin, greatly reducing the size of their silhouette. In addition, their whole bodies are covered in highly reflective silver. Just as a glass skyscraper can almost disappear against the sky when its windows reflect the patterns of clouds, the hatchetfish's reflective sides act like tiny mirrors, bouncing back remnants of blue light from the surface. As if these two disappearing tricks were not enough, hatchetfish have one other method of camouflage. All along their bellies they have a series of special light-producing cells called photophores. These can change colour to match the light penetrating from the surface and are thus very effective in breaking up the fish's silhouette from below.

One of the strangest of all deep-sea fish also uses bioluminescence for counter-illumination. *Opisthoproctus* not only has large, tubular eyes for looking at the surface, but behind its anus is a large gland that contains luminous bacteria. Its ventral surface has been flattened so that it looks rather like the bottom of an old steam iron. Light from the anal gland is transmitted to special cells on the flattened belly of the fish. The exact purpose of this wide, glowing belly is not clear, but it could certainly help to hide *Opisthoproctus*'s silhouette from below.

A wide range of other twilight zone fish, shrimps and squid also use photophores as a form of counter-illumination to disguise their silhouette. But in the constant arms race between predator and prey there is one more twist in the story. A number of predatory fish have developed massive eyes with special yellow lenses which are able to distinguish between the light coming from the surface and that produced by photophores. This means that even the hatchetfish's cleverest camouflage is cracked and that its silhouette is clearly visible from below.

2

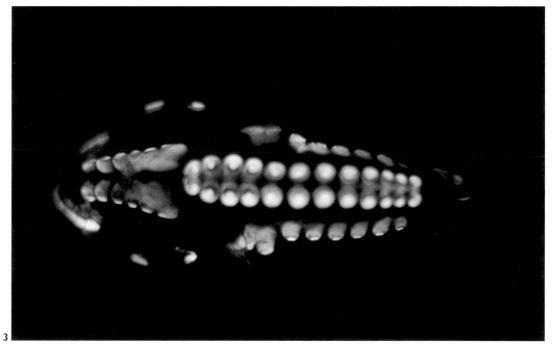

3

Of the 12,000 or so species of marine fish, only about 2000 live in the deep sea.

THE SEARCH FOR FOOD

The biggest problem faced by all animals living in the twilight zone is the chronic shortage of food. All the energy they require must come from the sunlit waters of the photic zone above, where photosynthesis is possible and plants can grow. Unfortunately, only about 20 per cent of the energy fixed in these shallow waters filters down to the twilight zone, and this has a dramatic effect on the animals living there. The fish, for instance, tend to be small,

but they make up for their diminutive size by looking absolutely terrifying. A good example is the aptly named viperfish, *Chauliodus*, which has a huge set of needle-like teeth that are too long to fit in its mouth; in fact, the lower teeth actually extend right up to the fish's eyes. What is more, these teeth are set in a hinged and highly extendible jaw, which gives the viperfish a massive rat-trap of a mouth.

The hunting strategy adopted by many twilight zone fish is not to waste energy swimming around searching for prey, but

1. Many fish that inhabit the twilight zone have impressive sets of teeth. Their food is so thinly spread that they must be able to deal with a wide range of prey in all sorts of different sizes.

2. Pteropods, or sea butterflies, are small snails that have modified their foot to form a pair of 'wings', which they use to move about in the water column.

simply to sit and wait. For this to be successful they have to be able to eat practically anything that comes by, whatever its size, and that is when a large extendible jaw, with enormous teeth, is particularly useful.

Another impressive predator from the twilight zone is *Barracudina*, a thin, sleek fish, with a sharply pointed snout and powerful teeth. This fish will hang absolutely vertical in the water column, looking straight up at the surface in order to spot the silhouettes of its prey. Another elegant, sit-and-wait predator is the long and sinuous snipe eel. Its mouth consists of an extraordinary bird-like beak whose two halves bend away from each other in two gentle curves. Each is covered in tiny, hook-like teeth, which are designed to trap the long antennae of passing shrimps as the snipe eel waits patiently in the gloom.

Vertical migration

Not all the animals that live in the twilight zone are willing to wait patiently for food to come to them. Each night under cover of darkness many journey up into the richer and shallower sunlit waters in search of food, returning to the depths during the day. This daily routine of vertical movement involves literally millions of tonnes of animals and is by far the largest migration of life on Earth, far outstripping the massed movements of wildebeest or migratory birds.

The full extent of this vertical migration was not really understood until after World War II, when sonar became more widely available. Sailors using sonar to map the depth of the ocean floor began to notice a surprising second echo coming back from shallower water at about 400 m (1312 feet). They were even more surprised that this second echo seemed to come from nearer the surface at night. They went on to discover that the echo came from greater depths on nights when the moon was 2

full, and drew closer when the moon went behind the clouds. Whatever was causing this echo was clearly very sensitive to light. What their sonar had revealed, of course, was the animals involved in vertical migration. The sailors called this 'false bottom' the deep scattering layer, and scientists used nets to discover the enormous number and variety of animals responsible for reflecting back the sonar's echo. Plankton, krill, shrimps, copepods, jellies and squid are all involved, but the most important members of the deep scattering layer seem to be fish, particularly lantern fish and bristlemouths.

Lantern fish, ranging in size from 5–15 cm (2–6 in), have large heads and big round eyes. They get their name from the array of light-producing photophores along their head, belly and sides. Bristlemouths are a similar size and are named after their mouthful of tiny, brush-like teeth. Unlike the sit-and-wait fish of the twilight zone, lantern fish and bristlemouths have strong muscular bodies and have retained their swim-bladders, which maintain and vary their buoyancy. These two species are the most abundant fish in the twilight zone and it is thought that the sonar echo from the deep scattering layer is produced mostly by reflections off their swim-bladders. In fact, bristlemouths are probably the most numerous fish in the sea, outstripping even the enormous shoals of herring and anchovies.

The extent of vertical migration varies a great deal between species. The smallest plankton, measuring less than a millimetre long, probably travel up only 10–20 m (33–66 feet) each night. Large plankton and copepods may rise 100–300 m (328–984 feet), while fish and larger animals might manage as much as 1000 m (3281 feet) every night. The real champion of vertical migration has to be the lantern fish, *Ceratoscopelus warmingii*, which nightly undertakes a three-hour journey from 1700 m (5577 feet) down, rising to within 100 m (328 feet) of the surface. In the morning, it repeats its three-hour journey in reverse.

Why do lantern fish and all the other vertical migrants expend so much energy in these nightly journeys? Nobody is absolutely sure, but the abundance of food plants in the photic layer must be the main attraction for the herbivorous animals. Non-vegetarian animals that make the journey upwards presumably have no option but to follow their prey into shallower water. Whatever their diet, all vertical migrants take a risk in coming nearer the surface because the density of predators is far greater there. Since most of the predators in shallow, sunlit waters hunt visually, vertical migrants are careful only to approach the surface under the cover of darkness. Even moonlight can be dangerous. By dawn, vertical migrants return to the safety of the endless gloom where they feel most at home. Vertical migration is vital for all life in the deep ocean. It represents a massive daily injection of new energy carried from the surface, which eventually will work its way down through the food chain to even the deepest ocean floor.

1. Lantern fish get their name from the light-producing photophores that cover their bodies.

2. This deep-sea heteropod is a transparent snail that has lost all but the remnants of its shell. At the end of its proboscis is a set of teeth, which it uses to dispatch its prey.

3. (opposite) The Paper nautilus, or Argonaut derives its name from the beautiful papery shell that surrounds the female and in which she broods her eggs.

THE DARK ZONE

Journey below 1000 m (3280 feet) and you leave the twilight zone for a mid-water world of perpetual darkness where not even the faintest glimmer of sunlight penetrates. Here the pressure is more than 100 times greater than at the surface, and the temperature is remarkably uniform and cold, typically 1–2 °C (34–37 °F). This is by far the largest single habitat on Earth, containing three-quarters of all the liquid water on our planet. Yet it is a world we hardly know: just a few hundred lucky people have had the chance to observe the life down here, through the reinforced portholes of submersibles. The enormous changes in pressure mean that practically all the animals caught from this depth are dead by the time they reach the surface. The animals we have brought to the surface in nets have some of the strangest body forms found anywhere on Earth. These are the real monsters of the deep, designed to live in a world of darkness where food is in very short supply.

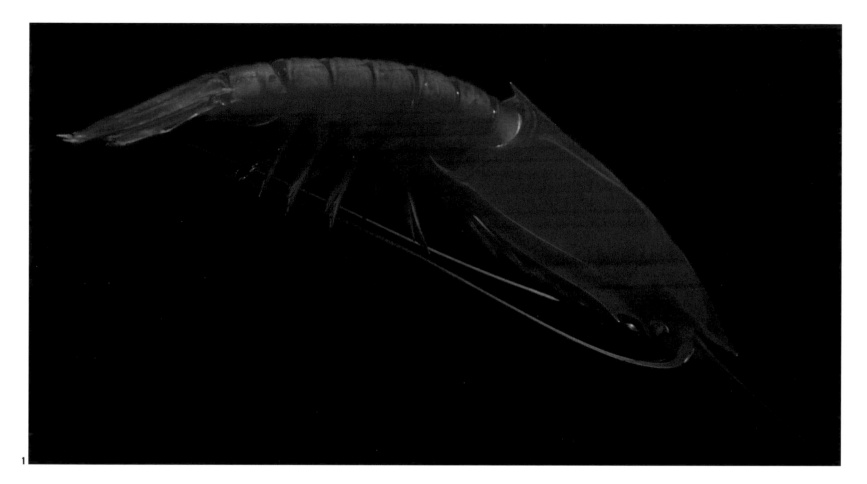

1

LIFE IN THE DARK ZONE

As the submersible travels beyond the twilight zone into the dark zone, glimpses of life become rarer and rarer. This is hardly surprising because life here is very sparse, and what does exist is designed to be hidden in the darkness. With no natural light penetrating this deep, there is no camouflage value to be gained from transparency or counter-shading. Instead, the animals here are usually either black or dark red. Deep-sea shrimps, for example, are the colour of blood, but this is visible only in white light. Down in the dark zone where there is no red light at all, these shrimps appear black and disappear into the darkness.

Practically all the fish down here are black, and many of them are alarming in

appearance. Most monstrous of all though are anglerfish. Most are far smaller than people expect at less than 10 cm (4 in) long, but all have a terrifying set of teeth and gigantic heads out of all proportion to the rest of their bodies. Their common names such as triple-wart sea devil and common black devil-fish are all suitably pejorative. Anglers are not only the most grotesque fish in the sea, but also among the most fascinating.

Desperate for food

Only 5 per cent of the energy generated in the sunlit waters of the shallow ocean makes it down to the dark zone, so food is extremely scarce. Animals down here cannot resort to the vertical migrations undertaken by those living in the twilight zone because the rich

1. The dark red colour of this dark-zone shrimp is perfect camouflage in a world where no red light penetrates down from the surface.

★ The largest deep-sea anglerfish can reach a length of 1 m (3 feet) and weigh as much as 9 kg (20 lb).

surface waters are just too far away and the changes in pressure too great. Instead, animals in the dark zone can do nothing but wait for their food to come to them.

The fish down here, such as deep-sea anglers, are mostly sedentary and sluggish, with flabby muscles and weak skeletons. Nearly all lack a functional swim-bladder, and they seem designed to use as little energy as possible while waiting in the water column for the next meal to come along. Catching that meal in the darkness is the challenge that has dominated the design of dark-zone fish. With no natural light at this depth, vision is not very helpful and most of the fish have very small eyes. Instead, many have become very sensitive to the smallest vibrations in the water. Some have thin, rod-like bodies that they try to keep completely straight. All along their sides are lateral lines of cells sensitive to tiny vibrations. By keeping their bodies rigid, they turn themselves into aerials, able to pick up the subtlest of signals. The aptly named fangtooth not only has a very impressive set of teeth, but its body is pockmarked with pores that are sensitive to the movements of its prey. But the ultimate listening stations in the darkness have to be the hairy anglers, which are covered with so many long, sensitive antennae that they look more like large hairy gooseberries than fish.

Since meals are so rare and unpredictable, fish in the dark zone have to be able to kill and eat anything that floats by, however large. That is why deep-sea anglers have such enormous mouths, powerful teeth and expandable stomachs. But the fish with the largest mouths of all are gulper eels, which are found at depths of 2000 m (6560 feet) or below. Their body consists almost entirely of mouth, with jaws that are loosely hinged and highly expandable, allowing them to eat prey at least as big as themselves. Hanging vertically in the water column, they have a thin, eel-like appearance, with a tiny eye on top of their heads. When their prey comes close enough, the mouth opens like an enormous umbrella and engulfs the meal.

Fishing for supper

Waiting for food to arrive is not acceptable to all dark-zone fish, and many have developed ▷▷

1. (opposite) The hairy angler is covered with antennae that are sensitive to the tiniest movements in the water. Its highly expandable stomach allows it to eat very large prey.

2. Like many dark-zone fish, anglerfish are black or dark brown for camouflage. Their flabby muscles and weak skeletons are suited to their sedentary energy-saving lifestyles.

Overleaf: The gulper eel's body consists almost entirely of one massive mouth which, combined with a highly expandable stomach, allows it to eat prey at least as big as itself. **2**

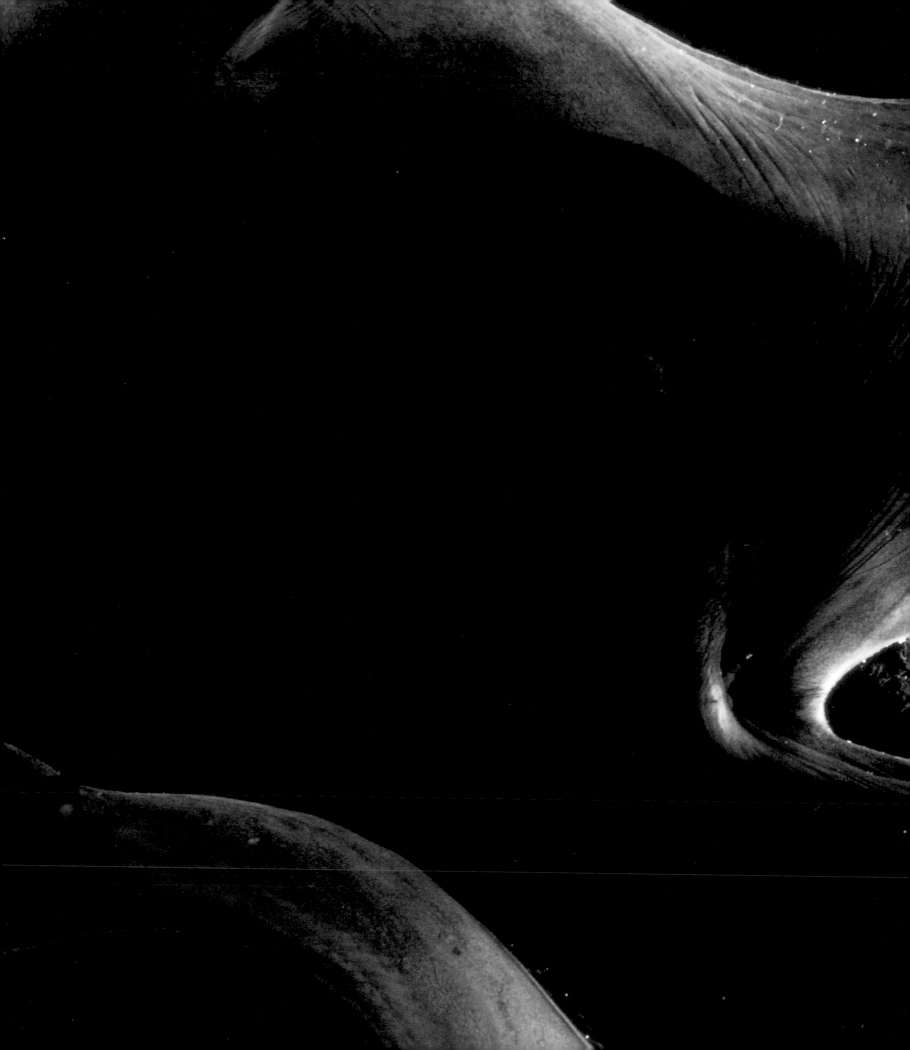

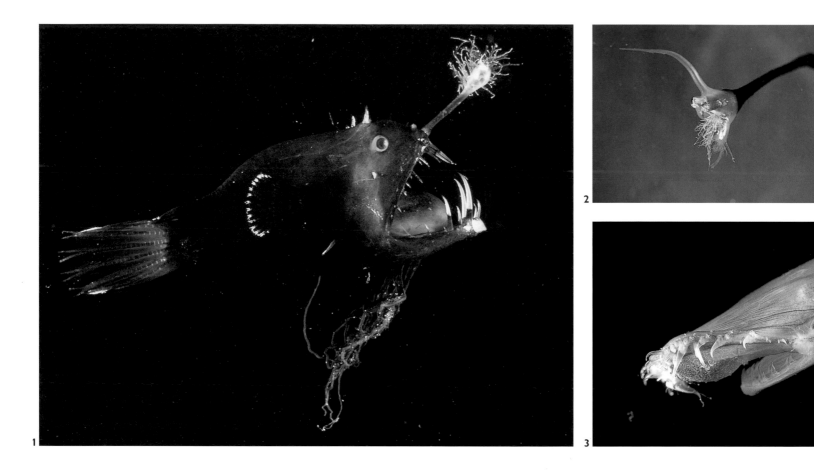

1. Anglerfish attract prey using a lure suspended on a specially adapted dorsal fin in front of their mouths.

2. An anglerfish lure is full of symbiotic bacteria that produce a bioluminescent glow.

3. The anglerfish *Thaumatichthys* have their lures hanging from the roof of their mouths, which are fringed with sharp teeth.

4. Many dragonfish have barbels hanging from their chins with luminous lures at the end. Exactly how these are used to attract prey remains a mystery.

clever ways of attracting prey. The masters at this are anglerfish, which get their name from their habit of 'fishing' for food using a glowing lure. Each species has a specially modified dorsal fin that sticks like a pole out of the top of their head. On the end of the pole is a lure full of symbiotic bacteria, which produces a bioluminescent glow. The lure is often decorated with filaments or branches that also glow in the dark, the aim being to make it more attractive. Anglerfish suspend the lure in front of their mouths and gently flash away. As any light is intriguing in a world of darkness, curious prey come closer and closer. Suddenly, like a mousetrap, the angler will snap up the surprised prey with its massive mouth and razor-sharp teeth.

The variety of anglerfish lures is as extraordinary as the fish themselves. Whip-nosed anglers have fishing poles that emerge from a position just above the mouth, and in some cases can be four or five times longer than the fish itself. The exact purpose of a lure so far from the mouth is difficult to imagine. One other group of anglers known as the *Thaumatichthys*, literally 'wonder fish', have their lure attached to the roof of their mouth, which is lined with long, sharp, teeth. What better place to attract the prey than into the mouth itself?

The *Linophryne* genus anglerfish (which literally means 'toad that fishes with a net') are unique in having two different lighting systems. In addition to the usual lure on their head, they also have an extraordinary barbel on their chins that generates its own light. In some species this barbel consists of tens of different branching filaments which look rather like a splendid hanging basket glowing in the darkness.

LIGHT IN THE DARK

While there is absolutely no sunlight in the dark zone, most of the animals that live there produce their own light. This biological light, or bioluminescence, is usually created by the animals themselves, but some animals, such as anglerfish, use bacteria living symbiotically in their bodies to produce the light for them.

Anglers are not the only deep-sea fish that use light to attract their prey. In the darker and deepest parts of the twilight zone there is a terrifying group of predators commonly called dragonfish. Although small, these fearful fish have large armoured heads and a mouthful of sharp teeth better described as fangs. But their most impressive weapons have to be the barbels that hang down from their chins and usually have luminous lures at the end. These barbels come in all shapes and sizes and often have many branching filaments resembling the root system of a plant – one 15-cm (6-in) dragonfish has a thin barbel that grows to

more than 2 m (6.5 feet). Exactly how these fish use their lures is still largely a matter of speculation. Very few have been caught alive, and only a small number of people have ever been lucky enough to watch their natural behaviour in situ from a submersible.

Dragonfish do not rely on glowing barbels alone to catch their prey. Many of them also have a large, light-producing organ, called a photophore, behind their eyes, which may act like a headlight. Being muscular fish by deep-sea standards, dragonfish may actively hunt for their prey using their built-in beam.

Practically all the bioluminescence created in deep waters is blue or bluey-green because these wavelengths penetrate the water best and most deep-sea animals have eyes sensitive to them. However, a few species, such as the loose-jawed dragonfish, have the ability to produce red light. In this case, only the fish itself can see the red light it produces, so it can illuminate unsuspecting prey while remaining undetected itself – a system not

4

 CREATING BIOLUMINESCENCE

Bioluminescence, or the emission of light by living organisms, is created through a process of oxidation, or burning: a substrate called luciferin is oxidized in the presence of a catalytic enzyme called luciferase. Animals are able to decide exactly when to produce light by controlling when the luciferin and luciferase are mixed together in light-producing cells called photophores. In many fish, crustaceans and squid these light-producing cells are associated with reflectors, light guides or filters, which can concentrate and direct the light as required. Almost all luciferin produces blue light – as in the case of the *Periphylla*, illustrated, right – which penetrates water well, but some animals create yellow, green and, in a few cases, red light. Most animals in the deep-sea can produce their own luciferins, but some get theirs from bacteria growing in their light organs. The lures of the anglerfish contain colonies of luciferin-producing bacteria, which are completely self-contained and isolated from the rest of the fish. Exactly how these precious bacteria are passed on from generation to generation remains a mystery.

unlike the night-vision scopes used by the military. The red light may also provide a secret channel of communication visible only to other dragonfish.

Light for escape

In the constant battle between predators and prey, bioluminescence has also been put to very effective use by animals that want to avoid being eaten. In the twilight zone, photophores are used by a variety of animals to break up their silhouette from below. In the dark zone there is no light from the surface, however, so counter-illumination is unnecessary. Instead, prey animals use bioluminescence to alarm or confuse their predators. Copepod crustaceans, for example, flash brilliantly when attacked and their call for help may serve to warn other copepods or even attract the assailants' own predators. Some species of copepod release packets of bioluminescence outside their bodies, which explode like tiny fireworks in the darkness. Sometimes the explosion of light is delayed so that it detonates away from the copepod that released it. This confuses the predator into chasing after the flash only to find that the copepod has long ago disappeared into the darkness.

Other creatures have different techniques. Certain shrimps spew out a sticky glowing liquid when approached which not only confuses the predator, but also leaves it covered with a bright glow that makes it obvious to its own predators. At least one squid, *Heteroteuthis*, also shoots out a cloud of bioluminescent confusion into the water. But it is the dark-zone jellyfish that produce

1. The loose-jawed dragonfish *Melanstomias* produces red light from a special organ beneath its eye, which it may use as a headlight to illuminate its prey in the darkness.

2. If attacked by a predator, the deep-sea jellyfish *Atolla* illuminates its whole body in a spectacular bioluminescent display that resembles a Catherine wheel.

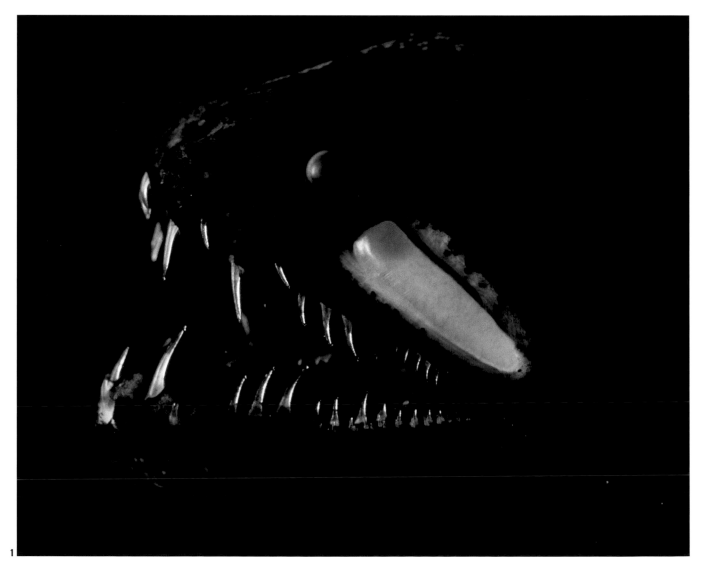

1

the most impressive firework displays. One moment they are floating gently through the dark, then suddenly, if touched by a predator, their bodies ignite with waves and pulses of bioluminesence. With the medusa *Periphylla*, the whole bell glows with a wave of light that runs right down to the tip of the tentacles, while the red, round *Atolla* jellyfish lights up like a Catherine wheel. The *Colobonema* jellyfish not only flashes its whole body, but also sheds some of its glowing tentacles. This sacrifice attracts the predator's attention while the jelly escapes.

Although most animals in the deep can produce light biologically, they use it very conservatively. Jellies, for instance, only flash when approached by predators in what is often called the 'burglar alarm' response. By creating light the jellies can attract predators to the scene, which might want to eat the animal threatening them. But the corollary of the burglar-alarm theory is the minefield theory. It suggests that the reason many animals try to hang motionless in the mid-water is to avoid setting off light explosions and attracting predators. It is a tense battle between seeing and avoiding being seen.

Only about five per cent of the food produced in the sunlit waters of the photic zone makes it down to the dark zone.

2

EXTRAORDINARY DEEP-SEA CEPHALOPODS

The deep-sea cephalopods – squid and octopus – have always been something of a mystery. Their agile, flexible bodies make them very difficult to catch in nets or trawls, and only recently have remote cameras and submersibles begun to reveal a little of their distribution and natural behaviour. Recorded now as deep as 5000 m (16,400 feet), the cephalopods include some of the strangest animals in the sea. The chambered nautilus is a living fossil, the last surviving representative of a group of animals that once ruled the ocean; *Vampyroteuthis* is a terrifying mixture of squid and octopus, while the giant squid is the largest invertebrate on Earth.

2. *Vampyroteuthis* – literally the 'vampire squid from hell' – is classified halfway between squid and octopus.

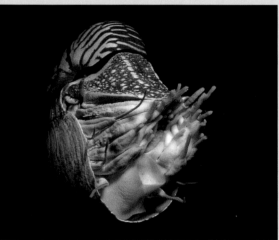

1. The chambered nautilus is the only cephalopod to have retained the hard outer shell characteristic of molluscs.

The chambered nautilus

While other cephalopods have lost practically all the hard outer shell that is characteristic of molluscs, the nautilus retains a large, heavy shell, which is divided into a series of sealed chambers. Only the last of these is occupied by the animal itself: all the other chambers are filled with gas to provide buoyancy and allow free movement in the water column. This adaptation allowed the nautiloids and their descendants to dominate the oceans for 200 million years, but then fish developed the swim-bladder, and the nautiloids found themselves outclassed. Most nautiloids therefore became extinct, and now only the nautilus survives. Found around 500 m (16,400 feet), very little is known about its biology. It appears to be primarily a scavenger, and when not feeding, spends most of the time 'asleep' in deep water, conserving energy.

Vampyroteuthis

Literally 'vampire squid from hell', *Vampyroteuthis* is about the size of a football.

It has a dark red body and menacing blue eyes, which, in proportion to body size, are the largest eyes in the animal kingdom. *Vampyroteuthis* is classified halfway between an octopus and a squid: it has eight arms linked by an umbrella of skin, but inside this web are two other thin arms that resemble the tentacles of a squid. At the opposite end of its body are two small, retractable fins. Living in the darkness at around 1000 m (3280 feet), *Vampyroteuthis* is completely covered in light-producing photophores. There are even two large photophores behind the fins with flaps of skin that work like eyelids, turning the light on and off. The really surprising thing about this animal only became clear when it was observed in its natural habitat by a remotely operated camera. *Vampyroteuthis* turned out to be a far faster-moving animal than its body design would suggest, and also had the ability to turn itself inside-out. Throwing its arms back over its mantle, it exposes its suckers to the

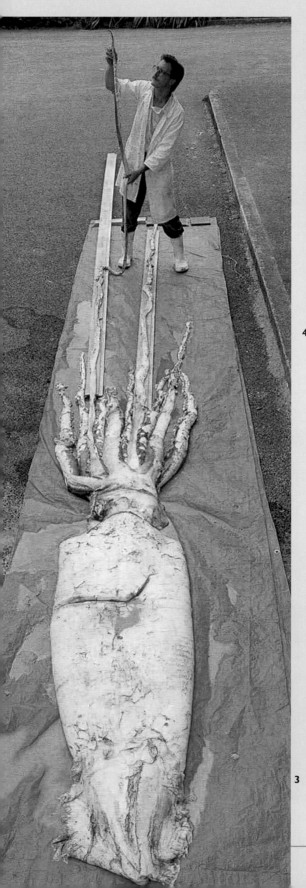

4

outside, giving it the appearance of a spiky pineapple. Nobody has yet explained this unusual behaviour.

Giant squid

At least 15 m (49 foot) long and weighing over a tonne, the giant squid is by far the largest animal without a backbone on land or sea, yet nobody has ever seen one alive. All our knowledge about the giant squid has come from dead specimens that get caught in fishing nets or wash up on beaches, particularly in New Zealand and Newfoundland. Their eyes, the size of dinner plates, suggest that the squid lives at the bottom of the twilight zone (▷ p. 314), where there is still some light to hunt. Alternatively, these huge eyes may be used to search for biolumines-cent prey at greater depths. Many sperm whales have sucker marks from giant squid, but these are probably inflicted when the whale tries to eat the squid rather than the other way round.

3

3. At over 15 m (49 foot) long, giant squid are by far the largest invertebrates on land or in the sea, but they have never been seen alive.

4. The deep-sea squid *Histioteuthis* has one larger eye, which it uses to look up at the surface for the silhouettes of its prey.

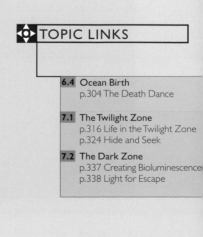

◆ TOPIC LINKS

6.4 Ocean Birth
p.304 The Death Dance

7.1 The Twilight Zone
p.316 Life in the Twilight Zone
p.324 Hide and Seek

7.2 The Dark Zone
p.337 Creating Bioluminescence
p.338 Light for Escape

SEX IN THE DARKNESS

Finding food in the vast, empty wastes of the dark zone is not the only problem faced by the animals that live there. With such small numbers of animals spread very thinly over an enormous area, it can be difficult to find a mate. One answer is to become hermaphrodite, and a good number of species do have both male and female gonads. For those that do not, bioluminescence can again prove very useful. All the many shrimps, squid and fish species with photophores have different light arrangements that are unique to each particular species. Often male and female light patterns vary too, and these differences may be very useful as animals try to search out a partner in the darkness. Predatory fish with lures may also use these attractive lights to signal to potential mates. Anglerfish certainly use their lures in one of the most extraordinary reproductive stories in nature.

Male anglerfish look completely different from their mates. They are far smaller, sometimes just a tenth of the female size, and, unlike their fat, sluggish partners, the males have muscular bodies for active swimming. For many years fish biologists were very confused by these differences and misidentified male and female anglers as completely different species. This was hardly surprising because these early scientists never saw the animals alive. All they had to go on were dead specimens, often damaged and misshapen by the enormous pressure changes and physical trauma of being dragged up from the depths. In 1922 an Icelandic biologist published a description of a large female anglerfish that had two small fish attached to its belly. He thought the two small fish were juveniles that had somehow become attached to their mother. It was not until three years later that another biologist dissected one of the small fish and realized it was male. The mystery was solved.

When they are born, male anglers have no other role but to search out a female. The free-swimming males have no lure, so they probably never feed. Instead they have large eyes, presumably for spotting the female's flashing lure, and a large organ in front of their eyes to sniff out chemicals released by the female to attract him. Once he has found a partner, the male angler bites into her belly, trying to form a permanent attachment.

Gradually the male and female become fused, and her circulation system completely takes over. The only function that remains with the male is breathing. During the fusing process, his mouth moves gradually backwards so that it remains free and open to provide water to his gills. In every other way, the male becomes no more than an appendage to the female: he knows he will never have to search for a mate again. She, meanwhile, gains a permanently attached testis, which will provide her with sperm whenever she needs it.

One female angler was found to have nearly 5 million eggs in her ovaries. A number of these are released outside her body, at any given moment, and the male must release his sperm at exactly the same time. To ensure this is coordinated, the female's sexual hormones take over and control the male. Once they have been fertilized, the eggs, which contain large oil droplets to give buoyancy, float to the ocean surface. For many months the young anglers can grow in the photic zone, where there is lots of food. Eventually, when large enough, they will sink back to the perpetual gloom of the dark zone.

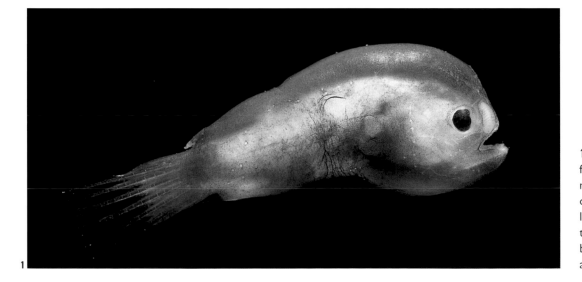

1. Male anglerfish are far smaller than their mates. The white organ in front of their large eyes is sensitive to chemicals released by the females to attract them.

2. (opposite) A female anglerfish with two males permanently attached. Her blood supply answers all their needs while they ensure she has a reliable source of sperm.

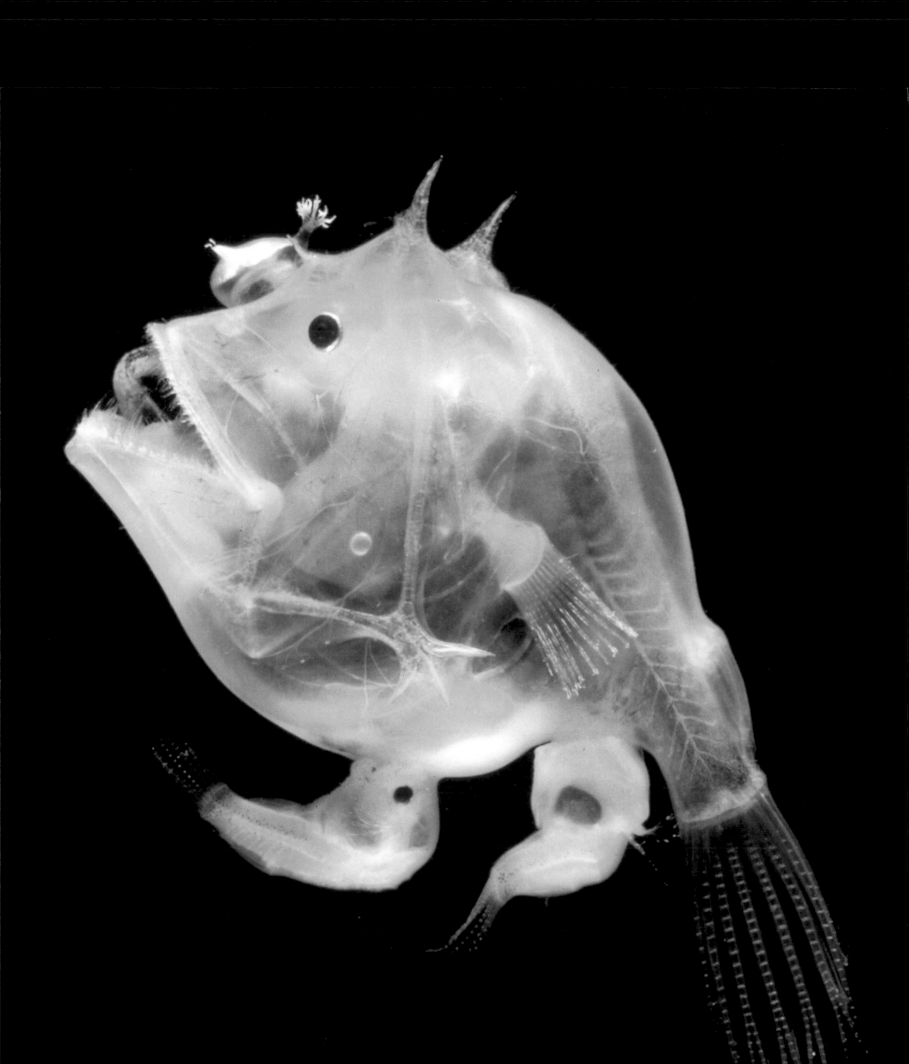

THE DEEP-SEA FLOOR

Animals living on the deep-sea floor face similar challenges to those faced by life throughout the deep ocean. There is no sunlight, water temperature is low, pressure is high and food is in short supply. However, while mid-water life is lived in three dimensions, sea-floor animals have largely two-dimensional lives. The majority are either permanently attached to the bottom or stay close to it. With few exceptions, they get all their food from the surface, and with 80 per cent of the ocean being more than 3000 m (9842 feet) deep, those supply lines can be very long. More than other factors, it is this scarcity of food that has shaped the bodies and defined the lifestyles of the animals that survive on the deep-sea floor. Human knowledge of the deep has been growing since studies began in the 1960s, but there is a great deal still to discover. So far, we have explored just 10 sq km (3.9 sq miles) of the deep-sea floor and have the best part of 300 million sq km (116 million sq miles) still to go …

LIFE ON THE BOTTOM

Arriving on the deep-sea floor in a submersible is both exciting and frightening. Great care must be taken to avoid landing too hard and damaging the vessel. There is a strong desire to get out and have a look around, but, of course, the enormous pressure outside the craft makes this impossible. Although the water at these great depths is crystal clear, what can be seen is limited by the power of the submersible's lights, so the view through the portholes is frustratingly restricted. Unlike astronauts, who have examined much of the moon lit by the sun, deep-sea explorers have seen less than 1 per cent of the sea floor. It is something of a cliché to say we know more about the surface of the moon than we do about the surface of our own planet, but it is true.

Once bearings have been established, the submersible starts its slow foray across the sea floor. Although the deep-sea bed has some of the largest and most spectacular geology on Earth, most of it is pretty flat, boring and apparently lifeless. But take a closer look at the sand and you soon notice that it is covered in evidence of animal activity. Every so often there are small volcano-shaped mounds surrounded by a series of holes, or a star shape of little trenches with a burrow entrance in the middle. In fact, tracks criss-cross the seabed in every direction. There is lots of life down here but much of it is hidden.

Although 60 per cent of the ocean is more than 1500 m (4921 feet) deep, there are only a handful of submersibles worldwide that can dive deeper than 1000 m (3281 feet).

1. This deep-sea anemone grows to more than 10 cm (4 in) tall, which helps with catching passing food.

THE SHAPE OF THE DEEP-SEA FLOOR

The deep-sea floor makes up 60 per cent of the Earth's surface and includes the world's highest peaks and longest mountain chain. Its shape is a balance between the parameters of new sea floor spreading out from the centre of the oceans and the constant deposition of organic and inorganic sediment. All the Earth's major landmasses are surrounded by relatively shallow, flat-bottomed seas around 200 m (656 feet) deep. These areas are called the continental shelf and extend about 65 km (40 miles) from the coast. However, on the Pacific coast of South America the shelf extends just 1 km (0.6 miles), while off Siberia it stretches about 750 km (466 miles) from the coast. At its furthest point, the shelf falls away into the deep sea, becoming known as the continental slope.

1. Diagram to show the key features of the continental margin, descending to the abyssal plain, or deep-sea floor.

The continental slope

Most of the continental slope drops away in a gradual gradient of 1:40, which is no more than a gentle hill. For the most part, the topography of the slopes is uniform and predictable, but in some places it is punctuated by steep terraces and deep canyons. Much of the slope is covered in sediment, which has either been carried into the sea by rivers and wind, or is the remains of innumerable marine animals and plants. At a depth of about 3000 m (9842 feet), the slope flattens out to a gradient of 1:100. This is called the continental rise and is typically a thick wedge of sediment that has gradually slipped down the slope itself. Together the continental slope and rise extend on average about 240 km (149 miles) from the coast.

The abyssal plain

At around 4000 m (13,123 feet) the seabed levels out again to an almost imperceptible gradient of 1:1000 or less. This is the abyssal plain, which covers over half of the ocean area and is the largest single environment on Earth. Even today, there are just a handful of manned submersibles that can reach it, and we have only explored a fraction of its surface. The abyssal plain's topography is not always uniform. In places volcanoes rise up from the sea floor. Where these volcanoes reach above the ocean surface, they form islands like the Hawaiian chain. If they reach just below the surface, the inactive volcanoes are called seamounts. In the empty blue expanses of the open ocean, seamounts often become oases that attract enormous numbers of oceanic species like tuna and billfish. In other areas the seabed drops suddenly away into deep trenches with water depths of 10 to 11 km (6 to 7 miles). The deepest point of all is called the Challenger Deep, which forms part of the Marianas Trench.

THE DEEP-SEA FLOOR

1

Continental shelf

Shelf break

Continental slope

Continental rise

Abyssal plain

Sediment

2. The mid-ocean ridges stretch for over 45,000 km (27,963 miles) and cross all the major oceans. They are the largest geological stuctures on Earth.

Mid-ocean ridges

The abyssal plains are broken up by huge mountain chains known as mid-ocean ridges. It is at these points that molten rock rises from deep within the Earth and spreads out to form a new sea floor; at about the same speed as our fingernails grow.

The sheer scale of the mid-ocean ridges is extraordinary: 3000 m (9842 feet) high, 50 km (31 miles) wide and over 45,000 km (27,963 miles) long, they cross all the major oceans except the North Pacific. None of the ranges or peaks on land come near their enormity. If we could drain away the water and fly above the mid-ocean ridges, the scenery would be the most spectacular ever seen. As it is, submersible lights have only illuminated a few hundred metres of these massive structures.

FORMATION OF THE MID-OCEAN RIDGES

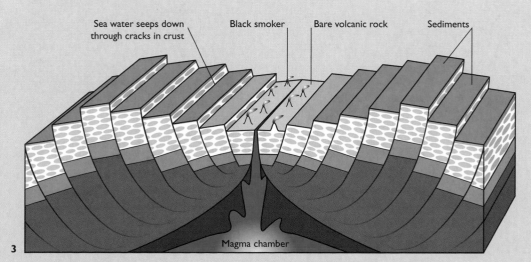

Sea water seeps down through cracks in crust   Black smoker   Bare volcanic rock   Sediments

Magma chamber

3. A cross-section of a mid-ocean ridge. Sea water percolates through fissures in the rock and is superheated by the rocks of the oceanic crust. It then rushes to the surface and gushes out as a hydrothermal vent.

◆ TOPIC LINKS

1.1 Water World
p.24 Mid-ocean Ridges
p.27 Seascapes

7.1 The Twilight Zone
p.315 Into the Gloom

7.2 The Dark Zone
p.331 Life in the Dark Zone

7.3 The Deep-Sea Floor
p.345 Life on the Bottom
p.354 Life on the Rocky Slopes

7.4 Life without the Sun
p.361 Hydrothermal Vents

Life in the mud

In the 1980s a team of deep-sea biologists spent two years taking hundreds of samples of mud from the deep-sea floor off the east coast of the United States. From an area of just 54 sq km (21 sq m), they identified 90,677 individual animals belonging to 798 species. Nearly 60 per cent were new to science, and on the basis of similar sampling experiments on land, the team calculated that it could expect to find one new species in every square kilometre of the deep-sea floor. Multiply this figure by the area of floor, and that means 100 million species are still to be discovered. Other scientists dispute this figure, but few would disagree that there should be at least a million undescribed animals down there. Considering that only around 230,000 marine species have been identified – a mere 9 per cent

of the 1.5 million species described for the whole planet – there is undoubtedly much to be discovered in the deep sea.

Most of the animals in the mud are just a few millimetres long, and by far the most numerous are the foraminiferans and their relatives. Indeed, their total weight probably outweighs all the other animals in the sediment. These single-celled animals feed off bacteria and other tiny pieces of organic matter, building themselves beautiful, intricate little homes out of mud and pieces of animal shell. The most numerous of the multi-celled animals are the nematodes or roundworms, which in the deep sea range in length from a few tenths of a millimetre to a centimetre or more. They vary from bacterial grazers to aggressive hunters that specialize in sucking the internal juices out of their prey.

Other common deep-sea animals are the isopods, which are familiar to us as terrestrial woodlice, and come in all shapes and sizes to help them move through the sediment. Tiny predatory polychaete worms are part of a complete food chain within the mud, which includes numerous small bivalve molluscs. These are relatives of shallow-water mussels and cockles, but unlike their filter feeding cousins, the deep-sea species gather food from the surface of the mud, and some have become specialized hunters. Perhaps the most surprising of all the deep-sea bivalve molluscs are those that feed off wood. Certainly the hulls of sunken ships provide good meals, but what did they eat before man arrived on the scene? The only likely source of food would have been coastal trees washed into the ocean and which eventually sank down to the depths.

1. Foraminiferans, the most numerous creatures living in the mud of the deep-sea floor, build themselves a wide variety of beautiful homes out of mud and pieces of animal shell.

2. Sea cucumbers travel across the deep-sea floor hoovering up sediment to extract its organic content.

Manna from heaven

With very few exceptions, all the animals on the deep-sea floor rely on food dropping down from the sunlit surface of the ocean. Most of this 'marine snow' arrives as particles of dead plants or dead animals and their faecal matter. Given its long journey from the surface, much marine snow is eaten by mid-water animals, who get to it first. The scraps that make it all the way down to the bottom really are the scrapings from the rich man's table above. However, while the mid-water animals have to grab the food as it passes, seabed creatures can wait for it to hit the sea floor, where it goes no further. Among the animals designed to take advantage of this are sea cucumbers, which are responsible for many of the tracks made across the muddy ▷▷ **2**

 ## UNDERTAKERS OF THE DEEP

Most of the food that drops to the deep-sea floor falls in small particles called marine snow. Occasionally, however, a larger animal — a fish, a dolphin or even a whale — will die and drop to the bottom. In 1998 biologists observed the plundering of a grey whale carcass. First to arrive at the body were swarms of amphipods, crustaceans just a few centimetres long, which have sharp jaws for cutting into flesh. These were followed by deep-sea fish, many of which were specialist scavengers with an acute sense of smell. Among them were eel-like hagfish, which rip off pieces of flesh by twisting their bodies into a knot to get extra torsion. Next to arrive were sleeper sharks, which took massive bites out of the carcass. Once the first wave of diners had feasted, another group of slower-moving scavengers arrived: brittle stars, polychaete worms and crabs slowly stripped the whale down, leaving only a clean white skeleton, such as the one illustrated, right. But even then, a further group of undertakers appeared, including worms, clams, mussels and, most importantly, chemosynthetic bacteria capable of breaking down the sulphide-rich bones. Some of these animals are exactly the same species as those found at hot vents (▷ p.361), suggesting that whale skeletons could be stepping-stones for the larvae of animals moving from one hot vent site to another.

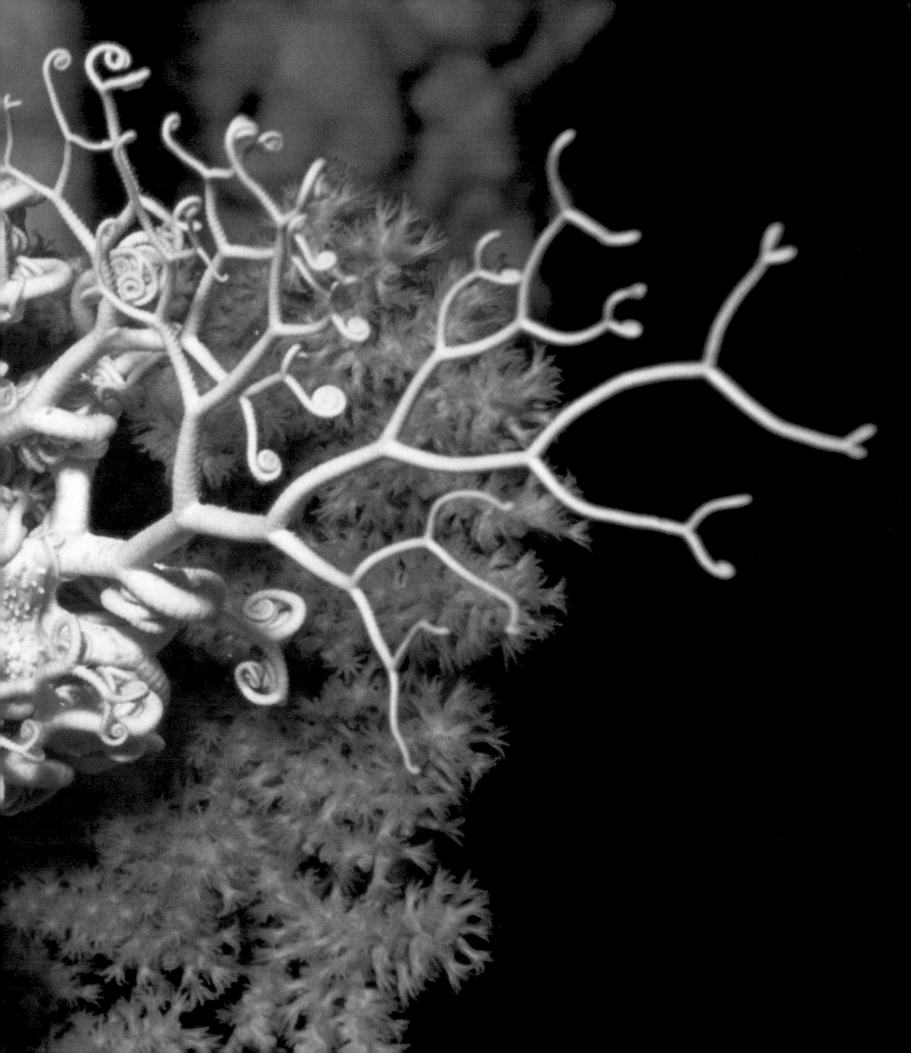

⭐ Sea cucumbers are probably the dominant life form on the deep-sea floor, representing as much as 95 per cent of the total biomass.

bottom. Sea cucumbers are echinoderms – the dominant sea-floor animal group, which includes starfish, sea urchins and brittle stars. Sea cucumbers vary in size from just a centimetre long to some football-sized giants, and feed by crawling over the sea floor sucking up the sediment to extract its organic content. Like shallow-water species, many of the deep-sea varieties resemble long, fat sausages, but some come in extraordinary shapes with long tentacles that look like legs, and even tall, sail-like structures that stick straight up out of their backs. One particularly spectacular sea cucumber called *Enypniastes* has developed webbed swimming structures at the front and back of its body, and, extraordinarily for this largely sedentary family, can actually swim off the sea floor and journey as much as 1000 m (3280 feet) up into the water column. It is

thought that these migrations help *Enypniastes* move to new feeding grounds and avoid predators. Its beautiful red skin is covered with hundreds of tiny, golden light-producing granules, which act as a defence mechanism. If the sea cucumber is attacked, its sticky skin peels off and sticks to the predator, which is left glowing dangerously in the dark.

Brittle stars and sea urchins are also common echinoderms of the deep-sea floor, sometimes numbering millions over a small area. Brittle stars are found worldwide as deep as 7000 m (22,966 feet) and have five long, slender arms attached to a central disc containing their mouth. They use these arms to sweep food off the sea floor, and sometimes stick them up into the water to catch passing particles. Sea urchins in the deep sea come in many variations of the basic spiny design.

Previous page: This medusa star has positioned itself up on a deep-sea coral, where it is in the current and can make better use of its long arms to catch passing particles of food.

1. This polychaete worm, *Biremas*, is unique in its group because it is able to swim from place to place on the deep-sea floor to find food and avoid predators.

2. This droopy sea pen comes from the same family as the jellyfish and comb jellies. This deep-sea species reaches up into the current above the sea floor to trap particles of food.

1

Some have long spines striped with candy pink; others have bendable spines from which a tiny round body is suspended. Most of them are omnivores and will eat anything they can find. Often they are found moving together in groups, which may be an efficient way of finding food, but may also be useful for reproduction. As elsewhere in the deep sea, the low density of animals on the sea floor can make it difficult to find a partner: moving in groups ensures that a potential mate is never far away.

The pressure to find food on the deep-sea floor has had a strong influence on the body design and lifestyles of many of the animals that live there. One of the most extraordinary adaptations to this demanding habitat can be seen in the deep-sea polychaete worm *Biremas*, which comes from a group of polychaete worms that typically live in tubes in the sediment. *Biremas* is different and lives out on the sea floor. If it is disturbed by a predator, or it needs to move to fresh feeding grounds, *Biremas* has a very clever trick. It can suddenly take off and swim, propelled by a tuft of tentacles around its mouth. This is extraordinary behaviour for a worm that one would normally expect to remain firmly within a burrow.

Many animals of the deep-sea floor, though, do not have the option of moving around to find their food. Animals like sponges, sea anemones, sea pens and tubeworms have a more sedentary life style where they just sit and wait for their food to come to them. Standing still is an energy-saving strategy in this low-energy world and as a life style it has evolved separately many times in the deep sea. In order to increase their chance of catching passing prey, animals on the deep-sea floor tend to be larger than their relatives in shallower water. One sea anemone, for instance, has a 10 cm (4 in) stalk which holds its feeding tentacles well up in the water column.

2

LIFE ON THE ROCKY SLOPES

Although much of the deep-sea floor is either completely flat or no more than a gentle slope, that you could easily tackle on a bicycle, there are areas where the gradient drops away far more steeply. These range from small rocky outcrops to seamounts that can rise several kilometres off the sea floor. Sometimes dramatic canyons can drop straight down thousands of metres; the Challenger Deep in the Pacific's Marianas Trench, for example, descends over 11 km (7 miles) and is the deepest place in the ocean.

Wherever the gradient is steep, deep-sea animals face a new set of challenges. Marine snow may not settle, but continue down to a flat seabed below. On the other hand, rocky outcrops can provide a good vantage place to catch food passing in the currents. It is because of these conditions that many deep-sea creatures appear more like plants than animals. Sea lilies or stalked crinoids, which look like flowers struggling towards the light, are actually echinoderms, but they have developed a long stalk and an umbrella of arms to catch passing prey. They bend together in the current, arranging their arms in a parabolic fan so that tiny particles of food get trapped in the thick mucus that runs along the length of them.

The corals are another animal group that have plant-like body structures. In shallow water they grow like this because they must have maximum exposure to sunlight to promote the growth of symbiotic algae, their resident source of food. In the darkness of the deep sea they have to catch all their food themselves, and, like the crinoids, are designed to catch particles suspended in the water. The gorgonians, or horny corals, for example, grow into spectacular bushes or long, corkscrew-type stalks that stick out into the current, fishing for food. Sometimes brittle stars will climb up gorgonians to get themselves into a better position for fishing. The soft corals of the deep include the beautiful mushroom coral, which,

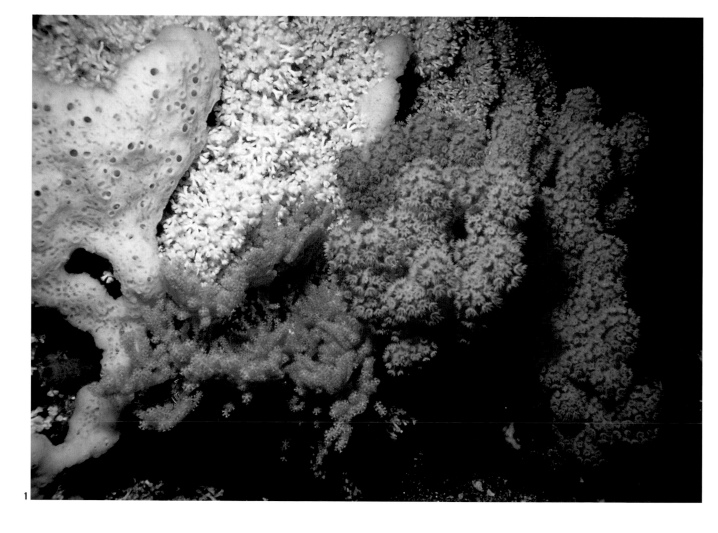

1. Coral reefs are not supposed to exist in the deep sea, but recently biologists discovered a 'reef' of this white, deep-water species *Lophelia* that stretched for 200 m (656 feet).

2. (opposite) The deep-sea mushroom coral has the largest polyps of any coral species, which allows it to catch a variety of different prey.

1

from a distance, looks like a pink mushroom with red palm trees growing out of the top. The 'palm trees' are in fact massive polyps – the largest of any coral in the ocean – which are crowned with an array of long tentacles for catching prey. Although the deep sea does not have the massive areas of reef-building corals typical of shallow tropical seas, some surprisingly large growths have been found. Using a remotely controlled submarine off Norway, biologists recently discovered a reef of the cold-water coral *Lophelia* at 300 m (984 feet); it measured over 30 m (98 feet) high and extended nearly 200 m (656 feet).

The severe shortage of food on the deep-sea floor has had a dramatic effect on the body structure and feeding habitats of a wide range of animals. Starfish, for example, are predators of slow-moving animals, such as snails, when in shallow water. In deep sea off the Bahamas, however, the bright red starfish called *Novodinea* behaves more like a filter-feeder and is an aggressive predator of shrimps and other fast-moving crustaceans. It sticks its arms, which are covered in tiny pincers, right up into the water to trap passing prey. But perhaps the most dramatic change in body form for life in the deep-sea is seen in the tunicate *Megalodicopia*. Most tunicates look like small, transparent balls attached to the seabed. Siphons on the side of their body draw in and expel water, extracting particles of food as they do so. *Megalodicopia* is unique among tunicates, however, because it is a carnivore. The siphon that carries water into the body has been massively enlarged and strengthened to produce an impressive set of 'jaws'. Looking rather like a boxing glove on a stalk, *Megalodicopia* opens and closes these jaws to grab any prey that comes within reach. Throughout the deep sea one finds similar examples of typical animal forms that have drastically changed to survive this harshest of habitats.

FISH OF THE DEEP-SEA FLOOR

The fish found on and around the deep-sea floor look very different from those that live in the three-dimensional mid-water world. Even by deep-sea standards, they are very ugly and tend to be brown or black. Gone are the delicate shapes of the twilight zone, and the intriguing barbels and lures of the dark zone. Sea-floor fish are usually larger, muscular animals with big heads and long tails. The record depth for a deep-sea fish goes to *Abyssobrotula galatheae*, an undistinguished specimen, which was found at the bottom of the Puerto Rico Trench, some 8400 m (27,558 feet) down.

Around 1500 different sea-floor species have been identified so far, and of those, the rat-tails or grenadiers are the most abundant. They are found from 250 m (820 feet) right down to the bottom of the deepest trenches, their large heads and long, tapering tails making them look rather like overgrown tadpoles. Rat-tails are the fish most commonly seen from submersibles and have a very characteristic position, their snouts angled down into the current, slowly sculling forward with their tails elevated. Having swim-bladders makes them neutrally buoyant and able to move freely up and down the water column. However, in order to save energy in this demanding environment, they tend to be slow-moving.

As food is in such short supply, the 200 or so different rat-tail species have a varied diet. Some feed on animals swimming just above the seabed, while others pick their food off the sea floor. Still others have hardened, pointed snouts and underslung mouths, which allow them to plough through the sediment of the sea floor searching for other small invertebrates. Special projections on the inner gill arches act as sieves to extract the food as sediment passes through. Many rat-tail species have a light-producing organ near their anus, which contains a lens and mirrors to direct the beam. Exactly what this is used for is still a mystery, but one theory is that it might be used as a searchlight to look for food.

1. *Megalodicopia* is unique among tunicates because it is a carnivore. One of its siphons has been massively enlarged and strengthened to produce a set of 'jaws'.

2. Rat-tail fish gather around a dolphin carcass. These scavengers are the most abundant fish of the deep-sea floor, found right at the bottom of the deepest trenches.

While rat-tails are active hunters, other fish of the deep-sea floor are not so mobile. Many prefer to save energy by sitting and waiting for food to come to them. They are helped in this by not having swim-bladders for buoyancy, and sink to the bottom if they stop swimming. The elegant tripod fish, so named because its fin-rays are enormously elongated to produce a tripod structure on which it stands, faces into the current completely motionless, waiting to snap up any passing prey. Its eyes are either tiny or very inefficient, so it has developed a sensitivity to even the tiniest vibrations in the water. Some species have long, extended fins on their heads, which they hold out in front of them like radio antennae to pick up the movements of potential food.

Another fascinating feature of tripod fish is that each individual has both male and female sex organs. While hermaphroditism is not uncommon in the natural world, the two sets of organs usually mature at different times, and rarely will an individual fertilize itself. In tripod fish, though, the testes and ovaries can become active at the same time. With few potential mates available on the deep-sea floor, this must be a useful last resort for fish that cannot find partners.

Deep-sea sharks

Sharks belong to the elasmobranchs – fishes with skeletons of cartilage rather than bone – which includes the rays and skates. Members of this group do not have swim-bladders, but obtain buoyancy from their oily livers, which are lighter than water. They hunt for food by moving slowly around the deep-sea floor. One of the largest fish in the deep sea is the sleeper or Greenland shark, which can grow to 7 m (23 feet) in length and is found at depths

1

1. Tripod fish get their name from their specially adapted fin-rays that produce a tripod structure on which the fish waits patiently for passing prey.

2. Six-gilled sharks are living fossils. For 150 million years they have existed unchanged in waters as deep as 2500 m (8202 feet).

3. *Chimaera*, or rabbit fish, are close relations of the sharks and grow to about a metre long. Their large eyes are probably designed to spot bioluminescence.

2

3

as great as 2200 m (7218 feet). Only the basking sharks, whale sharks and great white sharks of shallow waters grow any larger, but most of the 350 or so deep-water sharks are far smaller, with long, thin bodies that rarely exceed a metre. Indeed, the smallest of all – the pygmy or dwarf shark – is a deep-water species. It is cigar-shaped and cigar-sized, never being more than 25 cm (10 in) long. It lives down to 500 m (1640 feet) and the whole of its ventral surface is covered in photophores, which probably produce light to disguise its silhouette from below.

Although most deep-water sharks are small, many are also extremely strange and fascinating. The cookie-cutter shark gets its name from its habit of taking large, circular bites out of larger animals, such as billfish and even whales. Like many other deep-water sharks, it is also covered with bioluminescent organs so that its whole lower body glows a ghostly green. This may be a way of attracting inquisitive larger species so that the cookie-cutter can take a bite. Perhaps strangest of all are the goblin sharks. Their bodies, usually 3–4 m (10–13 feet) long, are mostly tail, and over their jaws extends a long, paddle-like blade. The exact purpose of this protrusion remains a mystery. Perhaps, like the head lobes of hammerhead sharks, it is loaded with sensory receptors, or it might be used to stir up sediment on the bottom.

Sea snails, a group of fish found at great depths, have a small suction disk on the bottom of their heads, which may help them to stay on the bottom.

7.4 LIFE WITHOUT THE SUN

Until 1977, it was believed that sunlight was the basis of every food chain on Earth. Without it, there could be no photosynthesis, no plants and ultimately no animals. But in that year a discovery was made in the deep sea that was to completely upturn our understanding of the limits of life on Earth. Geologists were exploring the mid-ocean ridge off the Galápagos Islands, looking for volcanic activity on the seabed over 2000 m (6562 feet) down. They found what they were after – hydrothermal vents – but were amazed also to discover a profusion of life like nothing that had ever been seen before. This oasis of life was living quite independently of energy from the sun and included a remarkable variety of species totally new to science. Since that original discovery, similar communities have been found at hydrothermal vents on mid-ocean ridges all over the world.

HYDROTHERMAL VENTS

Alien worlds are nearer than you think. To reach them you have to dive only 2000–3000 m (6562–9842 feet) below the waves to the crest of the mid-ocean ridges that extend 45,000 km (27,963 miles) along the middle of the world's oceans (▷ pp. 24, 347). These ridges are the largest geological structures on Earth – 80 km (50 miles) wide in places and rising up to 3 km (2 miles) off the sea floor. Nobody will ever see the extent of these spectacular features because submersible lights can illuminate only a tiny area.

The ridges are the site for the production of new sea floor, which rises as molten rock from deep within the Earth. Sea water percolates down through cracks and fissures left in the new sea floor as it solidifies. At a depth of just over 1 km (0.6 miles) below the sea floor, the water meets the hot rocks of the oceanic crust and is superheated before rushing back to the surface and gushing out as a hydrothermal vent. At some vents the water is as hot as molten lead – a staggering 350–400 °C (662–752 °F). Normally, water at that temperature would be steam, but under the pressures of the deep ocean, it remains in liquid form. The water comes up loaded with minerals from the deep rocks, and the coloured plumes of water are consequently known as 'black smokers' or

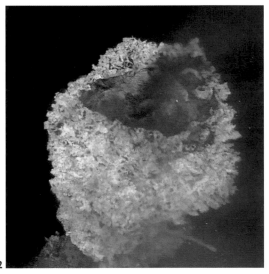

The largest black smoker yet discovered, Godzilla, is 45 m (148 feet) tall and 12 m (39 feet) in diameter.

1. A black smoker. Superheated water, coloured black by minerals from within the Earth's crust, gushes out of a hydrothermal vent.

2. The water that emerges from the vents is as hot as molten lead. Under the great pressures of the deep ocean it remains liquid and does not turn into steam.

'white smokers'. The minerals often crystallize as they encounter the cold sea water, and gradually deposit themselves as chimneys around the vents. These chimneys can grow to enormous heights, in one case becoming as tall as a 16-storey building. Entering a field of hydrothermal vents is rather like visiting a horrific vision of industrial hell. Tall black chimneys roar with the sound of escaping superheated water, and the water column is full of highly toxic gases. It is hard to imagine a less hospitable place for life, and yet here it is in extraordinary abundance.

Life at the hydrothermal vents

The equation, everyone thought, was simple: the deeper you travel into the ocean, the less life you find. Down on the ocean's abyssal plain, at depths of 4000 m (13,123 feet) and below, there is 1000 times less life than in the ocean shallows. As the mid-ocean ridges rise up from the abyssal plain, everyone expected them to be largely lifeless. But in 1979, when biologists visited the vents first discovered by geologists two years previously, they could hardly believe their eyes. Packed around some of the hot vent chimneys was a density and variety of animal life that exceeded anything found in the richest tropical jungle or coral reef. The vast majority had never been seen before, and some seemed to come from completely new animal groups. These oases of life were dominated by spectacular tubeworms up to 2 m (7 feet) long and as thick as a human arm. At the top of their white tubes were blood-red structures that looked like gills. The bottom of the stack of life was encrusted with hundreds of mussels and clams, all far bigger than the tiny bivalve molluscs found elsewhere in the deep sea. Literally hundreds of white crabs crawled between the tubeworms, and weird pink fish fed on thick swarms of amphipods. The array of previously unknown species was extraordinary.

Fuel for the system

At first, nobody could work out what was providing the energy to fuel this abundance of life. There was no sunlight, of course, and the tiny quantities of food that might find their way down from the surface would never have been enough to feed such a rich system. The mystery only deepened when the first tubeworms were brought to the surface and dissected in the laboratory. They had no mouth, anus or gut, and biologists called them *Riftia* and placed them in a new and distinct phylum: the Vestimentifera. How were *Riftia* getting their energy to grow to such a great size and in such profusion? Well, there had been one good clue right back in 1977, when geologists examined the first water samples from the hydrothermal vents: they reeked of rotten eggs – hydrogen sulphide. The water rushing out of the hot vents was clearly carrying sulphides leached from the hot rocks below. For most animals, hydrogen sulphide is a highly toxic substance, but the *Riftia* were not adversely affected by it.

Looking more closely at the tubeworms, scientists discovered that they are packed with chemosynthetic bacteria, which are able to use the energy in hydrogen sulphide molecules to make organic matter in much the same way as plants use light energy. Over half of the tubeworms' weight consisted of these bacteria, which provided Riftia with organic material in exchange for chemicals provided by the tubeworm. The red stuctures on the worms are gills packed with special haemoglobin, which fixes sulphides, carbon dioxide and oxygen and carries them ▷▷

1. The communities of animals that live around the hydrothermal vents in the Pacific are dominated visually by the red gills of the tubeworm *Riftia*.

2. Since hot-vent communities were first discovered in the 1970s, a new species has been described every ten days or so.

3. The bright red gills of the tubeworms carry sulphides and oxygen down to the bacteria that pack into their two-metre-long tubes.

EXPLORING THE ABYSS

The return of HMS *Challenger* to Britain in 1876 after its three and a half year circumnavigation of the globe probably marks the birth of deep-sea biology. Before that date, most people believed the conditions in the deep sea were too harsh to support life. But the scientists on board *Challenger* returned with over 4000 new species including the first ever anglerfish to be retrieved from the depths. The expedition established the foundations for deep-sea research and spawned a series of other major expeditions that all confirmed *Challenger*'s findings – the deep ocean is far richer in life than anyone had expected.

Dr Beebe's bathysphere

Until 1930, the only way to see the animals and plants of the deep ocean was to drag them up on to ships using nets and dregs. But in that year an American biologist, Dr William Beebe, became the first person ever to observe deep-sea animals alive in their natural habitat. His submersible, called the bathysphere, was a hollow sphere of steel about 1.5 m (5 feet) in diameter, with walls 4 cm (2 in) thick and windows of quartz glass. There was room inside for only two people, and the tiny door had to be fastened with 10 heavy bolts. Lowered into the water on a steel cable, the bathysphere made 32 dives off Bermuda, reaching a maximum depth of 805 m (2641 feet). Photography was impossible, but, the artist Else Bostelmann later produced vivid images based on Beebe's descriptions of life in the depths.

Down to the deepest ocean

After Beebe's successful dives, a number of different submersible designs were tried out. In 1948, the French scientist, Auguste Piccard, famous for journeys into the upper atmosphere, adapted the design of his high-altitude balloons for underwater use. The balloon's gasbag was replaced with a gas-filled float beneath which he hung a 10-tonne steel sphere. This bathyscaphe was used to dive in the Atlantic and Mediterranean as deep as 4000 m (13,123 feet). Eventually, in 1960, a second-generation bathyscaphe, the *Trieste*, carried Piccard's son Jacques and fellow scientist Don Walsh right to the bottom of the Challenger Deep, 11 km (7 miles) down in the Marianas Trench. They remain the only people to have reached this deepest spot in the ocean.

Trieste's main limitation was that it was really no more than a lift – excellent for going up and down, but very limited for horizontal

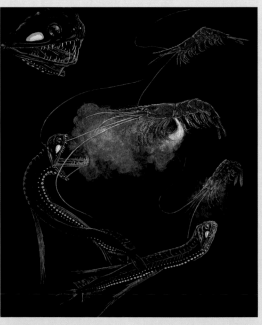

1. Dr William Beebe emerging from the bathysphere, in which he descended 805 m (2641 feet). He became the first person to observe deep-sea animals in their natural habitat.

2. Beebe described the things he saw to the artist Else Bostelmann, who then drew them. Here, a shrimp is shown releasing a cloud of bioluminescence to confuse its predators.

3. The submersible, *Alvin*, is operated by the Woods Hole Oceanographic Institute and can dive to 4500 m (14,764 feet).

4. In the 1950s, the French scientist, Auguste Piccard, used his experience with high-altitude balloons to design the bathyscaphe, which could travel as deep as 4000 m (13,123 feet).

exploration of the seabed. In 1964 the Woods Hole Oceanographic Institute in the United States launched *Alvin*, a 2-m (7-foot) titanium sphere able to hold a pilot and two observers. Although it could not dive as deep as its predecessor, it was far more mobile on reaching the bottom. *Alvin* quickly became the workhorse of deep-sea exploration, and went on to discover the hot vents and explore the wreck of the *Titanic*. It is still in active use today.

Modern deep-sea exploration

Modern deep-sea exploration still relies on many of the techniques used on HMS *Challenger*. Nets, trawls and dregs are still in regular use to study deep-sea animals, but they have been augmented by a wide range of electronic, and acoustic devices, which throw new light on the 'catches'.

Submersibles remain expensive and so are rationed in their use. Scientific opinion is divided on how best to use them. Some people believe that remotely operated vehicles carrying cameras are a more efficient way to study the deep sea, while others feel that observing in situ is essential, so, manned submersibles continue to be built. Among the most recent is the Johnson Sealink (JSL), built and operated by Harbour Branch Oceanographic Institute in Florida. It has a front sphere made out of plexiglass, which limits it to a depth of 1000 m (3280 feet) but gives the observer an unrestricted view of mid-water life.

Submarines are now being developed that roam the deep sea on their own. They return to the surface only occasionally, so that they can transmit their information to satellites, which beam it back to laboratories on land.

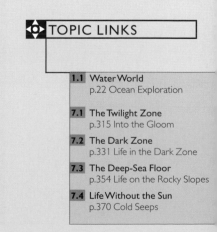

◆ TOPIC LINKS

1.1 Water World
p.22 Ocean Exploration

7.1 The Twilight Zone
p.315 Into the Gloom

7.2 The Dark Zone
p.331 Life in the Dark Zone

7.3 The Deep-Sea Floor
p.354 Life on the Rocky Slopes

7.4 Life Without the Sun
p.370 Cold Seeps

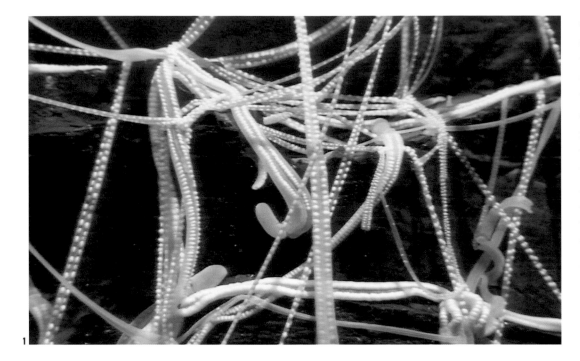

1

down the body to the bacteria. In most animals, hydrogen sulphide inhibits respiration by blocking the oxygen's binding sites on the haemoglobin molecule, but the tubeworms were able to control its toxic effects by binding the oxygen and sulphide molecules separately and simultaneously. In this way they could prevent the sulphide and the oxygen combining – a very poisonous cocktail. The mussels and clams were found to contain exactly the same chemosynthetic bacteria, providing their energy needs. These bivalve molluscs occur in such extraordinary densities at the eastern Pacific hot vents that scientists have given the sites names such as Clambake and Mussel Bed. The giant, white clams can grow to a length of 30 cm (12 in), and three-quarters of their gill tissue is made

1. A tangle of spaghetti worms, *Enteropneusta*, found near the hot vents in the Pacific.

2. This deep-sea octopus is nick-named Dumbo. Flaps of skin between its arms, and the fins above its eyes allow Dumbo to hover above the sea floor.

3. Pompeii worms live in their white tubes on the edge of the vents, close to where the hot water is emerging. They can survive in temperatures that average 65 °C (149 °F).

2

3

up of chemosynthetic bacteria. Although the mussels also get much of their energy from these sulphide-fixing bacteria in their gills, they still retain a fully functional mouth and gut to feed off other bacteria that covers the vents. All over and around the vent there were also enormous quantities of non-symbiotic bacteria fixing sulphides and providing food for all the other animals in the community.

Variety of life

Since the first visit to the Galápagos hydrothermal vents in 1979, a new species has been described at this location, on average, every week and a half. Among the giant tubeworms were other worms and molluscs, shrimps, crabs, sea anemones and even fish. One of the most fascinating creatures was the Pompeii worm, named after its ability to survive extreme temperatures. Pompeii worms live in white tubes and cluster in snowball-like masses on the side of the chimneys, close to where the hot water is emerging. Here they live in temperatures that average 65 °C (149 °F), and can survive occasional spikes of well above 80 °C (176 °F). What is even more surprising is the enormous gradients in temperature they can handle. They are just 10 cm (4 in) long and often have one end of the body in water 60 °C (140 °F) warmer than at the other end. No other creature on Earth could survive these conditions for more than a few minutes.

Approximately 20 different species of fish have been seen at the hot vents, but only one of these is an obligatory vent resident.

⭐ Individual hot vents are only active for a few decades before they close down, forcing all the life they support to move on.

After the initial discoveries at the Pacific mid-ocean ridges, the search began in other oceans to find new hydrothermal vent communities. Exciting discoveries were made along the mid-Atlantic ridge, which were both remarkably similar yet fascinatingly different from those in the Pacific. Although the communities were just as rich, with sulphide-fixing bacteria at the bottom of their food chain, they contained no giant tubeworms, mussels or clams. Instead, there were thousands of white shrimps, which completely covered the vent chimneys like swarms of bees. All about 5 cm (2 in) long, the shrimps belonged to several different species, which fed off bacteria growing around the vents and on their own bodies. Although at first they seemed to be completely blind, they were found to have two organs on their backs that seemed to have the structure of rudimentary eyes. What could be

the purpose of even limited vision in a pitch-black environment? This question was answered when a special low-light camera was taken down to the hydrothermal vents. This allowed the scientists to see that the vents glowed in the dark at very low levels. The shrimps' rudimentary eyes probably help them to find new vents in the darkness.

As scientists continue to investigate the mid-oceanic ridges they are discovering more and more of these oases of life. Even today it still seems truly remarkable that life can exist in such demanding conditions, with high pressure, no light, and waters that are laden with toxic substances. But some biologists have suggested that these conditions may be just those that existed when life began. By studying hot vent communities in detail, we may get a valuable insight into the conditions and pathways that sowed the seeds for life on Earth.

1

2

1. A sonograph of part of the mid-Atlantic ridge, south of Iceland.

2. One of two shrimp species discovered at the Pacific hot vents.

3. (opposite) The mid-Atlantic hydrothermal vents are swarming with the shrimp *Rimicaris*, which is about 5 cm (2 in) long.

COLD SEEPS

The existence of such rich ecosystems, at hydrothermal vents, parallel to those powered by the sun's energy, was extraordinary enough, but in 1984 deep-sea biologists working at the bottom of the Gulf of Mexico made another remarkable discovery. They came across communities of animals almost as rich and varied as those at the hot vents and once again the life forms were surviving independently of the sun's energy. There are no hot vents in the Gulf of Mexico but it is a key site for the United States oil and gas industry.

The rocks at the bottom of the Gulf are rich in hydrocarbons, and at certain places on the sea floor these seep out through the sediment and escape into the water column. These places are called cold seeps, and it was here that the new 'parallel' ecosystems were found. One of the richest sites discovered was initially spotted by the sophisticated sonar of a US Navy submarine, and when biologists first had a chance to visit it with a scientific submersible, they could hardly believe their eyes. Through the gloom the lights seemed to be illuminating a beautiful, calm lake on the bottom of the ocean. The lake gently lapped against what looked like a golden sandy shore. Of course, lakes cannot exist under water, so the pilot attempted to land on it and found that the submersible bounced up and down on the surface. The lake obviously consisted of a liquid denser than the surrounding water. The scientists named the site the Brine Pool because the liquid was very rich in salt that had seeped up from the rocks below. When they took a closer look at the 'golden sand', it turned out to be thousands of mussels, and living among them was a rich community of different animals not dissimilar to those found at a hot vent.

Energy at the cold seeps

The cold seeps are too deep to receive any sunlight, so, just as happened with the hot vents, the search began to discover what exactly was fuelling this rich new ecosystem. Looking closely at the mussel beds, biologists discovered that methane was continually bubbling up from the rocks below. Inside the mussels, in an extraordinary parallel with the hot vents, they found chemosynthetic bacteria that this time were fixing methane rather than hydrogen sulphide. These bacteria were providing the energy at the bottom of a food chain that included mussels, worms, crabs, isopods and even fish. In places the combination of high pressure and low temperatures had frozen the methane into a solid, ice-like material. Living among this strange habitat, biologists discovered dense aggregations of a new species of polychaete worm that they

1

⭐ Around 160 new species have been found at the hot vents and cold seeps, belonging to at least 16 previously unknown families.

2

christened 'ice worms'. They are still trying to work out how these worms survive in such toxic conditions. Near the Brine Pool they even discovered large fields of a new species of tubeworm that stretched in some places for hundreds of metres. Like the hot-vent tubeworms, these animals had no mouth, gut, or anus, but were full of chemosynthetic bacteria fixing hydrogen sulphide. This gas was seeping up through the rocks with the methane, and the tubeworms seemed to obtain it through their roots.

Cold-vent tubeworms are much thinner, more elegant animals than the hot-vent worms. At the top of their tubes their gills emerge in the shape of freshly opened rosebuds rather than large red plumes. But it was the similarities rather than the differences that amazed the biologists. When the hot-vent tubeworms were discovered, they were believed to be unique, so a new phylum was created for them.

Yet here was an animal, separated by hundreds of kilometres of barren sea floor from the nearest hot vent, that clearly belonged in exactly the same phylum.

As research continued, an interesting difference between the tubeworms did emerge. From what little we know about animals in the deep sea, the rate of growth generally seems to be very slow indeed. With so little food available, most species seem to take years, even decades, to reach full size. But the hot-vent tubeworm broke all the rules and appears to be able to do this in just a couple of years, rivalling the growth rate of almost any animal in the oceans. By contrast, the tubeworms at the cold vents grow so slowly that they take around 200 years to reach full size. If you exclude colonial animals, such as corals, this growth rate makes the cold-vent tubeworms the longest-lived invertebrates in the ocean.

1. Mussels found at the vents are full of a bacteria that can fix energy from methane, the gas that seeps from the sea floor.

2. The edge of the Brine Pool, in the Gulf of Mexico, is surrounded by thousands of mussels.

3. Tubeworms are some of the slowest growing invertebrates in the ocean, taking 200 years to grow to their full size.

4. The gills of cold-vent tubeworms only catch oxygen. Sulphides are supplied to their bacteria by their roots in the ground.

3

4

Glossary

abyssal plain   The flat plain that forms the greater part of the deep ocean floor. Its average depth is about 4000 m (13100 feet) below the surface.

algae (singular **alga**)   A very varied group of simple non-flowering plants that live mainly in water. The single-celled plants making up the **phytoplankton** are algae, as are all types of seaweeds.

amphipods   A widespread group of mainly small shrimp-like **crustaceans**, mostly living on or in the sea floor. Their bodies are usually flattened from side to side.

annelids   A **phylum** of invertebrate animals, also called segmented worms. They include earthworms, ragworms, most tube worms, and leeches. *See also* **polychaete, oligochaete.**

Antarctic circle   The line of latitude that lies at 66° 32′ south of the Equator. South of this line there is at least one day of perpetual darkness and one of perpetual sunlight per year. The equivalent line north of the Equator is the *Arctic circle*.

Antarctic convergence   The area in the Southern Ocean where cold Antarctic waters meet and sink below warmer northern waters.

Arctic circle *see* **Antarctic circle**

arthropods   The **phylum** of invertebrate animals that includes insects, spiders, **crustaceans**, and related creatures.

bacteria (singular **bacterium**)   Minute single-celled organisms, a major division of life on earth, occurring in their billions in all ecosystems. Bacterial cells, unlike those of animals and plants, contain no nuclei. *See also* **cyanobacteria.**

baleen   Large plates of horny **keratin** (sometimes called 'whalebone') found in the mouths of some whales. The baleen is used to filter food from the water.

barbel   A whisker-like projection around the mouths of some fish.

barrier reef   A coral reef growing parallel to a coastline and separated from it by a sheltered area of sea or broad lagoon.

basin *see* **ocean basin**

basket stars   Types of **brittle star**, having each arm divided into many branches.

benthos   General term for organisms living on or in the sea floor.

Beringia   The region now submerged beneath the Bering Sea between Alaska and Russia. It was dry land during the last ice age.

bioluminescence   The production of light by living organisms.

biomass   The total quantity (mass) of living material in any given context (e.g. the biomass of plankton in the ocean).

bivalves   **Molluscs** (shellfish) that have a shell made up of two halves – for example cockles, mussels and oysters.

bloom   A dense growth of **plankton** in water, often making it appear cloudy.

blue-green algae *see* **cyanobacteria**

brittle stars   A group of animals related to starfish (*see* **echinoderms**) but with thinner, more flexible arms.

bryozoans   Small colonial invertebrate animals, also called 'moss animals', that filter food from sea water. Each individual occupies a tiny box-like chamber.

carbon cycle   The global processes in which element carbon is cycled between living organisms (which are mainly made of carbon compounds) and the non-living environment.

cartilage   A tough elastic body tissue (colloquially 'gristle').

cephalopods   The group of **molluscs** that includes squid, octopuses, and cuttlefish.

chitons   A group of small **molluscs**, sometimes called coat-of-mail shells, that have a shell of eight protective plates running down their back.

chlorophyll   The green substance in plants that gives them the ability to **photosynthesize.**

clam   (1) Term used (especially in the US) for any kind of **bivalve** mollusc; (2) any of a number of individual kinds of bivalve, such as the giant clam.

Cnidaria   The **phylum** of animals that includes corals, jellyfish, sea anemones, and related creatures. Primitively, their life cycle includes a **polyp** and a **medusa** stage, although not all species have both these stages. Formerly known as **Coelenterata.**

Coelenterata   An older name for the **Cnidaria**, nowadays more usually used for the broader grouping that includes both the Cnidaria and the **ctenophores**.

cold seep   An area of the sea floor where energy-rich chemicals from surrounding rocks form the basis of a food chain that does not depend on **photosynthesis**. Unlike **hydrothermal vents**, they are not associated with high-temperature **tectonic activity**.

comb jellies *see* **ctenophores**

continental crust   That part of the Earth's crust that forms the continents. It is both thicker and less dense than **oceanic crust**. (Both types of crust rest or 'float' on the underlying **mantle**.)

continental drift   The slow movement of the Earth's continents relative to one another as a result of **plate tectonics**.

continental rise   A region of sea floor at the boundary of the **continental slope** and the **abyssal plain**, mainly formed from thick sediments coming from the adjacent continent.

continental shelf   The submerged edge of a continent. Made of **continental crust**, the continental shelf creates an almost flat sea bottom around 200 m (650 feet) deep around the margins of most continents.

continental slope   The true edge of a continent: the sloping region of sea floor that leads from the edge of the **continental shelf** down to the **continental rise.**

copepods   A group of small **crustaceans**, usually no more than a few millimetres long, that are an important part of the **plankton**.

coral bleaching   Loss of coloured symbiotic algae (**zooxanthellae**) from the bodies of coral animals, giving the coral colonies affected a bleached appearance.

coral head   A large individual growth of coral.

corals   Any of a variety of simple animals (**polyps**) that secrete an external 'skeleton' to support themselves. They are normally colonial. The 'true' or hard corals form heavy skeletons of calcium carbonate that eventually build up into reefs; other varieties include the horny corals (**gorgonians**).

coriolis effect   The effect by which winds and currents that would otherwise flow due north or south are deflected to the east or west as a result of the Earth's rotation.

crinoids   Relatives of the starfish (*see* **echinoderms**) that feed by filtering food from the water with long 'arms'. Some (the sea lilies) grow on stalks attached to the bottom, while others (feather stars) are able to move over the sea floor.

crustaceans   A very large and diverse group of mainly marine animals with jointed legs. Crustaceans include crabs, lobsters, **shrimps, amphipods**, barnacles, **copepods, isopods, and krill**.

ctenophores   A **phylum** of simple animals with jelly-like bodies and rows of beating hairs, distantly related to jellyfish (*see* **Cnidaria**). Also known as comb jellies or sea gooseberries, they feed on smaller planktonic animals.

cyanobacteria   Tiny single-celled organisms, also known as blue-green algae. Although related to **bacteria**, they can also **photosynthesize** like plants.

demersal   (of marine organisms) Living near the sea floor.

deposit feeding   Feeding on mainly dead material (**detritus**) trapped in the sediments of the sea floor.

detritus   Dead and decaying material, especially in the form of small fragments.

diatoms   Single-celled **algae** that form an important part of the **phytoplankton**. Each diatom cell is protected by a transparent and often ornate protective 'box' of **silica**.

dinoflagellates *see* **flagellates**

dorsal   (of an animal) Relating to the back or upper surface.

echinoderms   A **phylum** of invertebrate animals that is found only in the oceans. The group includes starfish, sea urchins, **brittle stars, crinoids**, and **sea cucumbers**.

El Niño   Event that occurs every few years in the tropical eastern Pacific, where the waters around Christmastime remain much warmer than usual, disrupting fisheries in the region. It is part of a larger phenomenon called the southern oscillation which can cause global disruption of weather systems.

estuary   A broad, usually sheltered river mouth. Life in estuaries is strongly affected by the combination of the tidal rhythms, deposition of **sediments**, and the mixing of salt- and freshwater.

filter-feeding   Obtaining food by filtering small particles from the water.

flagellates   Single-celled organisms that propel themselves by one or more microscopic 'hairs' (flagellae). Some photosynthesize and are classified as **algae**, while others have the lifestyle of tiny animals (**protozoa**). They include the *dinoflagellates*, a particularly important element of the **plankton**.

foraminiferans   A group of single-celled animals (*see* **protozoans**) that make up an important part of the **plankton**. Their empty, chalky skeletons commonly accumulate in marine sediments.

fringing reef   A coral reef lying close in to the shore.

fucoids   A group of **algae** that includes many familiar brown seaweeds found on the shore.

gastropods   A large group of **molluscs** that includes snails, slugs, limpets, and **pteropods** (sea-butterflies). The name means 'stomach-foot'.

genus   The first level of classification above species. (For example, in *Homo sapiens*, '*Homo*' is the genus name.)

gill rakers   Bony projections on the gill-supports of some fish, that allow them to **filter-feed** using their gills.

Gondwanaland   A former supercontinent lying in the Southern Hemisphere, comprising present-day Africa, Antarctica, Australia, South America, and India.

gorgonians   A group of colonial animals belonging to the **Cnidaria**, related to sea-anemones. They are also called horny **corals**. The skeletons of most gorgonians disintegrate after death, and so do not contribute to reef formation. Sea-fans, whose colonies grow in flat fan-shapes, are also gorgonians.

guyot   A flat-topped **seamount**.

gyre   A large-scale circular motion of ocean currents in subtropical regions.

high latitudes   Areas of the earth lying towards the Poles, where the lines of latitude have higher numbers (for example, 60° S).

holdfast   The 'anchor' used by a seaweed to attach itself to rocks. It is not designed for absorbing nutrients, and so is not a true root.

horny corals *see* **gorgonians**

hydroids   A group of colonial animals belonging to the **Cnidaria**, distantly related to sea-anemones. The individual animals (**polyps**) are usually very small, and the whole colony often looks seaweed-like.

hydrothermal vent   Site on the sea floor at which water from underlying rocks streams out at high temperature, carrying dissolved minerals such as sulphur compounds. Hydrothermal vents are the location of unique communities of marine organisms that depend on chemical energy rather than light from the sun. *See also* **cold seep**.

ice floe   An area of ice created when a larger extent of floating ice is broken up by storms. Collectively, ice floes form **pack ice**.

ice shelf   A large area of floating sea ice that is attached to land.

ice-sheet   A very extensive and thick layer of ice covering a major landmass – for example, the Antarctic ice-sheet. (The term *ice-cap* is sometimes used instead.)

infauna   Animals that live within sediments such as sand or mud.

invertebrate   An animal without a backbone.

isopods   A widespread group of **crustaceans** that includes many marine species as well as the terrestrial woodlouse.

kelp   A group of large brown seaweeds. They anchor themselves to the sea bottom by a **holdfast**. Some species can grow over 60 metres long.

keratin   Horny material, of which hair, scales, etc. are made.

krill   **Crustaceans** that are distant relatives of crabs and lobsters. They grow up to a few centimetres in length. Vast numbers of them occur especially in the Southern Ocean, feeding on plankton.

larva The young stage of an animal, especially when different in appearance and way of life from the adult.

larvaceans Small, free-floating invertebrate creatures that secrete a large, delicate structure of mucus called a 'house' that helps them **filter-feed** on minute plankton. They are a type of **tunicate**.

longshore drift The moving of shore material such as sand in one direction along a coastline, as a result of waves, wind and currents.

low latitudes Areas of the earth lying towards the Equator, where the lines of latitude have lower numbers (for example 10° N).

mangrove A tree or shrub specialized to live between the tidelines. Mangrove trees, which are frost-sensitive, belong to several different families of plants.

mangrove swamp Natural ecosystem dominated by mangroves which occurs on many tropical shorelines and estuaries.

mantle The layer of dense hot rock, nearly 3000 km (1860 miles) thick, that lies between the Earth's crust and its core. Over time it 'flows' like a very treacly liquid. Currents in the mantle produced by the Earth's internal heat are the driving force of **plate tectonics**.

medusa (plural, **medusae** or **medusas**) The swimming stage of a **Cnidarian**. They can be regarded as upside-down **polyps**. A jellyfish is an example of a medusa.

mid-ocean ridge Submarine mountain chain extending through the world's oceans. Hot rock rising from the **mantle** at mid-ocean ridges creates new **oceanic crust**, pushing continents apart via the process of *sea floor spreading*.

molluscs A very large group (**phylum**) of invertebrate animals. They are soft-bodied and usually have shells, or remnants of shells. The group includes **gastropods** (snails and slugs), **bivalves** (cockles, mussels, etc.) **cephalopods** (squid, octopus, etc), and **chitons**.

moss animal *see* **bryozoan**

neap tides *see* **spring tides**

nekton General term for free-swimming sea animals that are strong enough swimmers not to be at the mercy of ocean currents. (*Compare* **plankton**)

nematocysts Coiled, threadlike structures found in certain cells of jellyfish etc. (*see* **Cnidaria**), especially in the tentacles. They 'shoot out' when triggered by touching prey. Some inject poison, while others are sticky.

nematode A **phylum** of worms, also called roundworms or threadworms. Many are microscopic and occur in their billions in many environments. There are also parasitic species.

nemerteans/nemertines A **phylum** of marine worms, also called ribbon worms.

nudibranchs Sea slugs. They are often brightly coloured to warn predators that they are poisonous or distasteful.

ocean basin Low-lying region of the Earth whose edge is marked by the bottom of the **continental slope**. New ocean basins are created by sea floor spreading (*see* **mid-ocean ridge**).

oceanic crust That part of the Earth's crust that forms the bottoms of deep oceans. It is both thinner and denser than **continental crust**. New oceanic crust is created at **mid-ocean ridges** and destroyed (*subducted*) in the vicinity of deep ocean **trenches**.

oligochaetes A group of **annelid** worms that includes lugworms and many other marine species, as well as earthworms. The name means 'few bristles'. *See also* **polychaetes**.

osmosis Where two salt solutions of different strengths come into contact, water tends to move from the dilute into the more concentrated solution: this is osmosis. Many marine creatures avoid the danger of gaining or losing water in this way by keeping the overall salt concentration in their bodies similar to that of the sea. But animals in estuaries, for example, can be in danger of swelling up and bursting as they move into fresher (less salty) water. To avoid this, they must either quickly reduce the salt concentration in their own tissues, or have a way of 'baling out' the unwanted water as it enters their bodies.

pack ice Floating sea ice in polar regions, especially when not attached to the shore (*compare* **ice shelf**). It is formed of **ice floes**, either floating separately or frozen together.

Pangaea Supercontinent consisting of all the present-day continents combined, which existed on Earth from roughly 250 to 200 million years ago.

pectoral fins The front pair of fins of fishes.

pelagic (of marine organisms) Inhabiting open water, especially its upper layers. *Compare* **demersal**.

pelvic fins The hind pair of fins of fishes.

photic zone The surface waters of seas and oceans, where enough light penetrates to support photosynthesis by marine plants such as **phytoplankton**.

photosynthesis The chemical process occurring in plants by which carbon dioxide gas and water are combined to form simple sugars. The energy for this process is provided by sunlight.

phylum (*plural,* **phyla**) The highest category used to classify animals apart from *kingdom* itself. About 30 phyla are recognized, including **molluscs, annelids, arthropods**, and **echinoderms**. (Vertebrates, including humans, form only part of a single phylum, the chordates.)

phytoplankton Plants belonging to the **plankton**. They are mainly microscopic, single-celled **algae**.

planktivorous (of an animal) Eating plankton.

plankton Animals, plants and microorganisms that float freely in the ocean at the mercy of ocean currents. Most are small, but some large creatures such as jellyfish are classified as plankton. (*Compare* **nekton**.)

plate One of the large rigid units into which the surface of the earth is divided. A plate comprises a section of the earth's crust together with the uppermost part of the underlying **mantle**. Some plates, such as the African plate, comprise both **oceanic crust** and **continental crust**, while others such as the Pacific plate are purely oceanic.

plate tectonics The theory, now well established, that the earth's surface is divided into a number of large rigid **plates**, whose movement is responsible for continental drift, earthquakes, deep ocean trenches, and other phenomena.

Pleistocene Geological epoch characterized by repeated ice ages. It lasted from around 1.7 million to 10,000 years ago.

polychaetes A large group of **annelid** worms that includes both tube-worms that are anchored to one spot and **filter-feed**, and free-living species such as ragworms. The name means 'many bristles'. *See also* **oligochaetes**.

polynya A space of open water surrounded by ice.

polyp The attached stage of a member of the **Cnidaria** – for example, a sea anemone or individual **coral** animal. Polyps have a central cavity with a single opening (mouth) at the top, surrounded by tentacles. (*Compare* **medusa**)

pressure ridge A raised area formed when two **ice floes** collide.

productivity The rate at which living tissue is produced in any given ecosystem. *Primary productivity* normally refers to the production of plant tissue by **photosynthesis**.

protozoa Single-celled animals. There are a great variety of types. Important marine protozoans include **foraminiferans** and many **flagellates**.

pteropods Relatives of snails that can swim in open water using beating movements of their modified foot. Also called sea butterflies.

radiation (electromagnetic)
Electromagnetic radiation includes radio waves, infrared (heat) radiation, visible light, ultraviolet radiation, and x-rays. The atmosphere and oceans absorb different parts of this 'spectrum' to very different degrees.

reef flat The shallow, flattest part of a reef, often partly eroded and uncovered at low tide. It supports fewer species than the **reef slope**.

reef slope The seaward edge of a coral reef where it slopes down into deeper water. It is usually very rich in species.

salps Delicate, barrel-shaped, free-floating animals related to sea-squirts (*see* **tunicates**). They obtain food by filtering water. Some species grow very large.

salt marsh Ecosystem that can develop on the higher parts of muddy shores and estuaries in temperate regions. It consists of usually flat areas of salt-tolerant land plants, dissected by muddy tidal creeks.

scyphozoans The group of the **Cnidaria** that includes the jellyfish.

sea cucumbers A group of soft-bodied, usually tube-shaped animals related to starfish (*see* **echinoderms**). Most live on the sea floor, and they are often the commonest large animals at great depths.

sea fans *see* **gorgonians**

sea lilies *see* **crinoids**

seamount A submarine mountain, often an extinct volcano. *See also* **guyot**.

sea pens A group of colonial animals related to **gorgonian** corals. They are adapted to anchor themselves in soft mud.

sea slugs *see* **nudibranchs**

sea-squirts *see* **tunicates**

sediment Accumulation of solid particles that have settled out of water. Sediments may be coarse (sand and gravel) or fine (silt and clay).

shelf *see* **continental shelf**

shrimps Any of a number of different small **crustaceans**. The 'true' shrimps are close relatives of crabs and lobsters, but many other kinds of crustaceans may include *shrimp* as part of their name.

silica The mineral of which quartz and most sand is made: chemically silicon dioxide (SiO_2). It is used in the skeletons of some marine organisms, including **diatoms** and some sponges.

siphonophores A group of jellyfish-like animals belonging to the phylum **Cnidaria**, of which the best known is the Portuguese Man-of-War. They have long stinging tentacles. Each 'individual' actually comprises a whole colony of **polyps**.

splash zone The zone on the shore just above spring tide level which is regularly wetted by salt spray.

sporophyte A plant that produces spores.

spring tides Tides in which the high tide is at its highest and the low tide is at its lowest compared with the monthly average. Spring tides occur twice each lunar month of approximately 29 ½ days. The opposite of spring tides are *neap tides*.

subduction zone *see* **trench**

symbiosis (of different kinds of organism) Living together for mutual benefit. **Corals** and the algae (**zooxanthellae**) that live in their tissues are an example of symbiosis.

tectonic Relating to structural movements in the earth, especially those caused by **plate tectonics**.

thermocline A temperature boundary formed between different layers of the

ocean. A thermocline may be temporary or permanent.

trade winds Prevailing winds that blow towards the Equator. They blow from the northeast in the northern hemisphere and from the southeast in the southern hemisphere.

trench Deep area of ocean formed where two **plates** are colliding. The **oceanic crust** from one plate is slowly *subducted* (forced under the other plate), its rocks ultimately melting and merging with the **mantle**.

Tropic of Cancer The line of latitude lying at 23° 27′ north of the Equator. The area of the Earth between this and the *Tropic of Capricorn* (23° 27′ south) receives more of the sun's energy than does the rest of the planet.

tsunami So-called 'tidal wave', although nothing to do with the tides. It is a fast-moving, high-energy wave created by underwater earthquake activity that can cause devastation when it reaches a shoreline.

tube worm Any worm that lives anchored in a tube or burrow, often spreading out tentacles to **filter-feed**. Many of them are **polychaetes**.

tunicates A group of invertebrate animals that includes the *sea-squirts*. Sea-squirts are small creatures that live anchored on rocks, protected by a tough 'tunic' pierced by two holes, through which they draw water to **filter-feed**. They are quite closely related to vertebrates. **Salps** and **larvaceans** are also tunicates.

twilight zone The zone in the open oceans below the **photic zone**, where some light penetrates, but not enough to support **photosynthesis**.

ventral (of an animal) Relating to the front or lower surface.

vertical migration A daily cycle of movement of many **zooplankton**. It commonly involves rising to the surface at night-time and sinking down again during the day.

zooplankton The animals (mainly small) that belong to the **plankton**.

zooxanthellae Algae that live **symbiotically** in the tissues of animals, especially **corals**.

Acknowledgements

While making the television series that this book accompanies we were fortunate enough to travel to the far corners and deep depths of our ocean planet. The chapters that we have each written largely reflect the episodes in the series for which we were responsible. *The Blue Planet* series would never have been possible without the help of many marine biologists and naturalists from all around the world. There sadly is not enough space here to list all the names of those that freely gave us the benefit of their intimate knowledge of the oceans. Their research and experience was not just the life blood of the series but was also the inspiration of much in this book. We are extremely grateful for all their help as we are to the many boat skippers, diving buddies and submersible pilots who assured us many a safe passage. Thank you too to the field assistants who made life much easier for the cameramen and, in particular, Ben Osborne who also took a number of the photographs in this book.

Ultimately the quality of any natural history series lies literally in the hands of the camera team. Filming underwater provides very particular challenges but we were fortunate to work with the best in the business. Many of the still images they took while filming illustrate this book. We owe them all a particular vote of thanks.

Both the series and this book have relied more than anything else on the enormous contribution made by our own production team here in Bristol. Throughout the five years it took to complete the project they have worked tirelessly to make a television series that did justice to the oceans. Much of the research they undertook or the filming trips they organised have found their way into this book in text or photographs. Their names are listed, right.

Finally, a big thank you to the excellent team at BBC Books and, especially, our editor Rachel Copus who has been immensely patient with our very busy schedules and been relentless in her drive to get every detail just right.

CAMERA TEAM
Doug Allan
John Aitchison
Doug Anderson
Simon Carroll
Rod Clarke
Peter Coleman
Bob Cranston
Mike deGruy
Leo Dickinson
Steve Downer
Goran Ehlme
Yuri Farrant
Tom Fitz
Kevin Flay
Robert Fulton
Steve Gardner
Mark Gottlieb
Florian Graner
Simon King
Richard Kirby
Ian McCarthy
Neil McDaniel
Michael Male
Charles Maxwell
Hugh Maynard
Shane Moore
Didier Noirot
Peter Parks
Andrew Penniket
Michael Pitts
Mike Potts
David Reichert
Rick Rosenthal
Matt Ruglys
Peter Scoones
David Shale
Warwick Sloss
Paul Stewart
Gavin Thurston
Richard Wollacombe
Mark Yates

PRODUCTION TEAM
Penny Allen
Lynn Barry
Samantha Davis
Lizzie Esden
Sue Flood
Amanda Hutchinson
Roger Jones
Hugh Pearson
John Ruthven
Jo Ruxton
Jo Sarsby
Katie Walker

POST PRODUCTION TEAM
FILM EDITORS
Tim Coope
Martin Elsbury
Alan Hoida
Jo Payne

SOUND EDITORS
Paul Cowgill
Angela Groves
Kate Hopkins
Lucy Rutherford

DUBBING MIXERS
Chris Domaille
Graham Wild
Andrew Wilson

MUSIC
George Fenton
BBC Concert Orchestra
Magdalen College Choir

Picture credits

BBC Worldwide would like to thank the following for providing photographs and for permission to reproduce copyright material. While every effort has been made to trace and acknowledge all copyright holders, we would like to apologize should there have been any errors or omissions.

B & C Alexander pages 231 (David Rootes), 232–3 & 247; **Doug Allan** pages 80 *both* & 234; **Ardea** pages 28–29 *right* (D. Parer & E. Parer-Cook), 66 (S. Roberts), 117 (Valerie Taylor), 125 (Valerie Taylor), 160 (Adrian Warren), 164–5 *right* (François Gohier) & 271 *top* (Jean-Paul Ferrero); **Associated Press** pages 341 *left* & 364 *left*; **Auscape** pages 43 *bottom* (Mark Spencer), 62 (Tim Acker), 105 (D. Parer & E. Parer-Cook), 110 (Jean-Paul Ferrero), 136 *left* (Mark Spencer), & 144 (Kathie Atkinson); **BBC** pages 134, 224 *all bottom*, 321 *right* & 324 *all*; **BBC/OSF** page 340 *right*; **BBC/HBOI** page 258 *top*; **BBC/WHOI** pages 361 *right*, 363 *both*, 366 *both*, 367, 368 *bottom*, 370 *right* & 371 *both*; **BBC Natural History Unit Picture Library** pages 11 (Ben Osborne), 19 (Peter Scoones), 25 (Doug Allan), 31 (Jürgen Freund), 39 (Pete Oxford), 46–7 *centre* & *right* (Doc White), 50 (Jeff Foott), 56 *top* & 56–7 *centre* (Jeff Rotman), 58 (Nigel Bean), 63 (Chris Gomersall), 74 (Tom Vezo), 84–5 *right* (Torsten Brehm), 91 (Jürgen Freund), 96 (Klaus Nigge), 103 (Georgette Douwma), 107 *bottom* (Georgette Douwma), 115 (Jürgen Freund), 118 (David Hall), 127 (Jeff Rotman), 140 *right* (Jürgen

Freund), 150 (Jeff Foott), 151 (Jürgen Freund), 154 (Jeff Rotman), 167 *right* (Peter Scoones), 177 (Alan James), 188 *right* (Duncan McEwan), 194 *left* (Jeff Rotman), 195 (Georgette Douwma), 197 *top* (Thomas D. Mangelsen), 204 *left* (Alan James), 237 (Tom Vezo), 240 (David Tipling), 248 (Doug Allan), 249 (Mike Salisbury), 254 (Steve Packham), 255 *top* (Doug Allan), 256 (Martha Holmes), 271 *bottom* (Peter Reese), 282 (Sinclair Stammers), 295 (Avi Klapper/Jeff Rotman Photography), 298–9 *centre* (Tom Walmsley), 308 *left* (Jürgen Freund), 310–11 (Jeff Rotman), 329 (David Shale) & 340 *left* (Doc White); **William Boyce** pages 164 *left*, 285 *right*, 292 *left*, 296 *both*, 297, 305 *bottom*, 306 *both* & 307; **Bridgeman Art Library** page 23 *left*; **Andy Byatt** page 274; **Brandon D. Cole** pages 1, 182–3 & 199; **Bruce Coleman Collection** pages 33 *left* (Pacific Stock), 46 *left* (Kim Taylor), 51 (Malcom Hey), 76–7 *right* (Chris Gomersall), 90 *top* (Fred Bruemmer), 94 (John Shaw), 166 (Johnny Johnson), 189, 208 *left* (Kim Taylor), 212, 218 (Johnny Johnson), 253 (Staffan Widstrand), 257 (Staffan Widstrand), 258 (Tero Niemi), 263 (Pacific Stock), 281 (Pacific Stock); **Corbis** page 27

(© Digital image © 1996 CORBIS; original image courtesy of NASA/CORBIS); **Georgette Douwma** pages 52, 104, 107 *top*, 119, 122, 191 *bottom*, 194 *right*; **Steve Downer** page 124 *right*; **Göran Ehlmé** page 239 *top*; **FLPA** pages 181 (Roger Wilmshurst) & 309 (Flip Nicklin/Minden Pictures); **Sue Flood** pages 259 *bottom* & 268; **Florian Graner** pages 350–1, 354 & 359; **Robert Harding Picture Library** pages 61 (David Noton), 78 (Frans Lanting/Minden Pictures), 219 (Jim Brandenburg/Minden Pictures), 242–3 (Frans Lanting/Minden Pictures), 245 *left* (Frans Lanting/Minden Pictures), 265 (Flip Nicklin/Minden Pictures), 293 (Flip Nicklin/Minden Pictures), 327 (Flip Nicklin/Minden Pictures) & 378–9 (Flip Nicklin/Minden Pictures); **Guy Harvey** page 294 *top*; **P. J. Herring** pages 318–9, 325 *bottom*, & 341 *right*; **Martha Holmes** pages 20, 221, 222 *left*, 223, 238, 244, 245 *right*, 250 *top*, 251 & 259 *top*; **Image Quest 3-D/Peter Parks** pages 171, 172, 173, 174, 277, 301, 302 *top* & 317; **Innerspace Visions** pages 28 *left* (Doug Perrine), 57 *top right* (Bruce Rasner), 132 (Michel Jozon), 179 (Amos Nachoum), 192–3 (Phillip Colla), 208 *right* (Marty Snyderman), 209 (Jim Knowlton), 255 *bottom* (John K. B. Ford),

260 (Masa Ushioda/Seapics.com), 264 (Bob Cranston), 272 (Richard Herrmann), 273 (Doug Perrine), 284 *left* (Doug Perrine), 284–5 *centre* (Doc White), 286 (Mike Johnson), 287 (Doug Perrine), 289 *top* (Doug Perrine), *bottom* (Howard Hall), 290 (Bob Cranston), 291 (James D. Watt), 298 *left* (Michael S. Nolan), 299 *right* (James D. Watt), 305 *top* (Mark Conlin), 308 *right* (Doug Perrine), 315 (Doug Perrine) & 358 *bottom* (Bob Cranston); **Emma Jones** page 357; **Neil G. McDaniel** pages 6, 188 *left*, 197 *bottom*, 200, 202 *left* & 211; **George Matsumoto, MBARI** page 320; **National Geographic Society Image Collection/Else Bostelmann** page 364 *right*; **National Trust Photographic Library** page 38 (Paul Wakefield); **Natural Image/Bob Gibbons** page 83 *bottom*; **Natural Visions/Heather Angel** page 302 *bottom*; **Network** page 22 *left*; **NHPA** pages 21 (Tom & Therisa Stack), 49 *right* (A.N.T.), 131 (B. Jones & M. Shimlock), 142 *top* (John Shaw), *bottom* (Jean-Louis le Moigne), 147 (George Gainsburgh), 148 *left* (Norbert Wu), 157 (R. Sorenson & J. Olsen), 162 (Bill Coster), 163 (Ralph & Daphne Keller), 178 *bottom* (Peter Pickford), 226 (Lady Philippa Scott), 227 (Norbert Wu), 230 (Norbert Wu), 235 (Norbert Wu), 241 (Norbert Wu), 252 (Andy Rouse), 270 *left* (Roger Tidman), 278 (Peter Parks) & 348 (Peter Parks); **NOAA Photo Library** pages 34 *left* (EDIS), 36 *left*, 362 (NURP Collection), 365 *left* (NURP Collection) & 370 *left* (NURP Collection); **Didier Noirot** pages 137, 146 & 269; **Ben Osborne** pages 33 *right*, 36 *right*, 71, 81, 89 *both*, 92, 93, 95, 98, 236 *right* & 239 *bottom*; **OSF** pages 44–5 *left* (Doug Allan), 45 *right* (Mark Jones), 64–5 (Mark Hamblin), 73 (Tui de Roy), 75 (Rodger Jackman), 76 *left* (Ted Levin/Animals Animals), 79 *top* (G. I. Bernard), 79 *bottom* (Mark Jones), 88 (David B. Fleetham), 112–113 (Kathie Atkinson), 149 (Howard Hall), 152 *both* (Rudie Kuiter), 153 (Karen Gowlett-Holmes), 175 *left* (Peter Parks), 186–7 *right* (Karen Gowlett-Holmes), 196 (Norbert Wu), 202–3 (Mark Webster), 204 *right* (David Fox), 207 Howard Hall, 222 *right* (Colin Monteath), 225 (Konrad Wothe), 229 (C. J. Gilbert), 236 *left* (Ben Osborne), 275 (Norbert Wu), 279 (Peter Parks), 280 *top* (Richard Herrmann), 303 (Zig Leszczynski/ Animals Animals), 304 (Richard Herrmann) & 321 *left* (Peter Parks); **Planet Earth** pages 2 (Gary Bell), 4–5 (Norbert Wu), 53 (Norbert Wu), 54 (Linda Dunk), 55 (Gary Bell), 57 *bottom right* (Warren Williams), 67 *top* (Tom Brakefield), 70 *bottom* (Jim Greenfield), 87 (Darryl Torckler), 90 *bottom* (Mike Brock), 97 (Peter Scoones), 99 *left* (James D. Watt), *right* (Paul Hobson), 106 (Pete Atkinson), 116 *top* (Pete Atkinson), 120–1 *both* (Ken Lucas), 180 (James D. Watt), 205 (Marty Snyderman), 206 *top* (Mark Conlin), 210 (Andrew Mounter), 280 *bottom* (Marty Snyderman), 283 (Doug Perrine), 326 (Peter David), 336 *left* (Peter David), 337 *top* (Peter David), 343 (Peter David) & 372 (Mary Clay); **Popperfoto** page 365 *right*; **David Reichert** page 294 *bottom*; **Bruce Robison** pages 334–5 & 337 *bottom*; **Jan Rocha** page 41; **Rick Rosenthal** page 292 *right*; **Science Photo Library** pages 17 (NASA), 18 *top* (Space Telescope Science Institute/NASA), 26 (NASA), 32 (NASA), 37 (Bernhard Edmaier), 40 (NASA), 48 (Claude Nuridsany & Marie Perennou), 67 *bottom* (Simon Fraser), 100 (Bernhard Edmaier), 169 (Jan Hinsch), 216 (NASA), 220 (Bernhard Edmaier), 361 *left* (B. Murton, Southampton Oceanography Centre) & 368 *top* (Institute of Oceanographic Sciences/NERC); **Peter Scoones** pages 109, 123, 129 & 175 *right*; **David Shale** pages 23 *right*, 316, 325 *top*, 328 *right*, 331, 332, 333, 336 *bottom right*, 338, 342 & 352; **Craig R. Smith** page 349 *bottom*; **Southampton Oceanography Centre** pages 328 *left*, 336 *top right*, 339 & 345; **Jeremy Stafford-Deitsch** pages 130, 140 *left*, 143, 145 & 148 *right*; **Roger Steene** pages 124 *left*, 133, 135 & 136 *right*; **Still Pictures** page 139 *right* (M.& C. Denis-Huot); **Stone** pages 14, 18 *bottom*, 34 *right* & 35; **Mark Strickland/Oceanic Impressions** page 126; **Woodfall Wild Images** pages 43 *top* (David Woodfall), 70 *top* (Allan Watson), 82 (David Woodfall), 83 *top* (Steve Austin), 84 *left* (Mike Lane), 111 (Ted Mead), 116 *bottom* (L. Wood), 139 *left* (Alan Watson), 141 (David Woodfall), 167 *left* (David Woodfall), 170 *top* (Sue Scott), 176 (Sue Scott), 178 *top* (Sue Scott), 185 (Sue Scott), 186 *left* (Sue Scott), 190 (Sue Scott), 191 *top* (George Gornacz), 201 *left* (Sue Scott), *right* (Paul Kay), 206 *bottom* (Adrian Dorst), 215 (Paul Nicklen), 224 *top* (Paul Nicklen), 250 *bottom* (Tony Martin) & 270 *right* (Inigo Everson); **Woods Hole Oceanographic Institution** page 369; **David Wrobel** pages 312, 349 *top*, 353, 355 & 356.

The engraving on page 22 is from *The Depths of the Ocean* by Sir John Murray & Dr Johan Horst, pub. Macmillan, London, 1912.

Index

Page numbers in *italic* indicate pictures.

abyssal plains 28, 29, 346
Abyssobrotula galatheae 357
Adélie penguins
    breeding 231, 234-5
    chicks 239
    losses to leopard seals 241
alabaster nudibranch 200
albatrosses 95, 236, 270-1
    black-browed *36, 236*
algae 111
    Antarctic sea ice 226
    and territory defence, reef fish 118
    see also blue-green algae; green algae;
        red algae; seaweeds
Alvin, Woods Hole Oceanographic Institute
    365
amphipods
    Cystisoma 316, 317
    deposit feeders 205
    Phronima 316, 317, 320
    sandy coasts 76
ampullae of Lorenzini 290, 295
anchor ice 226, 227
Andean condors 81
Andes, formation of 24, 25-6
anemonefish 130, *131*
anemones *see* sea anemones
angelfish 120, 129, 133
anglerfish 331, 333
    attracting prey 336
    breeding and reproduction 342-3
    hairy *332, 333*
    symbiotic bacteria, bioluminescence 336
annelid worms 79
Antarctic 215
    autumn 239-41
    spring 229-31
    summer 234-5
    winter 241
Antarctic Circumpolar Current 36
Antarctic Convergence 215
Antarctica 216, 217
    plateau 218
    sea ice 219, 221, 226
    snowfall 222
    temperature ranges 217, 219
    wildlife 228-45
anthias 116, 117, 129, *129*
    Red Sea, feeding on reef *103*, 129
archerfish 146, *147*
Arctic 215
    autumn 257-8
    hunting 252-5
    people in 250-1
    prehistory 216, 217
    sea ice 220, 221

summer 253-7
temperature ranges 219
wildlife 246-59
Arctic foxes 93, 247
Arctic Ocean 216, 219
    continental shelves 227
    plankton blooms 225-6
    sea ice 220, 221
Arctic terns 258
Argonaut (Paper nautilus) 328, 329
arribada 71, 89
Atlantic lobsters 167
Atlantic mackerel 164
Atlantic Ocean 27, 28
Atlantic spotted dolphin 298-9
Atolla, jellyfish 338, 339
atolls 103, 104
auks 179
Aurelia aurita 174, 175
Australian soldier crabs 76

bacteria
    bioluminescence 336, 337
    hydrogen sulphide fixing 363, 366, 367,
        371
    methane-fixing 370
    ocean floor 53
    surface layer, oceans 281
Bahama banks *100*, 102
baitball 178-9
baleen whales 180, 287
    blue whales 46-7, 287
    bowhead whales 255, 258, 259
    fin whales 164, *164-5*, 287
    humpback whales 179, 181, 182-3, 235,
        308, 309
    migrations 235, 308-9
    right whales 162, 163, 180, 235
banded pilot fish 293
barnacles 74, 75, 143, 200
Barracudina 327
barrier reef 103, 104
basket stars 126
basking sharks 57, 176, 177
bathyscaphe 364-5
bathysphere 364
Bay of Fundy, Nova Scotia 41, 66, *160, 161,
    164-5*, 180
beach, zones on 70
Beebe, William 364
beluga whales 254, 255, 258, 259, *259*
Benguela Current 38
bergy bits 223
Bering Sea, grey whales 207
Bermuda, coral reefs 105
Beroë 282, 321
Big Bang 17-18
bigeye jacks 282, 283

billfish 291, 294-5
bioluminescence 170, 324, 337
    breeding and reproduction 342
    counter-illumination 325
    dark-zone fish 337-9
    deep-sea sharks 359
    escaping predators 338-9
    symbiotic bacteria 336, 337
bird colonies 92-6, 181
    Arctic, proximity to polynyas 258
    north Atlantic cliffs 74
Biremas 352, 353
bivalves 55, 204
    Arctic 227
    coral, damage to 112
    wood-feeding 348
black bear, scavenging stranded whale 80,
    81
black coral 107
black guillemots 95
black hamlet 129
'black smokers' 29, 361
black vultures 81, 89
black-browed albatross *36, 236*
blacksmiths 195
blue marlin *291, 294-5*
blue sharks *192-3, 272, 290*, 308
blue whales 46-7, 287
blue-barred parrotfish, primary males 130
blue-green algae 21, 111, 169
blue-spotted stingray, spiracle 54
blue-striped fang *104, 105*
bluefin tuna 163, 268, 269, 296, 297, 301
Boleophthalmus 146
bottlenose dolphin, mother and calf *310-11*
bowhead whale 255, 258, 259
boxfish 133
brash ice 223
Brine Pool, Gulf of Mexico 370, 371
bristlemouths 328
brittlestars 119, 126, 352
broadbill *see* swordfish
broadcast spawning 132, 133, 301
brown seaweed 188
Brünnich's guillemots 254
bryozoans (moss animals) 194
bull kelp *188*, 191
buoyancy 45
    deep-sea sharks 358
butterflyfish 120, 133

cabbage corals *106*
Calanus hyperboreus 253-4
California Current 275
California, kelp forest *154*, 190
Californian grunion 71, 90
Californian sea hare 194
Californian sea otters 195, 196-7

camouflage
    anglerfish 333
    counter shading 284, 290
    counter-illumination 325
    flying fish 284
    hatchet fish 324, 325
    reef fish 120, 122, 127
cannonball mangrove, roots 140
capelin 90
carbon cycle 49
cardinalfish 135, 147
Caribbean spiny lobsters *149*
central rift valley 29
cephalopods, deep-sea 340-1
    see also opctopus; squid
Ceratoscopelus warmingii 283, 328
Challenger Deep, Marianas Trench 346, 354
Challenger expedition, 1872 23, 364
chambered nautilus 340
chemical scents, sensitivity to 289-90
chimaera 358, 359
chinstrap penguins 93, 230, 231, 234
chronometer, invention of 23
Chrysaora hysoscella 176
cleaning fish 116
cliff-nesting, seabirds 74, 95, 180, *181*
climate control 37, 38-9
    see also El Niño-Southern Oscillation
climate currents 274
cnidarians 106
    medusae 175
    see also coral; jellyfish; sea anemones
coast 58-99
    breeding and reproduction 86-99
    as dynamic border 60-71
    erosion 61, 62, 149
    as habitat 43-4, 72-85
    scavengers 80-1
    shape of 61-3
cockles 78, 204
cod 210, 211
cold seeps 370-1
cold-vent tubeworms 371
cold-water currents 38, 269
cold-water overturn 265, 277
Colobonema jellyfish 339
comb jellies 282, 320-1
comet fish 120
commercial fishing *see* fishing industry
common eider and ducklings 64-5
compass jellyfish 176
continental drift 24, 25, 26, 104
continental edges 27-8
continental rise 28
continental shelves 27, 160, 227, 346
continental slope 28, 346
convergence zone, western Pacific 275
copepods 50, 172-3, 174, 181, 253-4

coral 106-9
  bleaching 107
  calcium carbonate, secretion 107, 108
  deep-sea 354, 355, 356
  fire coral 122, 123
  as food 122
  growth 112
  polyps 106-7, 108
  spawning 136-7
  zooxanthellae, symbiotic relationship
    with 108
coral atolls 103, 104
coral cay 112-13
coral reefs 43, 44-5, 102-13
  deep, cold-water 356
  distribution of 105
  erosion 111, 112
  food web 114-27
  formation of 103-5, 107, 108
  reproduction on 128-37
  shaping 110-13
  zonation 110-11
coral sands, creation of 111, 112
cord grass 82, 83
Coriolis effect 33
counter-current blood system 295, 296
counter-illumination 325
cowries 122
Crab Island, Australia 89
crabeater seals 226, 229, 230
crabs
  Australian soldier 76
  fiddler 143, 144-5
  ghost 76, 76-7
  grapsid 143
  horseshoe 90-1
  landcrabs 91
  mole crab 79
  porcelain 52, 53, 201
  red 91
  Sally lightfoot 74
  sand bubbler 76
  xanthid 124
crested auklets 94, 95, 96
crocodiles 89, 147
crown-of-thorns starfish 55, 124-5
ctenophores 170, 175, 282, 320-1
currents 36, 37, 268-9
Cyanea lamarckii 174, 175
cyanobacteria 21, 169
Cystisoma 316, 317

damselfish 116, 117, 129
dark zone 330-43
  bioluminescence 337-9
  breeding and reproduction 342-3
  life in 331-6
daylight hours
  polar regions 215, 216
  temperate regions 160, 161
deep layer, ocean 264
deep ocean circulation 37, 38
deep oceanic trenches 25

deep scattering layer 328
deep sea 312-71
  dark zone 330-43
  sea floor 344-59
  twilight zone 314-29
deep-sea floor 344-59
  cold seeps 370-1
  exploration 364-5
  fish 357-9
  hydrothermal vents 361-3, 366-9
  life at the bottom 345, 348-56
  shape 346-7
demersal fish 205, 208-11
demersal spawners 133
Dendronephthya 106
detritus, seabed 204
  detritus eaters 53
  marine snow 349
dhows 22
Diadema 117, 149
diatomaceous earth 169
diatoms 169, 171, 226, 277
dinoflagellates 170, 171
dog teams, Arctic 251
dog whelk 75
doldrums 32, 33
dolphin fish (dorado) 285, 293, 305
dolphins 298-9
  care of young 309, 310-11
  hunting 179, 296-7
  sonar 297
  spinner 260, 262, 298, 299
  strandings 79, 80
  tears 50
  and tuna fishing 306-7
Dover sole 208
dragonfish 337, 338
dugongs 151
Dumbo, deep-sea octopus 366
dwarf minke 287
dwarf shark 359

Earth, photographed from Apollo 17 17
Earth's polarity, periodic reversal 24
East-Pacific Rise 25
eel grass 148, 149
eelpout 324
eels
  European 302, 318-19
  gulper 333, 334-5
El Niño-Southern Oscillation 39, 275
electrical charges 210
electrical signals, sensitivity to 290, 295
elephant seals 97, 98, 98-9, 98, 237, 264
emperor penguins 92, 244-5
  chicks 242-3, 245
Enteropneusta 366
Enypniastes 352
enzymes, sub-zero conditions 224
equatorial currents 33
erosion
  coral reefs 111, 112
  rocky coasts 61, 62

Erythrymenia minuta 186
estuaries 62-3, 82-5
estuarine crocodiles 147
Euphausia superba 229
European eels 302, 318-19
evolution of life 16, 17, 21

fairy basslets see anthias
fangtooth 312, 333
fiddler crabs 143, 144-5
filter-feeders 52
  mangroves 143
  rocky coasts 201-2
fin whales 164, 164-5, 287
fire coral 122, 123
fish breeding on land 90
fish eggs 301
fishing industry 305
  albatross casualities of long-lining 271
  dolphin friendly tuna 306-7
  maximum sustainable yield 305
fishing quotas 305
flat fish 84, 208
flat-backed turtle, breeding 89
flood water and ocean nutrient levels 274
flotsam 292-3
flyingfish 284-5
  eggs in sargassum weed 302
  four-winged 284, 302
foraminiferans 348
frazil ice 219, 221
fringing reefs 103, 104
frozen seas 212-59
  Antarctic wildlife 228-45
  Arctic wildlife 246-59
  polar regions 214-27
fur seals 97, 99, 237, 238

Galápagos Islands 28-9
Ganges fan 28
gannets, nesting colonies 93
garibaldi fish 194, 195
ghost crabs 76, 76-7
ghost pipefish 122, 148, 149
giant Atlantic halibut 211
giant clams 136
giant kelp 154, 188, 190, 191, 194
giant petrels 81, 239
giant squid 341
giant sunfish 287
giant triton 124
gills 54
glaciers 219, 222-3
glasswort see samphire
Glaucus 278
global warming 221
glossary 373-7
glycopeptides, biological antifreeze 224,
  230
gobies 74, 117
goblin sharks 359
Gondwanaland 26, 217
grapsid crabs 143

gravitational pull 40, 41
gray whales 195, 206-7, 309
grease ice 221
Great Barrier Reef, Australia 104, 105, 110
  coral spawning 136
Great Ocean Conveyer Belt 38
great sheephead wrasse 195
great white sharks 56-7, 57
green algae 111, 112, 186
green chromis, spawning 133-4
green turtles 50, 51, 87, 88, 89
green wrasse 130-1, 133
greenhouse gases 37
Greenland 219
grenadiers 357
grey seals 98-9
grey-headed albatross 270
grizzly bears 67
ground-nesting birds 95
groupers 119, 120, 129
grunion 90
guillemots 44-5, 258
guitar fish 208
Gulf of Mexico, cold seeps 370-1
Gulf Stream 38, 39, 105, 268
gulper eels 333, 334-5
guyots 28
gyres 33, 36, 268

habitats 43-5, 687-69
  estuaries 62-3, 82-5
  intertidal 66-7, 68-9, 70-1, 74-5
  open ocean 266-7
  rocky coasts 61-2, 73-5
  sandy coasts 62, 76-9
  surf zone 76, 78
  temperate seas 158-9
hairy anglerfish 332, 333
Halimeda 112
hammerhead sharks 56, 57, 132, 295
harbour seals 195
hard corals 106
harlequin ghost pipefish 120
harlequin shrimps 118, 119
harp seals 247-8, 248
Hastings, depositional coastline 62
hatchetfish 324-5
hawk anthias 116, 117
hermaphroditism 120
  corals 137
  deep-sea fish 342
  see also protandrous fish; protogynous
    fish
herring 163, 177, 178-9
heteropods 320, 328
high pressure weather systems 66
  see also Southern Oscillation
high-energy coastlines 61-2
Himalayas, view from space 26
Histioteuthis 324, 341
hooded seals 248
Hopewell rocks, Bay of Fundy 66
horizon, open ocean 263

horn sharks 56, 57, 132, 208
horseshoe crabs 90-1
Humboldt Current 38, 269
humpback whales 179, 181, 182-3, 235, 308, 309
humphead parrotfish 122
hurricanes 32, 34
Hydrobia 84
hydrodynamic efficiency, ocean predators 290-1
hydrogen sulphide fixing bacteria 363, 366, 367, 371
hydroids 122
hydrological cycle 19
hydrothermal vents 29, 360-3, 366-9

ice
    floating 19-20
    frozen sea 219-21
    life beneath 227
    life with 224-7
    making 222-3
    see also sea ice
ice cliffs, polar seas 212
ice fish 230
ice floes, seals breeding on 97-8, 226, 230
ice sheet, movement of 222
ice worms 370, 371
ice-caps, Arctic and Antarctic 222
icebergs 223, 232-3
iguanas, marine 73, 73-4
infauna 205
insects, mangroves 142
intermediate layer, ocean 264
International Whaling Commission, 1965 46
intertidal region 43-4, 66-7, 74-5
    breeding 70-1
    drying out, risk of 75
    seaweed 185
    tropical, mangroves 139-40
Inuit 250-1
isopods 194, 348

jacks 116, 119
jellyfish 21, 174-6
    Atolla 338, 339
    Chrysaora hysoscella 176
    Colobenema 339
    Cyanea lamarkii 174, 175
    nematocysts 175
jewel anemones 202-3
Johnson Sealink 23, 365

katabatic winds 219
kelp 187, 188, 189
    bull kelp 188, 191
    forests 154, 190, 195
    as habitat 194-5
    holdfasts 188, 194
    paddies 191, 192-3
    and wave action 191
    see also giant kelp

kelp fishes 194
killer whales 179, 230, 235
king penguins 97, 236-7, 237
kittiwakes 180, 181
krill 229-30, 229
    whales feeding on 235

land
    fish breeding on 90
    marine mammals breeding on 97-9
    reptiles breeding on 87-9
land crabs, breeding 91
lantern fish 283, 328
lanugo, Arctic seal pups 248
larvaceans 281, 282
lateral line, vibrational sensitivity 290, 333
Laurasia 26
leafy seadragon 153
leatherback turtles 87, 273
lemon shark, live birth 308
leopard seals 230, 239, 241
Leptocephalus 318-19
life, evolution 16, 17, 21
light in the sea 28
    and seaweed growth 189
    twilight zone 316
    see also bioluminescence
limpets 75, 227
Linckia multifora 134
Linophryne anglerfish 336
lionfish 120, 121, 133
lion's mane jellyfish 174, 175
lithospheric plates 24
little terns 78, 93
live birth 305
    and care of young 308, 309, 310-11
    sharks 132, 308
lizardfish 119
lobsters 167
long-horned cowfish 120
long-spined sea urchins 117
Lophelia 356
low pressure weather systems 66
    see also Southern Oscillation
low-energy coastlines 62
lugworms 63, 84

macaroni penguins 236
mackerel, migration 164
mako sharks 289, 295, 305
males brooding eggs, reef fish 134, 135
    see also seahorses
mammals, marine *see* marine mammals
manatees 150, 151
mangroves 139-47
    animals 142-7
    forests 139
    roots 139, 140, 141, 142-3
    seeds 143-4
manta ray 280, 287
mantis shrimp 204-5
Manx shearwaters 162, 166, 167

Mappa Mundi 23
mapping the world 22-3
Marianas Trench 29, 315
    Challenger Deep 346, 354
marine iguanas, Galapagos 73-4
marine mammals
    breeding colonies 98-9
    breeding on land 97-9
    care of young 308, 309, 310-11
    fat storage 45
    pack hunting 296-7
marine snow 349
mass spawning 301-2
Mediterranean, tidal ranges 66
medusa stage, jellyfish 175
medusa star 350-1
Megalodicopia 356, 357
megamouth sharks 56, 57
meiofauna 205
Melanstomias 338
meroplankton 173-4
Mertz glacier 222
methane, cold seeps 370
Mid-Atlantic ridge 24, 368
mid-ocean ridges 24, 25, 29, 347, 361, 368
migrations
    baleen whales 235, 308-9
    beluga whales 254, 255, 259
    from polar regions 225
    north, Arctic summer 254-5
    of peoples 22
    to breeding grounds 166
    to feeding grounds 164
    to shelter of land 163
    to winter havens 162-3
    vertical 280-1, 327-8
mimic blenny 104, 105
Mississippi river fan 26, 27
Mnemiopsis 282
mole crab 79
monkfish 208
moon power 40-1
moorish idols 127
mountain ranges, creation of 25, 26
mudflats, estuaries 63, 64-5, 84-5
mudskippers 144, 145-6
multi-year ice 221
mushroom coral 354, 355, 356
mussels 70, 75
    surrounding cold seeps 370, 371
myctophids *see* lantern fish

narwhals 255
navigation, early 23
Nazca Plate 24, 25-6
nekton 50
nematocysts 122, 175
nematodes 348
nemertine worms 241
nesting places, sea birds 77, 93-5, 180, 181
nests, underwater 133-4
neuston layer 264, 277, 278-9
night feeders

coral reefs 126-7
    planktivores, open-ocean 283
night herons, preying on turtle hatchlings 89
North Atlantic Drift 39
North Atlantic gannets 162
North Atlantic grey seal 99
North Atlantic salmon 166
northern bluefin tuna 268
northern lights 216
northern right whales 180
Northwater, Baffin Bay 258, 259
Novodinea 356
nudibranch *see* sea slugs
nutrients
    floodwater 274
    marine snow 349
    recycling, cold-water overturn 277
    temperate seas 157, 160-1

ocean exploration 22-3
ocean floor 28-9
oceans
    and climate control 20, 37-9
    currents 36, 37, 38, 275
    layers 264, 265, 278
    main surface currents 36, 37
    origins 17-19
    source of fresh water 19
    see also open ocean
octopus
    deep-sea, Dumbo 366
    Pacific 210, 211
    twilight zone 320
Olive Ridley turtles 71, 81, 89
open ocean 45, 260-311
    breeding and reproduction 300-11
    drifters 276-87
    hunters 288-99, 295
Opisthoproctus 325
Orion Nebula 18
ospreys 84, 142
otters 82, 83, 93
    see also sea otters
oxygen minimum layer 265
ozone layer 21

Pacific ocean 263
    islands 273
    tidal patterns 41
Pacific octupus 210, 211
Pacific rim, continental shelves 27
Pacific walruses 256, 257
pack ice 220, 221
pair spawning 133
palm weed 189
pancake ice 221
Pangaea 24, 26
Panthalassa 26
paper nautilus 328, 329
parrotfish 112, 122, 127, 129, 130, 133
patch reefs 111
pelicans 78, 89

penguins
  Adélie 231, 234-5, 239, 241
  emperor 92, 244-5
  king 97, 236-7, 237
  leopard seals preying on fledgelings 239
  macaroni 236
  nesting 92, 234
  South Georgia 236
Periophthalmus 146
periwinkles 147, 227
Peruvian coast, upwelling 33, 38, 39
  El Niño 39
photophores 324, 325, 328, 337
photosynthesis 21
  phytoplankton 44
  seaweed 185
phronima 316, 317, 320
phytoplankton 44, 48-9, 168-71
  blooms 125, 170-1, 229
  open ocean 277
  seamounts, concentrations around 273
  seasonal distribution 170
Piccard, Auguste, bathyscaphe 364, 365
picoplankton 171, 172
pipefish 134, 135
plaice, larval 208
planktivores 177
  coral reefs 115-16
  filter-feeders 52
  giants 48, 49, 180
  kelp forests 195
  night feeders 126
  open oceans 283-7
plankton 168-77, 171, 181, 276
  blooms 49, 50, 116, 170-1, 181, 225-6
  seamounts, concentrations around 273, 292
  see also phytoplankton; zooplankton
plant-eaters, coral reefs 117-18
plate tectonics 24-6
plough snails 78
pneumatocysts, seaweed 185, 188, 190, 191
polar bears 218, 219, 224, 247
  Arctic summers 256-7
  female with cub 224-5, 224, 252, 253, 256
  hunting ringed seal pups 252-3
  swimming 256
  waiting for sea to freeze 258
polar regions 214-27
  daylight hours 215, 216
  habitat 44
  solar radiation 216
  see also Antarctic; Antarctica; Arctic
polychaete worms 78, 79, 348, 352, 353
polynyas 258-9
Pompeii worms 366, 367
porcelain crabs 52, 53, 201
Porites coral heads, reproduction 137
Porphyra 187
Portuguese man-of-war 278, 279
powder blue surgeonfish 118
pressure

dark zone 330
twilight zone 315, 317
primary males, protandrous fish 130-1
propagule 144
protandrous fish 129, 130
protogynous fish 129, 131
protozoans 170
protrusible mouths 116
pteropods 280, 281, 326, 327
pufferfish 120
puffins 95
purse-seine fishing 306
pygmy shark 359
pyramid butterflyfish 116
pyramids of life 48-51

quiet time, coral reefs 126

rabbit fish 117, 358, 359
rainbow runners 292, 293
rat-tails 357
rays 210
  live birth 305
  manta rays 280, 287
  sensory systems 290
  spiracles 54
  torpedo 208, 209, 210
red algae 111, 186, 186-7, 187, 188, 316
red crabs 91
red sea urchins, grazing kelp holdfasts 196, 197
reef plants 111
reef slope 111
  planktivores 115-16
Reeves glacier, Victoria Land 222
remoras 293
reptiles breeding on land 87-9
Riftia 362, 363, 363
right whales 163, 235
  northern 180
  southern 162, 163, 180
Rimicaris 368, 369
ringed seals 248, 249, 256, 258
  polar bears preying on pups 252-3
river fans 26, 27, 28
rock faces, temperate seas 199
rock-pools 75
rocky coasts 61-2, 73-5
  seabed 204-5
  underwater 199-203
rocky slopes, deep-sea 354-6
rogue waves 34
roundworms 348

sailfish 265, 269, 279
St Kilda, nesting colony 93
salinity 20, 21
  estuarine crocodiles 147
  fluctuations, estuaries 67, 82
  mangrove trees 140
Sally lightfoot crabs 74
salmon, migration 166
salp 172, 281, 282

invaded by *phronima* 316, 317
salt excretion, gills 54
salt marshes 83
salt spray, survival on coast 73
saltwater crocodiles 89
samphire 82, 83
sand
  burrowing in 78-9
  coral reefs 112
  finding food in 79
sand bubbler crabs 76
sand cay, development 112
sand dollars 79, 205
sand dunes 62
sand-hoppers 76
sanderling 78
sandy coasts 62, 76-9
Sargasso Sea 36, 302
sargassum fish 302, 303
scalefin anthias 129
scarlet ibis 142
schooling fish 177, 282, 283
  baitball 178-9
scorpionfish 54, 55
sea anemones 201, 202, 202-3
  deep-sea 345, 354, 355
  jewel anemones 202-1
  seagrass beds 149, 151
sea beans 80
sea birds
  breeding, timing of 50, 181
  colonies 74, 92-6, 181, 258
  ground-nesting 95
  kelp forests 195
  planktonivores 180, 287
sea butterflies 280, 281, 326, 327
sea cows 151
sea cucumbers 53, 200, 201, 348, 349, 352
sea fans 52, 107
sea gooseberry 170, 282
sea ice 215, 219-21
  living with 225-7
  maps of annual 217
  predators 247-9
  summer melt, Arctic 253-4
  see also polynyas
sea lettuce 186, 187
sea level 27, 29, 36
sea lions 45, 81, 98, 99, 195
sea mouse 204, 205
sea otters 195, 196-7
sea palms 189
sea pens 204, 205, 352, 353
sea slugs 120, 200, 278
sea snails 359
sea snakes 279, 305
sea squirts 52, 201
sea turtles *see* turtles
sea urchins 54, 200, 205, 352-3
  Diadema 117, 149
  grazing on kelp holdfasts 196, 197
  grazing seagrass beds 149
  long-spined 117

sea otters feeding on 196-7
sea-surface temperatures, pattern of 268, 269
seabed
  deep-sea 344-59, 364-5
  rocky coasts 204-5, 208-11
  see also cold seeps; hydrothermal vents
seagrass beds 148-51
seahorses 151, 152-3
seals
  breeding 97-9
  elephant 97, 98-9, 98, 237, 264
  fur seals 97, 99, 237, 238
  grey 98-9
  harbour 195
  harp 247-8, 248
  hooded 248
  leopard 230, 239, 241
  ringed 248, 249, 252-3, 256, 258
seamounts 28, 273, 292, 346
seas, formation of early 18
seascapes 27-9
seaweeds 67, 74, 75, 75, 184-97, 302
  see also algae
sediment, estuaries 82
sediment fans 26, 27, 28
sei whales 287
sensory systems
  basking sharks 177
  deep sea fish 333
  demersal fish 208, 210
  ocean hunters 289-90
Severn Estuary 66
sharks 56-7
  basking 57, 176, 177
  blue 192-3, 272, 290, 308
  breathing 54
  breeding 132
  bycatch, dolphin-friendly nets 307
  deep-sea 358-9
  fins for soup 308
  goblin 359
  guitar fish 208
  hammerhead 56, 57, 132, 295
  horn 56, 57, 132, 208
  hunting 57
  jaws and teeth 57
  live births 305, 308
  mako 289, 295, 305
  megamouth 56, 57
  pygmy or dwarf 359
  sensory systems 127, 210, 290, 295
  six-gilled 358
  swell 304, 305
  whale sharks 48, 57, 287
  white-tip reef 126, 127
  young 132
shearwaters 180
sheathbill 81
shell collectors 124
shortfin mako 289
shrimps 134, 204
  dark zone 331

hydrothermal vents 368, 368, 369
mantis 204-5
silver wahoo 293
simultaneous hermaphrodites 129
siphonophores 321
six-gilled sharks 358
skate 54, 211
skipjack tuna 274
sleeper gobies 53
snails
herbiverous 200
mangroves 147
surfing 78
vampire 126, 127
snapping shrimps 134
snipe eel 327
snow petrels 225
soft corals 106, 107, 201, 202
deep-sea 354, 355, 356
solar system, creation of 17-18
sooty terns 93
South American sea lions 45
South Georgia 97, 236-7, 238
southern lights 216
Southern Ocean 216
seabed 227
whaling industry 238
Southern Oscillation 39
southern right whale 162, 163, 180
spaghetti worms 366
sperm whale, twilight zone 315, 316
spine-cheek anemonefish 130, 131
spinner dolphin 260, 262, 298, 299
spiral eddies, strong currents 36
splash zone 73, 74
sponges 52, 53, 112
spotted dolphin 299
spring and neap tides 41
squid 304, 320
giant squid 341
Histioteuthis 324, 341
Vitronella 320, 321
stalked crinoids 354
starfish 55, 74, 75, 134, 356
crown-of-thorns 55, 124-5
Novodinea 356
sunstar 202
Steeple Jason, black-browed albatross 92, 93
Steller's sea eagle 95-6, 96, 97
Steller's sea lion 98, 99
storms, nutrient mixing 160, 161, 277
strand line scavengers 80
striped marlin 274, 294
subduction zone
plate tectonics 25
sun, moon and tides 40
sun, power of 30, 31-3
sunfish 286, 287
sunstars 202
surf zone 76, 78
surface currents 33
surface layer, ocean see neuston layer
surfbird 74

surfing snails, South Africa 78
surgeonfish 54, 116, 120, 127
powder blue 118
reproduction 132, 133
sushi 187
suspension feeders 79, 204-5
swell shark 304, 305
swordfish 294, 295
Synalpheus regalis 134

tabular icebergs 222, 223
Talan 95
Tees estuary 82
teeth, twilight zone fish 326
temperate seas 154-211
habitat 158-9
plankton 168-77
seabed 198-211
seaweed 184-95
web of life 181-3
temperature ranges
adaptation to polar 224-5
Antarctica 217, 218-19
Arctic 216, 217, 219
intertidal habitats 66-7, 74-5
polar regions 218-19
temperate waters 156
thermoclines 264-5
twilight zone 316
terns 93, 95
Tethys Sea 26, 104
Thames estuary 63
Thaumatichthys 336
thermoclines 160, 161, 264-5
thick-billed murre 254
thin tellin 78-9
tidal bores, estuaries 41
tidal ranges 66
tidal waves see tsunamis
tide-pools 75
tides 40-1
and habitats 66-7
and low-pressure weather systems 66
nutrient mixing 161
spring and neap 41
torpedo ray 208, 209, 210
trade winds 31, 33
trading networks 22
transparency, twilight zone 320, 324
Transpolar Drift 221
trenches, deep ocean 29
triggerfish 124-5, 134
tripod fish 358
tropical seas 100-53
breeding and reproduction 128-37
coral reefs 102-13
feeding habits 114-27
mangroves and seagrass beds 138-51
trumpetfish 120
trunkfish, pair spawning 133
tsunamis 34, 35, 41
Tubastraea 108, 109
tubeworms 115, 204

cold-vent 371
Riftia 362, 363, 363
tuna 50, 287, 296
bluefin 163, 268, 269, 296, 297, 301
breeding and reproduction 301-2
commercial fishing 306-7
larvae 301, 302
school chasing baitfish 296, 297
skipjack 274
yellowfin 292, 296, 297, 301, 305, 306-7
turtles 87-9
flat-backed 89
green 50, 51, 87, 88, 89
leatherback 87, 273
Olive Ridley 71, 81, 89
twilight zone 314-29
habitat 322-3
search for food 326-9
two moon jellyfish 174, 175

Ulva lactuca 186, 187
uplifted coasts 62
upwellings 33, 49, 272, 273, 277
Peruvian coast 33, 38, 39

vampire snails 126, 127
Vampyroteuthis 340, 341
Vellela 278, 279
vertical migration 280-1, 327-8
vibrations, sensitivity to 290, 333
Vitronella 320, 321
volcanic activity 18
islands 28, 28-9
tsunamis 34, 35, 41
see also seamounts

Waddenzee, Netherlands 63
wading birds 84, 84-5
walruses 44, 224
Arctic summers 257
Pacific 256, 257
pups 224
wandering albatross 236, 270-1, 271
warm pool, western Pacific 275
warm-water currents 268
Wash estuary 62, 63
water
basis of life-forms 21
and evolution of life 16
heat storage 20
hydrogen bond 19
nature of 19-20
oxygen concentration 21
waves 32, 33, 34-5
biggest accurately recorded 263
erosion of reefs 111-12
and seaweeds 189, 191
tsunamis 34, 35, 41
weather patterns, sun driving 31
Weddell seals 44, 97, 224, 240, 241
Wegner, Alfred, continental drift 24
westerlies 31
whale sharks 48, 57, 269, 287

whale strandings 79, 80, 81
whales 97
dwarf minke 287
fin whales 164, 164-5, 287
gray 195, 206-7, 309
hunting of 46-7
keeping warm 224
killer 179, 230, 235
migration 50
sperm 315-16
tears 50
see also baleen whales
whaling, Southern Ocean 238
whip-nosed anglers 336
white sand beaches, tropics 62
white shrimps, hydrothermal vents 368
'white smokers' 362
white whales see beluga whales
whitetip reef sharks 126, 127
willets 84, 84-5
Wilson's storm petrel 180
winds 31-3
winter
Antarctic 241
Arctic 258
climate effects on oceans 274
migrations 162-3
temperate seas 160-1
Winteria 324
wolves 247
World map 12-13
wrasses 129, 133

xanthid crabs 124

yellow-bellied sea snake 279
yellow-green kelp fish 194
yellowfin tuna 292, 296, 297, 301
captive breeding 305
fishing methods 306-7

Zavodovski island, chinstrap penguins 93, 234
zooplankton 49, 50, 172-6, 278, 280-2
Arctic 253-4
grazing on phytoplankton 170, 171
night feeders 126
reef fish feeding on 115-16
see also copepods; krill
zooxanthellae 108